D1604958

Social Work Practice Research
for the Twenty-first Century

Social Work
Practice Research
for the Twenty-first Century

Edited by
Anne E. Fortune,
Philip McCallion,
and Katharine Briar-Lawson

COLUMBIA UNIVERSITY PRESS   NEW YORK

Columbia University Press
Publishers Since 1893
New York   Chichester, West Sussex
Copyright © 2010 Columbia University Press
All rights reserved
Library of Congress Cataloging-in-Publication Data
Social work practice research for the twenty-first century / edited by
Anne E. Fortune, Philip McCallion, and Katharine Briar-Lawson.
  p.   cm.
  Includes index.
  ISBN 978-0-231-14214-4 (cloth : alk. paper) — ISBN 978-0-231-51264-0 (electronic)
  1. Social service—Research 2. Evaluation research (Social action programs) I.
Fortune, Anne E., 1945– II. McCallion, Philip. III. Briar-Lawson, Katharine. IV. Title.
HV11.S5886   2010
361.3'2—dc22

                                                        2009042015

To Bill Reid,
friend, colleague, innovator,
and leader in social work practice and research

Contents

Preface

Anne E. Fortune, Philip McCallion,
and Katharine Briar-Lawson

AT A TIME WHEN society faces serious social, economic, and planetary problems, the social work profession struggles to redefine its role in reducing those problems and their impact on individuals. At the same time, the pursuit of "social good" is no longer a valued outcome in itself. The profession must demonstrate its relevance and effectiveness to a broad constituency of legislators and the public as well as to clients and practitioners. An important asset is research on social work practice: research on what social workers actually do; variations; benefits; the processes, cultural competences, and ethics of practice; and effectiveness. Still, despite forty years of emphasis on empirically based clinical practice, the promotion of clinician-scientists, development of infrastructure for agency-based research, and more recently Evidence-Based Practice (EBP), the amount of intervention research comes up perilously short (Fraser 2004). The needs of underserved, diverse, and culturally identified populations are often poorly addressed.

This book provides a direction for social work practice research by reviewing the recent history of empirical practice, summarizing current knowledge in key areas, tracing an empirically developed social work model (task-centered practice), and developing an agenda for research in the twenty-first century. The book is a tribute to William J. Reid (1928–2003), a social work scholar who influenced social work in several areas: 1) with Laura Epstein, developing an evidence-based intervention model (1972) (see chapter 13 for a description of the task-centered model); 2) systematizing research methods and disseminating them to social workers (*Research in Social Work*, Reid and Smith, 1981); 3) integrating many approaches to research while other scholars squared off in epistemological debates; 4) assiduously promoting empirically based practice long before its current cachet;

and 5) more recently, synthesizing intervention knowledge and framing an agenda for future research (Reid 2000; Reid, Kenaley, and Burton 2004).

Part 1 reviews the development of social work research. Ronald A. Feldman (chapter 1) focuses on paradoxes inherent in the infrastructures that shape research over time: 1) landmark reports from external organizations (Flexner, Russell Sage Foundation, National Institutes of Mental Health); 2) growth in educational programs for MSWs without concomitant growth in doctoral programs to produce faculty and researchers; 3) minimal research instruction and competency at all program levels; 4) a proliferation of organizations that effectively separate practice, research, and education; 5) journals that have low impact ratings and publish little original research; and 6) a profession reluctant to legitimate research findings. In chapter 2, Anne E. Fortune traces the development of empirical practice in social work from Mary Richmond's "scientific art" (1917) to the current proliferation of Evidence-Based Practices. While the rest of the book describes primarily quantitative research, Ian Shaw (chapter 3) summarizes the contributions of qualitative research. Qualitative research enables one to study individual outcomes (not evaluate a program) and advance an emancipatory research agenda. It shifts research questions from academicians' concerns "to those that sufferers and survivors think are central" (page 35).

The second part of the book includes summaries of the current "state of the art" in key fields of social work service. EBP is currently defined in two ways. One way is "practice that uses knowledge and interventions with research validation" (Gellis and Reid 2004). This approach is sometimes called "EBP as a noun or product" (Proctor 2009), "evidence-supported intervention (ESI)," or "evidence-supported treatment (EST)" (Danya International 2008). It assumes that intervention guidelines can be crafted from available data or have been tested with randomized trials of manualized interventions. In most of social work, such forms of EBP are organized by problem or field of practice. This second part includes evidence on work with small groups to resolve individuals' problems (chapter 4, Charles D. Garvin); large-scale social development prevention programs designed to strengthen protection while reducing risk for children (chapter 5, Richard F. Catalano and colleagues), intervention for children's mental health (chapter 6, Mark W. Fraser and Mary A. Terzian), child welfare services (chapter 7, June G. Hopps, Tony B. Lowe, and Latrice S. Rollins), and aging (chapter 8, Barbara Berkman). Because validating effectiveness for different cultures is so important (Conner and Grote 2008), two chapters address culturally grounded approaches: drug prevention with Latino youth (chapter 9, Flavio Francisco Marsiglia) and development of interventions for poor inner-city African Americans with Alzheimer's disease (chapter 10, June G. Hopps, Tony B. Lowe, and Ollie G. Christian).

A second definition of EBP is as a process for practitioners to generate case-relevant questions and then find the evidence for effective intervention, normally using bibliographic and (now) computerized searches (Gellis and Reid 2004). Proctor (2009) calls it "EBP as a verb or process." This approach, championed in social work by Gambrill (1999) and Gibbs (2003), assumes that each practitioner will be an efficient retriever and critic of relevant research. Following this definition of EBP, Julia Littell (chapter 11) discusses the science of research synthesis: how to conduct a systematic literature review that reduces bias, the international efforts to make such systematic reviews readily available through the Cochrane and Campbell Collaborations, and misinterpretation when systematic review is not implemented.

The third part maps the development and dissemination of social work's only "homegrown" empirical practice model, Reid and Epstein's task-centered model for work with individuals, families, groups, administration, and supervision. Lynn Videka and James Blackburn (chapter 12) outline Reid (and Epstein's) contributions to social work practice research. Reid used research and development (R&D) (Thomas and Rothman 1994) over forty years to build a model with an eclectic, pragmatic, and above all empirical approach. The model generated much dismay among social work practitioners when it was introduced in the late 1970s. Ideas that were controversial in the then-dominant psychosocial practice community included focusing on client-acknowledged problems, focusing on delimited problems in living, taking action (tasks) to resolve problems, and practitioner collaboration with the client.

A focus on the task-centered model is important in the history of social work research because Reid was an early advocate of mixed research methods, integrating quantitative and qualitative approaches. He and colleagues used a wide variety of research approaches in developing the task-centered model. These included quantitative methods like small randomized clinical trials (e.g., Reid and Epstein 1972; Reid, Bailey-Dempsey, et al. 1995) and tests of discrete interventions like the task-implementation sequence (Reid 1975). Qualitative methods to develop and validate new micro-interventions included content analysis of sessions (Reid and Bailey-Dempsey 1994), Interpersonal Process Recall (Naleppa and Reid 1998), and critical events analysis (Davis and Reid 1988). Indeed, as a harbinger of next steps in practice research in the twenty-first century, Reid's last publication called for expanding the type of data used to support evidence-based practice to include practitioner-driven and local qualitative and quantitative research (Gellis and Reid 2004).

Subsequent chapters in part 3 focus on the dissemination of the task-centered model. Ronald H. Rooney (chapter 13) describes its contributions to American social work practice. Elsewhere, some countries adopted the task-centered model wholeheartedly. Social workers in Great Britain, the

Netherlands, and Norway developed programs of research and adaptation for their national contexts (chapter 14, Peter Marsh; chapter 15, Nel and Louwerus Jagt; and chapter 18, Rita Elisabeth Eriksen). With support from government, professional organizations, and systematic training, the task-centered model became the central framework for most social services and child protection in those countries.

In other countries, diffusion of the task-centered model was more limited. In Switzerland, it was subsumed in a broader intervention approach, a "service bundle" that included the task-centered model within the "counseling bundle" (chapter 17, Alexander Kobbel and Matthias Naleppa). In Australia and Hong Kong, it was integrated into eclectic intervention approaches (chapter 19, Christopher Trotter; chapter 23, Yueh-Ching Chou and Ronald H. Rooney). In some countries, only a few practitioners use the model, not always systematically (chapter 21, South Korea, Nam-Soon Huh and Yun-Soon Koh; chapter 22, Hong Kong, T. Wing Lo). The widespread international dissemination of the task-centered model suggests it is robust to cultural differences. It has adapted well to many worldviews of individual and situational difficulties and to different means of providing social welfare. Remarkably, the model appears to be useful with involuntary as well as voluntary clients. The range of problems with which it has been used is considerable, especially in an era where practice research focuses on specific problems rather than on generalizable interventions. Problems and populations include suicide and depression, addictions, sexual abuse, child neglect, frail elderly, maladaptive youth in treatment centers, homeless people with psychiatric difficulties, welfare and social services case management, schoolchildren, families of children with developmental disability, and substance abuse. Most of the research is on intervention with individuals—children, adolescents, adults, and elderly; some with families (especially those with child problems); some with treatment groups whose members share similar problems; and administration and supervision. The task-centered model is rarely used to address problems that have structural or societal causes; an exception is improving housing in Norway (chapter 18).

The fourth part of the book draws lessons learned from the practice research movement as well as visions for future agendas. In chapter 24, Enola K. Proctor argues that to date, social work researchers have missed the most important research questions. To develop useful, rich knowledge in this social-political era, Proctor's agenda includes five research questions: 1. What *do* social workers *do*? 2. How does practice *vary*? 3. What is the *value* of social work practice? 4. What practices *should* social workers use? 5. How can social work practice *be improved*?

While that agenda may be clear, whether the social work profession can conduct the needed practice research is a different issue altogether. Feldman (chapter 1) outlines efforts to improve social work's research infrastructure, culminating in recent widespread efforts of the National Institutes of Health (NIH) and other organizations such as the Society for Social Work and Research (SSWR) and the Institute for the Advancement of Social Work Research (IASWR) to train, mentor, promote, and fund social work researchers (Jenson, Briar-Lawson, and Flanzer 2008; Zlotnik and Solt 2008; Williams et al. 2008). Although the amount and quality of social work research has increased, the research agendas have not necessarily been practice oriented. At the end of the twentieth century, intervention research was still a very small portion of published research (Fraser 2004).

To remedy the situation requires building infrastructures that support both conducting and disseminating intervention research (Bellamy, Bledsoe, and Traube 2006). In chapter 25, Jack M. Richman reviews models for conducting research—practitioner-scientist, agency research unit, and agency-university partnership—and analyzes the likely buy-ins from various stakeholders who determine if research is conducted and of what quality. Lastly, in chapter 26, the book editors Anne E. Fortune, Philip McCallion, and Katharine Briar-Lawson review other issues in intervention research and propose practical, cost-effective models of research, and EBP dissemination.

Much of the material for this volume was presented in earlier versions at an International Practice Research Symposium held in June 2005 at the University at Albany, in honor of William J. Reid. The symposium was cosponsored by the National Institute of Drug Abuse (NIDA), the School of Social Welfare, and the Center for Excellence in Aging Services at the University at Albany.

Many chapters—particularly the reviews of current knowledge and visions of the future—began as invited presentations at the symposium. Other chapters, including the international dissemination of the task-centered model, were written later to complete the framework developed at the symposium. A different part of the conference—presentations of new research studies on social work intervention—was published separately as a special issue of the journal *Research on Social Work Practice* (vol. 18, no. 6, November 2008).

We acknowledge support offered by the National Institute on Drug Abuse through grant 5R01DA15376–5, an infrastructure grant, Child Welfare Drug Abuse and Intergenerational Risk (CWDAIR), awarded to the School of Social Welfare at the University at Albany. We especially thank then NIDA program officers Peter Delany, Ph.D., and Jerry P. Flanzer, Ph.D., for their help organizing the conference and encouraging the development of this book.

We also thank others who were so supportive of this volume—the staff and students at the Center for Excellence in Aging Services who organized and implemented the conference: James Caringi, Dennis G. Chapman, Manrong

Chen, Michael J. Eversman, Lisa A. Ferretti, Zachary Ferretti, Kristen Kirkland, Nancy Macy, Irene Manfredo, Dayna M. Maniccia, Michael B. Marks, Cristina Mogro-Wilson, Anne (Polly) Petruska, Marylou Schiro, Amanda Sisselman, Jessica Strolin, Mary Lou Weseman, and Monna Zuckerman. Randy Stetson and Deborah Reyome were invaluable collecting and editing the voluminous material from so many authors.

We also thank the late John Michel, Bill Reid's editor at Columbia University Press, and the patient current editor, Lauren Dockett, for believing in the legacy of Reid and our ability to honor it.

Robert K. Merton, the sociologist and National Medal of Science winner, used the phrase "standing on the shoulders of giants" to refer to paradigm leaders (1965). William J. Reid was such a giant in social work. When we stand on his shoulders, the imperative to foster and accelerate twenty-first-century practice research agendas is clear. Like Reid, when we advance social work practice research, we also advance the future of the profession and its effectiveness in delivering positive results to those we serve.

Anne E. Fortune

Philip McCallion

Katharine Briar-Lawson

References

Bellamy, J. L., Bledsoe, S. E., and Traube, D. E. (2006). The current state of evidence-based practice in social work: A review of the literature and qualitative analysis of expert interviews. *Journal of Evidence-Based Social Work 3* (1): 23–48.

Conner, K. O. and Grote, N. K. (2008). Enhancing the cultural relevance of empirically supported mental health interventions. *Families in Society 89*:587–595.

Danya International, Inc. (2008). *Research and empirical applications for curriculum enhancement in social work (REACH-SW): Advanced doctoral students or new instructors edition* [CD-ROM].

Davis, I. P. and Reid, W. J. (1988). Event analysis in clinical practice and process research. *Social Casework 69* (5): 298–306.

Fortune, A. E. and Reid, W. J. (1999). *Research in social work*. 3rd ed. New York: Columbia University Press.

Fraser, M. W. (2004). Intervention research in social work: Recent advances and continuing challenges. *Research on Social Work Practice 14*:210–222.

Gambrill, E. (1999). Evidence-based practice: An alternative to authority-based practice. *Families in Society 80*:341–350.

Gellis, Z. and Reid, W. J. (2004). Strengthening evidence-based practice. *Brief Treatment and Crisis Intervention 4* (2): 155–165.

Gibbs, L. E. (2003). *Evidence-based practice for the helping professionals: A practical guide with integrated multimedia*. Pacific Grove, CA: Brooks/Cole.

Jenson, J. M., Briar-Lawson, K., and Flanzer, J. P. (2008). Editorial: Advances and challenges in developing research capacity in social work. *Social Work Research 32*: 197–200.

Merton, R. K. (1965). *On the shoulders of giants: The post-Italianate edition.* Chicago: University of Chicago Press.

Naleppa, M. J. and Reid, W. J. (1998). Task-centered case management for the elderly: Developing a practice model. *Research on Social Work Practice 8* (1): 63–85.

Proctor, E. K. (2009, June). *From the task-centered approach to evidence-based practice.* School of Social Service Administration Centennial Symposium, Chicago, IL.

Reid, W. J. (1990). Change process research: A new paradigm? In L. Videka-Sherman and W. J. Reid (Eds.), *Advances in clinical social work research*, 130–148. Silver Spring, MD: NASW Press.

Reid, W. J. (2000). *The task planner.* New York: Columbia University Press.

Reid, W. J. (2002). Knowledge for direct social work practice: An analysis of trends. *Social Service Review 76*:6–33.

Reid, W. J. and Bailey-Dempsey, C. A. (1994). Content analysis in design and development. *Research on Social Work Practice 4* (1): 101–114.

Reid, W. J., Bailey-Dempsey, C. A., Cain, E., Cook, T. V., and Burchard, J. D. (1994). Cash incentives versus case management: Can money replace services in preventing school failure? *Social Work Research 18* (4): 227–236.

Reid, W. J. and Epstein, L. (1972). *Task-centered casework.* New York: Columbia University Press.

Reid, W. J. and Epstein, L. (1977). *Task-centered practice.* New York: Columbia University Press.

Reid, W. J., Kenaley, B., and Burton, J. (2004). Do some interventions work better than others? A review of comparative social work experiments. *Social Work Research 28* (2): 71–81.

Reid, W. J. and Smith, A. D. (1981). *Research in social work.* New York: Columbia University Press.

Richmond, M. (1917). *Social diagnosis.* New York: Russell Sage Foundation.

Rothman, J. and Thomas, E. J. (1994). *Intervention research: Design and development for human service.* New York: Haworth Press.

Williams, J. B. W., Tripodi, T., Rubin, A., Hooyman, N., Allen-Meares, P., Padgett, D. K., and Fortune, A. E. (2008). A historical account of the Society for Social Work and Research: Presidential perspectives on advances in research infrastructure. *Social Work Research 32*:208–219.

Zlotnik, J. L., and Solt, B. E. (2008). Developing research infrastructure: The Institute for the Advancement of Social Work Research. *Social Work Research 32*:201–207.

Tribute

William J. Reid: A Personal Remembrance

Stuart A. Kirk

IN 1969, I WAS a twenty-four-year-old MSW student at the University of Illinois in Urbana-Champaign. I was perplexed by the discrepancies between the profession's aspirations that practice should be grounded in science and the vague, frequently unfounded claims made in social work journal articles and practice textbooks, still infused with psychoanalytic theory and practices. I was confused by exactly how the methods of science were to shape the practice of social work.

I stumbled on a recently published small monograph that compared the outcomes of short-term versus long-term casework treatment. It was an uncommonly masterful empirical test of one of social work's sacred cows: namely, that the widely preferred long-term treatment was better for clients. Based on the study data, however, long-term treatment was not better, a surprise even to the researchers. Although undoubtedly the findings were disheartening to traditionalists, I was encouraged and impressed—not because I harbored a bias with regard to the preferred length of treatment, about which I knew little, but because I had found critically minded social work scholars who were using scientific methods to examine significant practice issues, and who exercised care and courage in interpreting the findings. This book, *Brief and Extended Casework*, by Bill Reid and Ann Shyne (1969), was a model of applied social work research. At the time, I had never heard of William J. Reid, who was in his mid-thirties and a professor of social work at the University of Chicago. I was unaware that this marvelous study was one of Bill's earliest publications and his first book. I certainly couldn't have forecast that it would be the beginning of four decades of outstanding scholarship, in which he would be in the forefront of empirical practice, a tough-minded and rigorous academic, but one with an eye for practice realities and applications. Bill Reid's work inspired me and many others.

Scholarship

His professional achievements are now well known: distinguished university professor; author of nearly 200 publications, including 18 books; founding editor of the journal *Social Work Research*; winner of national awards for his research contributions; developer and ardent proponent of task-centered practice; and mentor to generations of doctoral students at the University of Chicago and the University at Albany.

He was one of very few researchers whose body of work has made a difference in both what we teach and how we deliver services. A pioneer in using empirical methods to develop knowledge for practice, he was one of the leaders and champions in what was perhaps the most influential development in social work practice in the last half of the twentieth century, a movement that led directly to what is now labeled Evidence-Based Practice.

In a 2003 article, coauthors and I surveyed dozens of leaders in social work, asking them to list the top researchers who had made the most significant contributions to the profession. When we published the results, we listed the names, but deliberately did not identify the specific ranking of the individuals who were among the top group. When we immediately started getting e-mails from colleagues asking how they personally ranked, we decided not to reveal the specific ranks to anyone because of the instability of such scores. Even though one of the coauthors and I had known Bill for decades, he would never have asked such a question and wouldn't have been interested in the answer anyway. Nevertheless, in drafting this tribute, my coauthors agreed that I could make an exception and reveal that in our survey, Bill Reid's reputation as a researcher ranked first nationally. I now wish that I had shared that with him.

He did not gain his prominence in the profession, however, in the usual ways—consciously promoting himself, elbowing his way into positions of leadership, skillfully cultivating friends in high places, crafty political maneuvering, or gaining renown by natural charisma. His prominence came from the significance of his written work and his steadfast commitment to studying interventions empirically. This modest, soft-spoken, slightly disheveled, self-effacing professor actually seemed uneasy with his public reputation and more at home in his study, surrounded by books and piles of articles, than at the podium.

To me, another indicator of his stature was how he achieved his stunning record of publications. In most disciplines, hundreds of publications are the result of a senior investigator overseeing teams of researchers, supported by large foundation and federal grants, cranking out dozens of group-written articles carrying the senior investigator's name. Bill's contributions are not the products of the largesse of foundations or national institutes. Although he received many small grants for his work, he managed to remain an independent, incredibly productive scholar through sheer energy, dedication, and involvement in the practice world.

He was not, however, an isolated scholar, a recluse working alone. Many of his articles and books were coauthored, usually with his current or former doctoral students. Such collaborations are a testament to his role as a mentor and role model to young scholars. In fact, through his prodigious writings, he served as a mentor to many others who were not necessarily young and who never had the opportunity to work directly with him. I had known Bill for years before I worked with him as a colleague at Albany, and while we didn't publish together during those years, we certainly worked together on many educational projects and reports. A decade after I left Albany, I had the good fortune to work with Bill on a book addressing the very topic that had concerned me as an MSW student thirty years before, about which this young University of Chicago professor had been an inspiration. As it turned out, it was the only publication we wrote together. I could hardly ask for a more personally meaningful collaboration. He was an ideal partner—responsive, helpful, reassuring, and fully engaged. As many know from personal experience, Bill was a precise and skilled writer and editor. Never had co-authoring been as easy or rewarding for me.

Institution Building

In 1979 I accepted the deanship at the School of Social Welfare at Albany. It was an incredible opportunity. The school was young and underdeveloped. The university's president, Vincent O'Leary, encouraged us to develop a top-tier school of social welfare. The challenge required recruiting the best senior and junior faculty in the country, building a research-oriented program, and initiating the first Ph.D. program in social welfare in the state university system.

In the year of transition as I moved to Albany, we hired six new faculty to build on the existing core of very fine scholars already there. One of the new recruits stood out: we had enticed Professor William J. Reid to join us from the University of Chicago. That one hire was, in my opinion, the catalyst for the future development and growth at Albany. Bill's arrival attracted the attention of the national social work academic community and encouraged all the school faculty to have higher aspirations for the program and their own work. It allowed us to develop a proposal for a credible research-oriented Ph.D. program and confirmed the campus administration's faith in the future of the school. Equally important, it helped us continue recruiting other superb faculty within the next five years. The scholarly productivity of the school's faculty jumped from a rank of 57th (Jayaratne 1979) into the top five or ten, a coveted position maintained for over 20 years (Feldman 2006).

Bill did not hide in his office and write articles; he was actively engaged in this transformation. As soon as he arrived at Albany he took a critical and influential, if partly behind the scenes, role in helping to reshape the school—its directions, its academic standards, and its commitment to practice research. For example, within the first few months I asked him to help me shape a proposal for the new Ph.D. program. In keeping with his incredible task focus, Bill had the essence of the program designed in about four days. As was common for the SUNY bureaucracy, it took about four years for the program to be reviewed and approved. The fact that he directed the Ph.D. program for so many years must have given him great and deserved satisfaction. Although I left Albany as it commenced, his leadership allowed me to know over the years that the program we started was in very good hands.

As a young dean, I was learning as I was leading, and relying heavily on the wisdom of others. Having Bill in the school's hallways, at faculty meetings, and available as an advisor was an enormous asset. His presence was reassuring and his encouragement about what we might achieve collectively was an inspiration to me and others.

Personal

Among Bill's remarkable personal qualities were his modesty and reserve. He was comfortably unpretentious. I can't remember ever hearing him boast of his achievements, expect deference, or seek praise. He never pursued fame or prominence. He was a very private person, cautious and reserved, not quick at a social gathering to tell you his life story or his wide-ranging interests. I didn't know, for instance, that he played cards well, until some faculty invited him to join our poker group and he lightened our wallets. Many know he was a prodigious scholar and workaholic, but few knew he loved the outdoors. One winter, I invited him to UCLA to talk at a doctoral seminar. He arrived in California with his wet suit, ready to do some body surfing. He was a swimmer, hiker, and naturalist. Not exactly the athleticism you'd expect from a seventy-year-old professor ensconced in a crowded office writing book after book.

His subdued, restrained personal style also characterized his scholarship, which was deliberate and careful. His academic work never consisted of showmanship, deliberately meant to entertain or provoke. He quietly pursued his own agenda, avoiding as best he could the many distractions that derail most scholars. He was absorbed and energized by his own projects that he relished and pursued vigorously. I have met very few professors in my life with as much focus and persistence, and not a single one who sustained such a high level of craftsmanship for as long as Bill did. When he was in his late sixties, I asked Ricky Fortune if Bill was thinking of retiring. She told me he never would. I think that was what I personally wanted to hear. Bill retiring was simply unimaginable.

Despite his inner-directedness, Bill was always available to work for the collective good, and was gracious with his assistance. You would've thought that someone as well read and accomplished as he would have trouble suffering fools. Not so. It was remarkable to me how even-handed and judicious he was in his criticism of others' work. He had, of course, a definite point of view and strongly held opinions, but he used them to gently persuade if he could, not to put others down. He had the wisdom to know that nothing useful could be accomplished by sharpening conflict. Bill was not only a social work scholar of the first order but also a very decent man.

Bill was a scholar's scholar, an ideal colleague, a trusted friend. In the profession of social work, he was a giant among us. I miss his friendship, but I am grateful that his significant contributions to social work will endure. In 1969 I was a student and Bill was a teacher. Now, after forty years, I'm still learning from him.

References

Feldman, R. A. (2006). Reputations, rankings, and realities of social work schools: Challenges for future research. *Journal of Social Work Education 42* (3): 483–505.

Jayaratne, S. (1979). Analysis of selected social work journals and productivity rankings among schools of social work. *Journal of Education for Social Work 15* (3): 72–80.

Reid, W. J. and Shyne, A. (1969). *Brief and extended casework.* New York: Columbia University Press.

PART ONE | *A Historical Mapping of*
Social Work
Practice Research

1 | Critical Infrastructures for Social Work Practice Research

Pondering the Past, Framing the Future

Ronald A. Feldman

THIS CHAPTER FOCUSES ON critical infrastructures that have shaped the current status of social work practice research and, in turn, will shape the course of future research. It sets forth a partial and selective perspective that no doubt will be augmented and complemented by the views of others. Additional relevant infrastructures are not examined here due to space constraints; they are considered in substantial detail in a more comprehensive companion paper (Feldman 2005). Ultimately, an authoritative history of social work research must examine all facets of the research enterprise and synthesize the perspectives of multiple observers.

The Practice Research Enterprise

The most determinate factor in the development of meaningful practice research is the extent to which critical infrastructures are created to promote and sustain the research enterprise over the long run. However, it is difficult, if not impossible, to fully comprehend the complexities of practice research without recognizing its three central and interrelated aspects: research development, research dissemination, and research utilization. Each is critical to the advancement of social work practice. Indeed, the development of research-based knowledge is of little consequence if it is not followed by effective dissemination and utilization. Although social work has made substantial strides in research development and, to some extent, in research dissemination over the years, relatively few gains have been made in actual utilization by practitioners. In its own right, the latter topic merits heightened attention on the part of social work scholars.

In considering research development, three critical infrastructures are reviewed here: landmark reports and task forces; significant educational trends; and major associational structures. Other relevant, but less determinate, infrastructures discussed elsewhere include important conferences and meetings; research centers and institutes established at schools of social work; research programs conducted at social work agencies; international research consortiums and collaborations; public and private funding sources for research; and prestigious awards and prizes for exemplary research (cf. Feldman 2005).

In considering research dissemination, one major infrastructure will be examined in particular detail, namely, professional journals and books. Other dissemination infrastructures are discussed elsewhere (Feldman 2005) and include conferences and reports; electronic dissemination mechanisms; and agency-based, school-based, and associational research dissemination efforts. Research utilization is considered here only briefly.

Research Development

Social work research suffers from a fundamental paradox. The dimensions and importance of the paradox will become increasingly evident as the following infrastructures are examined.

Landmark Reports and Task Forces

Since the very inception of social work, important new directions for the profession have been galvanized by landmark reports and task forces. These include, of course, the classic Flexner Report delivered ninety years ago at a meeting of the National Conference of Charities and Corrections (Flexner 1915) and, in later years, the Tufts Report issued under the aegis of the Russell Sage Foundation (Tufts 1923) and seminal reports about social work education such as those by Hollis and Taylor (1951) and Boehm (1959). However, landmark reports and task forces are more often the exception than the rule. Far more numerous are the countless reports that come to naught. Yet even these can inform our understanding of the formidable challenges that beset efforts to advance social work research.

An example is a promising report issued in 1989 by a Task Force on the Future of Social Work Education, formed by the National Association of

Deans and Directors of Social Work Schools (NADD). Titled "Proposal for a Comprehensive Study of Social Work Education," the report asserted that "the time is nigh for social work to conduct a comprehensive and in-depth study of the present state and future needs of social work education" (National Association of Deans and Directors 1989:4).[1] The task force members recommended that a central concern be "the nature of the knowledge base of social work." They observed that "it will be useful to articulate the extent to which social work knowledge should be endogenous (that is, generated primarily within the profession) or exogenous (that is, generated outside of the social work profession, but adapted or modified for social work education and practice)" (Ibid. 21). The report especially emphasized the importance of examining "the range and quality of social work scholarship and the extent to which the scholarly literature is incorporated into professional training" (Ibid. 21). Anticipating that such a study would cost slightly more than $1 million, NADD then decided to form a second task force to seek funds to implement it. However, that task force faltered and a unique opportunity to strengthen and refine social work research failed to materialize.

In sharp contrast, a particularly influential report was issued in 1991 by the National Institute of Mental Health (NIMH) Task Force on Social Work Research.[2] That task force directly addressed many of the extant challenges to practice research in social work and, more important, yielded unprecedented results in advancing social work research. Declaring that a "crisis" existed, the report's authors forcefully asserted:

- There is a paucity of social work research and researchers in critical areas of social work practice.
- A critical gap exists between the studies being carried out by researchers in schools of social work and the knowledge needs of social work practitioners and the service agencies in which they work.
- Extant patterns of research dissemination are fragmented and inefficient in getting research-based information to social work practitioners.
- There are critical problems in how research is taught at every level of social work education and, in particular, in social work doctoral programs.
- Existing organizational and funding resources are not sufficient to support research development in social work.
- Few social work researchers are included in the national bodies that determine research priorities and government research policies pertinent to social work practice.

Importantly, these concerns and others articulated in the report also were accompanied by a detailed plan of action that called for:

- An Office of Social Work Mental Health Research Development in NIMH that is responsible for an expanded program of recruitment, research training, and research career development related to mental health research priorities.
- A program of Social Work Research Development Center awards, including flexible funds for research infrastructure development and the support of developmental research projects in mental health.
- A National Institute for the Advancement of Research in Social Work with responsibility for supporting research development throughout the profession in all practice areas with the support of national professional associations in social work.
- A staff position for research development advocacy in NASW and a staff position for research education development in CSWE.
- Improved research education in baccalaureate and master's degree programs.
- Corresponding changes in the policies and standards for accrediting schools of social work.
- Improved research education in doctoral programs.
- Strengthened research support structures in schools of social work.
- Development of research partnerships between schools of social work and service agencies.

In a subsequent report published eight years later, the chairman of the NIMH Task Force inventoried the impressive progress that had been made (Austin 1999). For instance, NIMH had funded nine research centers at schools of social work in the United States and had sponsored important programs of technical and educational assistance for social work researchers. In 1993 the Institute for the Advancement of Social Work Research (IASWR) emerged from the task force's recommendations. The chairman of the NIMH Task Force served on IASWR's first board of directors and IASWR's interim director also had been a member of the task force. Regrettably, current data about NIMH funding of social work research are not available. NIMH reportedly no longer publishes funding allocations by awardees' disciplinary or professional affiliation.

Despite the significant advances stimulated by the report of the NIMH Task Force, certain recommendations remain unrealized. Research training has improved markedly in many doctoral programs, but much less so in others. Neither NASW nor CSWE has yet established a staff position dedicated expressly to the advancement of research for social work practice. Nor has it yet proved possible to secure sufficient congressional support to establish a National Center for Social Work Research at NIH. In this regard and others, social work has yet to attain parity with some allied mental health professions. Since the NIMH Task Force on Social Work Research was formed in 1989 and its report released in 1991, it appears timely for a second NIMH Task Force to be convened and, even more, for social workers to explore the feasibility of similar initiatives at other units of NIH such as the National Institute for Drug Abuse (NIDA), the National Institute of Aging (NIA), and the National Institute of Child Health and Human Development (NICHD).

Significant Educational Trends

The last half century has witnessed unprecedented growth in social work education programs. In 1953, for example, the United States had only 53 graduate schools of social work. By 1992, there were 114 graduate programs plus 302 undergraduate programs, a total of 416. Today there are 191 accredited MSW programs and 460 accredited BSW programs—an increase of 63 percent since 1992! Although many, and perhaps most, social workers look favorably upon such rapid expansion of the profession's educational sector, significant liabilities attend this rate of growth.

From a research development perspective, the nearly unbridled proliferation of educational programs in social work can be regarded favorably only to the extent that it is accompanied by corresponding advances in research productivity and knowledge development. Data regarding the growth of doctoral education in social work are illustrative in this regard. In 1960, for example, only 10 social work doctoral programs existed in the United States. This number grew to 32 in 1980 and 46 in 1993. Today there are 73 doctoral programs. But while the total number of programs has increased steadily, their annual number of graduates has not. Instead, throughout the last three decades the average number of doctorates awarded in social work has remained stable, between roughly 200 and 300 per year. Whereas 243 social work doctorates were awarded in 1992, for instance, there were only 250 in 2002. Hence, while baccalaureate and master's programs in social work (and, correspondingly, their cumulative numbers of graduates) have proliferated over the years, the average number of doctoral graduates in social work has remained inordinately stable—some would say stagnant—for at least three decades. Moreover, only a fraction of doctoral graduates embark upon careers in education and/or research.

Barring significant shifts in educational policy or unforeseen technological breakthroughs, these trends portend that the present and projected numbers of social work doctoral graduates will be grossly inadequate to staff our profession's current education and research programs, much less those educational programs that will enter candidacy for CSWE accreditation in the coming years. In fact, if each of the current educational programs were to hire merely one new faculty member per year, the extant supply would still fall far short of demand. Indeed, if only *half* of the currently existing programs were to hire just a single new faculty member per year, it would be necessary for every doctoral graduate of every annual cohort to pursue a career in social work education. It is unlikely in the extreme that existing programs, on average, will hire only one new faculty member per year. It is absolutely inconceivable that 100 percent of social work doctoral graduates will embark upon academic careers and, if so, that all would have the career commitments and research competencies necessary to become productive practice researchers.

In short, the unprecedented proliferation of social work education programs has not been accompanied by corresponding growth in the number of doctoral graduates required to staff them and to conduct sound research aimed at advancing the knowledge base of social work practice. To the contrary, the educational sector confronts a steadily widening and perhaps irreversible gap between demand and supply for doctoral-trained social work researchers and educators. Given the above-described trends, it is nearly certain that the limited pool of qualified doctoral-level educators will be fragmented among many different programs that, on average, yield fewer graduates per program than in previous years. Furthermore, the disparity between the total number of social work education programs and the number of doctoral graduates available to teach in them will continue to grow and, in fact, accelerate. These trends seriously threaten the long-term quality of social work education and social work practice. From virtually every perspective, they bode ill for the cost-effectiveness, success, credibility, public acceptance, and future well-being of the social work profession. Several strategies for possibly resolving this conundrum are discussed elsewhere (Feldman 2005), but none offers an easy or assured solution. Perhaps the most productive would entail vigorous efforts to steeply raise the accreditation standards for *all* social work education programs, particularly with regard to the required ratios of doctoral-trained faculty.

A closely related topic is the content and substance of research training in social work education. Especially germane in this regard is the "foundation" curriculum content required for CSWE accreditation at the baccalaureate and master's levels. Due in part to the report of the NIMH Task Force and subsequent lobbying by numerous organizations and individuals, CSWE's accreditation policies and standards concerning research education in social work have been upgraded appreciably in recent years. The latest revision of accreditation standards incorporates many new requirements concerning research (Council on Social Work Education 2003). Students now are required to know more about research methods, the importance of research, and evaluation of their own practice interventions. But, importantly, CSWE's accreditation standards typically are sufficient rather than optimizing. The standards for research training remain minimal in most respects.

Similar concerns pertain to doctoral education in social work. To date, social work educators have strongly resisted efforts to establish accreditation policies, standards, and mechanisms for doctoral education. Many observers rightly attribute this to dissatisfaction about the barriers to curriculum innovation often imposed by CSWE accreditation policies. However, paralleling the trends observed in baccalaureate and master's education, social work doctoral programs with scant or questionable resources have proliferated rapidly in recent years. Therefore, it appears timely to seriously consider the accreditation of doctoral programs in social work. If meaningful leadership is to be exercised in this realm, however, it must be by institutions whose overarching interest is in doctoral education and research. Moreover, any such initiative should seek to optimize the quality of doctoral education rather than solely set forth minimal standards for accreditation. Finally, with regard to advanced education, it is germane to note that very few postdoctoral programs exist in social work. The dearth of such programs needs to be addressed if the profession is to progress toward higher levels of research productivity and practice excellence.

Major Associational Structures

Throughout its history social work has been shaped by numerous associations and organizations that have sought to advance the profession or certain of its special interest constituencies. Among relevant examples are:

1917 National Conference of Charities and Corrections (subsequently became National Conference of Social Work and then National Conference on Social Welfare)
1917 National Social Workers' Exchange
1918 American Association of Hospital Social Workers
1919 National Association of School Social Workers
1919 American Association of Training Schools for Professional Social Work
1921 American Association of Social Workers (evolved in part from former National Social Workers' Exchange)
1926 American Association of Psychiatric Social Workers
1927 American Association of Schools of Social Work (evolved in part from former American Association of Training Schools for Professional Social Work)
1930 American Public Welfare Association

1935 National Conference on Social Work (evolved in part from former National Conference of Charities and Corrections)

1936 American Association for the Study of Group Work

1942 National Association of Schools of Social Administration

1946 Association for the Study of Community Organizations

1946 National Council on Social Work Education

1946 American Association of Group Workers (evolved in part from former American Association for the Study of Group Work)

1949 Social Work Research Group

1949 Committee on Inter-Association Structure

1950 Temporary Inter-Association Council of Social Work Membership (evolved in part from former Committee on Inter-Association Structure)

1952 Council on Social Work Education (evolved in part from former National Council on Social Work Education and former American Association of Schools of Social Work)

1955 National Association of Social Workers (evolved in part from seven earlier groups: American Association of Group Workers; American Association of Medical Social Workers; American Association of Psychiatric Social Workers; American Association of Social Workers; Association for the Study of Community Organization; National Association of School Social Workers; Social Work Research Group)

1968 National Association of Black Social Workers

1970 Association of American Indian Social Workers

1971 National Association of Puerto Rican/Hispanic Social Workers

1971 National Federation of Societies for Clinical Social Work

1981 Group for the Advancement of Doctoral Education

1982 American Association of Industrial Social Workers

1982 National Conference of Deans and Directors of Graduate Schools of Social Work

1984 National Association of Deans and Directors of Schools of Social Work (evolved from former National Conference of Deans and Directors of Graduate Schools of Social Work)

1994 Society for Social Work and Research

2000 St. Louis Group for Excellence in Social Work Research and Education

Today there are perhaps forty to fifty associations and organizations whose members are predominantly professional social workers. However, they vary considerably with regard to priorities and membership. Importantly, most of the above-mentioned associations now are defunct, perhaps the foremost being the National Conference on Social Welfare. Few ever regarded the advancement of social work practice research as a top priority and many others devoted substantially greater effort to rhetoric about the importance of research than to actions aimed at developing and conducting research. More detailed information about many of these associations can be found in discussions by Alexander (1987), Bernard (1987), Brieland (1987), Goldstein and Beebe (1995), Lloyd (1987), Polansky (1977), Popple (1995), Tourse (1995), and Williams (1987).

A particularly notable, albeit short-lived, advance in associational infrastructures for social work research was the Social Work Research Group. Established in 1948–1949 under the aegis of NASW, it brought together some 600 members with interests in social work research. As described elsewhere (Maas 1977), the group's members were responsible for a series of documents on the "functions" of social work research and for sponsorship of research meetings at the National Conference on Social Welfare. Shortly after its formation, however, the Social Work Research Group lost its separate identity when NASW terminated all of its special interest subgroups and merged them into a centralized association with a more generalist orientation toward social work. After evolving into the Research Section of the newly organized National Association of Social Workers, the Social Work Research Group was for a short time responsible for a research segment of NASW's journal. It also generated a series of small research conferences, beginning in the mid-1950s with a meeting on research in the children's field.

Since its formation in 1955 NASW has played a noteworthy role in advancing social work research. Among many contributions, it is responsible for introducing *Social Work Research and Abstracts* to the professional literature, producing the *Encyclopedia of Social Work*, and publishing numerous texts and compendia that have contributed to the advancement of practice research. Many of NASW's recent publications are useful resources for both social work researchers and practitioners. NASW also has been a key partner in providing financial support for the Institute for the Advancement of Social Work Research (IASWR). Nevertheless, only a very small portion of NASW's financial resources are directed toward research development. Instead, issues like licensing, public image, and social workers' salaries are among its foremost priorities (see, for instance, *NASW News* September 2001:3). Ironically, it would seem that the latter concern can be addressed most fruitfully by means of compelling research that demonstrates to a skeptical public what many social workers already know, namely, that social work constitutes one of the best possible investments of scarce societal resources. It is there that NASW can profitably redirect more of its own fiscal resources.

Since 1952 CSWE also has played a key role in promoting social work research. It too provides ongoing, albeit modest, financial support for IASWR.

For decades, CSWE's annual conferences have featured research studies, workshops, and informational sessions about funding sources for social work research. In recent years, however, its contributions in this regard have been eclipsed by the Society for Social Work and Research (SSWR). To date, neither CSWE nor NASW has established a formal staff position dedicated expressly to promoting advances in social work research. Moreover, as CSWE has grown in size, many of its key decision makers seemingly have become less receptive than before to the needs of research-oriented schools of social work.

The National Association of Deans and Directors of Schools of Social Work (NADD) was established in 1984 by social work deans and directors who were, in large part, concerned about CSWE's impact on social work research and education, or lack thereof. The vast majority of its original members were deans and directors of educational institutions strongly committed to social work research. Over the years NADD task force reports have advocated vigorously for the advancement of social work education through rigorous research (see, for example, National Association of Deans and Directors 1989, 1997). In recent years, however, as in CSWE, the rapid growth of NADD's membership seemingly has weakened its capacity to address the interests of research-oriented schools of social work and to significantly advance research.

The most recent professional association formed expressly to advance social work research is the St. Louis Group for Excellence in Social Work Research and Education, created in June 2000 when the deans and directors of 29 research-intensive social work schools convened in St. Louis, Missouri.[3] The criterion for participation was an active research portfolio with at least $3 million of extramural funding. The overarching purpose of the group was to strengthen social work education by means of research. Among other initiatives, the group has sought significant modifications in CSWE accreditation policies regarding social work research. However, as with CSWE and NADD previously, the St. Louis Group has expanded very rapidly in only a few years. By 2005, it had 55 members—an increase of 90 percent in merely five years. Although this rate of growth might be regarded as an indicator of potential to advance social work research, the criterion for participation in the St. Louis Group gradually has been relaxed in recent years. The group's commitment and capacity to spearhead significant advances in social work research and education may decline accordingly. Its long-term impact remains uncertain.

Despite these mixed efforts to build associational infrastructures for social work research, two uniquely promising research-oriented organizations have been formed by social workers in the last thirty years, namely, the Group for the Advancement of Doctoral Education (GADE) and the Society for Social Work and Research (SSWR). The former, formed in 1981, consists of the directors of all social work doctoral programs in the United States and Canada.

It has played an integral role in improving and expanding research-oriented doctoral education in social work. A major contribution was made in 1992 when GADE issued a landmark report that set forth guidelines for strengthening the quality of doctoral education in social work (Group for the Advancement of Doctoral Education 1992). The membership of GADE currently consists of the directors of 73 doctoral programs in the United States plus an additional seven from Canada, and one from Israel.

SSWR, established in 1994, now has some 1,300 members.[4] More than any other association in social work's modern history, its members are actively engaged in practice research. Its annual meetings provide invaluable opportunities to present and discuss research, attend workshops that provide training and funding opportunities, and recognize the achievements of both accomplished and beginning investigators through conferral of highly regarded research awards. Even more, through its sponsorship of *Research on Social Work Practice*, it plays an ongoing role in strengthening and extending the dissemination of research-based practice knowledge. At this juncture of its development, perhaps SSWR's primary challenges are twofold: first, to assure that its members do not unduly neglect the other central components of the research enterprise, namely, dissemination and utilization, and second, to encourage approaches to research and publication that extend beyond many of the traditional, formulaic, or sterile models that often characterize social science research. If these pitfalls cannot be avoided, SSWR could inadvertently contribute to a widened gap between research and practice not unlike those found in allied professions with different membership organizations for researchers and practitioners.

Because individual research careers often are guided more by the availability of funds from federal and private sources than by the urgent needs of practitioners, SSWR can potentially play a central role in the future of social work research by conducting large-scale assessments of the profession's knowledge base and informational needs and, even more, by helping its members to forge some degree of consensus about the most pressing research challenges and priorities. Likewise, it can advance the enterprise by promoting studies and convening special conferences on the utilization of research, bringing together working groups of researchers and practitioners, and sponsoring special journal issues that improve linkages among research development, research dissemination, and research utilization. In short, as SSWR promotes research development, it needs also to recognize continuously the importance of initiatives in the other two central components of the research enterprise, dissemination and utilization.

SSWR's membership of some 1,300 researchers appears impressive in view of the fact that this organization has existed for hardly more than a decade.

Its current size suggests that a critical mass of researchers now may be developing in social work. Yet it also must be recognized that 152,000 social workers currently are members of NASW and there may be 300,000 to 400,000 more social workers who are not members. Absent dramatic breakthroughs in research and/or technology, these figures again raise the question of whether or not there are enough social work researchers to service the knowledge development needs of the profession. Equally sobering is the realization that the current membership of SSWR is only slightly more than double the 600-person membership of the Social Work Research Group that existed some five decades ago. From an associational perspective, it seems obvious that the growth rate of the research sector in social work has not kept pace with the growth rate of the practice sector.

Research Dissemination

Despite noteworthy progress in research development, such advances will amount to little if they are not disseminated effectively to practitioners. Until recent years, the dissemination of practice research in social work has been accomplished by highly traditional mechanisms such as conferences, workshops, and professional publications.

In the last two decades social work has seen a marked upsurge in print and electronic publications. Examples include refereed professional journals and targeted book publication programs under the imprimatur of major presses such as Oxford University Press, Columbia University Press, Sage Publications, Lyceum Books, John Wiley and Sons, Haworth Press, and others. Some of the latter products are extensive syntheses and compilations of practice-relevant research while others are textbooks and resource compendiums (cf., for example, Bloom, Fischer, and Orme 2006; Potocky-Tripodi and Tripodi 1999; Rapp-Pagliacci, Dulmus, and Wodarski 2004; Reid and Smith 1989; Roberts and Yeager 2004; Rothman and Thomas 1994). However, the quality of these products varies considerably. To date, only a handful of books and journal articles effectively link research and practice in ways that can systematically guide practitioners' assessments and interventions.

The existence of a vast array of books and journals of varying quality poses formidable problems of selection for social work practitioners. The library of one major school of social work, for instance, offers readers access to nearly 600 professional journals, of which approximately 250 appear in print version. But it is doubtful that most practitioners can subscribe to more than a few journals. This author recently surveyed 52 journals of particular interest to professional social workers. Of these, 18, or 35 percent, have been launched within the last two decades. Yet it is virtually impossible to gauge the actual impact of these and other professional journals upon social work practice. Despite repeated requests, for example, circulation data were not available for 28, or 54 percent, of the journals. Seventeen, including many sponsored by national social work associations, treat their readership as classified proprietary information. Eleven more did not reply to repeated inquiries about their circulation. Hence, it is impossible to determine even the readership of many social work journals. More important, there have been very few efforts to gauge the relative impact of various social work journals on the actual behavior of practitioners. In its own right, this topic constitutes an underrepresented and much-needed area of research inquiry.

Among major social work journals, circulation data could not be obtained for *Social Work, Social Work Research, Social Work Abstracts, Social Service Review, Health and Social Work, Journal of Social Work Research and Evaluation,* and *Journal of Evidence-Based Social Work.* Of the research-oriented journals for which data were available, *Research on Social Work Practice* reported a relatively impressive circulation of 2,003. This has been achieved in part by offering subscriptions to the journal in conjunction with SSWR membership. In contrast, the *Journal of Social Service Research* reported a circulation of merely 135. Both figures pale in comparison to the reported circulation for *American Journal of Psychiatry*: 37,568.

Given recent advances in reproducing professional journals and circulating their contents electronically, subscriptions alone are an inadequate indicator of the actual readership and/or utilization of most journals. Nevertheless, it is essential for a research-based profession to be able to gauge the relative and overall impact of its professional journals. This is especially the case when questions abound concerning the rigor, quality, and effect of journals. In social work, vigorous debates have emerged in recent years not only about the quality of journals but also about the credentials and expertise of editorial "gatekeepers" (see, for instance, discussions by Browning and Winchester 1999; Epstein 1999; Ginsberg 1999; Karger 1999; Kreuger 1999, Lindsey 1999; Midgley 1999; Pardeck and Meinert 1999a, 1999b; Reamer 1999). Given numerous questions about quality, it is far from certain that the proliferation of social work journals in recent decades has been accompanied by corresponding gains in rigor and utility. Such concerns warrant examination on the part of those who wish to advance social work research and its application by practitioners.

To effectively employ research findings, social work practitioners must identify the most rigorous and applicable journals and eschew those that fail to meet acceptable standards. Beginning progress is being made in this realm of inquiry. For example, in a study of 299 research-based articles that were nominated for SSWR's outstanding research awards, Craig, Cook, and Fraser (2004) found that more than one third had appeared in merely three journals, namely, *Research on Social Work Practice* (13 percent), *Social Work* (11 percent), and *Families in Society* (11 percent). The criteria for nomination included social significance of the problem being addressed; suitability of the research design; appropriateness of data, text analysis, and interpretation; potential for replicability; clarity of application to social work; and attention to gender, race, socioeconomic status, and other issues of difference. Among the remaining top 10 journals were *Social Work Research* (6 percent), *Journal of Social Work Education* (5 percent), *American Journal of Orthopsychiatry* (4 percent), *Child and Youth Services Review* (3 percent), *Child Abuse and Neglect* (3 percent), *Social Service Review* (3 percent), and *Psychiatric Services* (3 percent). From the perspective of rigor and applicability, it seems that social work practitioners might be well advised to subscribe mainly to these journals.

In one of the few studies concerning the impact of social work journals on citations and the work of fellow scholars, Lindsey and Kirk (1992) observed that the social work profession is served well by several core journals that have consistently improved their contributions over the years. These journals publish information that others read and use in subsequent work, thus leading to the accretion of a cumulative knowledge base. Lindsey and Kirk's analysis indicated also that some journals publish work that is seldom used and apparently has little effect on the profession. They comment that these need to ensure broader dissemination if their articles merit reading and use. If, however, their articles are of limited value, editors need to further examine their editorial policies to ensure that the profession will benefit from their journals. In a more recent study, Lindsey (2002) analyzed the relative impact of child welfare journals of special interest to social workers by determining how often their articles appeared in research cited in the *Journal Citation Report* of the Institute for Scientific Information. Respectively, the four journals with the greatest impact were *Children and Youth Services Review, Social Work, Health and Social Work,* and *Social Service Review.*

In a study of eight refereed journals that often publish articles on social group work, Feldman (1986) found that only 10 percent of the articles on this topic exemplified research or surveys. Of these, very few were characterized by statistical tests, control groups, baseline periods, or the analysis of more than a score of subjects. The preponderance of publications were merely anecdotal descriptions of group work programs that provide few reliable guidelines for practitioners. An updated analysis examined 254 articles on group work that appeared in *Social Work Abstracts* from 1977 through 2003. Fewer than a dozen entailed research employing a true experimental design, and none constituted a large-scale multifactorial field experiment (Feldman 2004).

A more comprehensive study by Rosen, Proctor, and Staudt (1999) analyzed 1,849 articles in 13 social work journals and found that less than half actually qualified as research. Moreover, only 15 percent of the research-based articles actually tested an intervention. Of those, less than half contained enough information to permit replication. Similarly, the analyses reported by Craig, Cook, and Fraser (2004) indicate that the vast preponderance of journal articles nominated for SSWR outstanding research awards (67 percent) are mere surveys. Of the quantitative studies nominated for a SSWR award, only 14 percent were experimental. Others were quasi-experimental (14 percent) or pre-experimental (4 percent). The authors duly note, "Compared with survey methods, intervention research, which should obtain high priority in a practice profession, is less frequently nominated [for SSWR awards]" (51).

These reports point clearly to the need for increased rigor and practice relevance in the articles published by social work journals. Editorial practices, the expertise of editorial boards, and the actual readerships of social work journals merit closer attention from researchers and practitioners. The publishers of social work journals should be urged to place information about their circulation in the public domain. Strengthened efforts should be made to publish professional journals that aim expressly to apply research to social work practice in ways more readily useful to practitioners. Moreover, at least a few journals ought to be primarily "translational," that is, designed to interpret the findings of research studies in ways that are clearly comprehensible and applicable to practice. In addition, more studies need to be conducted about the relative impact of major social work journals. Attention should be directed especially to their rigor, utility, applicability, and overall influence on social work practice.

Greater emphasis also needs to be placed upon the publication of in-depth syntheses, compendia, and meta-analyses of the research literature in various fields of social work practice. Examples include publications such as *Social Workers' Desk Reference* (Roberts and Greene 2002), *Evidence-Based Practice Manual* (Roberts and Yeager 2004), and the *Encyclopedia of Social Work, 20th ed.* (Mizrahi and Davis 2008). Additionally, researchers should be encouraged to report their findings in practice-oriented monographs, books, and manuals as well as journals. Such publications are more likely than journals to reflect the real intricacies of social work practice and to lend themselves to the elaboration of detailed interventions that can be of use to practitioners.

It should be noted also that rapidly evolving information technologies are exerting a profound influence on the dissemination of many kinds of knowledge. Electronic journals are emerging in social work. Web sites are being employed to greater advantage in order to disseminate the findings of research studies conducted by social workers and to distribute information about funding opportunities for investigators. Examples include sites sponsored by the Institute for the Advancement of Social Work Research and the Society for Social Work and Research, and the "Information for Practice" site developed at the New York University School of Social Work. Concurrently, management information systems that draw upon recent advances in storage, retrieval, and transmission of data are being employed increasingly by social work agencies.

A wide array of allied organizations also disseminate research-based knowledge that can be of particular value to social workers. The Substance Abuse and Mental Health Services Administration (SAMHSA), for example, compiles and disseminates information regarding model intervention programs for substance abuse and related problems that have proved effective on the basis of rigorous research. Likewise, private foundations such as the William T. Grant Foundation and Casey Family Programs have created Web sites that disseminate the practical findings of research they fund. Finally, research dissemination is being advanced by a wide range of other mechanisms, including video conferencing, live video streaming, and geographic information systems. The extent to which these advances can be harnessed successfully by social work researchers and practitioners is bound to shape the future of the profession.

Research Utilization

By far the least developed leg of the tripartite social work research enterprise is research utilization. Major social work conferences often offer workshops, seminars, or lectures that introduce social work practitioners to new interventions. However, relatively few are grounded in rigorous empirical research. Moreover, such learning opportunities typically are compressed into brief sessions of merely an hour or two. Among the more fruitful initiatives are multiweek courses offered by the continuing education programs of social work schools and various service delivery organizations. With a few exceptions (cf., for instance, Grasso and Epstein 1992), only a handful of books and journal publications concerning research utilization have appeared in the social work literature.

Much remains to be done if social work is to develop effective mechanisms for apprising large numbers of practitioners about research-based interventions and how best to apply them. The potential consumers of research-based knowledge—namely, practitioners—may be better positioned than the producers of such knowledge to determine when and how it can be best utilized. Therefore, it is timely for direct service agencies to experiment with innovative mechanisms for facilitating and expediting the application of research-based knowledge by their practitioners. Among other things, it may be profitable for social work agencies to establish in-house units that collect and translate research findings for their own practitioners and, subsequently, to develop pilot programs that test and refine promising research-based practice interventions. In its own right, research utilization is a young science that is insufficiently studied and calls for much greater research inquiry on the part of the social work profession.

Due to significant advances in many areas, the social work research enterprise never has been stronger or better developed than it is now. Yet, relative to present and emerging needs, the research enterprise arguably has never been weaker or less adequately prepared for the challenges at hand. This is one of many fundamental paradoxes that must be addressed if social work practice is to be improved by means of rigorous and meaningful research. The profession's policy makers must recognize the major forces that need to be addressed in all key domains. Above all, attention must be directed toward strengthening, refining, and expanding the most critical infrastructures for social work research, including especially those discussed here.

Notes

1. The members of the task force were Shanti Khinduka (chair), June Gary Hopps, Mark Battle, Don Beless, Scott Briar, Richard English, Patricia L. Ewalt, Ronald Feldman, Merl Hokenstad, Julia Norlin, Alvin Sallee, Barbara Shore, and Neilson Smith.

2. The members of the task force were David Austin (chair), Ronald Feldman (vice-chair), Glenn Allison, Scott Briar, Elaine Brody, Claudia Coulton, King Davis, Patricia L. Ewalt, W. David Harrison, Steven Segal, Barbara Solomon, Tony Tripodi, and Betsey Vourlekis.

3. The co-convenors of the June 2000 meeting were Paula Allen-Meares, Richard Edwards, Ronald Feldman, Marilyn Flynn, Shanti Khinduka, Edward Lawlor, James Midgley, and Ira Schwartz. Representatives attended from Boston University; Columbia University; Florida International University; Florida State University; Howard University; Portland State University; University of California, Berkeley; University of California, Los Angeles; University of Chicago; University of Georgia; University of Houston; University of Illinois, Urbana-Champaign; University of Iowa; University of Kansas; University of Maryland; University of Michigan; University of Minnesota; University of North Carolina, Chapel Hill; University of Pennsylvania; University of Pittsburgh; University of South Carolina; University of Southern California; University of Tennessee; University of Texas, Arlington; University of Texas, Austin; University of Washington; University of Wisconsin, Madison; University of Wisconsin, Milwaukee; and Washington University, St. Louis. Also invited, but unable to attend the meeting, were representatives from: University of Alabama; State University of New York, Albany; State University of New York, Buffalo; and University of California, Berkeley.

4. The members of SSWR's founding board were Janet B.W. Williams, Ronald Feldman, Charles Glisson, Mark Mattaini, Bruce Thyer, Joanne Turnbull, and Betsy Vourlekis.

References

Alexander, C. A. (1987). History of social work and social welfare: Significant dates. In A. Minahan (Ed.-in-Chief), *Encyclopedia of social work,* 18th ed., 1:777–788. Silver Spring, MD: NASW Press.

Austin, D. M. (1999). A report on the progress in the development of research resources in social work. *Research on Social Work Practice 9* (6): 673–707.

Bernard, L. D. (1987). Professional associations: Council on Social Work Education. In A. Minahan (Ed.-in-Chief), *Encyclopedia of social work,* 18th ed., 2:330–333. Silver Spring, MD: National Association of Social Workers.

Brieland, D. (1987). History and evolution of social work practice. In A. Minahan (Ed.-in-Chief), *Encyclopedia of social work,* 18th ed., 1:739–754. Silver Spring, MD: NASW Press.

Boehm, W. M. (1959). *Objectives of the social work curriculum of the future* (Vol. 1 of the social work curriculum study). New York: Council on Social Work Education.

Bloom, M., Fischer, J., and Orme, J. G. (2006). *Evaluating practice: Guidelines for the accountable professional,* 5th ed. Boston: Pearson.

Council on Social Work Education Commission on Accreditation. (2003). *Handbook of accreditation standards and procedures,* 5th ed. Alexandria, VA: Council on Social Work Education.

Craig, C. D., Cook, P. G., and Fraser, M. W. (2004). Research awards in the Society for Social Work and Research, 1996–2000. *Research on Social Work Practice 14* (1): 51–56.

Edwards, R. L. (Ed.). (1995). *Encyclopedia of social work,* 19th ed. Washington, DC: National Association of Social Workers.

Epstein, W. (1999). Of newsletters and scholarly journals. *Research on Social Work Practice 9* (1): 11–112.

Feldman, R. A. (1986). Group work knowledge and research: A two-decade comparison. *Social Work with Groups 9* (3): 7–14.

——. (2004). Principles, practices and findings of The St. Louis Conundrum: A large-scale field experiment with antisocial children. In A. R. Roberts and K. R. Yeager (Eds.), *Evidence-based practice manual: Research and outcome measures in health and human services,* 827–837. New York: Oxford University Press.

——. (2005). Social work practice research: Mapping the past, pondering the future. Unpublished manuscript.

Flexner, A. (1915). Is social work a profession? In *Proceedings of the national conference on charities and corrections,* 576–590. Chicago: Hildeman.

Goldstein, S. R. and Beebe, L. (1995). National Association of Social Workers. In R. L. Edwards (Ed.-in-Chief), *Encyclopedia of social work,* 19th ed., 2:1747–1764. Washington, DC: NASW Press.

Grasso, A. J. and Epstein, I. (Eds.). (1992). *Research utilization in the social services: Innovations for practice and administration.* New York: Haworth Press.

Group for the Advancement of Doctoral Education (1992). *Guidelines for quality in social work doctoral programs.* Washington, DC: Author.

Hollis, E. V. and Taylor, A. L. (1951). *Social work education in the United States.* New York: Columbia University Press.

Karger, H. J. (1999). The politics of social work research. *Research on Social Work Practice 9* (1): 96–99.

Lindsey, D. (1999). Ensuring standards in social work research. *Research on Social Work Practice 9* (1): 115–120.

——. (2002). Building a research journal in child welfare. *Children and Youth Services Review 24* (12): 881–883.

Lindsey, D. and Kirk, S. A. (1992). The role of social work journals in the development of a knowledge base for the profession. *Social Service Review 66* (2): 295–310.

Lloyd, G. A. (1987). Social work education. In A. Minahan (Ed.-in-Chief), *Encyclopedia of social work,* 18th ed., 2:695–705. Silver Spring, MD: NASW Press.

Maas, H. S. (1977). Research in social work. In J. B. Turner (Ed.-in-Chief), *Encyclopedia of social work,* 17th ed., 2:1183–1194. Washington, DC: NASW Press.

NASW News. (2001). Image seen as key to social work's future. September 3. Washington, DC: NASW Press.

National Association of Deans and Directors Task Force. (1997). *Challenges and opportunities for promoting federally funded research in social work programs.* Washington, DC: Institute for the Advancement of Social Work Research.

National Association of Deans and Directors of Social Work Schools, Task Force on the Future of Social Work Education. (1989). *Proposal for a comprehensive study of social work education.*

Pardeck, J. T. and Meinert, R. C. (1999a). Scholarly achievements of the Social Work editorial board and consulting editors: A commentary. *Research on Social Work Practice 9* (1): 86–91.

——. (1999b). Improving the scholarly quality of Social Work's editorial board and consulting editors: A professional obligation. *Research on Social Work Practice 9* (1): 121–127.

Polansky, N. A. (1987). Research in social work: Social treatment. In A. Minahan (Ed.-in-Chief), *Encyclopedia of social work,* 18th ed., 2:1206–1213. Silver Spring, MD: NASW Press.

Popple, P. R. (1995). Social work profession: History. In R. L. Edwards (Ed.-in-Chief), *Encyclopedia of social work,* 19th ed., 3:2282–2292. Washington, DC: NASW Press.

Potocky-Tripodi, M. and Tripodi, T. (Eds.). (1999). *New directions for social work practice research.* Washington, DC: NASW Press.

Rapp-Pagliacci, L., Dulmus, C. N., and Wodarski, J. S. (Eds.). (2004). *Handbook of preventive interventions for children and adolescents.* Hoboken, NJ: Wiley.

Reid, W. J., and Smith, A. D. (1989). *Research in social work,* 2nd ed. New York: Columbia University Press.

Roberts, A. R. and Greene, G. J. (Eds.). (2002). *Social workers' desk reference.* New York: Oxford University Press.

Roberts, A. R. and Yeager, K. R. (Eds.). (2004). *Evidence-based practice manual: Research and outcome measures in health and human services.* New York: Oxford University Press.

Rosen, A., Proctor, E. K., and Staudt, M. M. (1999). Social work research and the quest for effective practice. *Social Work Research 23*:4–14.

Rothman, J. and Thomas, E. J. (Eds.). (1994). *Intervention research: Design and development for human service.* Binghamton, NY: Haworth Press.

Tourse, R. W. C. (1995). Special interest professional associations. In R. L. Edwards (Ed.-in-Chief), *Encyclopedia of social work,* 19th ed., 3:2314–2319. Washington, DC: NASW Press.

Tufts, J. H. (1923). *Education and training for social work.* New York: Russell Sage Foundation.

Williams, L. F. (1987). Professional associations: Special interest. In A. Minahan (Ed.-in-Chief), *Encyclopedia of social work,* 18th ed., 2:341–346. Silver Spring, MD: NASW Press.

2 | Empirical Practice in Social Work

Anne E. Fortune

THE CURRENT INTEREST IN empirical clinical practice in the United States reflects a confluence of several efforts to place social work practice on a more "scientific" basis. We focus on clinical practice—practice with individual, families, and small groups—because only recently has community organization been included (Ohmer and Korr 2006). These twentieth-century efforts to make social work "scientific" include legitimating research as a source of data for intervention knowledge; researching the outcomes of social work practice; building empirical practice models; and several forms of evidence-based interventions and decision making.

Establishing Relevance of a Scientific Approach

Beginning with Mary Richmond (1917), social work researchers attempted to structure intervention with systematic rational decision making based on empirical knowledge (Kirk and Reid 2002; Reid 1994). Shortly after World War II, as specialist social work groups began talking about joining forces, researchers organized to define their roles and contribution to social work (Graham, Al-Krenawi, and Bradshaw 2000). In 1949, they founded the Social Work Research Group (SWRG). In 1955, SWRG was one of seven professional groups that formed the National Association of Social Work (NASW); from 1963 to 1974 it was a "council" within NASW; and then in a reorganization of NASW, it was dropped. SWRG's substantial accomplishments over these twenty-five years included defining social work research; integrating research into the role and curricula of schools; disseminating research results through conferences, a newsletter, and the first database of social work research, —*Social Work Abstracts*; and improving capacity through workshops and the first social work research textbook, Polansky's (1960) *Social Work Research* (Graham, Al-Krenawi, and Bradshaw 2000; Kirk and Reid 2002).

Research on Social Casework

During the same period, from the 1950s to the 1970s, social work researchers conducted multiple ambitious, large-scale social experiments. These studies for the first time assumed that there were measurable outcomes and that it was desirable to study those outcomes. Examples include intensive individual psychodynamic services for predelinquent boys (the Cambridge-Somerville study) (Powers and Witmer 1951), services for mentally impaired older persons in need of protective services (the Benjamin Rose study) (Blenkner, Bloom, and Nielsen 1971), and psychodynamic services for public assistance families (the Chemung County study) (Wallace 1967). All together, the studies included predelinquent and delinquent boys, girls on probation, bright disadvantaged minority youth, high school girls, new AFDC recipients and longer-term multiproblem families, and older individuals. The interventions included predominantly psychodynamic approaches, individual and group services, and help with environmental resources. When the studies were reviewed, reviewers suggested that social work intervention was ineffective or even detrimental (Mullen and Dumpson 1972; Fischer 1973). These unwanted results spurred two efforts: an "age of accountability" where practitioner-researchers attempted to infuse practice with evaluation and measureable outcomes and a reexamination of the principles of casework, including application of psychodynamic as well as new approaches such as task-centered, cognitive-behavioral, and systems approaches (Kirk and Reid 2002).

Beginnings of Empirical Practice

Reid defined scientifically based or empirical practice as including five elements: 1) empirical language in which key terms can be tied to measurable indicators; 2) use of well-explicated practice models that link interventions and change; 3) priority of research-based knowledge as a means of making assessments and selecting interventions; 4) use of scientific reasoning, rather than intuition or faith, to make decisions; and 5) use of research methods as an integral part of practice (e.g., gathering data for assessment and evaluation) (Reid and Smith 1981:16–22). These assumptions were a response to the interest in effective practice but also a direct challenge to the prevailing psychodynamic and functional interventions.

The new ideas about empirical practice developed initially at the Columbia University School of Social Work doctoral program in the late 1950s and early 1960s. The context of scientific skepticism and dissatisfaction with psychodynamic casework stimulated a cohort of doctoral students who would become leading proponents of scientific practice (Kirk and Reid 2002; Reid 1994). After graduation, they clustered at five schools—University of California, Los Angeles; University of Washington; University of Michigan; University of Wisconsin-Madison; and University of Chicago. At each, they established systematic research programs to improve social work interventions. Columbia graduate Scott Briar championed the "clinical scientist" and practitioner contribution to intervention knowledge through single-system designs (Blythe, Tripodi, and Briar 1995). Edward J. Mullen worked on practitioners' individualized models of evidence-based practice, a precursor to the current EBP (Mullen 1978). Several clusters of faculty refined behavioral group and individual interventions based on cumulative research programs with their graduate students. These included Edwin J. Thomas and Sheldon Rose (Michigan graduates), Elsie Pinkston (a University of Kansas graduate) and Columbia graduates Richard Stuart, Tony Tripodi, Irwin Epstein, and Arthur Schwartz (Thomas 1974; Pinkston and Linsk 1984; Stuart 1977; Schwartz and Goldiamond 1975; Tripodi and Epstein 1980; Ivanoff, Blythe, and Tripodi 1994). William J. Reid and Laura Epstein (a Chicago graduate) (1972) developed a new practice approach—the task-centered model—based not on behavioral methods but on the results of research on psychodynamic practice. Despite their differences, these faculty (and their students) shared a commitment to developing practice through empirical means, and they influenced one another's work. All were prolific writers who attempted to integrate their research results and theoretical foundations into new formulations of social work practice that challenged the prevailing psychodynamic interpretations. They in turn influenced scores of students to continue the development of empirical practice and research on interventions.

While the proponents of empirical practice focused on developmental research, social work intervention theories generally blossomed as scholars developed models that integrated new ideas from various sources. These non-empirical models included several versions of the generalist model (Compton and Galaway 1975; Pincus and Minahan 1973), the Life Model (Germain and Gitterman 1980), problem solving (Perlman 1957), general systems (Goldstein

1973), family systems (Hartman and Laird 1983), and ecosystems (Meyer 1976). While these nonempirical models dominated in education and practice (for example, U.S. accreditation standards required generalist practice), gradually the empirical and nonempirical models influenced each other. For example, behavioral (learning) theory became cognitive-behavioral theory; task-centered practice incorporated systems theories; and generalist practice included notions of client determination and contracts.

In practice and in teaching, both empirical and nonempirical models were discrete wholes; a practitioner did "generalist practice" or "cognitive-behavioral practice." Although social workers were intensely interested in assessment and problem classification (Kirk and Reid 2002), the emphasis was differential diagnosis within a practice model. For example, Reid and Epstein (1972) included a typology of target problems in their initial formulation of the task-centered model and later attempted to link interventions to the problem type (Reid 1992).

Evidence-Based Interventions

In the mental health field outside of social work, intervention research was linked primarily to the problem, with interventions being eclectic or nontheoretical. For example, the (now) National Institutes of Health are organized by area, e.g., aging, mental health, drug abuse, etc. When the federal government agreed to bolster the research infrastructure for social work (the 1988 NIMH Task Force on Social Work Research) (see Feldman, chapter 1), not surprisingly, that funding was problem based. Each of the eight research centers focused on a specific area of mental health, as did the research methodology workshops for faculty (Austin 1999). Currently, the directory of federally funded grants maintained by the Institute for Advancement of Social Work Research (IASWR 2009) indicates the specific, focused, and problem-oriented nature of social work research. For example, research topics include adherence to a low-fat diet, motivational enhancement for drug addicts, treatment of depression among older alcoholics, reducing HIV risk among drug users, etc.

Most of the research on social work practice since 1988 is problem specific. Because the eclectic interventions in recent research are usually based on "best known" practice, the interventions favor those already supported by evidence, e.g., structured interventions, cognitive-behavioral methods, group interventions, and primary prevention (Reid and Fortune 2003). As a consequence, there are multiple evidence-supported interventions (EBP as a noun) for narrowly defined problems, while many of the popular social work interventions have not been tested.

A related development in empirical practice was the study of how social workers make decisions about interventions. Many of the Columbia University pioneers had been influenced by James Bieri, who studied clinical decision making (Reid 1994). Edward J. Mullen's (1978) personal practice model was a form of decision making using research evidence. Aaron Rosen and Enola K. Proctor (1978) studied clinician decision making from several perspectives. Eventually they developed and tested a structured decision-making system (Systematic Planned Practice) (Rosen 1993) and specified the necessary components of practice guidelines (Rosen and Proctor 2003). In the mid-1980s, Leonard Gibbs began advocating better reasoning in clinical practice and preparing curricular materials to teach critical thinking (1985; 2003). Gibbs joined Eileen Gambrill (a graduate of Thomas's Michigan program and an ardent behaviorist) to promote critical thinking in the United States (Gambrill 1990; 1993). Their model was heavily influenced by Sackett's Evidence-Based Medicine (1997), adopted in 1991 by the United Kingdom Health Service (including British social workers). It includes a seven-step process of motivation to use EBP: defining an answerable (practice) question; finding best available evidence to answer it; assessing the evidence; integrating it with practice experience, client values, and other relevant factors; implementing the intervention; evaluating it; and teaching others (Gibbs 2003; Gibbs and Gambrill 1999).

The concurrent development of problem-based research and critical, rational decision making in the 1980s and 1990s allowed the two to be melded into the Evidence-Based Practice (EBP) decision-making process. Evidence-supported interventions from problem-based research could be retrieved, evaluated, and implemented using this process. The difficulty, of course, is that the supply of well-validated evidence-supported interventions is much slimmer in social work than in medicine. Despite the dramatic increase in research infrastructure due to the NIMH efforts after 1988 (Austin 1999), relatively little of the new research focused on practice interventions. Further, the criteria for adequate evidence are controversial. For clients with multiple and varied problems, the array of evidence-based guidelines is overwhelming and may not be appropriate for comorbidity. To make the evidence-supported interventions more accessible and understandable to practitioners, several organizations assess research in a particular area and summarize the findings. Notable are the British Cochrane Collaboration in medicine, founded in 1993, and the Campbell Collaboration, founded in 2000 for education, criminal justice, and social welfare. In the United States, particularly rich sources of evidence-supported interventions are available at the National Institutes of Health and several foundations. (For in-depth discussion of EBP retrieval and limits, see Fraser and Terzian, chapter 6; Littell, chapter 11; and Fortune, McCallion and Briar-Lawson, chapter 26).

In 2008, the Council on Social Work Education mandated that evidence-based interventions be included in the curricula of U.S. schools of social work. It did not define "evidence-based intervention," though, and there is considerable ambiguity about its meaning. However, the National Institutes of Mental Health contracted with Danya International to develop a social work EBP curriculum in collaboration with six social work organizations, including CSWE, and many scholars of EBP. Their curriculum, based on the Sackett-Gibbs-Gambrill decision-making process, has been disseminated to graduate and undergraduate programs in the United States (Danya 2008).

Thus, at the beginning of the twenty-first century, social work interventions include four streams: nonempirical practice theories, empirically based models, eclectic problem-specific evidence-supported interventions (EBPs), and a critical thinking decision-making process (EBP) that structures use of evidence-supported interventions. Each stream has strengths and weaknesses, so it would be a shame to overlook one of them in the quest for effective practice. The theory-based interventions can be tested (if their epistemology allows). Empirically based models can be refined for specific problems, as indeed they have been (see, for example, Reid 2000). Problem-specific EBPs may be integrated by finding common elements, as Bruce Chorpita has done with behavioral interventions for children (Chorpita 2007) and Horvath and colleagues with the working alliance (Horvath and Greenberg 1994). And critical thinking can be integrated into any approach that allows choice of intervention. These four streams may eventually be reconciled through research or (more likely) consensual co-optation. Or they may stand alone as different approaches to resolving human ills.

References

Austin, D. M. (1999). A report on progress in the development of research resources in social work. *Research on Social Work Practice 9* (6): 673–707.

Blenkner, M., Bloom, M., and Nielson, M. (1971). A research and demonstration project of protective services. *Social Casework 52*:483–499.

Blythe, B.J., Tripodi, T., and Briar, S. (1995). *Direct practice research in human service agencies.* New York: Columbia University Press.

Chorpita, B. F. (2007). *Modular cognitive-behavioral therapy for children.* New York: Guilford.

Compton, B. R., and Galaway, B. (1975). *Social work processes.* Homewood, IL: Dorsey Press.

Danya International, I. (2008). *Research and empirical applications for curriculum enhancement in social work (REACH-SW): Advanced doctoral students or new instructors edition* [CD-ROM].

Fischer, J. (1973). Is casework effective? A review. *Social Work 18* (1): 5–20.

Fortune, A. E. (1992). Inadequate resources. In W. J. Reid (Ed.), *Task strategies: An empirical approach to clinical social work*, 250–279. New York: Columbia University Press.

Gambrill, E. (1990). *Critical thinking in clinical practice: Sources of error and how to avoid them.* San Francisco: Jossey-Bass.

——. (1993). What critical thinking offers to clinicians and clients. *Behavior Therapist* 16:141–147.

Germain, C. B. and Gitterman, A. (1980). *The life model of social work practice.* New York: Columbia University Press.

Gibbs, L. E. (1985). Teaching critical thinking at the university level: A review of some empirical evidence. *Informal Logic 7* (2/3): 137–149.

——. (2003). *Evidence-based practice for the helping professions: A practical guide with integrated multimedia.* Pacific Grove, CA: Brooks/Cole Thomson Learning.

Gibbs, L. E., and Gambrill, E. (1999). *Critical thinking for social workers: Exercises for the helping professions,* 2nd ed. Thousand Oaks, CA: Pine Forge Press.

Goldstein, H. (1973). *Social work practice: a unitary approach.* Columbia: University of South Carolina Press.

Graham, J. R., Al-Krenawi, A., and Bradshaw, C. (2000). The Social Work Research Group/NASW Research Section/Council on Social Work Research, 1949–1965: An emerging research identity in the American profession. *Research on Social Work Practice 10* (5): 622–643.

Hartman, A., and Laird, J. (1983). *Family-centered social work practice.* New York, London: Free Press; Collier Macmillan.

Institute for the Advancement of Social Work Research (IASWR). (2009). Directory of social work research grants awarded by the National Institutes of Health 1993–2009 Updated June 2009. http://www.charityadvantage.com/iaswr/NIHSWRDatabaseRevJUNE2009.pdf (accessed June 29, 2009).

Ivanoff, A. M., Blythe, B. J., and Tripodi, T. (1994). *Involuntary clients in social work practice: A research-based approach.* Hawthorne, NY: Aldine de Gruyter.

Kirk, S. A. and Reid, W. J. (2002). *Science and social work.* New York: Columbia University Press.

Meyer, C. H. (1976). *Social work practice,* 2nd ed. New York: Free Press.

Mullen, E. J. (1978). The construction of personal models for effective parctice: A method for utilizing research findings to guide social interventions. *Journal of Social Service Research, 2* (1): 45–63.

Mullen, E. J. and Dumpson, J. R. (Eds.). (1972). *Evaluation of social intervention.* San Francisco: Jossey-Bass.

Ohmer, M. L. and Korr, W. (2006). The effectiveness of community practice interventions: A review of the literature. *Research on Social Work Practice 16* (2): 132–145.

Perlman, H. H. (1957). *Social casework, a problem-solving process.* Chicago: University of Chicago Press.

Pincus, A. and Minahan, A. (1973). *Social work practice: model and method.* Itasca, IL: F. E. Peacock.

Pinkston, E. M. and Linsk, N. L. (1984). *Care of the elderly: A family approach.* New York: Pergamon Press.

Polansky, N. A. (Ed.). (1960). *Social work research: Methods for the helping professions.* Chicago: University of Chicago Press.

Powers, E. and Witmer, H. (1951). *An experiment in the prevention of delinquency—The Cambridge-Somerville Youth Study.* New York: Columbia University Press.

Proctor, E. K. and Rosen, A. (2003). The structure and function of social work practice guidelines. In A. Rosen and E. K. Proctor (Eds.), *Developing practice guidelines for social work intervention: Issues, methods, and research agenda,* 108–127. New York: Columbia University Press.

Reid, W. J. (1994). Field testing and data gathering on innovative practice interventions in early development. In J. Rothman and E. J. Thomas (Eds.), *Intervention research,* 245–264. New York: Haworth Press.

——. (2000). *The task planner: An intervention resource for human service professionals.* New York: Columbia University Press.

Reid, W. J. and Epstein, L. (1972). *Task-centered casework.* New York: Columbia University Press.

Reid, W. J. and Fortune, A. E. (2003). Empirical foundations for practice guidelines in current social work knowledge. In E. K. Proctor and A. Rosen (Eds.), *Developing practice guidelines for social work intervention: Issues, methods, and research agenda,* 59–79. New York: Columbia University Press.

Reid, W. J. and Smith, A. D. (1981). *Research in social work.* New York: Columbia University Press.

Richmond, M. (1917). *Social diagnosis.* New York: Russell Sage Foundation.

Rose, S. D. (1980). *A casebook in group therapy: A behavioral-cognitive approach.* Englewood Cliffs, NJ: Prentice-Hall.

Rosen, A. (1993). Systematic planned practice. *Social Service Review 67* (1): 84–100.

Rosen, A. and Proctor, E. K. (1978). Specifying the treatment process: The basis for effectiveness research. *Journal of Social Service Research 2* (1): 25–44.

Sackett, D. L., Richardson, W. S., and Haynes, R. B. (1997). *Evidence-based medicine: How to practice and teach EBM.* New York: Churchill Livingstone.

Schwartz, A. and Goldiamond, I. (1975). *Social casework: A behavioral approach.* New York: Columbia University Press.

Stuart, R. B. (1977). *Behavioral self-management: Strategies, techniques and outcomes.* New York: Brunner/Mazel.

Thomas, E. J. (1974). *Behavior modification.* Chicago: Aldine.

Tripodi, T. and Epstein, I. (1980). *Research techniques for clinical social workers.* New York: Columbia University Press.

Wallace, D. (1967). The Chemung County evaluation of casework service to dependent multi-problem families: Another problem outcome. *Social Service Review 41:*379–389.

3 | Qualitative Social Work Practice Research

Ian Shaw

IN THIS CHAPTER, I primarily outline ways qualitative research methodology not only enriches but also expands the challenges posed for and by practice research. I will suggest how qualitative approaches challenge how we think about the *design* of practice research, *fieldwork* within it, and *analysis*. I will also touch on developments in *qualitative synthesis*. I will close by briefly suggesting broader issues that inescapably surface as we begin to think in this way.

Social work practice research is defined relatively widely for this chapter—in both scope and methodology. In scope, practice research for our purposes is any disciplined empirical inquiry (research, evaluation, analysis), conducted by researchers, practitioners, service users/caregivers or others, that is intended, wholly or to some significant degree, to shed light on or explain social work intervention/practice with the purpose of achieving the goals of social work within or across national cultures.

My concern for breadth is intended in part to bring practitioners of social work and human services into active conversation with colleagues in other professions and disciplines. However, I wish to avoid too easy assumptions regarding the feasibility of mutual accommodations between disciplines and methodologies. Trend's long-ago advice was "that we give the different viewpoints the chance to arise, and postpone the immediate rejection of information or hypotheses that seem out of joint with the majority viewpoint" (Trend 1979:84).

Although I am stressing the contribution that qualitative methodology might make to social work practice research, a couple of cautions are in order. First, this chapter should not be read as a claim that qualitative research is better equipped than more traditional approaches to generate *foundationalist* knowledge of policy and practice outcomes. This would be crass. "*Nothing* can guarantee that we have recalled the truth" (Phillips 1990:43). Second, this is not a plea to replace one uniformitarian orthodoxy with another. On the one hand, a notion that only qualitative methods can examine unique, complex cases is clearly not accurate, as there is an interesting history of idiographic and ipsative quantitative methods for individual case analysis in psychology in the work of people such as Rogers, Allport, Cattell, and Kelly. On the other hand, I am not convinced that all forms and traditions of qualitative methodology lend themselves equally or even directly to practice research purposes.

Third, changing contexts push us to integrate and formalize the contribution of qualitative methods within evaluative research (e.g., Spencer et al. 2003; NIH 2001). Within social work and the evaluation field, there has been much talk of moving beyond the "paradigm wars." At one extreme, this "moving beyond" has led to an unhelpful polarization and to a response marked by naïve pragmatism and a rejection of anything that seems to place "theory" close to "method." In its more helpful manifestations it has led to considered efforts at *epistemological conversation* and a general reluctance to adopt strong versions of incommensurability arguments (e.g., Greene and Caracelli 1997; Reichardt and Rallis 1994).

Qualitative Practice Research

A qualitative approach is valuable where issues or problems are poorly understood, where a researcher wants to explore a policy context, where evaluation criteria are not clear or alternative criteria are sought, where it is important to understand practices in detail or it is important to discover how a scheme was actually implemented, or where an evaluator wants to know about people's subjective experience of outcomes. (Spencer et al. 2003:36)

Practice Research Design and Strategy

Case Study Research

Michael Patton has illustrated how "well-crafted case studies can tell the stories behind the numbers, capture unintended impacts and ripple effects, and illuminate dimensions of desired outcomes that are difficult to quantify"

(Patton 2002:152). He makes a familiar distinction between program improvement and individual outcomes, and argues that qualitative case studies offer a method for capturing and reporting individualized outcomes. Insofar as it is necessary to understand individual outcomes—and in many human services interventions, it is vital—then quantitative, standardized measures will be inappropriate. Take, for example, human services programs that aim at some form of individual autonomy and independence. "Independence has different meanings for different people under different conditions. . . . What program staff want to document under such conditions is the unique meaning of the outcomes for each client." "Qualitative methods are particularly appropriate for capturing and evaluating such outcomes," through the use, in particular, of inductive description (Patton 2002:158, 476).

Simulations

A rather different design solution for practice research is offered by qualitative simulation designs, which have the potential to provide "a unique and innovative tool that has not yet been widely applied" (Turner and Zimmerman 1994:335). They have two main applications—first as an evaluative test for service discrimination and second as a qualitative proxy for control within a natural setting. The second and much less appreciated application adopts the logic of quantitative research, but in the context of a thoroughgoing qualitative strategy.

One particular example of simulation—the simulated client—represents an advance on the use of vignettes in policy and practice research. Those who evaluate the process of professional practice come face to face with its invisibility. How may we learn the ways social workers practice? How would different professionals deal with the same case? Wasoff and Dobash used a promising innovative method in their study of how a specific piece of law reform was incorporated into the practice of solicitors in the UK (Wasoff and Dobash 1992; Wasoff and Dobash 1996). The use of simulated clients in "natural" settings allowed them to identify practice variations that could be ascribed with some confidence to differences between lawyers rather than taken as artifacts of differences between cases. Suppose, for example, that one wishes to carry out a qualitative evaluation of decisions made by housing managers, medical staff, and social workers regarding the allocation of care management packages. Evaluators using simulated clients would prepare a small number of very detailed case histories designed to test the practice decisions under consideration. Adopting this as a script, a researcher or evaluator would take on the role of the client. The housing manager, relevant medical staff, and social workers each interview the "client" within the "natural" settings of their own work, and the practice is compared across settings while the "case" is held significantly more constant than would be possible in, say, ethnographic fieldwork.

User-Led Practice Research

In social work it is often claimed that an emancipatory research agenda, delivered prominently through the involvement of service users and caregivers in the research process, is part and parcel of good research. It is also (sometimes) claimed that qualitative commitments better serve this purpose than quantitative methods. David Hamilton, in a little noticed argument, concluded several years ago that "its commitment to participate rationally in the prosecution of worthwhile, even emancipatory, social change is probably the most enduring tradition of qualitative research" (Hamilton 1998:127). This is by no means a universal stance. Walter Lorenz, for example, believes that

> It is not the choice of a particular research method that determines social work's position socially and politically. Rather it is the ability to engage critically in the political agenda of defining the terms on which knowledge and truth can be established which should form the basis for the search of appropriate research approaches in social work. (Lorenz 2000:8)

In a thoughtful analysis of black research, Stanfield concludes that "even in the most critical qualitative research methods literature there is a tendency to treat 'human subjects' as the passive prisoners of the research process" (Stanfield 1994:168). A similar argument has been put forward by participatory researchers such as John Heron.

Others have been more optimistic regarding the affinity of qualitative methodology with moral or political agenda. Riessman, for example, has written about narrative methods through which "an individual links disruptive events in a biography to heal discontinuities—what should have been and what was" (1994:114). She makes a more general link between qualitative methodology and liberatory positions. "Because qualitative approaches offer the potential for representing human agency—initiative, language, emotion—they provide support for the liberatory project of social work" (1994:xv).

The sociologist Robert Dingwall arrives at a similar conclusion, albeit from a different standpoint, in a form that is insightful for social work practice research. In his consideration of the moral discourse of interactionism, he is impatient with the postmodern repudiation of moral concerns and is concerned with how the moral and the empirical fit together. He reaches back to the philosophy of Adam Smith, for viewing sociology as studying the very preconditions for mutual society. "If we have a mission for our discipline, it may be to show the timeless virtues of compromise and civility, of patient change and human decency, of a community bound by obligations rather than rights" (Dingwall 1997:204). This quotation has been deliberately chosen in contrast to emancipatory models of research, to show that the qualitative analysis "of what it might take to live a moral life" (204) is neither novel nor the exclusive province of any single political position. My own position is close to that of Riessman. Qualitative research informed by critical concerns "must neither ignore instrumental issues nor privilege them" (Vanderplaat 1995:94).

Social workers, to borrow apt phrasing from Robert Stake, have become "reluctant to separate epistemology from ideology, findings from yearnings" (Stake 1997:471). But is advocacy research a *sine qua non* of good (qualitative) practice research? I would claim it is a necessary part of the overall research mission, but not a necessary dimension of each and every research project. User-led research widens and challenges the foci from what academics and practitioners think are key questions, extends what is regarded as good intervention, and provides a powerful sense of what is stigmatizing (cf. Hanley 2005).

For example, qualitative user-led research and evaluation shifts the focus from what practitioners or researchers think are key questions for research to those that sufferers and survivors think are central. These are likely to include:

- Coping
- Identity
- Information needs
- Support needs
- Self-help
- Caregivers
- Women's issues
- Rights and opportunities[1]

This anchors an abiding tension in applied qualitative research—that between expertise and democratizing values. I think I detect an emerging level of accommodation, or at least conversation, in this vexed field. Thus, Hammersley concedes that

> if we can see how educational research could be characterized by competing paradigms (in a non Kuhnian sense) . . . and therefore necessarily divided by allegiances to discrepant world-views, then we perhaps should resist any inclination to dismiss paradigm differentiation as entirely the product of bias, theoretical or methodological fashion, career building, etc as some of us (myself included) sometimes do. (Hammersley 2005)

Qualitative Practitioner Research

Empirical practice—whether it be a mode of intervention or a commitment to doing small-scale rigorous research—has been almost exclusively modeled on logic borrowed from the experimental tradition. Reid's paper on empirical practice (Reid 1994), and his cowritten subsequent analysis (Reid and Zettergren 1999), taken together, offer a fine perspective on this tradition.

It seems to me that there are three aspects to the question of how we may advance qualitative practitioner research. First, we know all too little regarding the nature of practitioner research. The literature has focused too much on the promotion of a particular ideology of research practice and insufficiently on a more inductive and empirical account. Kirk and Reid were correct to observe the absence of empirical evidence on practitioners' epistemologies, just as they were right to drive the empirical agenda in arguing that "The bottom line for research utilization is what happens in the field among practitioners" (Kirk and Reid 2002:194). I have tried elsewhere to address this lacuna (Shaw 2005; Shaw and Faulkner 2006). The second point follows closely from this, and relates to the absence of interest in qualitative analysis of such work, or in developing qualitative practitioner research projects.[2] Finally, there has been an unduly individualist understanding of how such research should develop.

Interactionist Practice Research

Finally, a different story for qualitative practice research is suggested by *interactionist approaches* from within sociology. Interactionism in sociology goes back to Chicago and hence is tied to the history of social work through the emergence of the School of Social Service Administration. The Chicago school led to a growing awareness of qualitative methods as methodological issues rather than just common-sense practice. Interactionism has led to a focus on settings as sites of moral work as well as technical professional decision making.

Viewing moral orders as outcomes calls for a different take on social work intervention. Professional and personal identities are ascribed and negotiated. There was some early work in social work on this, though not explicitly attributed to interactionism (e.g., Hall 1971), and the general perspective is represented in two collections of work (Sherman and Reid 1994; Kirk 1999). This probably influenced social work as much through Erving Goffman as anyone else, and through Lemert and others' labeling theory. We are pushed to see how the collective responses of social institutions shape identities. Intervention research influenced by interactionist sociology would thus start with a different stance.

The general point here is that interactionism is a genuinely social approach, whereas some intervention research is not, and will yield evidence consistent with its approach. Miller's example from the field of nursing care illustrates the point above about moral orders and enriches our understanding of the importance of context in qualitative practice research.[3] He discusses ways that institutional texts constructed to explain past decisions inevitably gloss over the openness and complexity of the decision-making process (Miller 1997). He gives the mundane example of evaluation research on managing continence problems in a nursing home. The evaluation consisted of counting when and how patients had continence problems. The program was judged to have a successful outcome if patients used a toilet or bedpan and to be ineffective for those who continued soiling beds. One patient had soiled her bed. Ethnographic methods enabled the researcher to observe a nursing aide contesting the definition of this incident as "failure," on the grounds that the patient knew what she was doing and had soiled her bed as a protest act against staff favoring another patient. This illustrates how mundane, everyday life is illuminated by observing the context of text construction. This would not have found a way into the formal outcome record. Text production in institutions is "micropolitically organized," and this includes textual outcome records.

Fieldwork in Qualitative Practice Research

Change-Process Research

Bill Reid's work in this field has been far too little exploited as a form of practice research that is neither straightforwardly outcome nor process focused. Reid did not, of course, reject the role of controlled experiments, but concluded that "practical and ethical constraints on experiments necessitate a reliance on the naturalistic study of these relations" (Reid 1990:130). This entails a focus on the processes of change during the period of contact between the professional helper and the client system. Rather than relying on aggregated, averaged summary measures of outcomes, this approach focuses on micro-outcomes.

A systemic view of intervention is at its root, when professionals and service users are viewed in a circular, mutually influencing interaction. In this model "conventional distinctions between intervention and outcome lose their simplicity" (135). "It then becomes possible to depict change-process research as a study of strings of intermixed . . . interventions and outcomes" (136). Although Reid defended experiments throughout his career, he suggested a more naturalistic stance when he said, "averages of process variables that are devoid of their contexts at best provide weak measures" (137). Two radical conclusions follow: we cannot divide intervention and outcomes in any clear way; and evaluation does not work well when we try to evaluate a group, especially when it ignores context.

A different and interesting argument for using qualitative methods as a means of understanding microprocesses has been suggested by McLeod in a thoughtful assessment of the potential of such methods for understanding outcomes of counseling. He suggests that qualitative interviews are more likely than questionnaires to elicit critical perspectives, arising from the "demand characteristics" of extended interviews. "In terms of producing new knowledge that contributes to debates over evidence-based therapy, it would appear that qualitative evaluation is better able to explore the limits of therapeutic *ineffectiveness*" (McLeod 2001:178). Combined with their potential for eliciting positive relations between intervention and outcome, he concludes, not unlike Patton, that "Qualitative interviews appear to be, at present, the most sensitive method for evaluating the harmful effects of therapy and also for recording its greatest individual successes" (179).

Evaluating in Practice

> Historically, the influence of science on direct social work practice has taken two forms. One is the use of the scientific method to shape practice activities, for example, gathering evidence and forming hypotheses about a client's problem. The other form is the provision of scientific knowledge about human beings, their problems and ways of resolving them. (Reid 1998:3)

Reid's distinction is fundamental and too little appreciated. It is the first "form" that is of interest. I have tried to develop an example of this approach through work on evaluating-in-practice (e.g., Shaw 1996). Three aspects of the approach need emphasizing. First, evaluating in practice is not about the application of research findings to practice but about the method of inquiry and evaluation. We may label this the difference between research as "source" for practice and research as "model" for practice. Second, evaluating-in-practice is a cluster of practice skills and not research skills as such. Third, my own orientation draws primarily on the rich literature and practice of qualitative inquiry and evaluation.

A demanding set of skills is necessary to achieve this shaping of practice—skills that I convey through the use of metaphors such as "translation" and "countercolonizing" and through ideas of transfer of learning. Implicit in this argument is a challenge to conventional ways of seeing expert/beneficiary relationships. "Countercolonization" is an allusion to the typical dominance of social science and research "experts" over practice "beneficiaries" and suggests in a contrary fashion the potential for practice to challenge social science.

A wide range of qualitative methods awaits such translation and counter-colonization: narratives, different forms of interview, private and public documents, focus groups, life histories, visual methods, auto-ethnography—to name just a few. For example, a recent book explores the use of "systematic self-observation" (SSO) as a research strategy (Rodriguez and Ryave 2002). As a qualitative research tool, they see SSO as training informants "to observe and record a selected feature of their everyday experience" (2). The focus is on understanding the ordinary, in particular the covert, the elusive, and the personal. In an effort to overcome the "numbness to the details of everyday life" (4), respondents are asked to observe "a single, focused phenomenon that is natural to the culture, is readily noticeable, is intermittent . . . is bounded . . . and is of short duration" and also to focus on the subjective (5).

The recording involves writing a narrative about the situation, the participants, what occurred, the words spoken and thoughts/feelings experienced at the time (i.e., not retrospectively), and doing it as soon as possible after the event. In observing they are instructed in no way to act differently than usual, to never produce instances or judge the propriety of the action—"do not judge it, do not slow down, do not speed up, do not change it, do not question it—just observe it" (17). They refer to a key skill as gaining a "new mindfulness" about everyday life. In their own studies they have used the method to research telling lies, telling secrets in everyday life, withholding compliments, and the role of envy in making social comparisons in everyday life. As a research strategy this raises several questions. For example, how can one know if a problem is "generic" and hence generalizable? How many instances are missed by informants? Is reporting selective? Does the "new mindfulness" lead to a problem of reactivity?

Is a research method like this "translatable" for evaluating in practice? Probably. Indeed, they suggest it has application within therapy in that:

- Naming something can help.
- The task of observing without judging "accesses the roots of the trouble in the tacit dimension" (57), for example, by identifying triggers/antecedents to problem behavior, etc.
- The write-up can act as therapeutic "time out."
- Submitting data to others is a public "owning up."
- Sharing with others who are doing the same activity gives a sense of not being alone with a problem.

They are being speculative, not having tried it in this way—and so am I. But I would suggest a wider potential use that does not assume the "client" is also the target for change. SSO may well be better than single-system designs in two respects: it would allow a more contextualized and richer understanding of the nature of a problem in a service user's life, as part of an assessment and planning process; and because single-system approaches are committed to behavioral approaches that typically proceed by counting and measuring incidence and prevalence of problems, SSO is, as we have noted, "more appropriate for the study of hidden or elusive domains, like the motives, memories, thought processes, withheld actions, thoughts and/or emotions that accompany overt behaviours" (11).

Evaluating in practice approaches is as relevant to the practitioner as it is to the service user. For example, on self-observing, I have been attracted by the interesting work done by the American sociologist Grant McCracken on what he calls a "cultural review," whereby the "interviewer's" prior knowledge of something is made explicit (McCracken 1988; cf. Shaw and Gould 2001). Second, I do not see this kind of practice evaluation and inquiry as a solitary activity, but as one involving communities of practice. Peter Reason's cycles of action and inquiry can be seen in this context. So can some interesting recent work by Tineke Abma on communities of practice in responding to coercion in psychiatry, which included collegial meetings of project leaders (Abma 2007).

An encouraging sign is the almost taken-for-granted way practice-translatable qualitative work is appearing in the journals. Work stimulated by narrative methodology has been remarkably fruitful when viewed from this perspective. Neander and Stott (2006) offer an incisive and upbeat account of families that have struggled with their relationships to their children, and who have identified people who have had a positive influence on the child. In their contact with these "important persons" new narratives of emerging trust, which overcomes obstacles, replace old negative narratives. They conclude that utmost care should be taken to safeguard and nourish these unpredictable "important meetings" where "ordinary magic" may happen. This is a cogent, insightful, and indeed captivating paper.

Wahlström (2006) approaches his theme from the directions of counseling, psychotherapy, and family therapy. Expressing the fundamental technical problem of counseling and psychotherapy as "how to establish change facilitating conversational formats," the article shows how such a reflective process took place in one consultation, using a "reflective team" approach. He draws on the valuable work, too little appreciated in social work, of John McLeod. The role of the reflective team is likely to be especially interesting in, for example, reformulating clients' problems. His extended use of the idea of "voice" in the narrative elements of the consultation is also insightful. Thompson and Holland (2005) describe the evolution of the "memory book" in biographical research. The research and practice border-crossing interest in narrative is captured in McLeod's book (McLeod 1997). The participatory inquiry field is proving equally fertile. Kearney and Hyle (2004) explore the use of participant-produced drawings in a study of the emotional impact of change on individuals in educational institutions. Forbat and Atkinson explore the relationship between research and social work in their discussion of participatory research in learning disability (Forbat and Hyle 2005; cf. Forbat 2005). Interesting work is also emerging from ethnographers, distinctively so from Riemann (Riemann 2005). As Bloor expresses it, "practitioners . . . are able imaginatively to juxtapose their own everyday practices with the research description" (Bloor 2001:184).

Qualitative Analysis of Practice Research

I want to suggest the work of Patton, and Miles and Huberman, as having special resonance for thinking about qualitative contributions to practice research analysis. I have picked them, as with most of the sources mentioned in this chapter, because they address the "tough" version of qualitative practice research, i.e., how it may contribute to outcomes of practice.

"The conventional view is that qualitative studies are only good for exploratory forays, for developing hypotheses—and that strong explanations, including causal attributions, can be derived only through quantitative studies." Miles and Huberman describe this view as "mistaken" (1994:147), and insist that qualitative evaluation research can identify causal mechanisms, deal with complex local networks, and sort out the temporal dimension of events. They also argue that it is well equipped to cycle back and forth between different levels of variables and processes, and that a selective adoption of analytic induction provides a way of testing and deepening single-case explanations.

Miles and Huberman develop analytic methods that address causal attribution in both single- and multiple-case explanations. For example, they advocate the use of field research to map the "local causal networks" that informants carry in their heads and to make connections with the evaluator's own emerging causal map of the setting. Such maps start from "causal fragments," which lead to linked building of logical chains of evidence. Such causal networks "are not probabilistic, but specific and determinate, grounded in understanding of events over time in the concrete local context—*and* tied to a good conceptualization of each variable" (Miles and Huberman 1994:159).

Patton gives an example of how the creation of qualitative matrices is especially useful for exploring linkages between process and outcome. The analytic sequence entails the development of categorizations of types and levels of outcomes and of program processes. The categories are developed through orthodox qualitative analysis. The relationships between processes and outcomes may come either from participants or through subsequent analysis.

In either case, the process/outcomes matrix becomes a way of organizing, thinking about, and presenting the qualitative connections between program implementation dimensions and program impacts (Patton 2002:472). The following extract gives an illustration of how this approach can operate.

> Suppose we have been evaluating a juvenile justice program that places delinquent youth in foster homes. . . . A *regularly recurring process theme* concerns the importance of "letting kids learn to make their own decisions." A *regularly recurring outcome theme* involves "keeping the kids straight." . . . By crossing the program process ("kids making their own decisions") with the program outcome ("keeping the kids straight"), we create a data analysis question: What actual decisions do juveniles make that are supposed to lead to reduced recidivism? We then carefully review our field notes and interview quotations looking for data that help us understand how people in the program have answered this question based on their actual behaviors and practices. By describing what decisions juveniles actually make in the program, the decision makers to whom our findings are reported can make their own judgments about the strength or weakness of the linkage. (472–473)

Hence, while qualitative evaluation cannot resolve the problems of causal conclusions any more than quantitative evaluation, it can assess causality "as it actually plays out in a particular setting" (Miles and Huberman 1994:10).

Recurrent Issues

Qualitative Synthesis

A brief aside is in order. We are part way through a rapid expansion of frameworks and projects to develop the synthesis of qualitative research studies. The relevance of this development to the argument of this chapter is that most of this work is driven, as with the work of the Cochrane and Campbell collaborations, by a concern to derive practice guidance. For example, qualitative synthesis has been seen by some writers as one way of addressing the issue of developing generalizable statements from qualitative research. Meta-ethnography, thematic synthesis from within grounded theory, synthesis of qualitative and quantitative research, the development of quality criteria that can be applied in a transferable way across most research, and ecological triangulation methods are but some of the developments taking place (cf. Popay and Roen 2003 for a brief overview written for a human services audience).

The work of James Banning at the State University of Colorado is among the more interesting developments for our purposes because it is concerned with evidence about outcomes. His recent work has included systematic reviews designed to assist secondary-aged students with disabilities ("What Works for Youth with Disabilities Project"). He and his colleagues use both qualitative and quantitative studies in the same review and N-Vivo to do the synthesis. They have developed the concept of ecological triangulation, where theory, method, interventions, people, settings/environments and outcomes, and the transactional relationship among these variables are the focus. They are interested in theoretical frameworks (metatheory), methods (metamethod) and what interventions with what individuals under what conditions produced what outcomes (meta-analysis). Through their process synthesis, they seek interventions that have positive outcomes that can be described in relation to theory, method, people, and settings/environments.

Cause and Effect

Qualitative researchers have been diffident about cause-and-effect arguments. I checked the indices of several leading qualitative texts, to find no listing of "cause." Yet qualitative research entails recognition of the irony of social causes and consequences. Much of the sociology of deviance was based on just this sense of irony, with its exploration of deviant roles as doing necessary "dirty work." It leads to the question of what functions are served by a particular practice that would not be served by its absence. What are the typical results of this phenomenon in this setting, and what ends are served thereby?

Lofland and Lofland make the important observation that causal answers are by and large based on *passivist* conceptions of human nature. Qualitative inquiry has often steered away from causal accounts, not because the methodology is weak in that area, but because of a commitment to an *activist* conception of human nature. The Loflands argue that an activist conception will lead to a focus on questions that address both structures and strategies. This will involve "deciphering and depicting exactly what sort of situation the participants are facing" (Lofland and Lofland 1995:146) and understanding the "incessantly fabricated" strategies people construct to deal with the situation.

Take, for example, Silverman's work on HIV counseling. He is right to conclude that "it is usually unnecessary to allow our research topics to be defined in terms of . . . the 'causes' of 'bad' counseling or the 'consequences' of 'bad' counseling" (Silverman 1997:34), insofar as such topics reflect the conceptions of social problems as recognized by professional or community groups. Nonetheless, this does not require the abandonment of causal inquiry in qualitative evaluation. Inquiry into the ways professionals incessantly fabricate service forms and structures does promise a better way to understand causes.

There has been a plausible argument that randomized control trials are not the best way of tackling some causal questions (Long 2006). This is the case, Long suggests, when:

- The purpose is to illustrate possible mechanisms of effect.
- The causal chains are more complex. In such cases, "Observational studies built on designs based on the plausibility of the theoretically predicted causal chain may be the only feasible option" (Long 2006:463).
- "[A] qualitative research design would enable the generation of insight and understanding into how, and in what contexts, the intervention might work and achieve its outcomes" (464).

Values and Theory

These approaches share a tendency to give greater place to theory—e.g., *how* something might work—and to helpfully emphasize that theory often is implicit in hypotheses. As House expresses it, quoting from Kidder and Fine, "all research is a form of story telling, some more obvious than others. Randomized experiments are the least obvious. . . . Nonetheless, beneath the technical language is a story about how people behave under various conditions" (1994: 18).

Qualitative approaches to practice research tend to give greater prominence to theorizing. Finch argues, "First, that a concern with theory is quite compatible with qualitative research; second that a blend of theory and data is the hallmark of good qualitative work; and third, that this particular blend produces precisely the kind of work which is likely to make an impact upon policy because it offers theoretical insights grounded in evidence" (174).

Greene (1993) specifies what this might entail. We should:

- Explicate our own theoretical predispositions.
- Describe locally held theories ("locally meaningful theoretical perspectives in data interpretation") (Greene 1993:38).
- Attend to emergent theoretical issues.
- Integrate substantive theory into research conclusions and recommendations.

Finally, qualitative practice research facilitates the *valuation of outcomes*, and is opposed to the technicalization of outcome research. While this is not exclusively the province of qualitative research, more conventional and strictly evidence-based varieties of outcome research tend to treat such issues as technical matters. This links to the broader question of value and political issues. "Evidence on effectiveness and outcomes and an emphasis on health gain and health outcome provide an apparently value-neutral, rational approach and means for rationing health and social care. Beneath the range of technical issues in assessing outcomes are political and social values that need to be explicit" (Long 1994:175).

In closing, I am reminded of Stake's remarks regarding the nature of qualitative research methodology: "'to the qualitative scholar, the understanding of human experience is a matter of chronologies more than cause and effect" and that "the function of research is not . . . to map and conquer the world but to sophisticate the beholding of it" (Stake 1995:39, 43).

I have sought in this chapter not to "map and conquer the world but to sophisticate the beholding of it" (Ibid. 1995), with the aspiration that qualitative methodology will be explored by the social work community as an avenue to both extensive and penetrating practice research.

Notes

1. This list is drawn from discussions at a national seminar of user researchers in the UK mental health field.

2. This comment applies more to the United States than to the United Kingdom. Indeed, a weakness of the multitude of such projects in the UK is the risk of superficiality in the qualitative project designs.

3. See also Mohr 1997 for a discussion of how Denzin's interactionist work contributes to outcomes and intervention research.

References

Abma, T. A. (2007). Situated learning in communities of practice: Evaluation of coercion in psychiatrist as a case. *Evaluation 13* (1): 32–47.

Atkinson, P. and Delamont, S. (1993). Bread and dreams or bread and circuses? A critique of case study research in evaluation. In M. Hammersley (Ed.), *Controversies in the classroom*, 26–45. Buckingham, England: Open University Press.

Atkinson, P., Delamont, S., Coffey, A., Lofland, L., and Lofland, J. (2001). *Handbook of ethnography.* London: Sage.

Bloor, M. (2001). The ethnography of health and medicine. In P. Atkinson, S. Delamont, A. Coffey, L. Lofland, and J. Lofland (Eds.), *Handbook of ethnography*, 177–187. London: Sage.

Dingwall, R. (1997). Conclusion: The moral discourse of interactionism. In G. Miller and R. Dingwall (Eds.), *Context and method in qualitative research,* 198–205. London: Sage.

Finch, J. (1986). *Research and policy: The uses of qualitative methods in social and educational research.* London: Falmer Press.

Forbat, E. (2005). *Talking about care.* Bristol, England: Policy Press.

Forbat, E. and Atkinson, D. (2005). Research as social work: Participatory research in learning disability. *British Journal of Social* Work *35* (4): 425–434.

Gilgun, J. (2003). Conjectures and refutations: governmental funding and qualitative research. *Qualitative Social Work 1* (3): 359–373.

Greene, J. (1993). The role of theory in qualitative program evaluation. In J. Flinders and G. Mills, *Theory and concepts in qualitative research.* New York: Teachers College Press.

Greene, J. and Caracelli, V. (1997). Advances in mixed method evaluation: The challenge and benefits of integrating diverse paradigms. *New directions for evaluation,* No. 74. San Francisco: Jossey-Bass.

Hamilton, D. (1998). Traditions, preferences and postures in applied qualitative research. In N. Denzin and Y. Lincoln (Eds.), *The landscape of qualitative research,* 60–69. Thousand Oaks, CA: Sage.

Hammersley, M. (2003). Social research today: Some dilemmas and distinctions. *Qualitative Social Work 2* (1): 25–44.

——. (2005). Methodological disagreement and the problem of quality. Paper for seminar on Assessing Quality in Case Study and Qualitative Research, forming part of the ESRC TLRP Seminar Series on "Quality in Educational Research."

Hanley, B. (2005). *Research as empowerment?* York, England: Joseph Rowntree Foundation.

Heurtin-Roberts, S. (2003). Thoughts on qualitative research methods at NIH. *Qualitative Social Work 1* (3): 376–379.

House, E. (1994). Integrating the quantitative and qualitative. In C. S. Reichardt and S. F. Rallis (Eds.), The qualitative-quantitative debate: New perspectives. *New directions for program evaluation,* No. 61. San Francisco: Jossey-Bass.

Kearney, K. S. and Hyle, A. E. (2004). Drawing out emotions: The use of participant-produced drawings in qualitative inquiry. *Qualitative Research 4*(3): 361–382.

Kirk, S.A. (Ed.). (1999). *Social work research methods: building knowledge for practice.* Washington, DC: NASW Press.

Kirk, S. and Reid, W. J. (2002). *Science and social work.* New York: Columbia University Press.

Kushner, S. (2005). Qualitative control. *Evaluation 11* (1): 111–122.

Lofland, J. and Lofland, L. (1995). *Analyzing social settings.* Belmont, CA: Wadsworth.

Long, A. (1994). Assessing health and social outcomes. In J. Popay and G. Williams (Eds.), *Researching the people's health.* London: Routledge.

——. (2006). Health services evaluation. In I. Shaw, J. Greene, and M. Mark (Eds.), *Handbook of evaluation: Policies, programs and practice,* 461–485. London: Sage.

Lorenz, W. (2000). Contentious identities—social work research and the search for professional and personal identities. Paper from ESRC seminar series, "Theorizing Social Work Research." http://www.scie.org.uk/publications/misc/tswr/seminar4/lorenz.asp.

Macdonald, G. (1999). Social work and evaluation. In F. Williams, J. Popay, and A. Oakley, *Welfare research: A critical review.* London: UCL Press.

McLeod, J. (2001). *Qualitative research in counseling and psychotherapy.* London: Sage.

Miles, M. and Huberman, A. (1994). *Qualitative data analysis: An expanded sourcebook.* Thousand Oaks, CA: Sage.

Miller, G. (1997). Contextualizing texts: Studying organizational texts. In G. Miller and R. Dingwall (Eds.), *Context and method in qualitative research,* 77–91. London: Sage.

Mohr, W. K. (1997). Interpretive interactionism: Denzin's potential contribution to intervention and outcomes research. *Qualitative Health Research 7* (2): 270–286.

National Institutes of Health (2001). *Qualitative methods in health research.* http://obssr.od.nih.gov/publications/qualitative.pdf

Neander, K. and Stott, C. (2006). Important meetings with important persons: Narratives from families facing adversity and their key figures. *Qualitative Social Work 5* (3): 295–311.

Patton, M. Q. (2002). *Qualitative research and evaluation methods.* Thousand Oaks, CA: Sage.

Pawson, R., Boaz, A., Grayson, L., Long, A., and Barnes, C. (2003). *Types and quality of knowledge in social care.* London: Social Care Institute for Excellence.

Phillips, D. (1990). Postpositivistic science: Myths and realities. In E. Guba (Ed.), *The paradigm dialog,* 31–45. Newbury Park, CA: Sage.

Pithouse, A. (1998). *Social work as an invisible trade.* Aldershot (England): Avebury.

Popay, J. and Roen, K. (2003). *Using evidence from diverse research designs.* London: Social Care Institute for Excellence.

Popay, J. and Williams, G. (1998). Qualitative research and evidence-based healthcare. *Journal of the Royal Society of Medicine 901* (Supplement 35): 32–37.

Reichardt, C. S. and Rallis, S. F. (Eds.). (1994). The qualitative-quantitative debate: New perspectives. *New directions for program evaluation,* No. 61. San Francisco: Jossey-Bass.

Reid, W. (1990). Change-process research: a new paradigm? In L. Videka-Sherman and W. Reid (Eds.), *Advances in clinical social work research,* 130–148. Silver Spring, MD: NASW Press.

Reid, W. (1994). The empirical practice movement. *Social Service Review 68* (2): 165–184.

Reid, W. and Zettergren, P. (1999). A perspective on empirical practice. In I. Shaw and J. Lishman (Eds.), *Evaluation and social work practice,* 41–62. London: Sage.

Riemann, G. (2005). Ethnographies of practice—practicing ethnography. *Journal of Social Work Practice 19* (1): 87–101.

Riessman, C. K. (Ed). (1994). *Qualitative studies in social work research.* Thousand Oaks, CA: Sage.

Shaw, I. (2003). Qualitative research and outcomes in health, social work and education. *Qualitative Research 3* (1): 57–77.

——. (2005). Practitioner research: evidence or critique? *British Journal of Social Work 35* (8): 1231–1248.

——. (2006). Social work and the human services. In I. Shaw, J. Greene, and M. Mark (Eds.), *Handbook of evaluation: Policies, programs and practice,* 486–511. London: Sage.

Shaw, I. and Faulkner, A. (2006). Practitioner evaluation at work. *American Journal of Evaluation 27* (1): 44–63.

Shaw, I., and Gould, N. (2001). *Qualitative research in social work.* London: Sage.

Sherman, E. and Reid, J. (Eds.). (1994). *Qualitative research in social work.* New York: Columbia University Press.

Silverman, D. (1997). *Discourses of counselling.* London: Sage.

Social Care Institute for Excellence (2006). *The conduct of systematic research reviews for SCIE knowledge reviews.* London: SCIE.

Spencer, L., Ritchie, J., Lewis, J. and Dillon, L. (2003). *Quality in qualitative evaluation: A framework for assessing research evidence.* London: Cabinet Office. http://www.policyhub.gov.uk/docs/qqe_rep.pdf.

Stake, R. (1995). *The art of case study research.* Thousand Oaks, CA: Sage.

Thompson, R. and Holland, J. (2005). "Thanks for the memory": Memory books as a methodological resource in biographical research. *Qualitative Research 5* (2): 201–219.

Thyer, B. (1989). First principles of practice research. *British Journal of Social Work 19* (4): 309–323.

Trend, M. G. (1979). On the reconciliation of qualitative and quantitative analyses. In T. Cook and C. Reichardt, *Qualitative and quantitative methods in evaluation research.* Beverly Hills, CA: Sage.

Turner, M. and Zimmerman, W. (1994). Acting for the sake of research. In J. Wholey, H. Hatry, and K. Newcomer (Eds.), *Handbook of practical program evaluation.* San Francisco: Jossey-Bass.

Vanderplaat, M. (1995). Beyond technique: Issues in evaluating for empowerment. *Evaluation 1* (1): 81–96.

Wahlström, J. (2006). Narrative transformations and externalizing talk in a reflecting team consultation. *Qualitative Social Work 5* (3): 313–332.

Wasoff, F. and Dobash, R. (1992). Simulated clients in "natural" settings: Constructing a client to study professional practice. *Sociology 26* (2): 333–349.

——. (1996). *The simulated client: a method for studying professionals working with clients.* Aldershot, England: Avebury.

PART TWO | *Status of Evidence-Based Practice in Selected Areas of Social Work*

4 | Group Work Research

Past, Present, and Future

Charles D. Garvin

IN THIS CHAPTER, we will present our views of the evolution of research on group work practice, examine issues that pose challenges for the researchers who investigate group work practice, and discuss the current situation with regard to such research. Drawing from this analysis, we shall make recommendations regarding the future group work research agenda. We define group work research as investigations of groups facilitated by social workers or conducted in settings in which social workers play a major role.[1] Such groups, by definition, include so-called task groups to carry out projects beneficial to the agency or community, but this chapter primarily focuses on groups conducted to help members prevent or overcome individual problems in functioning.

Group work represents one of the major vehicles for the delivery of social work services. Although this has been true since the beginning of the profession of social work, group work has not always been accepted as a legitimate enterprise by many social workers who tended to have a view of their services as offered on a one-to-one, so-called casework, basis. There were many different reasons for this, not the least of which was that casework focused on helping individuals overcome personal problems while group work took place in community agencies that sought to help individuals with the issues of urban living, typically in inner-city communities. The prototypical site of early casework was the charity organization society; that of early group work was the settlement house.

The goals of casework were thought of in terms of individual change as this practice spread into such settings as child welfare, psychiatric, medical, school, public welfare, and correctional institutions. These objectives could be examined in terms of such changes as child placement, recovery from illness, and cessation of criminal behavior. The goals of group work were originally spoken of in terms of participation in community change, enhancement of community life, socialization to the requirements of urban living, and enrichment of life experience. Research on social work practice was limited in the beginnings of the profession, but it was certainly easier to examine the number of children placed than the ways life was enriched in the community. In fact, early social work researchers were more interested in community surveys than in either individual or community change.

The Beginnings of Group Work Research

It was essential, however, if research of any sort was to be done in group work, that the method be specified. This is precisely the task to which the early group work writers were devoted. It was essential; otherwise what was being investigated would be amorphous. The problem was compounded when different models emerged and questions arose as to precisely what group work consisted of. Papell and Rothman (1966) performed an important service when they pointed out that three major approaches to group work practice had developed in the few decades that group work had existed in social work.

A set of different issues for group work scholarship emerged, however, in the 1950s when group work practice began to expand beyond the community agencies into many, if not all, of the same agencies that previously had only provided service on a one-to-one, and later family, basis. Group work was employed, for example, to aid people recovering from illness, to help students succeed in school, to enable workers to find employment, and to prevent delinquent and criminal behavior. One might even think of the "old" community forms as preventive work for "people at risk." A major question that emerged from this evolution of group work was the comparative effectiveness of individual versus group treatment; we shall discuss this issue later.

The problem of group work research was compounded when practitioners offering services to individuals, families, and groups began to employ behavioral, cognitive-behavioral, humanistic, psychoeducational, solution-focused, strength-based, and ego-psychological interventions in group contexts, thus paralleling the array of approaches developed to help individuals.

At the same time, several authors charged that social work practice, especially casework, was ineffective (Fischer 1973). Although they might have also questioned the evidence for group work effectiveness, they did not focus on this, perhaps because studies of group work effectiveness or ineffectiveness were not as numerous as studies of individual work. This may also have been because group work had not been clearly established as a treatment modality rather than a socialization one. Writers such as Robert Vinter (1959) challenged group workers to give a higher priority to service to the victims of socially adverse conditions than to the members of groups in many community agencies who were being helped to adapt to their environments. He urged the employment of group workers in the many agencies that served people with serious problems in functioning. His model also emphasized the articulation of goals as a necessary precondition to evaluation. He pressed for several developments in group work that would precede group work research as he envisioned it, namely the utilization of social science and a better specification of what he termed the "essential components of social group work" (Vinter 1985).

Group work research, as it first emerged, was more likely to focus on studies of processes in social work groups than on the outcomes for group members. This was due, in my opinion, to the fact that group work was seen as a general method applied in a similar way to various types of groups. This work was often done in the form of doctoral dissertations. An early example was the dissertation in sociology of Grace Coyle, who is usually cited as a major creator of group work in social work (Coyle 1930). Her dissertation clarified such concepts as group formation, structure, and decision making.

As social work schools developed their own doctoral programs, additional dissertations emerged. For example, Marjorie Main (1964) explored events that occurred in the beginning phases of group work; Margaret Hartford (1962) examined group formation; and Charles Garvin (1968) investigated the effect of the group workers' correct or incorrect perceptions of member expectations. These studies were completed at the University of Chicago and may have been made possible because the school had employed a faculty member, Mary Louise Somers, who herself had completed a dissertation at Case Western Reserve University that focused on group work. At the University of Michigan, where Robert Vinter was developing his new model of group work drawing heavily on the social sciences, Ronald Feldman (1966) completed a dissertation during the same period in which he investigated the phenomenon of social integration as it operated in small groups.

It would be incorrect to state that all important early research on group work dealt only with group processes. Wilbur Newstetter at Case Western University had a long commitment to contributing to the creation of a scientific base for group work, and he and his colleagues saw this as being demonstrated in ways that also included studying the outcomes for members. He, Mark Feldstein, and Theodore Newcomb (the latter an eminent pioneer in social psychology) conducted a research project at a camp in Ohio that examined the interpersonal relations between boys who were referred to the camp by a child guidance clinic because of relationship problems (Newstetter, Feldstein, and Newcomb 1938). This study indicated that the children's relationships could be improved through group experience. The authors, incidentally, concluded that group experiments could and should be carried out in such natural settings.

Problems in Carrying out Group Work Research

As Brower, Arndt, and Ketterhagen (2004) state: "Conducting research on social work groups is difficult" (435). They indicate that a major source of such difficulty lies in the complexity of group phenomena:

> But how do we capture a group's complexity and unpredictability using methods that require us either to take snapshots of an ongoing process or to focus our attention on some aspects of the group and not others? How do we study cohesion, for example, without examining this one process within the context of membership or group goals or any number of structural elements of the group (setting, time, etc.)? How do we study individual outcomes, for example, without examining any number of interpersonal and group-level dynamics that contribute directly and indirectly to these outcomes? How do we even examine something like the interaction of member gender and leadership, for instance, knowing that this interaction itself is dependent on any number of other factors (such as structure, development, group purpose, and even current political and social climate? (436)

Nevertheless, group work research was being undertaken two thirds of a century ago, and doctoral research relevant to group work was being conducted within the next few decades, although this type of research was confronted by challenges that were not encountered in research on one-on-one helping. These challenges are present today and account for some of the weaknesses of much of current group work research. We will describe some of these issues and how they have been approached before discussing recent group work research.[2]

Group Creation

One category of challenge is that a group must be created, if it is not already in existence (e.g., an adolescent neighborhood gang; a residential unit in a psychiatric facility), before the research can be done. Most groups conducted by social workers are of this kind in that the worker recruits the members (as opposed to studying an extant group). Once the investigator determines the type of population to be served (e.g., depressed individuals, abused wives), she or he must find individuals who meet the recruitment criteria and are able to meet at the same time and place and commit to attending the group for the designated length of time. It is not easy to do this when one depends on referrals and publicity. The task is further complicated if these potential members are required to possess additional attributes such as willingness to attend, ability to interact with others in a constructive manner, and demographic characteristics that the worker deems necessary for purposes of group composition, such as designated ages, gender, and so forth.

Random Assignment to Groups

This task is more complicated in project designs that require more than one group because it is impossible to ensure that each group is identical. There will always be ways members differ, and these differences are likely to have consequences for the way the group evolves even if the group intervention is prescribed, such as through the use of a manual. The usual solution is to make a random assignment of members to each group, but this requires a good-sized pool of potential members. This random approach is also needed for assignment of individuals to a control group, thus introducing the usual decisions regarding control groups, such as whether they will consist of a no-treatment or alternative treatment condition. Group work researchers have often created an alternative group for the control condition. There also has been some use of single-case designs in which members essentially function as their own controls (Toseland and Rivas 2001:414–416).

Group Development

Brower, Arndt, and Ketterhagen (2004:440) suggest that the way to capture the "natural unfolding of groups" is "to describe the group as a case study." In their survey of recent group work research articles that met their criteria for research standards, they found four such publications. They describe as a good example a publication by Racine and Sevigny (2001).

> This study describes a board game devised by the researchers to generate both solutions to life situations and research data with women living in a homeless shelter in Montreal. In their study, Racine and Sevigny describe how the women used their game to solve problems in their lives and how their group interactions changed as a result of their participation. Characteristic of this type of research study is its careful attention to detail in its descriptions of the sample, the group setting, researcher objectives and biases, and the range of interactions that took place over the life of the group. The level of detail is important in these studies for two reasons: It allows readers both to evaluate the quality of the work being described and to determine the study's generalizability. In other words, case studies use descriptive detail to determine both internal and external validity. (440)

Brower and his colleagues also recommend the use of videotaping and act-by-act scoring systems. They note the use of SYMLOG (Bales and Cohen 1980) as a scoring system for this purpose. In the studies they examined, twelve used videotapes to record sessions and four of these used SYMLOG to code group actions.

Other Issues in Group Creation

Other circumstances around the creation of the group that are likely to have a significant impact on the group outcome but are seldom sufficiently examined are the selection and training of the group worker, the impact of her or his demographic characteristics (age, sex, ethnicity) on the group, and the impact of her or his style of work on the group. Seldom explored, also, is the impact of agency conditions on the group, such as allocation of resources and protection from interference. It would be considered a significant breach of professional conduct for a staff member to interrupt a counseling session, but this is not true when a member is called out of a meeting.

Measurement of Group Process

Another major challenge to group work research is the clear evidence that outcomes of the group experience for members are as likely to be determined by the processes that occur in the group as by the practice theory and practice approach utilized by the worker. As Burlingame, MacKenzie, and Strauss (2004) state:

> Leaders guided by small-group process principles understand that the therapeutic environment of the group is a potent and independent source of patient change. For instance, members who experience a greater sense of acceptance, belonging, and support from their group, regardless of for-

mal change theory, typically report more post-treatment improvement. Moreover, since the group is an evolving entity, group process principles (e.g., timing of feedback) must be understood and differentially applied to potentiate this therapeutic environment over the life of the group. Group therapy is not merely individual therapy offered in the context of the group! (649)

These authors discuss and provide evidence for the proposition that "group process theories might explain an independent portion of improvement in group treatment" (666). They cite some studies that do consider group processes; these tend to be multiple studies of a group intervention or to comprise a larger program of group research. Some of the process variables examined included those associated with group development, group cohesiveness, degree of member disclosure of personal material, group climate, and problem-solving behavior change.

A major approach to studying process variables evolved from the concept of therapeutic factors in groups. Yalom and Leszcz (2005) made major contributions to the study of such factors when they sought to determine the identifiable elements that might account for the impact of the group on its members, using instruments administered to members. Bloch and Crouch (1985) performed a significant service by reviewing all of the studies that contributed to an understanding of the creation of these factors or their consequences. Examples of these factors are installation of hope, universality, learning from interpersonal action, and self-disclosure.[3] Burlingame, MacKenzie, and Strauss (2004:675) indicate that the identification of these factors should have promoted progress in group work research. They attribute the lack of advancement to an inability to compare findings because of variations in measurement, lack of relationship to outcomes, and absence of reference to stages of group development.

There are several reasons investigators are not likely to collect data on process variables along with outcome variables in evaluation studies. One is the additional expense of data collection. Another is the fact that each additional set of data places requirements on sample size in order to determine the significance of results. A third is the lack of agreement among group theorists and researchers on a theoretical model of group work that indicates which process variables are important in terms of how they relate to the model.

Beck and Lewis (2000) have produced a volume that will benefit all who study group processes in relationship to outcomes in group therapy. It provides information on each of the major systems for studying therapy group processes and assesses the strengths and weaknesses of each for group therapy research. These systems include, for example, the now classic interaction process analysis, the group emotionality rating system, the Hill Interaction Matrix, and Group Development Process Analysis Measures.

Observational Nonindependence

Often the source of data utilized in group work research is the group member. Inasmuch as group members usually become well acquainted, it is difficult to tell whether their responses are independent or the members have influenced one another. In addition, if members provide ratings at successive sessions, it is difficult to tell whether responses from one session influence their responses to another. Third, when the investigator pools member responses to say something about the group, the nature of the variance among the members is obscured. Brower, Arndt, and Ketterhagen (2004:441–442) discuss the use of statistical methods (structural equation modeling and hierarchical linear modeling) to deal with this issue. They cite the work of Kivlighan and Lilly (1997), who used the latter approach to explore how dimensions of group climate related to therapeutic outcomes.

The Unit of Analysis Problem

Brower, Arndt, and Ketterhagen (2004:443) cite a review by Burlingame, Kircher, and Taylor (1994), who found that "almost 90% of group psychotherapy research published between 1980 and 1992 analyzed individual level data without correcting for, or sometimes even acknowledging, the nonindependence problem." Available statistical techniques to deal with this issue are not often used, although Brower and his colleagues cite articles that present easy-to-follow procedures for using them.

The Use of the Group to Promote Individual Change

Traditionally, group work practice theory in social work has promoted the idea that the worker should help the group to function as a mutual aid system. This means that the worker helps to bring about a group that will, in turn, help the members to attain their goals. If this is the platform from which the worker is operating, then the investigator must be able to analyze this path. As Brower and Garvin (1989) state: "Group work research designs must, consequently, be conducive to an examination of the enactment of a view of practice that sees the worker's role as either intervening in group processes or mediating between individual and group requirements" (94).

Multivariate Analyses

It should be evident from the preceding discussions that group work research should ideally take into consideration a number of variables, such as the group work approach employed (e.g., cognitive-behavioral, "mutual aid,"[4] psychoeducational), group composition, worker variables, and process variables—particularly stage of group development. This increases the cost of the research when the investigator collects and analyzes data on multiple variables as well as increases the sample size to accommodate the requirements of the analysis. Even qualitative research must provide for adequate collection of data on these variables and a coding scheme that pays attention to them.

Another solution to the problem is to limit the number of values of a variable. As Brower and Garvin (1989) state: "The validity of generalizing the findings to other conditions is limited but this is in the nature of the research enterprise. We need, therefore, *programs* of research that systematically vary the conditions of the research—a hard but not impossible task in today's funding environment" (94).

Now that we have identified some of the major challenges to group work research, we turn to a summary of contemporary group work research, examining both research done by social workers and research done on group therapy that is similar to that done by social workers. The inclusion of this broad review is justified, we believe, by the applicability of much group therapy research to social work with groups as well as the limitations of the body of research on the latter.

Current Group Work Research

In this discussion, we limit ourselves primarily to studies that have been published since 1990. This section draws heavily on the work of Burlingame, MacKenzie, and Strauss (2004), who have done a much more thorough review of this literature than we have the resources for. We have supplemented their review, however, with group work research articles that have appeared since 2001, the year they discontinued their sampling. It is important, however, for us to describe an important study that was published earlier than 1990 by Feldman, Caplinger, and Wodarski (1983) because, as Feldman (2004) states, it "represents perhaps the largest and most rigorous field experiment concerning group intervention to be found in the social work literature" (827). Feldman supports this allegation by noting that he examined "abstracts of 254 articles on group work research that appeared in *Social Work Abstracts* from 1977 through 2003. Fewer than a dozen publications employed a true experimental design, and none constituted a large-scale multifactorial field experiment."

These authors conducted an experiment that offered group work services to treat antisocial youths. Questions can be raised today about some of the aspects of this study, but these are not relevant to the current discussion. This work still stands as an unrivaled representation of a research design that incorporates some of the multivariate features essential for good group work research. The project started with the premise that grouping people with problems was dysfunctional and that the concept of mainstreaming in education should also apply to group treatment. The authors therefore arranged for antisocial youths to be served in a community agency established to serve a larger population.

In designing their experiment, Feldman and his colleagues included the following:

> a multifactorial design; randomized assignment of group workers, subjects, and treatment methods; comparison groups for the main independent variables; a no-intervention baseline period; trained nonparticipant observers who were tested for reliability on a biweekly basis; a multiple time series research design; measures that account for subjects' prosocial and nonsocial behavior, as well as their antisocial behavior and further, each subject's proportionate behavioral profile; multiple independent judges, including referral agents, group workers, parents, nonparticipant observers, and the participating youths themselves; measures of the extent to which the treatment variable actually was implemented; a blind intake criterion applied by two sets of independent judges; a standard measure of manifest aggression, arcsine transformations of proportionate data; reliability-corrected analyses of covariance that adjust for differences in the subject's pretest behavioral profiles; multiple discriminant analyses; and end point, dropout, and survivor analyses. (835)

Space does not permit a full discussion of the findings from this study. We only note here that the authors demonstrated the value of mixed groups for prosocial and antisocial youths while at the same time identifying the differential effects of worker training, treatment methods, and group composition.

Before we explore the current body of group work research, we should note the valiant efforts of Sheldon Rose and many of his colleagues at the University of Wisconsin to advance the cause of group work research over many years. It should also be noted that Rose was a staunch advocate of the group worker's attention to group processes. In addition to his work at that university, Rose took the lead in organizing an annual symposium on empirical group work that continued through the 1990s and into the current century before running its course. Rose essentially established a center on group work research in which investigators, largely his doctoral students, were able to use a campus site, if needed, to work with groups and to do relevant research. The group work method was primarily cognitive-behavioral in orientation and many studies were produced that demonstrated the effectiveness of this approach. This included work with socially isolated children (Edleson and Rose 1981), adolescents with deficits in social competence (LeCroy and Rose 1986), parenting issues (Magen and Rose 1994), assertiveness training (Rose 1978), and older adults (Toseland and Rose 1978). In an event honoring Rose held during one of the annual empirical group work symposia, a mock "genealogy" was drawn that portrayed his impact on many generations of group work scholars.

A significant development that should reinforce the need for group work research is a good deal of recent thinking about "evidence-based group work." MacGowan has substantially advanced our understanding of this approach in his recent book *Evidence-Based Group Work* (MacGowan 2008).

We now turn to an examination of a broad range of research findings with respect to group work and, as stated above, draw heavily on the work of Burlingame, MacKenzie, and Strauss (2004). These authors conducted a computer search of PsychLit and Medline utilizing the keywords "group psychotherapy," "group counseling," and "group therapy." The original search yielded 1,823 studies. They narrowed these to empirical studies published between January 1990 and January 2001 of treatment offered to clinically relevant populations that either employed designs that used randomized assignment of members to treatment and control conditions or that only obtained pre- and post- data.

They excluded reports that were exclusively case studies, used nonstandardized measures, had small sample sizes (n < 12), had high attrition rates, or did not appropriately use statistical procedures. They did not include self-help, mutual support, or 12-step programs unless these were used as controls. They also examined meta-analyses of treatment effectiveness. The final sample consisted of 107 studies and 14 meta-analyses. These studies were organized under the following diagnostic categories: mood, anxiety, eating, substance abuse, personality, and psychotic disorders and the following patient populations: elders, domestic violence victims, sexual abuse victims, and mentally ill. Finally they reported studies that compared individual with group treatment. We now present some of the highlights of their findings. We also cite some summary articles that have appeared since their work was accomplished.

Group Versus Individual

The studies and meta-analyses typically did not find differences between these two modalities and "both formats produced large pre-to-post-treatment gains." There are a few studies that show either superiority of individual treatment or the reverse. In some instances in which the group is superior, the outcome measure reflects unique features of the group, such as social support. There may be differences related to specific disorders, but the authors state that there are too few studies or too small sample sizes to draw any conclusions and hope this situation may change in the future.

Mood Disorders

The studies showed the efficacy of group cognitive-behavioral therapy (CBT) even when the treatment did not explicitly attend to group process principles. Another issue is that a number of studies compared CBT to medication, but methodological problems limit the conclusions that can be drawn. Other studies examined approaches that addressed group processes such as member interaction or the operation of the therapeutic factors defined by Yalom. Burlingame, MacKenzie, and Strauss (2004) did not consider these studies to be as strong methodologically as the CBT ones and they urged research that directly compare these two approaches when used with the same population. Finally, these authors concluded that the evidence for the effectiveness of group treatment for these disorders was mixed. They also stated that "the action of small group process principles was proffered as one explanation for the results of these four studies" (656). These were the studies that failed to find differences between experimental and control conditions. A more recent summary of research on group treatment of depression utilizing cognitive-behavioral approaches has also appeared (Chen, Jordan, and Thompson 2006).

Anxiety Disorders

Burlingame, MacKenzie, and Strauss (2004) present separate discussions of group treatment of agoraphobia/panic disorders, obsessive-compulsive disorders (OCD), and social phobia. The dominant change theory for group treatment in the first category was CBT. While most of the studies showed positive outcomes, Burlingame, MacKenzie, and Strauss conclude that there were many problems in the study designs and recommend better-constructed research be conducted in the future.

The studies of group treatment of OCD primarily utilized a behavioral group approach (BG) as well as an educational one. One incorporated group process principles. Burlingame, MacKenzie, and Strauss saw many limitations in the methodology of these studies and refrained from endorsing such groups on the basis of research findings.

Social phobia studies typically utilized a CBT approach. Many of these investigations were conducted by Richard Heimberg and his colleagues (Heimberg et al. 1990). The Heimberg team sought to determine the potency of different components of their treatment package. Burlingame, MacKenzie, and Strauss found the evidence of these studies for the effectiveness of CBT groups compelling. They did note findings supporting the effects of group processes, so the next steps in this line of inquiry will be to explore such forces. Similar findings were also reported in a more recent summary of research on this topic (Coles and Hart 2005).

Eating Disorders

CBT models were among the most frequently employed for these conditions, although some studies incorporate attention to group processes. Research also found the length of treatment to be an important variable. CBT applications were found to be effective; other approaches such as interpersonal therapy (IPT) were also found to be so.

Groups for Elders

The group treatment of elders typically attends to depressive symptoms and adjustment disorders. The techniques used in these groups are most frequently cognitive and cognitive-behavioral, although reminiscent, psychodynamic, behavioral, and eclectic treatments are also reported. According to Burlingame, MacKenzie, and Strauss (2004:659), "Virtually all focus on resolving problems, sharing memories and feelings, and increasing self esteem and life satisfaction." These authors conclude, on reviewing more than 100 studies, that the evidence is mixed when comparing individual to group treatment, although the group studies show pre-to-post improvement of subjects. Methodological problems in these studies led the authors to call for more rigorous comparative designs.

Substance-Related Disorders

Substance abuse programs typically include many components, although the group one is usually central and is seen as especially useful in confronting denial. A major problem in these programs is the high drop-out rate. Much more research needs to be done to determine the impact of twelve-step models that were often employed in these programs as well as of the supportive atmosphere created by the groups. A recent summary of research in this area by Weiss, Jaffee, and de Menil (2004) provides support for the effectiveness of group treatment in this area.

Sexual Abuse and Domestic Violence

In relationship to sexual abuse, several studies pertained to women abused as children. The groups were time-limited and used psychoeducation and process approaches. Evaluation of these groups indicated the members ended with lower levels of depression and higher levels of self-esteem and social adjustment. This conclusion has been supported by a more recent summary of research (Callahan, Price, and Hilsenroth 2004).

Group models have been developed for victims as well as perpetrators of domestic violence. Burlingame, MacKenzie, and Strauss (2004:662) conclude that these approaches appear promising, but the research has limitations in the definition of the treatment, lack of appropriate controls, and use of a common set of outcome measures. Nevertheless, a more recent summary of research by Carney and Buttell (2006) supports the use of group treatment in this area.

Medical Illness

There are many studies of the use of groups with cancer and human immunodeficiency virus (HIV) patients. For those with cancer, psychoeducational, time-limited, and supportive groups predominate. Changes found in patients consisted mainly of reduced emotional distress and improved coping. There was little evidence that group therapy had an impact on physical condition as such.

Two kinds of groups work on either preventing HIV or working with those who have been afflicted by it. The former focus on reducing high-risk behaviors and the latter on reducing stress, increasing coping, and providing social support. Burlingame, MacKenzie, and Strauss (2004:664) expressed optimism about the use of these groups when they reviewed the findings.

Severe Mental Illness

As we have stated elsewhere, group approaches with these individuals are prominent, and a major reason is the deficit in social skills found among them and the many opportunities groups provide to make up for this (Garvin 2005). An important contribution to this work comes from the psychosocial rehabilitation field, which encourages these group members to develop to their fullest capacities through learning new skills while acquiring environmental supports. Specific group approaches, according to Burlingame, MacKenzie, and Strauss (2004), include social skills training, psychoeducation, cognitive information processing, and CBT; many groups combine several of these. These authors present strong evidence for the effectiveness of social skills groups and less evidence for psychoeducational and cognitive-information processing groups. The CBT and cognitive treatment studies were fewer in number and their designs were weaker. Although many practitioners do utilize psychodynamic, Gestalt, and process approaches, the studies of these modalities are limited.

Personality Disorders (PD)

Burlingame, MacKenzie, and Strauss (2004:665) found mostly literature regarding the treatment of borderline personality disorder (BPD). This literature demonstrated a reduction in depression and suicidal tendencies, increased interpersonal functioning, and life satisfaction and adjustment. It was limited from the standpoint of efficacy research, as these authors state: "comparative summaries (e.g., meta-analyses) are difficult owing to the diversity of the models, lack of controlled studies, and limited number of studies. . . . Nevertheless, the available evidence indicates that group can be a beneficial and economic approach to the treatment of PD" (666).

Recent Social Work Studies

Articles that we have reviewed in the social work research literature are consistent with the findings of Burlingame, MacKenzie, and Strauss (2004). We are pleased to report that almost every issue of *Research on Social Work Practice* published in the last three years includes one or more research reports on the effectiveness of a group work intervention. Some fall under the categories utilized by Burlingame and his colleagues (health disorders, serious mental illness); others deal with populations that are of special interest to social workers because of the settings in which they practice, such as aggressive or defiant children (Martsch 2005; Ronen 2005); use of group approaches with people of color (Shin 2005); and use of spiritual content (Layer, Roberts, Wild, and Walters 2005).

Another category of group service, using such technological applications as telephone and computer groups, has also been studied by social workers; we believe more use should be made of these. Pioneers in this field are Maeda Galinsky and her colleagues (Galinsky, Shopler, and Abell 1997), who have reported on the success of such groups. Meier has produced a highly informative summary of these technologies and the research associated with them (Meier 2004).

Finally, we should note the emergence of young social work scholars who have been studying group processes, creating new instruments, and applying these findings to special populations. An example is the work of Mark MacGowan, who has been developing measures of group affiliation, creating valid and reliable measures of this phenomenon, and demonstrating the use of these measures in refining practice (MacGowan 2003; MacGowan and Levenson 2003).

The above summary of the group work research literature indicates the use of groups in all practice settings and the positive results of these applications. Though there is a need for more research and better designs, the evidence clearly supports the widespread use of group work and the value of allocating research resources to further determining which group approaches work best with which client populations, and with what quality of professional leadership. In making the best use of such resources, however, we have a number of recommendations regarding the shape of the group work research endeavor.

Recommendations Regarding Future Group Work Research

Based on the above discussion, we have several recommendations to make with respect to future group work research.

Multivariate Research

We would not discourage investigators from utilizing simple pre-post designs when limited resources and sample sizes mandate this. They are better than simple descriptive case studies in building the empirical base for group work. Simple descriptive studies have many limitations, as we have noted above, and far too many studies are of this nature exist. Measuring a full range of variables may not be possible in every research project, but we recommend that the investigator measure the compliance of the intervention with the theory and model that are utilized, some of the process variables that theory indicates are likely to affect outcome in the given instance, and the nature of the worker's training in the use of the intervention. It is important to add that there is great value in utilizing outcome measures that have been used and validated in other studies so that evidence on effectiveness can be cumulative.

In many situations, sound qualitative analysis procedures will be useful in identifying the interactions among several sets of variables. As described in the work of Beck and Lewis (2000), many process measures have been developed and their usefulness in group work research demonstrated.

Programs of Research

It is difficult to accumulate evidence on effectiveness when the study is a "one-shot" enterprise. Group work research desperately needs programs of research that undertake multiple studies conducted over periods of time that build on one another. We have described the work of Rose and his colleagues over many years at the University of Wisconsin, which built on a CBT theoretical base informed by sound group work process principles. Their findings were well disseminated through the social work literature as well as published books and their methods were presented at the annual meetings of the Empirical Group Work organization that has ceased operation. We heartily urge an effort to resuscitate that organization.

Action Research

An approach to building knowledge of group work that has been largely neglected is "action research" and the related "community-based research partnerships." These methods should be of considerable interest to group workers, historically committed to the ideas of empowerment and self-determination, as they promote the involvement of the group members in the evaluation and evolution of the intervention. Each successive application incorporates improvements based on inputs from members and other stakeholders (Schultz, Israel, and Lantz 2004). These inputs are another way of examining many of the variables that affect the outcomes.

We are currently engaged in research of this nature. Our project is now in its fourth year and involves using groups to train high school students to take leadership in the peaceful negotiation of intergroup conflicts. Our project makes use of principles of developmental research (Thomas 1984) in that it began with creating a model from a study of existing theory and research as well as case studies of exemplary programs. Developmental research also stresses successive iterations based on outcome data. This project has been jointly governed by faculty of the University of Michigan and of the high schools where implementation is taking place, and students from the schools are also represented. The program is now in its second implementation, which was developed out of an analysis of quantitative and qualitative data from the first one.

Accumulation and Retrieval of Evidence

There have been a few efforts to summarize the evidence of the effectiveness of social work with groups (Feldman 1987; Tolman and Molidor 1994). The most recent of these is now more than ten years old and new studies have appeared in the interim. It would be valuable to have an up-to-date compendium of this research. There is also a desperate need to identify process and outcome measures that are particularly useful to social workers with groups.

In this chapter, we have extensively drawn upon a summary of group work research prepared by scholars who are not social workers, and we know of no sound reason why group workers seeking to operate from an empirical base should not consult evidence on effective approaches wherever it may be found. There may be some value, however, in screening this data for the applications most compatible with social work values and the realities of social work practice settings. In addition, there are group approaches widely used by social workers that have not been studied sufficiently, for example, the hallowed concept of "mutual aid." Research could illuminate considerably the processes by which members come to help one another and the various ways this happens.

Summary and Conclusion

In this chapter we have described the evolution of group work and the role research has played in this development. We then discussed the issues that confront the researcher who investigates this type of practice. We presented a summary of recent research by social work scholars as well as those from other disciplines and professions. Finally, we made some recommendations with reference to the future of group work research.

We conclude that group workers can draw upon a rich array of group work research in determining the empirical support for many of their interventions. Nevertheless, a great deal of work remains to be done. It entails an examination of the interaction of variables that produce both processes and outcomes. It also involves work to resolve doubts about conclusions regarding the effectiveness of given interventions caused by weaknesses in measurement, design (especially with respect to suitable control groups), and adequate replication, and even doubts about the fidelity of the actual intervention. There are also many aspects of widely used social work models that have scarcely been investigated. Qualitative research designs have a major role to play in group work research but have not been applied with rigor.

The evidence supports the idea that group interventions have the potential to become even more potent as research and development proceed apace. A major task is to convince funders that group work research is valid while also convincing them that it will be different from individual research in the control of group processes, the recruitment of group members, and the establishment of control conditions. Good group research will also be expensive. We believe, however, that a growing recognition of the value of group experience in ameliorating many human problems will eventually overcome barriers to its continued development.

Notes

1. We do not exclude laboratory or other similar groups established to provide answers to questions relevant to the practice of group work.

2. This discussion draws on our earlier consideration of design issues in group work research (Brower and Garvin 1989).

3. Garvin (1997:138–153) discusses the application of these factors to social work with groups.

4. While many group workers indicate they promote mutual aid among members, this term has also been adopted to describe a particular model (Gitterman 2004).

References

Bales, R. F. and Cohen, S. P. (2001). *SYMLOG: A system for the multiple level observation of groups*. New York: Free Press.

Beck, A. P. and Lewis, C. M. (Eds.). (2000). *The process of group psychotherapy: Systems for analyzing change.* Washington, D.C.: American Psychological Association.

Bloch, S. and Crouch, E. (1985) *Therapeutic factors in group psychotherapy.* New York: Oxford University Press.

Brower, A. M. and Garvin, C. D. (1989). Design issues in social group work research. *Social Work with Groups 12* (3): 91–102.

Brower, A. M., Arndt, R. G., and Ketterhagen, A. (2004). Very good solutions really do exist for group work research design problems. In C. D. Garvin, L. M. Gutiérrez, and M. J. Galinsky (Eds.), *Handbook of social work with groups,* 435–446. New York: Guilford.

Burlingame, G., Kircher, J., and Taylor, S. (1994). Methodological considerations in group psychotherapy research: Past, present, and future practices. In A. Fuhrman and G. Burlingame (Eds.), *Handbook of group psychotherapy: An empirical and clinical synthesis,* 41–80. New York: Wiley.

Burlingame, G. M., MacKenzie, K. R., and Strauss, B. (2004). Small group treatment: Evidence for effectiveness and mechanisms of change. In M. J. Lambert (Ed.), *Bergin and Garfield's handbook of psychotherapy and behavior change,* 647–696. New York: Wiley.

Callahan, K. L., Price, J. L., and Hilsenroth, M. J. (2004). A review of interpersonal-psychodynamic group psychotherapy outcomes for adult survivors of childhood sexual abuse. *International Journal of Group Psychotherapy 54* (4): 491–519.

Carney, M. M. and Buttell, F. P. (2006). An evaluation of a court-mandated batterer intervention program: Investigating differential program effect for African-American and white women. *Research on Social Work Practice 16* (6): 571–581.

Chen, S-Y., Jordan, C., and Thompson, S. (2006). The effect of cognitive-behavioral therapy (CBT) on depression: The role of problem solving appraisal. *Research on Social Work Practice 16* (5): 500–510.

Coyle, G. L. (1930). *Social process in organized groups.* New York: Smith.

Edleson, J. L. and Rose, S. D. (1981). Investigations into the efficacy of short-term group social skill training for socially isolated children. *Child Behavior Therapy 3* (2): 1–16.

Feldman, R. A. (1966). *Three types of group integration: Their relationship to power, leadership, and conformity behavior.* Unpublished Ph.D. diss., University of Michigan.

——. (1987). Group work knowledge and research: A two-decade comparison. In S. D. Rose and R. A. Feldman (Eds.), *Research in social group work,* 7–14. New York: Haworth Press.

——. (2004). Principles, practices, and findings of the St. Louis Conundrum: A large-scale field experiment with anti-social children. In. A. R. Roberts and K. R. Yeager (Eds.), *Evidence-based practice manual: Research and outcome measures in health and human services,* 827–836. Oxford: Oxford University Press.

Feldman, R. A., Caplinger, T. E., and Wodarski, J. S. (1983). *The St. Louis Conundrum: The effective treatment of anti-social youths.* Englewood Cliffs, NJ: Prentice-Hall.

Fischer, J. (1973). Is casework effective? A review. *Social Work 28:*5–30.

Galinsky, M. J., Shopler, J. H., and Abell, M. D. (1997). Connecting members through telephone and computer groups. *Health and Social Work 22* (3): 181–188.

Garvin, C. (1968). *Complementarity of role expectations in groups: Relationship to member expectations and group problem solving.* Unpublished Ph.D. diss., University of Chicago.

——. (2005). Group work with seriously mentally ill people. In G. L. Grief and P. H. Ephross, *Work with populations at risk*, 2nd ed., 31–45. Oxford: Oxford.

——. (1997). *Contemporary group work*, 3rd ed. Boston: Allyn and Bacon.

Gitterman, A. (2004). The mutual aid model. In C. D. Garvin, L. M. Gutiérrez, and M. J. Galinsky, *Handbook of social work with groups*, 93–110. New York: Guilford.

Hartford, E. (1962). *The social group worker and group formation*. Unpublished Ph.D. diss., University of Chicago.

Heimberg, R. G., Dodge, C. S., Hope, D. A., Kennedy, C. R., Zollo, L. J., and Becker, R. J. (1990). Cognitive-behavioral group treatment for social phobia: Comparison with a credible placebo control. *Cognitive Therapy and Research 14*:1–23.

Kivlighan, D. M. and Lilly, R. L. (1997). Developmental changes in group climate as they relate to therapeutic gain. *Group Dynamics 1* (3): 208–221.

Layer, S. D., Roberts, L., Wild, K., and Walter, J. (2005). Post abortion grief: Evaluating the possible efficacy of a spiritual group. *Research in Social Work Practice 14* (5): 344–350.

LeCroy, C. W. and Rose, S. D. (1986). Evaluation of preventive intervention for enhancing social competence in adolescents. Social *Work Research and Abstracts 22*:8–17.

MacGowan, M. J. (2003). Increasing engagement in groups: A measurement-based approach. *Social Work with Groups 26* (1): 5–28.

——. (2003). Psychometrics of the group engagement measure with male sex offenders. *Small Group Research 34* (2): 155–169.

——. (2008). *Evidence-based group work*. New York: Oxford.

Main, M. W. (1964). *Selected aspects of the beginning phase of social group work*. Unpublished Ph.D. diss., University of Chicago.

Martsch, M. D. (2005). A comparison of two group interventions for adolescent aggressiveness: High process versus low process. *Research in Social Work Practice 15* (1): 8–18.

Meier, A. (2005). Technology-mediated groups. In C. D. Garvin, L. M. Gutiérrez, and M. J. Galinsky (Eds.), *Handbook of social work with groups*, 479–503. New York: Guilford.

Newstetter, W. I., Feldstein, M. J., and Newcomb, T. M. (1938). *Group adjustment—A study in experimental sociology*. Cleveland: Western Reserve University.

Papell, C. P. and Rothman, B. (1966). Social group work models: Possession and heritage. *Journal of Education for Social Work 2* (2): 66–77.

Racine, G. and Sevigny, O. (2001). Changing the rules: A board game lets homeless women tell their stories. *Social Work with Groups 23* (4): 25–38.

Ronen, T. (2005). Students' evidence-based practice intervention for children with oppositional defiant disorder. *Research on Social Work Practice 15* (3): 165–179.

Schultz, A. J., Israel, B. A., and Lantz, P. (2004). Assessing and strengthening characteristics of effective groups in community-based participatory research partnerships. In C. D. Garvin, L. M. Gutiérrez, and M. J. Galinsky (Eds.), *Handbook of social work with groups*, 309–325. New York: Guilford.

Shin, S. (2005). Effects of culturally relevant psychoeducation for Korean-American families of persons with chronic mental illness. *Research on Social Work Practice 14* (4): 231–239.

Thomas, E. J. (1984). *Designing interventions for the helping professions*. Beverly Hills, CA: Sage.

Tolman, R. M. and Molidor, C. E. (1994). A decade of social group work research: Trends in methodology, theory, and program development. *Research on Social Work Practice* 4:142–159.

Toseland, R. and Rose, S. (1978). Evaluating social skills training for older adults in groups. *Social Work Research and Abstracts 14* (1): 25–33.

Toseland, R. W. and Rivas, R. F. (2001). *An introduction to group work practice,* 4th ed. Boston: Allyn and Bacon.

Vinter, R. D. (1959). Group work: Perspectives and prospects. In *Social work with small groups,* 128–149. New York: NASW Press.

———. (1985). The essential components of group work practice. In M. Sundel, P. Glasser, R. Sarri, and R. Vinter (Eds.), *Individual change through small groups,* 2nd ed., 11–24. New York: Free Press.

Weiss, R. D., Jaffee, W. B., and de Menil, V. P. (2004). Group therapy for substance abuse disorders: What do we know? *Harvard Review of Psychiatry 12* (6): 339–350.

Yalom, I. D. and Leszcz, M. (2005). *The theory and practice of group psychotherapy,* 5th ed. New York: Basic Books.

5 | Social Development Interventions Have Extensive, Long-Lasting Effects

Richard F. Catalano, Karl G. Hill, Kevin P. Haggerty, Charles B. Fleming, and J. David Hawkins

Social development approaches to prevention target risk and aim to provide protection across childhood and adolescence. This chapter examines two studies conducted by the Social Development Research Group, the Seattle Social Development Project (Hawkins, Catalano, Kosterman, Abbott, and Hill 1999; Hawkins, Kosterman, Catalano, Hill, and Abbott 2005) and Raising Healthy Children (Brown, Catalano, Fleming, Haggerty, and Abbott 2005; Catalano et al. 2003). These studies demonstrate that a social development approach can reduce risk and enhance protection in the family, school, and peer environments, and improve behavior.

Social development interventions are guided by evidence that adolescent problems, including substance use, delinquency, violence, teen pregnancy, school dropout, and depression, are influenced by multiple, often overlapping risk and protective factors that exist in individuals and in their social environments (Hawkins, Catalano, and Miller 1992; Mrazek and Haggerty 1994; Pandina and White 1987). Some predictors of adolescent problems have a constant effect, while others increase or decrease in importance over the course of child and adolescent development.

Approaches to prevention target both the individual and the environment across childhood and adolescence. Exposure to early risk factors often impairs the course of development, leading to early developmental failures and a "snowball" effect, with risk factors in subsequent developmental stages tending to adhere and accumulate as a consequence of earlier problems (Mitchell, Spooner et al. 2001). For children who do not have early life risk exposure but engage in problem behaviors, the effect of risk may be more analogous to a "snowstorm" in which adolescents are exposed to models of problem behavior, favorable attitudes toward problem behavior, and peer engagement in problem behavior (Toumbourou and Catalano 2005). Even those without early risk may succumb if they experience a lengthy exposure without protection.

Social development interventions are designed to strengthen protection while reducing risk (Coie et al. 1993). The social development model is a theoretical framework that explains how protective factors work together to reduce risk (Catalano and Hawkins 1996). Social development interventions seek to strengthen protection by: 1) enhancing meaningful opportunities for youth to contribute to their family, school, and prosocial peer groups; 2) teaching appropriate skills so that they can be effective in their contribution; and 3) reinforcing effort and accomplishment so that they will be motivated to keep contributing to the social unit (the family, school, or peer group). When these three processes are supported, youth develop bonds to the social unit. When they develop bonds to those who hold prosocial values, they are more likely to adopt those values.

Seattle Social Development Project

The Seattle Social Development Project (SSDP) was initially implemented in 1981 among first-grade students in randomly assigned classrooms in eight public schools serving high-crime areas in Seattle, Washington. These students and those in control classrooms in the eight schools were followed prospectively to 1985. When the children entered the fifth grade, the study was expanded to include fifth-grade students in 10 additional schools. All 18 schools were then nonrandomly assigned to conditions in the fall of 1985. Thereafter, all fifth-grade students in each school received the intervention according to their school's intervention assignment: 10 schools assigned to the intervention, 5 schools assigned to control, 3 schools assigned to "parent training only." This resulted in a nonrandomized controlled trial with four conditions: 1) the full-intervention group ($n = 156$) consisted of those who received at least one semester of intervention in grades 1 through 4 and at least one semester of intervention in grades 5 and 6, with an average of 4.13 years of intervention exposure; 2) the late-intervention group (n = 267) consisted of those who received the intervention during grades 5 and 6 only, with an average of 1.65 years of exposure; 3) the "parent-training only" group (n = 141) (which is not discussed in this article) and 4) the control group (n = 220), who received no intervention. The late intervention and control groups included a mix of students from the original control classrooms in grades 1–4 and students added to the panel at grade 5.

The goal of the intervention was to improve the socialization experience of children within schools, families, and peer groups, and thereby affect multiple risk and protective factors. Parents and students attending schools in high-crime neighborhoods were asked to participate in program or comparison conditions (Hawkins et al. 1999).

During the elementary school years children learn patterns of behavior from the family and school socializing units, with peers playing an increasing role as children progress through the elementary years. Risk factors that were targeted by the SSDP intervention during elementary school included poor family management, family conflict, parental involvement in and favorable attitudes toward problem behaviors, academic failure, exposure to negative peer influences, favorable attitudes toward problem behaviors, and early antisocial behavior. The protective factors fostered by the intervention included healthy beliefs and clear standards; bonding to prosocial individuals, institutions, and groups; appropriate and meaningful opportunities for involvement; the social, emotional, and cognitive skills to be successful in those involvements; and recognition for effort and accomplishments. Additionally, we tested whether delivering the intervention package for the duration of elementary school (full intervention) had greater effects than delivering the intervention just prior to adolescence (late intervention) or providing no project intervention.

Teacher Component

Each year, as the study children moved through the elementary grades, teachers in intervention classrooms received five days of in-service training that consisted of a package of instructional methods with three major components: proactive classroom management, interactive teaching, and cooperative learning (Slavin 1980).

Child Component

First-grade teachers of the full treatment group also received instruction in the use of a cognitive, emotional, and social skills training curriculum. Interpersonal cognitive problem solving (Shure and Spivack 1982) teaches children to think through and use alternative solutions to problems with peers. This curriculum seeks to develop children's social skills for involvement in cooperative learning groups and other social activities without their resorting to aggressive or other problem behaviors. In addition, when students in both intervention conditions were in grade 6, they received training from project staff in skills to recognize and resist social influences to engage in problem behaviors, and to generate and suggest positive alternatives in order to stay out of trouble while still keeping friends.

Parent Component

Parent training classes appropriate to the developmental level of the children were offered to parents or adult caretakers of children. Parents in the full intervention condition were offered training in child behavior management skills when their children were in the first and second grades through a seven-session curriculum, "Catch 'Em Being Good" (McCarthy and Brown 1983). In the spring of second and third grades, parents of children in the full intervention also were offered a four-session curriculum, "Supporting School Success®," to strengthen their skills for supporting their children's academic development. When their children were in grades 5 and 6, parents of children in both the full and the late intervention conditions were offered a five-session curriculum, "Guiding Good Choices®" (Kosterman, Hawkins, Haggerty, Spoth, and Redmond 2001; Mason et al. in press; Park et al. 2000), to enhance family bonding and strengthen parents' skills to reduce their children's risks for drug use.

SSDP Intervention Findings

The SSDP intervention has demonstrated positive effects on child and adolescent development. At the end of the second grade, following two years of intervention, teachers rated experimental group males as less aggressive than controls, and experimental group females as less self-destructive than controls (Hawkins, Von Cleve, and Catalano 1991). At the start of fifth grade, intervention group children reported less initiation of delinquency, higher attachment to family, and higher school bonding compared to controls (Hawkins, Catalano, Morrison et al. 1992). SSDP had specific effects for low-income students. At the end of sixth grade, intervention group low-income girls reported more classroom learning opportunities, more classroom participation, and more bonding to school compared to controls. Low-income boys in the intervention group displayed better social skills, schoolwork skills, school bonding, achievement test scores, and grades than controls and were less likely to have antisocial peers (O'Donnell, Hawkins, and Abbott 1995). By age eighteen, fewer full intervention youth reported lifetime violence, lifetime sexual activity, and lifetime multiple sex partners than controls (Hawkins et al. 1999). They also reported improved school bonding and achievement and reduced school misbehavior compared to controls. Also at age eighteen, the intervention had specific benefits for students from low-income families, including better bonding to school and better academic achievement, and fewer were held back in school, engaged in school misbehavior, or drove after drinking. We have also found intervention effects preventing decline in bonding to school during high school, with students who received the full intervention showing less decline (Hawkins, Guo, Hill, Battin-Pearson, and Abbott 2001).

Further, SSDP intervention effects have been found in young adulthood. At age twenty-one, nine years after the program was delivered, the full intervention group reported fewer sexual partners and a greater probability of condom use at last intercourse, compared to controls. Fewer females in the full intervention had become pregnant and fewer had given birth. After controlling for socioeconomic status, the intervention was effective in reducing sexual risk behavior among African Americans,; those in the full intervention condition were more likely to use a condom and fewer had contracted a sexually transmitted disease (Lonczak, Abbott, Hawkins, Kosterman, and Catalano 2002). Also, compared to controls, fewer participants from the full intervention group were involved in a wide variety of crimes at age twenty-one, including property crimes, violent crimes, and fraud. Full intervention students are functioning better as young adults: they had completed more education, were more likely to be constructively engaged in school or work, were less likely to have changed jobs in the past year, and had more responsibility at work. Full intervention students were more likely to have positive emotional regulation (less depression, suicide ideation, and social phobia) and were less likely to have comorbid substance use and mental health disorders (Hawkins et al. 2005).

Raising Healthy Children Project

The Raising Healthy Children project (RHC) began in 1993 and, like SSDP, tested a social development approach to prevention with strategies that focused on three key socializing domains: school, family, and peer/individual. RHC was implemented in a suburban school district where ten schools were chosen because students' families had the lowest average income and children had higher rates of academic problems. The schools were randomized to experimental or control conditions.

In the experimental condition, RHC replicated the components of the SSDP intervention and extended the social development approach. Enhancements are described below.

Teacher Component

Because reading has been identified as a predictor of academic success, RHC trained teachers in effective strategies for teaching reading. RHC teacher training in elementary school was delivered to the whole school so that teachers gained experience with the practices before RHC program students entered their classrooms. In addition, the teacher component was extended to the first year of middle school to help maintain the child's commitment, which often drops off during the transition to middle school (Harachi, Abbott, Catalano, Haggerty, and Fleming 1999).

Family Component

RHC used a variety of recruitment efforts with parents that resulted in increased exposure to (greater involvement with) parenting programs. A variety of delivery mechanisms included parenting skills workshops delivered in single- to five-session formats, an all-day family fair offering multiple parenting skills sessions, and individual sessions with parents in their homes. Parenting content was reinforced and extended through a monthly newsletter distributed to all families in intervention schools. As a support component, families most at risk received twelve weeks of home-based services that provided the content of the curricula. During middle and high school, in-home, two-session family visits were offered to families with youth up to age eighteen at each of three developmental milestones: moving into high school (Brown et al. 2005), getting a driver's license (Haggerty, Fleming, Catalano, Harachi, and Abbott 2006), and transitioning out of high school.

Child Component

RHC augmented the SSDP child component in several ways. Teachers learned to provide direct instruction in social, emotional, and cognitive skills in the classroom through developmentally appropriate units across grades 1–6, creating a schoolwide scope and sequence of these skills. Interpersonal and problem-solving skills were integrated with literature and social studies. A schoolwide focus on staff development encouraged schools to adopt a "skill-of-the-month" to further enhance implementation (Haggerty, Cummings, Harachi, and Catalano 2004). RHC also extended learning opportunities beyond the school day by providing an after-school study club and a two-week, half-day summer camp to reinforce social, emotional, and cognitive skills. RHC offered tutor training to seventh-grade program students who were having academic difficulties, and these seventh-grade students tutored fourth-grade students. Special retreats offered middle school students the opportunity to learn and practice skills for recognizing and resisting social influences to engage in problem behaviors, and to generate and suggest positive alternatives in order to stay out of trouble while keeping friends.

RHC Intervention Findings

Effects of the intervention were examined at several time points by comparing students who were assigned to receive the RHC program to those who were not assigned to receive the intervention. After eighteen months, RHC students in intervention schools had significantly higher academic performance and a stronger commitment to school compared to their peers in the control group. Similarly, teachers rated RHC students as less involved in antisocial behaviors and as having higher social competence than their peers in control schools (Catalano et al. 2003).

Substance use during middle and early high school was also examined. Results indicated that intervention students had less growth in the frequency of alcohol and marijuana use over this time, and by tenth grade they used both substances less frequently than the nonintervention students (Brown et al. 2005).

We examined driving-related outcomes when study participants were in eleventh and twelfth grades and found that program students and parents were more likely to have a written driving contract than students in the control group. Program students also were less likely to report driving while under the influence of alcohol or riding in a car driven by a minor who had been drinking (Haggerty et al. 2006).

Summary

These two studies provide evidence that a social development approach to prevention can be reliably effective. The Seattle Social Development Project and Raising Healthy Children both addressed early life risk exposure and enhanced protection to stop the snowballing of accumulated risk. RHC added new components to extend the social development approach through middle and high school and provide added preparation for adolescents as they enter the snowstorm years, when they are exposed to peer models of problem behavior and favorable attitudes toward substance use and have weakening protection from the family. Both interventions have reduced risk factors, enhanced protective factors, and reduced problem behaviors. Young adults in the full intervention condition of SSDP continue to demonstrate enhanced outcomes nine years after the intervention was completed.

The Social Development Research Group gratefully acknowledges our partnership with the following school districts that we have worked with over the past twenty-five years: Edmonds School District #15, Renton School District, and Seattle Public Schools. We especially thank the principals, teachers, counselors, and district staff who have made this partnership successful. We also acknowledge our funding agencies, the National Institute on Drug Abuse, the National Institute on Alcohol Abuse and Alcoholism, the National Institute of Mental Health, the Office of Juvenile Justice and Delinquency Prevention, the Robert Wood Johnson Foundation, the Burlington Northern Foundation, and the Safeco Insurance Company.

References

Brown, E. C., Catalano, R. F., Fleming, C. B., Haggerty, K. P., and Abbott, R. D. (2005). Adolescent substance use outcomes in the Raising Healthy Children Project: A two-part latent growth curve analysis. *Journal of Consulting and Clinical Psychology* 73:699–710.

Catalano, R. F. and Hawkins, J. D. (1996). The social development model: A theory of antisocial behavior. In J. D. Hawkins (Ed.), *Delinquency and crime: Current theories,* 149–197. New York: Cambridge University Press.

Catalano, R. F., Mazza, J. J., Harachi, T. W., Abbott, R. D., Haggerty, K. P., and Fleming, C. B. (2003). Raising healthy children through enhancing social development in elementary school: Results after 1.5 years. *Journal of School Psychology* 41:143–164.

Coie, J. D., Watt, N. F., West, S. G., Hawkins, J. D., Asarnow, J. R., Markman, H. J., et al. (1993). The science of prevention: A conceptual framework and some directions for a national research program. *American Psychologist* 48:1013–1022.

Haggerty, K., Cummings, C., Harachi, T. W., and Catalano, R. F. (2004). Raising Healthy Children: School intervention strategies to develop prosocial behaviors. *Social Spectrum* 3:8–11.

Haggerty, K. P., Fleming, C. B., Catalano, R. F., Harachi, T. W., and Abbott, R. D. (2006). Raising healthy children: Examining the impact of promoting healthy driving behavior within a social development intervention. *Prevention Science* 7:257–267.

Harachi, T. W., Abbott, R. D., Catalano, R. F., Haggerty, K. P., and Fleming, C. B. (1999). Opening the black box: Using process evaluation measures to assess implementation and theory building. *American Journal of Community Psychology* 27:711–731.

Hawkins, J. D., Catalano, R. F., Kosterman, R., Abbott, R., and Hill, K. G. (1999). Preventing adolescent health-risk behaviors by strengthening protection during childhood. *Archives of Pediatrics and Adolescent Medicine* 153:226–234.

Hawkins, J. D., Catalano, R. F., and Miller, J. Y. (1992). Risk and protective factors for alcohol and other drug problems in adolescence and early adulthood: Implications for substance-abuse prevention. *Psychological Bulletin* 112:64–105.

Hawkins, J. D., Catalano, R. F., Morrison, D. M., O'Donnell, J., Abbott, R. D., and Day, L. E. (1992). The Seattle Social Development Project: Effects of the first four years on protective factors and problem behaviors. In J. McCord and R. E. Tremblay (Eds.), *Preventing antisocial behavior: Interventions from birth through adolescence,* 139–161. New York: Guilford Press.

Hawkins, J., Guo, J., Hill, K. G., Battin-Pearson, S., and Abbott, R. D. (2001). Long-term effects of the Seattle Social Development Intervention on school bonding trajectories. *Applied Developmental Science* 5:225–236.

Hawkins, J. D., Kosterman, R., Catalano, R. F., Hill, K. G., and Abbott, R. D. (2005). Promoting positive adult functioning through social development intervention in childhood: Long-term effects from the Seattle Social Development Project. *Archives of Pediatrics and Adolescent Medicine* 159:25–31.

Hawkins, J. D., Von Cleve, E., and Catalano, R. F. Jr. (1991). Reducing early childhood aggression: Results of a primary prevention program. *Journal of the American Academy of Child and Adolescent Psychiatry* 30:208–217.

Kosterman, R., Hawkins, J. D., Haggerty, K. P., Spoth, R., and Redmond, C. (2001). Preparing for the drug-free years: Session-specific effects of a universal parent-training intervention with rural families. *Journal of Drug Education* 31:47–68.

Lonczak, H. S., Abbott, R. D., Hawkins, J. D., Kosterman, R., and Catalano, R. F. (2002). Effects of the Seattle Social Development Project on sexual behavior, pregnancy, birth, and sexually transmitted disease outcomes by age 21 years. *Archives of Pediatrics and Adolescent Medicine* 156:438–447.

Mason, W. A., Kosterman, R., Hawkins, J. D., Haggerty, K. P., Spoth, R. L., and Redmond, C. (in press). Influence of a family-focused substance use preventive intervention on growth in adolescent depressive symptoms. *Journal of Research on Adolescence.*

McCarthy, S. P. and Brown, E. O. (1983). *Catch 'em being good.* Seattle, WA: Center for Law and Justice.

Mitchell, P., Spooner, C., et al. (2001). *A literature review of the role of families in the development, identification, prevention and treatment of illicit drug problems.* Commonwealth of Australia, National Health and Medical Research Council Monograph.

Mrazek, P. J. and Haggerty, R. J. (Eds.), Committee on Prevention of Mental Disorders, Institute of Medicine. (1994). *Reducing risks for mental disorders: Frontiers for prevention intervention research.* Washington, DC: National Academy Press.

O'Donnell, J., Hawkins, J. D., and Abbott, R. D. (1995). Predicting serious delinquency and substance use among aggressive boys. *Journal of Consulting and Clinical Psychology* 63:529–537.

Pandina, R. and White, H. R. (1987). The relationship between alcohol and marijuana use and crime: Implications for intervention and prevention. In C. Hampton and I. Silverman (Eds.), *Drug abuse, mental health, and delinquency,* 238–281. Rockville, MD: ADAMHA.

Park, J., Kosterman, R., Hawkins, J. D., Haggerty, K. P., Duncan, T. E., Duncan, S. C., et al. (2000). Effects of the "Preparing for the Drug Free Years" curriculum on growth in alcohol use and risk for alcohol use in early adolescence. *Prevention Science* 1:125–138.

Shure, M. B. and Spivack, G. (1982). Interpersonal problem-solving in young children: A cognitive approach to prevention. *American Journal of Community Psychology* 10:341–356.

Slavin, R. E. (1980). *Using student team learning.* Baltimore, MD: Johns Hopkins University Press.

Toumbourou, J. W. and Catalano, R. F. (2005). Predicting developmentally harmful substance use. In T. Stockwell, P. Gruenewald, J. W. Toumbourou, and W. Loxley (Eds.), *Preventing harmful substance use: The evidence base for policy and practice,* 53–65. London: Wiley.

6 | Advances in Children's Mental Health

Mark W. Fraser and Mary A. Terzian

THE PURPOSE OF THIS CHAPTER is to describe recent advances in mental health services for children and adolescents. It is divided into three sections, covering the prevalence of mental disorders in childhood and adolescence; the development of mental health disorders; and the effectiveness of interventions and services for children and adolescents. We conclude by considering system-level reforms and challenges in transferring advances in knowledge to mental health practice.

Two bodies of knowledge inform practice in the field of children's mental health: advances in developmental psychopathology, an area of research integrating knowledge of normative child development with knowledge of the etiologies of mental disorders; and advances in the design of interventions for children with mental disorders. When practitioners, advocates, policy makers, and researchers speak of mental health, they often focus on child and adolescent mental disorders described in the *Diagnostic and Statistical Manual* (*DSM*) of the American Psychiatric Association (American Psychiatric Association 2000). However, many terms other than those employed in the *DSM* are used to describe children and adolescents with mental health problems. These terms often focus on functional abilities more than nosological classification and include expressions such as serious emotional disturbances (SED) and emotional and behavior disorders (EBD). SED is used to describe any psychiatric disorder that produces serious functional impairment at home, in school, or with peers (Kazdin 2003). Used more in educational settings, EBD refers to impaired emotional or behavioral responses that occur over a long duration; diverge from generally accepted, age-appropriate, ethnic, or cultural norms; and adversely affect personal, social, academic, and behavioral functioning in at least two different settings, one of which must be school-related (Forness et al. 1998). Though conceptually related, the terms SED and EBD are not considered synonymous.

For this review, we consider SED and EBD, but we emphasize common *DSM* disorders, including disruptive behavior and emotional disorders. In childhood and adolescence, disruptive behavior disorders (DBDs) include oppositional defiant disorder (ODD), conduct disorder (CD), and attention-deficit/hyperactivity disorder (ADHD). Emotional disorders include mood disorders and anxiety disorders. A companion paper focuses on substance-related disorders, and these, in addition to developmental disorders, suicide, and adjustment/reactive disorders, are not included in our review.

The Prevalence of Mental Health Disorders in Childhood and Adolescence

Studies suggest that 8 percent to 14 percent of children and 17 percent to 42 percent of adolescents experience diagnosable emotional and behavior problems (Anderson, Williams, McGee, and Silva 1987; Kazdin 2003; Roberts, Attkisson, and Rosenblatt 1998; Simonoff et al. 1997; Simpson, Scott, Henderson, and Manderscheid 2002). Using 1998 and 1999 data from the National Health Interview Survey (N = 26,555), Simpson et al. (2002) found almost 1 in 7 U.S. youths ages 5 to 17 years (13.6 percent) had experienced at least 1 type of mental health impairment in their lifetime. Rates of psychiatric disorder among youth receiving services in mental health, juvenile detention, and educational facilities are higher, with some estimates approaching 80 percent (Garland et al. 2001; Mattison, Morales, and Bauer 1992; Teplin, Abram, McClelland, Dulcan, and Mericle 2002).

Among psychiatric disorders affecting normative samples of youth, disruptive behavior disorders are the most common (Anderson et al. 1987). According to the fourth and current edition of the *DSM* (*DSM-IV*), rates of ODD range from 2 to 16 percent, rates of CD range from 1 to 10 percent, and rates of ADHD range from 3 to 12 percent of children and youth between the ages of 6 and 18 (American Psychiatric Association 2000; Froehlich, Lanphear, Epstein, Barbaresi, Katusic, and Kahn 2007). Anxiety and mood disorders affect a lower proportion of children and adolescents: Generalized Anxiety Disorder (GAD) has a lifetime prevalence rate of 5 percent and Separation Anxiety Disorder (SAD) has a lifetime prevalence rate of 4 percent (American Psychiatric Association 2000). Depressive disorders are less commonly diagnosed in childhood, but 3-month point prevalence rates among youth ages 8 to 16 years range from 2 percent to 12 percent (Egger, Costello, and Angold 2003; Simonoff et al. 1997).

Prevalence rates for mental health disorders vary according to the diagnostic criteria, informant, time period, and population considered (Brown et al. 2001; Loeber, Burke, Lahey, Winters, and Zera 2000). For instance, using criteria from the *DSM-IV*, ODD has been found to affect approximately 2 to 3 percent of youth ages 9 to 17 years (Roberts, Roberts, and Xing 2007; Rowe, Maughan, Pickles, Costello, and Angold 2002). However, using criteria from the earlier *DSM III-R*, as many as 14 percent of youths ages 10 to 20 have ODD (Cohen et al. 1993). The annual prevalence of ADHD in a nationally representative sample of children ages 8 to 15 (Froehlich et al. 2007) was recently estimated at 8.7 percent using *DSM-IV* criteria from the caregiver module of the *Diagnostic Interview Schedule for Children* (*DISC*).

Compared with parent reports of youth behavior, child and adolescent self-reports result in lower prevalence rates and have less test-retest reliability (Breton et al. 1999; Shaffer et al. 2000). In addition, prevalence rates increase with longer time periods. Some studies have measured lifetime prevalence (Beals et al. 2005), while others have assessed three-month (Egger, Costello, and Angold 2003), six-month (Breton et al. 1999; Teplin et al. 2002), and one-year prevalence rates (Froehlich et al. 2007; Garland et al. 2001; for prevalence rates obtained from various U.S.-based studies, see table 6.1).

Gender, age, and socioeconomic differences in prevalence and symptom-growth rates have been identified for a variety of mental health disorders. Whereas girls and older youth are more likely to be diagnosed with depression (Cole et al. 2002) and anxiety (Lewinsohn, Gotlib, Lewinsohn, Seeley, and Allen 1998), boys are more likely to be diagnosed with disruptive behavior disorders (Cuffe, Moore, and McKeown 2005; Nock, Kazdin, Hiripi, and Kessler 2007; Shastry 2004). Gender differences in ADHD and CD are particularly pronounced. Epidemiological studies suggest that ADHD is at least twice as common in boys as in girls (9 percent versus 4 percent respectively; Dey and Bloom 2005) and that CD is 9 times more common in boys (Shastry 2004). Gender differences appear to be less pronounced for ODD (Nock, Kazdin, Hiripi, and Kessler 2007), with some studies reporting no gender differences (Loeber et al. 2000; Rowe et al. 2002). In contrast, age differences for ODD are more pronounced. A study conducted in Ontario, Canada with 2,674 youths, ages 4 to 16 years, and their parents (Offord et al. 1987) observed an average 3-month prevalence rate for ODD of 4.2 percent in 4- to 11-year olds and 7.3 percent in 12- to 16-year-olds.

Table 6.1 Prevalence Rates of Psychiatric Disorder Without Impairment Among School-age Youth (Unweighted)

| | Sample Characteristics | | | Methods | | | Percent of Sample with DSM-III or IV Diagnosis | | | | | |
| | | | | | | | Disruptive Behavior Disorders | | | Emotional Disorders | | |
Study/Source	N	Age	Population	DSM	Instrument		ADHD	ODD	CD	GAD	SAD	Depressive
Egger et al. 2003	1422	9–16	Normative sample of rural youth	IV	CAPA (caregiver and youth report; 3 mo. prevalence)		7.6%	24.3%	12.9%	5.2%	7.5%	12.6%
Simonoff et al. 1997	2762	8–16	Normative sample of Caucasian twins	III-R	CAPA (caregiver and youth report; 3 mo. prevalence)		2.4%	3.9%	6.6%	10.8%	7.2%	1.3%
Garland et al. 2001	1618	6-18	Indicated sample of service-involved youth	IV	DISC-IV (caregiver and youth report; 1 year prevalence)		24.4%	17.4%	24.9%	1.2%	4.9%	6.0%
Teplin et al. 2002*	1829	10–18	Indicated sample of juvenile detainees	III-R	DISC 2.3 (youth report; 6 mo. prevalence)		18.3%	15.6%	38.8%	7.2%	15.0%	12.0%
Beals et al. 1997	109	13–18	High-risk sample of American Indians	III-R	DISC 2.1c (youth report; 6 mo. prevalence)		10.6%	2.9%	3.8%	1.9%	1.9%	4.7%

Note: CAPA = Child and Adolescent Psychiatric Assessment; DISC = Diagnostic Interview Schedule for Children; ADHD = Attention Deficit/Hyperactivity Disorder; ODD = Oppositional Defiant Disorder; CD = Conduct Disorder; GAD = Generalized Anxiety Disorder; SAD = Separation Anxiety Disorder
*Prevalence estimates reflect rates of diagnosis with impairment rather than rates of diagnosis only, thus their values are conservative.

Age differences have also been observed for SED and psychiatric disorder, with nonlinear trends for SED and linear increases for psychiatric disorder. In a longitudinal study of 1,420 children ages 9 to 16 years, the percentage of children with a *DSM*-classified psychiatric disorder was highest among 9-year-olds, then declined until the age of 12, and sharply increased during adolescence (Costello, Mustillo, Erklani, Keeler, and Angold 2003). Over the same period, Costello and her colleagues found the percentage of children with SED steadily increased with age. Finally, a recent study conducted by Froelich and her colleagues (2007) found that the poorest children—in the bottom 20 percent of family income distribution—were more than twice as likely than the wealthiest children (in the top 20 percent) to fulfill criteria for ADHD (adjusted odds ratio [AOR] = 2.3, 95 percent confidence interval [CI] = 1.4–3.9). On balance, prevalence rates seem to vary by both age and gender; however, the relative differences have measurement variance, due to different methods and sources of data collection.

Because of the limitations of available epidemiological data, the prevalence of psychiatric disorders in children and adolescents must be inferred from a variety of studies. Unlike Australia (see Sawyer et al. 2001) and England (see Ford, Goodman, and Meltzer 2003; Meltzer, Gatward, Goodman, and Ford 2000), the United States has not funded a routine national survey of children to estimate the prevalence of mental disorders using common diagnostic assessment tools, such as the *Diagnostic Interview Schedule for Children* (Shaffer and Fisher 1997) or the *Child and Adolescent Psychiatric Assessment* (Angold et al. 1995). Consequently, we are limited to comparing rates obtained from studies using different sampling procedures. Moreover, few studies have attempted to explore differences between socioeconomic, racial, and ethnic groups. Developing a better understanding of the prevalence of mental health disorders among low-income communities and communities of color is particularly important, given evidence for income-based and ethnic/racial disparities in the provision of mental health services (see, e.g., Simpson et al. 2002). Advances in knowledge of the prevalence of disorders by race/ethnicity, socioeconomic status, age, and gender have the potential to contribute to the design of developmentally appropriate, culturally relevant mental health services, but the knowledge base is surprisingly thin.

Advances in Understanding Mental Disorders in Childhood and Adolescence

Recent advances in understanding mental health disorders are related in part to the emergence of a risk and resilience perspective in child development (Fraser 2004b).[1] A "risk factor" is any influence that increases the chances for harm, or, more specifically, any influence that increases the probability of onset, digression to a more serious state, or maintenance of a problem condition. Risk factors range from prenatal biological complications to negative family circumstances to toxic environmental conditions. The term "risk mechanism" refers to the process whereby related risk factors contribute to heightened vulnerability for a mental disorder or for other poor developmental outcomes.

The study of resilience—prevailing over adversity—emerged from the search for risk factors. In the 1960s and 1970s, researchers began to notice that some children who faced stressful, high-risk situations fared well in life (Garmezy 1971, 1985; Rutter 1987; Werner and Smith 1977). Initially, they were puzzled by this finding and surprised that children's responses to stress varied so widely. They began to search for factors that might promote successful adaptation in the face of risk. In part, the assets and strengths perspectives in social work and allied health disciplines represent this view (Saleebey 2000). In much the same way that assets and strengths are conceptualized as protecting children from risk, the term "protective" factors is used to describe factors that reduce risk or exposure to risk.

Protective factors occupy an increasingly important but often misunderstood position in developing knowledge of psychopathology. When a social, psychological, or environmental influence promotes healthy development regardless of risk, it is called a "promotive factor." We reserve the term "protective factor" to refer to those individual and environmental resources that buffer children from risk (for a discussion of protective versus promotive factors, see Sameroff and Gutman 2004). Protective factors operate in the presence of risk and, as with an immunization, they confer no particular benefit in the absence of a pathogen or, more broadly, a risk. Because they directly reduce risk or operate to ameliorate its effects, protective factors—to the extent we understand them—may be useful in the design of more effective services. Interventions can be conceptualized as systematic strategies intended to strengthen protective factors, both environmental and personal resources, for children at risk of a mental disorder or other poor life course outcomes.

The Biopsychosocial Perspective in Developmental Psychopathology

The ideas of risk and protection along with advances in genetics have led to the emergence of a biopsychosocial model of developmental psychopathology in the field of children's mental health. This model is based on a growing understanding of the developmental trajectories that characterize many childhood mental health disorders. In this context, no single risk factor or highly distinctive set of risk factors appears to produce mental health problems. Rather, it is the accumulation of risk in the absence of protection that appears to produce disruptive behavior, mood disturbances, and other social and health problems (Sameroff, Bartko, Baldwin, Baldwin, and Seifer 1999). To be sure, some disorders have strong biological bases. However, even in these disorders, environmental and biological risks appear to interact to affect actual vulnerability.

Two core ideas contribute to this biopsychosocial model. They integrate research from behavioral medicine, criminology, developmental psychology, genetics, neuroscience, sociology, and other fields. The first is that the manifestation of genetic risk is environmentally conditioned: symptoms for many disorders with genetic bases are exacerbated by psychosocial factors. The second, based on advances in cognitive science, focuses on the relationship between early life experiences and later behavior. It argues that early life experiences provide children with social knowledge and skills that influence developmental outcomes. Hence, the effect of early life experiences on later behavior problems is mediated in part by cognitions. We turn briefly to each of these ideas.

Genetic Risk Is Environmentally Mediated

Genetic influences are increasingly conceptualized as being facilitated by and exerting effects under certain environmental conditions (Rutter 2005). That is, genes may directly affect a child by interacting with environmental conditions (e.g., a certain trait may be expressed only in the presence of a certain condition) or may indirectly influence a child by influencing the environment (e.g., a child's temperament may influence parenting style, which in turn affects a child's behavior).

From this perspective, genetic influences potentiate the expression of mental health disorders; however, they may be insufficiently strong by themselves to produce problem behavior. For example, temperamental children whose stubborn, oppositional styles of interaction have genetic links may create such stress for their parents that child monitoring and parent-child attachments are weakened. In such a case, genetic risk potentiates the expression of a disorder both directly through temperament and indirectly through transactions with environmental conditions. Recent studies support both kinds of effects (Meyer et al. 2000; Roy, Rutter, and Pickles 2000; Rutter 2000; Rutter, Pickles, Murray, and Eaves 2001).

This understanding has an important practice implication for social work and other mental health professions. Children with high genetic risk may vary in their actual vulnerability because of environmental conditions. The likelihood that they will become symptomatic may be at least partly affected by family, school, and peer conditions that vary over time. Thus, at any point in a child's development, features of the social and physical environment may mediate genetic risk. In this sense, *the expression of genetic vulnerability is regulated, in part, by social contextual factors that are potentially malleable* (Rutter 2005; Sameroff 1995).

Indeed, a recent study of the relationship between poverty and mental disorders in childhood and adolescence demonstrates the potential impact of social and environmental conditions. As a part of the Great Smoky Mountains longitudinal study of children, Costello, Compton, Keeler, and Angold (2003) followed a sample of 1,420 children selected from a population of 20,000. American Indian children made up about 25 percent of the participants in the study. In the midst of the 8-year data collection, a gambling casino opened on tribal lands, and, as a result of an agreement with the casino operators, every man, woman, and child on the reservation received a percentage of the profits. The casino not only dramatically affected the incomes of tribe members but also created jobs in casino-related businesses such as hotels and restaurants. The "casino intervention" provided an opportunity to assess the effect of changes in income on the prevalence of mental health disorders among American Indian and non-American Indian children who moved out of poverty or failed to move out of poverty. American Indian and non-American Indian children who moved out of poverty showed a 40 percent decrease in disruptive behavior symptoms compared to children who remained in poverty or who were never poor. No significant differences were observed for mood disorders. Mediational analyses suggested that 77 percent of the effect of change in poverty level was explained by changes in parental supervision. In a natural experiment where changes in poverty were largely uncorrelated with family characteristics, the findings support the view that environmental resources may affect both the development and the remission of disruptive behavior disorders.

More broadly, then, some mental health disorders appear to have high contextual dependence or sensitivity. The context appears to affect behavior in many ways—in this case, by its effect on parental supervision, mediated by changes in income. The context potentiates genetic expression and is the medium through which experience accrues. Thus, contextual risk factors affect developmental trajectories by directly exposing children to hazards (e.g., environmental toxins, dangerous neighborhoods) and by indirectly influencing the resources available to and the actions of parents, teachers, and others.

Cognitive Processes Mediate Early Risk

The second emerging concept in developmental psychopathology is that mental processes mediate, in part, the effect of early childhood experiences on later developmental outcomes, including the development of mental health problems (Dodge and Pettit 2003). Mental processes are defined as learned scripts, schemata, skills, and beliefs that draw on social knowledge and influence behavior. Conditioned on emotions and emotional regulation skills that organize and motivate decisional processes, six steps in processing information have been identified: encoding social and environmental cues; interpreting cues; selecting social goals; identifying possible responses; making a response decision; and enacting a selected response. Of course, in real time, the way children process information is not so linear. It occurs in the blink of an eye and has many feedback loops. Research on cognition provides important new information on how early experiences affect later behavior.

At each step in this process, decision making is vulnerable to disruption by unregulated emotions, impulses, and accrued social knowledge, all of which have the potential to "bias" decision processes. Though it is used in the literature, the term "bias" may not be the right word because children make use of their experiences, whatever they may be. In fact, their life experiences influence every step in the process though scripts, schemata, and other rules of thumb for interpreting social interactions and guiding future behavior. For example, children who have been physically abused may have learned that adults can inflict harm, and they are especially vigilant for harmful potential in new social situations with adults. This can affect the way children process social information. Studies suggest that children exposed to abuse tend to encode fewer cues before coming to a decision, and they may conclude that a particular person is potentially harmful, when he or she is not (Dodge, Bates, and Pettit 1990). This is called "hostile attribution bias" or falsely attributing hostility to another (Crick and Dodge 1994; Lemerise and Arsenio 2000). Because behavior appears to be guided in part by attributions of intent, children who make mistakes in interpreting others' intentions may incorrectly adopt defensive postures that alienate them from peers, teachers, and others. Through research in developmental psychopathology (e.g., Lengua 2003; Prinstein, Cheah, and Guyer 2005), we are beginning to understand how early experiences affect cognitions, which in turn influence subsequent behavior. To the extent that we understand them, these social-cognitive skills and the social knowledge that children use in making daily decisions may be malleable in intervention.

Cumulative Risk and Specific Risk Mechanisms: A Stress-Vulnerability Model?

Based on the relationship between cumulative risk and developmental outcomes, a stress-vulnerability model with cognitive features is beginning to take shape. Cumulative stress is thought to potentiate the expression of disorders, including many that have biological bases. For example, poor parental monitoring of children (which can be a function of stress or other factors) may be related to a variety of disorders because poor monitoring creates circumstances where children develop poor social-cognitive skills, wander and associate with other poorly supervised children, and have opportunities to get into trouble. For some disorders, poor monitoring may also be a function of a child's difficult behavior. That is, hostile, unresponsive, or bizarre behavior may strain the parent-child attachment and weaken parental supervision. The dynamic and nonlinear relationships that affect vulnerability in combination with the cognitive features of adaptation (e.g., skills in processing social information, the steeling effects of moderate risk exposure, and hardiness in the face of adversity) hold the potential to affect the way interventions are designed; however, research on stress vulnerability and other risk mechanisms is in its infancy.

The Coercion Mechanism

One of the few clearly articulated risk mechanisms involves coercive parent-child interactions. Using a social interaction learning perspective, researchers at the Oregon Social Learning Center (OSLC 2005a) have been studying family and peer processes in the development of DBDs since the 1960s. In the course of their studies, they have observed a specific microsocial communication pattern that appears to reinforce antisocial behavior. It begins in the family as a pattern of interaction in which parents inadvertently reward their children's coercive behavior by acquiescing to it. Although acquiescence can occur for a variety of reasons, the result is that children learn that aggressive behavior produces benefits. Through positive reinforcement by siblings and peers, this behavioral style becomes covert in elementary school. By middle school, this behavior is characterized by a high level of "deviant" talk and association with delinquent peers. Studies show that this coercion risk mechanism is predictive of delinquency, drug use, high-risk sexual behavior, and—in young adulthood—domestic violence (Forgatch, Bulloch, and Patterson 2004).

The coercion risk mechanism specifies a causal sequence that leads to DBDs. In dozens of studies, researchers at the OSLC have shown that child developmental outcomes are mediated in early childhood by parenting practices and in adolescence by association with deviant peers (see Forgatch, Bulloch, and Patterson 2004; OSLC 2005b). Moreover, this putative risk mechanism identifies positive reinforcement of a child's overtly aggressive behavior as a key target for intervention. The parenting interventions developed by OSLC have been shown effective in interrupting that positive reinforcement. In adolescence, exposure to deviant talk and association with delinquent peers have proven more difficult to change, but they are the target of current studies.

The articulation of risk mechanisms such as the coercion mechanism or, more broadly, the stress-vulnerability mechanism is a major challenge in continuing to develop knowledge of the etiology of mental disorders. To date, researchers are divided between those who believe that interventions should focus on specific risk mechanisms and those who argue that cumulative risk, more than specific putative risk processes, elevates vulnerability. It is likely that we will find both to be important. Specific risk mechanisms may operate for specific disorders, and the stress-vulnerability mechanism may exacerbate specific risk processes and vulnerabilities, further potentiating problem behavior.

Advances in Knowledge Regarding the Effectiveness of Interventions and Services

Advances in knowledge regarding risk and protective factors for mental health disorders have led to a dramatic increase in the number of prevention and treatment trials funded by the National Institutes of Health (NIH) and other federal, foundation, state, and other agencies. In this section, we briefly review findings from studies of the effectiveness of psychosocial and pharmacological interventions. We then discuss research on the concept of systems of care for children and adolescents.

Advances in Psychosocial Interventions

Psychosocial interventions in mental health can be classified on a continuum from process-oriented to relatively structured change strategies. Sometimes process-oriented interventions are called "unfocused" interventions, because they tend to be open-ended and target strengthening attachments, recovering from trauma, or making broad developmental or social adjustments (Lock 2004). In contrast, structured interventions are called "focused," because they address highly specified problems, for example fire setting, dysfunctional fear (e.g., fear of crowds), or binge eating. Focused interventions are usually time limited and activities are typically spelled out in treatment manuals or protocols; they include behavioral and cognitive-behavioral programs, such as parent training and social problem-solving skills training. Both unfocused and focused interventions can be part of overarching services such as case management, residential treatment, wilderness experience or challenge camps, therapeutic foster care, psychiatric hospitalization, day treatment, psychosocial rehabilitation, after-school supervision, and secure care. Moreover, they can be provided in individual, family, small group, multifamily, and even social network formats.

The Effectiveness of Children's Mental Health Interventions

More than 1,500 controlled studies of the effectiveness of child and adolescent interventions have been completed, and the quality of studies continues to improve. On balance, children who receive a research-based intervention fare better than children who do not participate in intervention programs or who receive routine mental health services (Kazdin 2004; Weisz 2000). The greatest advances in knowledge have arisen from research on focused interventions (for a review of interventions for specific social and health problems, see Allen-Meares and Fraser 2004). Increasingly designed to interrupt risk mechanisms or to strengthen protective factors such as social competence, focused interventions are characterized by highly specified activities sequenced in a logical form to reduce a problem behavior.

Shown in table 6.2, a number of interventions have sufficient empirical support to be called "established" or evidence based. The supporting evidence may not be as strong as one might like, and there is substantial variation in the criteria used by the various authorities that evaluate the research evidence for interventions in the field of children's mental health. On balance, these authorities, ranging from governmental agencies like the Model Programs of the U.S. Department of Health and Human Services Center for Substance Abuse Prevention (http://www.samhsa.gov/centers/csap/modelprograms) and the What Works Clearinghouse of the U.S. Department of Education (http://www.w-w-c.org/whatwedo/overview.html) to nongovernmental organizations like the American Psychological Association Division 12 (http://www.apa.org/divisions/div12/rev_est/index.html), the American Psychiatric Association (http://www.psych.org/psych_pract/treatg/pg/prac_guide.cfm), the Campbell Collaboration (http://www.campbellcollaboration.org/), Child Trends (http://www.childtrends.org/_catdisp_page.cfm?LID=91F45245–56E6–4782–9807023A43EEB254), Cochrane Collaboration (http://www.cochrane.org), and Rand Corporation (http://www.promisingpractices.net/), rely on careful reviews of controlled studies. Some require that studies be conducted using treatment manuals. Others will accept practice guidelines instead. Some place greater emphasis on group designs, ignoring single-subject studies. Others will consider single-subject designs, if they are replicated. Some focus on the heterogeneity of the sample, the adequacy of the sample size, and intent-to-treat analyses. Though all seek rigor and have produced helpful reviews of the effectiveness of interventions for children and adolescents, the findings differ because criteria differ. Nonetheless, it is possible now—as never before—to identify a variety of potentially effective interventions for many children's mental health disorders.

Using Evidence in Practice

A striking feature of the contents of table 6.2 is that the recommended interventions are not those generally offered through mental health agencies (Weisz 2000). Compared to these, interventions in children's mental health tend to be less focused, less manual based, and more based on attributions to authority or beliefs (Gambrill 1999). In short, there seems to be a disjuncture between what is known from research and what is done in practice.

Another way to think about this phenomenon is that the difficulty in transferring knowledge from research to practice is vastly underestimated. In contrast to the adoption of new drugs in the medical fields, the mental health field has neither good mechanisms for disseminating knowledge nor incentives for changing routine practices. The problem arises, in part, because the ways we develop and test interventions bear little resemblance to the ways

Table 6.2 Effectiveness of Interventions for Mental Disorders in Childhood and Adolescence (adapted from Ollendick and King 2004)

Type of Disorder	Intervention	
	Established	Promising
Attention Deficit Hyperactivity Disorder Behavioral modification in classrooms	Behavioral parenting training	Cognitive behavioral therapy
Anxiety Disorders (Generalized Anxiety Disorder, Separation Anxiety Disorder)	None	Cognitive behavioral therapy Cognitive behavioral therapy plus family anxiety management
Depression	None	Behavioral self-control therapy Cognitive behavioral coping skills training
Obsessive-Compulsive Disorder	None	Exposure/response prevention
Oppositional Defiant Disorder	Behavioral parent training Functional family therapy	Anger control training with stress inoculation
Conduct Disorder	Multisystemic family therapy Videotape modeling	Anger coping therapy Assertiveness training Cognitive behavioral therapy Problem-solving skills training Rational-emotive therapy Time out plus signal seat treatment
Phobias	Graduated exposure Participant modeling Reinforced practice	Imaginal desensitization In vivo desensitization Live modeling Filmed modeling Cognitive behavioral therapy

Note:
Established = at least two controlled studies showing efficacy relative to pill, placebo, or another treatment, or a series of at least nine single-subject designs showing efficacy relative to another intervention, with treatment manuals, and with effects demonstrated by two different investigators.
Promising = at least two studies showing efficacy relative to wait-list control; or at least three single subject designs or one experiment meeting "established" criteria.

that interventions are implemented *in vivo*. Not only are the knowledge transfer mechanisms less well developed in mental health than in medicine, but the processes and structures that underpin research in mental health exist or are altered substantially in practice. In research, children and adolescents with identified problems—and usually a single diagnosis—are recruited as study participants. In practice, they are usually referred for treatment, and they often have multiple problems that are comorbid for several diagnoses. In research, incentives for participation—including transportation, child care, and food—are routinely offered. In practice, incentives for participation are rarely offered. In research, children and their caretakers participate voluntarily and can drop out of services without penalty. In practice, children and their families may be compelled to participate by court mandates or the threat of an out-of-home placement. In such situations, dropout can have dire consequences. In research, children and their families know that they are a part of an experimental study and may be receiving an innovative service. In practice, children and their families usually do not feel that they are part of an innovation. In sum, the conditions under which an intervention is developed differ markedly from those in which services are provided. Further complicating the problem, research-based interventions are often complex and require specific sequences of activities that build upon one another. In practice, the sequencing of activities is more process oriented, related in part to case flow, consumer preferences, and available resources. Thus, practice research differs significantly from practice in an agency or psychiatric hospital. Aside from the fact that ways must be found to adapt and implement research-based interventions in practice, we might draw at least one conclusion from this: we should expect effects to be smaller when established and promising interventions are brought to scale.

Advances in Psychopharmacology

The growth of knowledge regarding the effectiveness of psychosocial interventions has paralleled remarkable advances in psychopharmacological interventions for children and adolescents. In the 1950s and 1960s, the advent of chlorpromazine accelerated the deinstitutionalization of thousands of people with serious mental illnesses. Rapid advances in therapies based on lithium and tricyclic antidepressants followed. In the 1980s, significant advances were made with the introduction of selective-serotonin reuptake inhibitors and atypical antipsychotic agents. These pharmacological discoveries were applied first to adults, and more recently both these and new drugs have been tested with children and adolescents (Chang 2004).

More children than ever before—approximately 6 percent of all youths—are maintained on at least one psychoactive medication (Zito et al. 2003), with stimulants the most commonly prescribed (Jensen et al. 1999). This up-surge has resulted from a number of factors including the growing number of studies showing the effectiveness of pharmacological interventions with children, the increasing delivery of psychopharmacotherapies by family practitioners, the growing view that many childhood disorders are "brain diseases," changes in the way mental health services are provided to children, and aggressive marketing by pharmaceutical companies. In a recent study of 900,000 youths served by two large health maintenance organizations, overall drug prescriptions increased two- to threefold during the ten-year period from 1987 to 1996. The majority of this increase was observed in stimulants and antidepressants (Zito et al. 2003; Zuvekas, Vitiello, and Norquist 2006).

It may not be coincidence that increases in pharmacological interventions for children have occurred at the same time that for-profit health care organizations have claimed increasingly larger care responsibilities in the field of children's mental health. These behavioral health care organizations manage costs by setting time limits on services and by hiring fewer and less well-trained therapists. Medications are charged to medical budget lines, while psychosocial treatments are charged to highly scrutinized behavioral budget lines. Thus, "the incentives are aligned to use medication" (Jellinek 2003:15).

For a variety of other reasons, the rapid increase in the use of psychoactive medications is puzzling. Although knowledge of the effectiveness of pharmacological interventions for children is established in some areas of practice (e.g., ADHD) and is rapidly developing in other areas, it is not well established in all areas. Even though only promising, the evidence for psychosocial intervention may be stronger than the evidence for psychopharmacological intervention for anxiety, conduct, depressive, and eating disorders (Biederman, Spencer, and Wilens 2004; Lock 2004). Moreover, many of the newer medications have very limited longitudinal trials with children. The long-term effects are not clear. In addition, potentially elevating the cost of medications, the way medications are managed appears related strongly to outcomes. In the Multimodal Treatment study of children with ADHD sponsored by the National Institute of Mental Health, well-managed medications (i.e., once-per-month medications management office visits of thirty minutes, solicitation of teacher input to adjust dose, and higher dosages) proved superior in symptom reduction over behavior therapy alone and routine community care with typical medication (i.e., twice per year office visits of eighteen minutes each; Hoza et al. 2005; MTA Cooperative Group 1999). So in the context of important pharmacological discoveries, challenges remain in managing medications in practice and combining medications with psychosocial interventions. It does not appear that research-based advances in drug treatment fully explain the growing tendency to use psychopharmacological interventions (Saunders and Heflinger 2003).

At the confluence of advances in psychosocial and pharmacological interventions are systems reforms such as privatization and managed care, which bring marketplace pressures to bear on the design and delivery of mental health services. In the next section, we review attempts to alter the way that services are provided to children and their families. Begun in the 1980s, many of these reforms were meant to create systems or networks of care for children with serious emotional disturbances. At about the same time, performance-based contracting, privatization of services, accountability for service outcomes, and managed care were introduced to provide incentives for delivering cost-calibrated services.

Systems of Care: A Reform Too Late?

After years of criticism that states were failing to provide adequate mental health services for children (Knitzer 1982; National Alliance for the Mentally Ill 2001), Congress passed the Children's and Community Mental Health Services Improvement Act in 1992. This act created the Comprehensive Community Mental Health Services for Children and Their Families Program, which provided federal grants to states to develop "systems of care" (SOC) for children. SOC were intended to provide a coordinated network of need-based services for children with SED (Stroul and Friedman 1986). Based on interagency agreements, SOC require blending funding across child-serving agencies (e.g., mental health and child welfare), providing a continuum of services, treatment in the least restrictive setting, family involvement in the design and provision of services, and culturally sensitive individualized case plans.

The Cost-Effectiveness of Systems of Care

The initial vision of SOC was that expanded community-based services could be funded by shifting costs from expensive inpatient care to less expensive outpatient care and partial hospitalization. An evaluation of SOC in Ventura County in California suggested that it could indeed reduce hospitalizations and expand coverage, reducing racial/ethnic disparities of the provision of mental health services (Shortz 2003). However, recent data suggest that cost savings in inpatient care may not cover expenses in expanding community-based care. In a comparison of two Ohio counties in which one provided SOC-based mental health services and the other did not, Foster and Conner (2005) found that youths under the SOC approach stayed longer in treatment, but returned less often after the close of treatment. Moreover, they were less likely to receive inpatient treatment and to become involved in the juvenile justice system. Summing costs across the mental health, child welfare, special education, and justice systems, they found that SOC expenses were 18 percent higher than traditional services. To date, then, the data suggest that SOC can provide higher quality care, yet at a slightly greater cost.

Systems of Care and Other Mental Health Reforms

A looming challenge in mental health services for children and adolescents is the integration of SOC with other mental health care reforms. In many parts of the country, just at the time when the evidence base for services has expanded dramatically and the concept of SOC has begun to take hold, public community mental health systems have been restructured. In most states, public service systems have been reduced in size, supplanted in part by privatized managed care systems in which a variety of not-for-profit and for-profit organizations compete for contracts to provide mental health services.

The services offered by these new behavioral health agencies are often time limited and controlled by cost contingencies. Services in many states are tied through contractual agreements to the evidence base for mental health interventions, and providers are expected to offer effective or promising programs. However, pressures for cost containment may not necessarily operate to produce evidence-based interventions, especially if faithful implementation costs more. To assure that managed care agencies provide evidence-based services, many states are relying on credentialing to promote the selection of competent providers and quality assurance systems comprised of various performance-rating systems to ensure that services meet treatment standards. In addition, reimbursement formulas are linked in principle to evidence-based interventions, such that reimbursable services are those rated as promising or well established. It remains to be seen whether these measures will provide controls sufficient to produce high quality services in the context of profit-oriented management. As it stands now, the children's mental health system is a patchwork of loosely coordinated reform efforts undertaken with good reason but inadequate resources.

Implications of Advances in Developmental Psychopathology and Intervention Research

Amid the turmoil that currently characterizes children's mental health care, two related ideas are beginning to emerge from the research. These hold the potential to guide practitioners and agencies in developing and implementing psychosocial and pharmacological interventions during this time when systems are rapidly changing, knowledge bases are rapidly growing, and cost containment underpins many reforms. First, *services should be designed to reduce risk and promote protection*. This involves directly identifying and interrupting risk mechanisms (e.g., the coercion mechanism) and directly identifying and strengthening protective factors (e.g., parental supervision) that ameliorate risk exposure. For children and adolescents, this implies that services must be:

- based on careful functional assessments, including assessments of cumulative risk and protective factors and the identification of putative risk mechanisms;
- comprehensive in addressing both specific risk mechanisms and the accumulation of risk;
- family centered with high family or caregiver involvement, where possible;
- sensitive to race, culture, gender, language, and religion; and
- developmentally appropriate.

Second, *psychosocial services should be comprised of evidence-based interventions* focused, at least in part, on the environmental and other conditions that may interact with biological risk factors, and on the acquisition of social-cognitive skills, including skills in regulating emotions.

What types of practice should emerge? Clearly, practice should address a range of risk factors, and it should promote protection. It should address concrete environmental problems that disrupt support systems, including parental monitoring. It should involve families or seek to create caring, familylike communities. It should build social, academic, and vocational competencies by altering social knowledge and strengthening a variety of skills. On the face of it, few tested interventions do all this.

However, some aspects of practice may be more closely related to these guidelines than we think. To the extent that a stress-vulnerability mechanism potentiates mental health problems, practice may aggregate youths with a variety of case profiles. For example, psychoeducation programs such as the City Lights School in Washington, D.C. provide a developmentally appropriate hierarchy of academic and work opportunities, skills in daily living, vocational experiences with support, and a family-friendly community that expresses care throughout the ups and downs of living with a SED (Brown 2002). Hard to evaluate because they are so comprehensive and have no ready control condition, therapeutic milieu programs such as City Lights rely on modeling, peer support, skills training with supervised practice, and a structured environment that maintains high expectations in the context of high support. If it is cumulative risk more than a specific risk chain that triggers disruptive behavior and emotional disorders, broadly focused programs that change social knowledge, build skills in processing social information, and provide opportunities for academic and vocational achievement have some of the features of potentially effective interventions. To be sure, these programs must incorporate skills training and other programs for which there is strong research evidence. In practice, then, the challenge is not so much to develop such programs from scratch as it is to select evidence-based program components, train staff, and deliver services in a manner faithful to the original research.

The Sciences-to-Services Challenge

Is the workforce prepared to work in more cost-oriented settings, to provide focused interventions that are clustered in comprehensive programs like City Lights, and to address the contextual influences of family, school, and peer relationships that may moderate high risk? This is a tall order. Three core enterprises, shown in figure 6.1, are necessary to promote a sciences-to-services paradigm that is implied by evidence-based practice: continued research and development; careful implementation and monitoring; and translation and dissemination (New Freedom Commission on Mental Health 2005).

FIGURE 6.1   Sciences to Services: Three Core Activities to Implement and Sustain Evidence-Based Practice in Children's Mental Health

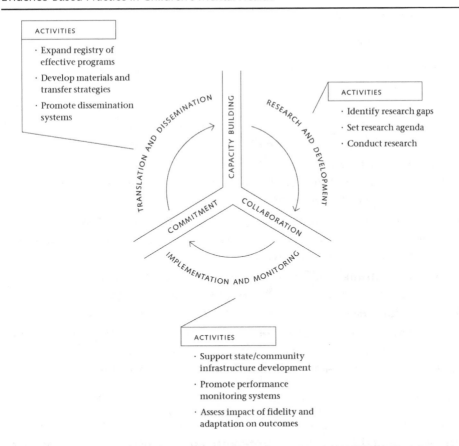

ACTIVITIES

· Expand registry of effective programs
· Develop materials and transfer strategies
· Promote dissemination systems

ACTIVITIES

· Identify research gaps
· Set research agenda
· Conduct research

TRANSLATION AND DISSEMINATION

CAPACITY BUILDING

RESEARCH AND DEVELOPMENT

COMMITMENT

COLLABORATION

IMPLEMENTATION AND MONITORING

ACTIVITIES

· Support state/community infrastructure development
· Promote performance monitoring systems
· Assess impact of fidelity and adaptation on outcomes

Source (public domain): New Freedom Commission on Mental Health (2005, April). *Subcommittee on Evidence-Based Practices: Background Paper* (Pub. No. SMA-05-4007). Rockville, MD: Department of Health and Human Services, p. 11.

Continued Research and Development

The vitality and effectiveness of services in mental health rest on continuing to make advances in developmental psychopathology and the design of interventions. The research agenda should be driven in part by feedback from the field on what is working and what is not working. That is, the scientific mission should be informed by the effect of interventions when they are brought to scale or tested under the intent-to-treat principle. When an intervention is intended for a particular population, the variation in dose response should be the basis for future research on both improving the response to treatment and developing mechanisms to better recruit and retain people in treatment. This will be particularly important in designing interventions that can be tailored to gender, race/ethnicity, culture, language, and religious differences. The challenge of developing new interventions and tailoring existing promising interventions so that they are effective *in vivo* looms large in ethnopsychopharmacological as well as psychosocial intervention.

Implementation and Monitoring

The development of state and community infrastructures to transfer knowledge from sciences to services will involve creating SOC-like linkages across state-level agencies and between state agencies and the core mental health disciplines—nursing, psychiatry, psychology, and social work. To implement services faithful to the growing evidence base for practice, staff must be properly trained at the preservice and in-service levels. Many schools of social work have not fully embraced a risk factor perspective and evidence-based practice. Moreover, the profession has so completely embraced ecological theory that students graduate with only the barest patina of knowledge regarding cognitive-behavioral, social learning, and other theories that underpin many of the interventions shown in table 6.2. Efforts to ensure faithful implementation through performance-based contracting and quality-assurance monitoring may be useful, but it is not yet clear that they are sufficient. At the core, reimbursement schema (e.g., Medicaid) that are linked to specific, well-defined intervention protocols and the training of mental health practitioners are likely to be crucial in transforming recent research knowledge into more effective mental health services for children and adolescents.

Translation and Dissemination

As implied in figure 6.1, the translation and dissemination of advances in children's mental health care will require creative new structures, some of which may be independent of state/community agencies and institutions of higher education. As in the dissemination of new pharmaceuticals, a private-sector marketplace must be created in which scientific knowledge is the basis for implementing evidence-based programs. Ventures might include developing private certification for specific interventions and marketing detailed materials related to evidence-based programs. Programs such as multisystemic family therapy (MST), assertive community treatment (ACT), and Fountain House psychosocial clubhouses have successfully developed registration and certification programs. Other programs such as the Skills, Opportunities, and Rewards (SOAR) program of the Channing Bete Company, which is linked to programs developed by the Social Development Research Group at the University of Washington in Seattle, have developed successful for-profit enterprises that promote sciences to services. These represent new mechanisms—beyond traditional academic journals and books, in-service training, and conferences—for the translation and dissemination of science-based knowledge.

Conclusion: The Challenges Implicit in the Work of William J. Reid and His Colleagues

From the sciences-to-services perspective, many challenges confront social work and the other mental health professions. Too many bright scholars—pressured by tenure, the difficulty of obtaining extramural funding, and inadequate research support in their agencies and universities—are not committing themselves to the development of interventions. As exemplified by the work of Reid and his colleagues, evidence-based programs develop from a period of sequential experimentation in which a variety of research designs and measures are used to test an evolving intervention (Reid 1994, 1997). In social work, too few of us are doing this vital work (Fraser 2004a). If, in the course of our careers, we each conduct just one controlled trial of an intervention that we think holds promise and develop just one treatment manual on a social or health problem that interests us, we will dramatically affect the evidence base.

As shown in figure 1, advances in both developmental psychopathology and intervention knowledge pose systems-level problems in dissemination. How can practitioners in child welfare, education, juvenile justice, and mental health collaborate to use new knowledge on the development of mental disorders and the effectiveness of mental health services? In addition, because organizational contingencies such as reimbursement protocols and performance standards affect practice, we are confronted with new questions: Will states provide fiscal support and adequate quality assurance to align incentives to support the development of evidence-based programs? How can managed-care organizations, faith-based programs, and other behavioral health agencies learn to use treatment manuals and to implement science-based services that are faithful to the research? How do practitioners within these organizations faithfully implement tested interventions—both psychosocial and psychopharmacological—and tailor them on the basis of race/ethnicity, gender, age, language, religion, and other risk factors? Will the core mental health professions continue to take leading roles in preparing the workforce and in contributing to the base of knowledge about the effectiveness of interventions? In children's mental health care, it is a time of great change and great opportunity.

Note

1. They are related also to significant advances in research methods (e.g., growth curve modeling), decisions by federal agencies in the 1980s and 1990s to fund longitudinal studies of children, and biological research in genetics and neuroscience.

References

Allen-Meares, P. and Fraser, M. W. (Eds.). (2004). *Intervention with children and adolescents: An interdisciplinary perspective.* Needham Heights, MA: Allyn and Bacon.

American Psychiatric Association. (1980). *Diagnostic and statistical manual of mental disorders III.* Washington, DC: American Psychiatric Association.

——. (1987). *Diagnostic and statistical manual of mental disorders III-R.* Washington, DC: American Psychiatric Association.

——. (2000). *Diagnostic and statistical manual of mental disorders IV-R.* Washington, DC: American Psychiatric Association.

Anderson, J. C., Williams, S., McGee, R., and Silva, P. A. (1987). DSM-III disorders in preadolescent children: Prevalence in a large sample from the general population. *Archives of General Psychiatry 44*:69–76.

Angold, A., Prendergast, M., Cox, A., Harrington, R., Simonoff, E., and Rutter, M. (1995). The Child and Adolescent Psychiatric Assessment (CAPA). *Psychological Medicine 25*:739–753.

Beals, J. et al. (1997). Psychiatric disorder among American Indian adolescents: Prevalence in Northern Plains youth. *Journal of the American Academy of Child and Adolescent Psychiatry 36*:1252–1259.

Beals, J., Manson, S. M., Whitesell, N. R., Spicer, P., Novins, D. K., and Mitchell, C. M. (2005). Prevalence of DSM-IV disorders and attendant help-seeking in 2 American Indian reservation populations. *Archives of General Psychiatry 62*:99–108.

Biederman, J., Spencer, T., and Wilens, T. (2004). Psychopharmacology. In J. M. Wiener and M. K. Dulcan (Eds.), *Textbook of child and adolescent psychiatry,* 931–974. Arlington, VA: American Psychiatric Publishing.

Birmaher, B., Ryan. N. D., Williamson, D. E., Brent, D. A., Kaufman J., Dahl, R. E., et al. (1996). Childhood and adolescent depression: A review of the past 10 years. Part I. *Journal of the American Academy of Child and Adolescent Psychiatry 35*:1427–1439.

Breton, J. et al. (1999). Quebec child mental health survey: Prevalence of DSM-III-R mental health disorders. *Journal of Child Psychology and Psychiatry 40*:375–384.

Brown, A. W. (2002). The state of mental health services for children and adolescents: An examination of programs, practices, and policies. In S. D. Miller (Ed.), *Disability and the black community*, 139–153. New York: Haworth Press.

Brown, R. T. et al. (2001). Prevalence and assessment of Attention-Deficit/Hyperactivity disorder in primary care settings. *Pediatrics 107* (3). http://pediatrics.aappublications.org/cgi/content/full/107/3/e43 (accessed October 1, 2007).

Chang, K. D. (2004). Pediatric psychopharmacology: An overview. In H. Steiner (Ed.), *Handbook of mental health interventions in children and adolescents*, 247–257. San Francisco: Jossey-Bass.

Cohen, P. et al. (1993). An epidemiological study of disorders in late childhood and adolescence, I: Age and gender-specific prevalence. *Journal of Child Psychology and Psychiatry 34*:851–867.

Cole, D. A. et al. (2002). Individual differences in the emergence of depressive symptoms in children and adolescents: A longitudinal investigation of parent and child reports. *Journal of Abnormal Psychology 111*:156–165.

Costello, E. J., Compton, S. N., Keeler, G., and Angold, A. (2003). Relationships between poverty and psychopathology: A natural experiment. *Journal of the American Medical Association 290*:2023–2029.

Costello, E. J., Mustillo, S., Erklani, A., Keeler, G., and Angold, A. (2003). Prevalence and development of psychiatric disorders in childhood and adolescence. *Archives of General Psychiatry 60*:837–844.

Crick, N. R. and Dodge, K. A. (1994). A review and reformulation of social information-processing mechanisms in children's social adjustment. *Psychological Bulletin 115*:74–101.

Cuffe, S. P., Moore, C. G., and McKeown, R. E. (2005). Prevalence and correlates of ADHD symptoms in the National Health Interview Survey. *Journal of Attention Disorders 9*:392–401.

Dey, A. N. and Bloom, B. (2005). Summary health statistics for U.S. children: National Health Interview Survey, 2003. *Vital Health Statistics 10*:1–78. http://www.cdc.gov/nchs/data/series/sr_10/sr10_223.pdf (accessed May 14, 2005).

Dodge, K. A., Bates, J. E., and Pettit, G. S. (1990). Mechanisms in the cycle of violence. *Science 250*:1678–1683.

Dodge, K. A. and Pettit, G. S. (2003). A biopsychosocial model of the development of chronic conduct problems in adolescence. *Developmental Psychology 39*:349–371.

Egger, H. L., Costello, E. J., and Angold, A. (2003). School refusal and psychiatric disorders: A community study. *Journal of the American Academy of Child and Adolescent Psychiatry 42*:797–807.

Ford, T., Goodman, R., and Meltzer, H. (2003). The British Child and Adolescent Mental Health Survey 1999: The prevalence of DSM-IV disorders. *Journal of the American Academy of Child and Adolescent Psychiatry 42*:1203–1211.

Forgatch, M. S., Bulloch, B. M., and Patterson, G. R. (2004). From theory to practice: Increasing effective parenting through role-play. In H. Steiner (Ed.), *Handbook of mental health interventions in children and adolescents,* 782–813. San Francisco: Jossey-Bass.

Forness, S. R. et al. (1998). Special education identification of Head Start children with emotional and behavioral disorders in the second grade. *Journal of Emotional and Behavioral Disorders* 6:194–204.

Foster, E. M. and Connor, T. (2005). Public costs of better mental health services for children and adolescents. *Psychiatric Services* 56:50–55.

Fraser, M. W. (2004a). Intervention research in social work: Recent advances and continuing challenges. *Research on Social Work Practice* 14:210–222.

Fraser, M. W. (Ed.). (2004b). *Risk and resilience in childhood: An ecological perspective.* 2nd ed. Washington, DC: NASW Press.

Froehlich, T. E., Lanphear, B. P., Epstein, J. N., Barbaresi, W. J., Katusic, S. K., and Kahn, R. S. (2007). Prevalence, recognition, and treatment of Attention-Deficit/ Hyperactivity Disorder in a national sample of US children. *Archives of Pediatric Medicine* 161:857–864.

Gambrill, E. (1999). Evidence-based practice: An alternative to authority-based practice. *Families in Society: The Journal of Contemporary Human Services* 80:341–350.

Garland, A. F., Hough, R. L., McCabe, K. M., Yeh, M., Wood, P. A., and Aarons, G. A. (2001). Prevalence of psychiatric disorders in youths across five sectors of care. *Journal of the American Academy of Child and Adolescent Psychiatry* 40:409–418.

Garmezy, N. (1971). Vulnerability research and the issue of primary prevention. *American Journal of Orthopsychiatry* 41:101–116.

——. (1985). Stress-resistant children: The search for protective factors. In J. E. Stevenson (Ed.), *Recent research in developmental psychopathology,* 213–233. Tarrytown, NY: Pergamon Press.

Hoza, B. et al. (2005). Peer-assessed outcomes in the multimodal treatment study of children with attention-deficit/hyperactivity disorder. *Journal of Clinical Child and Adolescent Psychology* 34:74–86.

Hyman, S. E. (2001). Mood disorders in children and adolescents: A NIMH perspective. *Biological Psychiatry* 49:962–969.

Jellinek, M. S. (2003). Mirror, mirror on the wall: Are we prescribing the right psychotropic medications to the right children using the right treatment plan? *Archives of Pediatrics and Adolescent Medicine* 157:14–16.

Jensen, P. S., Bhatara, B. S., Vitiello, B., Hoagwood, K., Feil, M., and Burke, L. B. (1999). Psychoactive medication prescribing practices for U.S. children: Gaps between research and clinical practice. *Journal of the American Academy of Child and Adolescent Psychiatry* 38:557–565.

Kazdin, A. E. (2003). Psychotherapy for children and adolescents. *Annual Review of Psychology* 54:253–276.

——. (2004). The state of child and adolescent psychotherapy research. *Child and Adolescent Mental Health* 7:53–59.

Knitzer, J. (1982). *Unclaimed children.* Washington, DC: Children's Defense Fund.

Lemerise, E. A. and Arsenio, W. F. (2000). An integrated model of emotion processes and cognition in social information processing. *Child Development* 71:107–118.

Lengua, L. J. (2003). Associations among emotionality, self-regulation, adjustment problems, and positive adjustment in middle childhood. *Applied Developmental Psychology* 24:595–618.

Lewinsohn, P. M., Gotlib, I. H., Lewinsohn, M., Seeley, J. R., and Allen, N. B. (1998). Gender differences in anxiety disorders and anxiety symptoms in adolescents. *Journal of Abnormal Psychology 107*:109–117.

Lock, J. (2004). Psychotherapy in children and adolescents: An overview. In H. Steiner (Ed.), *Handbook of mental health interventions in children and adolescents,* 485–497. San Francisco: Jossey-Bass.

Loeber, R., Burke, J., Lahey, B., Winters, A., and Zera, M. (2000). Oppositional defiant and conduct disorder: A review of the past 10 years. *Journal of the American Academy of Child and Adolescent Psychiatry 39*:1468–1484.

Mattison, R. E., Morales, J., and Bauer, M. A. (1992). Distinguishing characteristics of elementary schoolboys recommended for SED placement. *Behavioral Disorders 17*:107–114.

McGarvey, E. L. and Waite, D. (2000). Mental health needs among juveniles committed to the Virginia Department of Juvenile Justice. *Developments in Mental Health Law 20*:1–24.

Meltzer, H., Gatward, R., Goodman, R., and Ford, T. (2000). *The mental health of children and adolescents in Great Britain.* London: Office for National Statistics. http://www.dh.gov.uk/PublicationsAndStatistics/Publications /Publications Statistics/PublicationsStatisticsArticle/fs/en?CONTENT_ID=4019358andchk=V6aYxg (accessed May 25, 2005).

Meyer, J. M. et al. (2000). Familial aggregation for conduct disorder symptomatology: The role of genes, marital discord and family adaptability. *Psychological Medicine 30*:759–774.

MTA Cooperative Group. (1999). A 14-month randomized clinical trial of treatment strategies for attention-deficit/hyperactivity disorder. *Archives of General Psychiatry 56*:1073–1086.

National Alliance for the Mentally Ill. (2001). *Families on the brink: The impact of ignoring children with serious mental illness.* Arlington, VA: Author.

New Freedom Commission on Mental Health (2005, April). *Subcommittee on evidence-based practices: Background paper* (Pub. No. SMA-05-4007). Rockville, MD: Department of Health and Human Services.

Nock, M. K., Kazdin, A. E., Hiripi, E., and Kessler, R. C. (2007). Lifetime prevalence, correlates, and persistence of oppositional defiant disorder: Results from the National Comorbidity Survey Replication. *Journal of Child Psychology and Psychiatry 48*:703–713.

Offord, D. et al. (1987). Ontario Child Health Study II: Six-month prevalence of disorder and rates of service utilization. *Archives of General Psychiatry 44*:832–836.

Ollendick, T. H. and King, N. J. (2004). Empirically supported treatments for children and adolescents: Advances toward evidence-based practice. In P. M. Barrett and T. H. Ollendick (Eds.), *Handbook of interventions that work with children and adolescents,* 3–25. New York: Wiley.

Oregon Social Learning Center (2005a). History. http://www.oslc.org/history.html (accessed May 2, 2005).

——. (2005b). Publications. http://www.oslc.org/publications.html (accessed May 2, 2005).

Prinstein, M. J., Cheah, C. S. L., and Guyer, A. E. (2005). Peer victimization, cue interpretation, and internalizing symptoms: Preliminary concurrent and longitudinal findings for children and adolescents. *Journal of Clinical Child and Adolescent Psychology 34*:11–24.

Reid, W. J. (1994). The empirical practice movement. *Social Service Review 68*:165–184.

———. (1997). Long-term trends in clinical social work. *Social Service Review 71*:202–212.

Roberts, R. E., Attkisson, C. C., and Rosenblatt, A. (1998). Prevalence of psychopathology among children and adolescents. *American Journal of Psychiatry 155*:715–725.

Roberts, R. E., Roberts, C. R., and Xing, Y. (2006). Prevalence of psychiatric disorders among African American, European, and Mexican American adolescents. *Journal of the American Academy of Child and Adolescent Psychiatry 45*:1329–1337.

Rowe, R., Maughan, B., Pickles, A., Costello, E. J., and Angold, A. (2002). The relationship between DSM-IV oppositional defiant disorder and conduct disorder: Findings from the Great Smoky Mountains Study. *Journal of Child Psychology and Psychiatry 43*:365–373.

Roy, P., Rutter, M., and Pickles, A. (2000). Institutional care: Risk from family background or pattern of rearing? *Journal of Child Psychology and Psychiatry and Allied Disciplines 41*:139–149.

Rutter, M. (1987). Psychosocial resilience and protective mechanisms. *American Journal of Orthopsychiatry 57*:316–331.

———. (2000). Resilience reconsidered: Conceptual considerations, empirical findings, and policy implications. In J. P. Shonkoff and S. J. Meisels (Eds.), *Handbook of early childhood intervention*, 2nd ed., 651–682. New York: Cambridge University Press.

———. (2005, April). Identified gene-specific environment interactions in relation to psychopathology. Presentation at the Biennial Meeting of the Society for Research in Child Development, Atlanta, GA.

Rutter, M., Pickles, A., Murray, R., and Eaves, L. (2001). Testing hypotheses on specific environmental causal effects on behavior. *Psychological Bulletin 127*:291–324.

Ryan, E. P. and Redding, J. D. (2004). A review of mood disorders among juvenile offenders. *Psychiatric Services 55*:1397–1407.

Sawyer, M. G., Arney, F. M., Baghurst, P. A., Clark, J. J., Graetz, B. W., Kosky, R. J., et al. (2001). The mental health of young people in Australia: Key findings from the child and adolescent component of the national survey of mental health and well-being. *Australian and New Zealand Journal of Psychiatry 35*:806–814.

Sameroff, A. J., Bartko, W. T., Baldwin, A., Baldwin, C., and Seifer, R. (1999). Family and social influences on the development of child competence. In M. Lewis and C. Feiring (Eds.), *Families, risk, and competence*. Mahwah, NJ: Erlbaum.

Sameroff, A. J., and Gutman, L. M. (2004). Contributions of risk research to the design of successful interventions. In P. Allen-Meares and M. W. Fraser (Eds.), *Intervention with children and adolescents: An interdisciplinary perspective*. Boston: Pearson Education.

Saunders, R. C. and Heflinger, C. A. (2003). Access to and patterns of use of behavioral health services among children and adolescents in TennCare. *Psychiatric Services 54*:1364–1371.

Shaffer, D. et al. (1996). The NIMH Diagnostic Interview Schedule for Children Version 2.3 (DISC 2.3): Description, acceptability, prevalence rates, and performance in the MECA study. *Journal of the American Academy of Child and Adolescent Psychiatry 35*:865–877.

Shaffer, D. and Fisher, P. (1997). *NIMH—Diagnostic Interview Schedule for Children: Child Informant.* New York: New York State Psychiatric Institute.

Shaffer, D., Fisher, P., Lucas, C. P., Dulcan, M. K., and Schwab-Stone, M. E. (2000). NIMH Diagnostic Interview Schedule for Children Version IV (NIMH DISC-IV): Description, differences from previous versions, and reliability of some common diagnoses. *Journal of the American Academy of Child and Adolescent Psychiatry* 39:28–38.

Shastry, B. S. (2004). Molecular genetics of attention-deficit hyperactivity disorder (ADHD): An update. *Neurochemistry International 44*:469–474.

Shortz, M. (2003). *The tale of two settings: Institutional and community-based mental health services in California since realignment in 1991.* Oakland: California Protection and Advocacy.

Simonoff, E. et al. (1997). The Virginia twin study of adolescent behavioral development: Influences of age, sex, and impairment on rates of disorder. *Archives of General Psychiatry 54* (9): 801–808.

Simpson, G. A., Scott, G., Henderson, M. J., and Manderscheid, R. W. (2002). Estimates of attention, cognitive, and emotional problems, and health service use by U.S. school-age children. http://www.mentalhealth.samhsa.gov /publications/all-pubs/SMA04–3938/Chapter09.asp (accessed May 24, 2005).

Stroul, B. and Friedman, R. (1986). *A system of care for severely emotionally disturbed children and youth.* Washington, DC: CASSP Technical Assistance Center, Georgetown University.

Teplin, L. A., Abram, K. M., McClelland, G. M., Dulcan, M. K., and Mericle, A. A. (2002). Psychiatric disorders in youth in juvenile detention. *Archives of General Psychiatry 59*:1133–1143.

Weisz, J. R. (2000). State of the evidence on treatments, services, and systems of care and financing: Prevention, early intervention, and community-based services. In *Report of the Surgeon General's Conference on Children's Mental Health: A National Action Agenda,* 35–36. Washington, DC: U.S. Department of Health and Human Services, U.S. Public Health Service. http://www.surgeongeneral.gov/topics/cmh/default.htm (accessed May 25, 2005).

Werner, E. E. and Smith, R. S. (1977). *Kauai's children come of age.* Honolulu: University of Hawaii Press.

Zito, J. M., Safer, D. J., dosReis, S., Gardner, J. F., Magder, L., Soeken, K., et al. (2003). Psychotropic practice patterns for youth: A 10-year perspective. *Archives of Pediatrics and Adolescent Medicine 157*:17–25.

Zuvekas, S. H., Vitiello, B., and Norquist, G. S. (2006). Recent trends in stimulant medication use among U.S. children. *American Journal of Psychiatry 163*:579–585.

7 | Evidence-Based Services to Children in a Conservative Environment

June G. Hopps, Tony B. Lowe, and Latrice S. Rollins

THIS CHAPTER WILL EXAMINE services to children and research during the conservative decades most strongly identified initially with the Reagan-Bush years (1980–1988), but lasting for many more, including the three following administrations: Bush, Clinton, and G. W. Bush. Reagan's 1980 landslide victory over incumbent President Jimmy Carter ended the Democrats' fifty-year sway over American political thought and presented what his administration considered a mandate to tackle economic troubles—runaway inflation, unemployment, poor rates of productivity, declining investment, and stagflation—and to attack big government and make massive changes in approaches to social welfare, including services to children and their families. The Reagan "revolution" was driven by supply-side economics. In historical contrast, President F. D. Roosevelt's approach, the 1930s New Deal, was driven by Keynesian economics and represented a seismic shift in social welfare: government's role became larger than that of the private sector and remained dominant until the latter part of the twentieth century (Dinitto 2000; Hopps and Lowe 2008; Karger and Stoesz 2006). At that time, retrenchment became real in both public policy and social programs. Evaluation and accountability became not just an expectation but a mandate (Sze and Hopps 1973).

A Conservative Environment

Reagan successfully mobilized the elites, corporate leaders, and a disaffected middle class with antiwelfare and anti-big government arguments. Hallmarks of the new administration included: taxation policy favoring the haves and have-mores, deregulation of industry and finance, reversal in civil rights, expansion in defense spending, domestic program cuts, and a major uptick in the national deficit—some $207 billion in 1983. Reagan spoke harshly to and about the poor, referring to them as "cheats" and "freeloaders" and insisting that provision of welfare was not the responsibility of the national government, but rather of loyalty-based charities (Barusch 2009), which sounded much like nineteenth-century interventions. Under the Democratic leadership of William Jefferson Clinton (1992–2000), more centrist than liberal, a major sixty-year-old New Deal entitlement program, Aid to Families and Dependent Children, was reorganized into the Personal Responsibility and Work Opportunity Reconciliation Act of 1996. Clinton raised taxes. His policies generated prosperity for some, increased economic expansion, created a government surplus, supported family leave, and managed to maintain relatively peaceful international relations. Although a notable attempt to draft national health care was made by the First Lady, Hilary Clinton, it failed. Clinton's policy approach was called enterprise economics because policies benefited individuals through education and training, and improved technology and communication systems (Dinitto 2000). Others, however, remained concerned about the status of the poor, especially children, and were outraged that Clinton had signed off on the major social insurance program for this vulnerable population, devolving responsibility of AFDC from the federal government to the states via the Temporary Assistance to Needy Families (TANF) block grant program. The election of George W. Bush as the forty-third President in 2000 signaled a return to supply-side economics, tax cuts beneficial to the haves, expanded privatization of services, conservative appointments to the courts, continued devolution of welfare programs to the states, and an emphasis on faith-based services (Dinitto 2000; Hopps and Lowe 2008; Karger and Stoesz 2006). The Iraq War and economic meltdown may well be the administration's signature legacies, as its public rating was among the lowest since such recordings began.

Is the Reagan influence receding? As this is written, there seems to be an expectation that the Reagan spell is showing signs of decline; some even say it has ended (Fukuyama 2008). What exists is a troubled economy where petroleum on the mainland reached over $4 per gallon (and $10 in Alaska), declining employment, lower productivity, extreme stock market volatility, a devalued dollar, the near collapse and subsequent nationalization of mortgage giants Freddie Mac and Fannie Mae and a federal bailout of American International Group (AIG), the demise of major investment banks, and the need for a $700 billion rescue plan for the economy. These predicaments and crises are only part of the scenario. The 2008 election results of President Obama and a Democratically led Congress speak to the country's readiness for a new ideology moving away from neoconservative thought and toward social democracy or regulatory capitalism. This contextual overview is important because it shows, albeit briefly, significant shifts in approaches to social welfare since President Roosevelt initiated the New Deal to address problems arising from the depression. Less clear, but certainly undergirding service philosophy toward children and families, are attitudes about women. Oftentimes that philosophy focuses on their morality and character, and the temptation to use social welfare programs to legislate morality still exists (Barusch 2009). How else can one explain that 13 million children in the United States live in poverty, over 30 percent of the poor are children, and more striking, 21 percent are under 5 years old (U.S. Census Bureau 2007)? Little attention has been directed to the character of fathers; however, an emerging area of responsible fatherhood initiatives, targeted toward low-income men, is one step forward addressing their concerns (Hill 2007; Rollins and Lowe, in progress). Ironically, it was the dedicated conservative President Richard Nixon who actually suggested a war on welfare but in the end proposed the most supportive, universal, friendly child-family initiatives since the emergence of the New Deal philosophy. However, the negative income tax strategy, called the Family Assistance Plan (FAP), which would have put a minimum national income in place, failed. Nixon did sign into law, among other programs, the Earned Income Tax Credit, expansion of food stamps, and Title XX amendments to the Social Security Act, which provided social services to welfare recipients (Barusch 2009). Still, the United States remains the only industrialized country without social insurance for children (Briar-Lawson and Drews 2000; Waldfogel 2000). This raises the question: "Is America supportive of children and service provision necessary for their development?" (Hopps 1987).

Enhancing Reciprocity Among Stakeholders

The hallmark of a mature human service profession is its capacity to legitimize its role to an increasingly watchful and apprehensive society that is suspicious of public service. One way to achieve this is by establishing a record of good stewardship in the use of public and private resources and clearly demonstrating the effectiveness of such use. Under this mandate, evidence-based human services, referred to as evidence-minded or "research informed" (McNeish et al. 2002), have become the goal for children and others.

Since as far back as 1931, practitioners have been "admonished to assess the significance of their practice processes and to determine the effectiveness of their intervention efforts. . . . Not until some forty years later did social work practice begin to act on this concern" (Hopps et al. 1995:66). Social workers, along with members of other human service professions, responded through advocacy for and use of evidence-based practice (Hopps and Lowe 2008). Still, there is a serious void in the profession's understanding of forces that impede scientification and the use of evidence-based practice (Aaron 2005; Burns, Haywood, and Mrazer 1999; Garland, Kruse, and Aarons 2003; Glisson 1992; Hoagwood, Burn, Kiser, Ringeison, and Schoenwald 2001; as cited in Aaron and Palinkas 2007) despite evidence of improved services and benefits.

No one would argue that progress in research on practice, and on practice with children, has not been made. However, what knowledge is available is largely underutilized by practitioners (Mullen and Bacon 2004; Weissman and Sanderson 2001). Similarly, no rational thinker would argue that reciprocity between practitioners and researchers, two key stakeholders, must be accelerated. An important step is to reduce the fierce resistance to both practice-based research and its subsequent dissemination, which in other areas (e.g., health care) has been termed "formidable" (Barnatt 2003:143). Of note is the concern that dissemination and utilization of evidence-based practice is even more problematic in child welfare than other areas of practice (Tomlison 2003).

It has been reported that there is uneasiness and at times polarization relative to the evidence-based approach. Thus, there are no easy solutions to gaining acceptance of evidence-based practice and its vision and framework, which incorporate organizational, legal, political, and social complexities that require a number of interventions. At the outset, the social work/social welfare enterprise must cultivate the environment and insist that practitioners have the freedom to challenge assumptions, old underpinnings and verities about practice interventions and whether or not it is effective. In fact, evidence-based practice can be defined as "a way of assessing, intervening, and evaluating based on a set of assumptions and values" (Mullen, Bledsoe, and Bellamy 2008:326). Increasing scientification and professionalization will be required (Cnaan and Dichter 2008). Implied in the use of evidence-based practice is the notion that practitioners will become more intent on pursuing and developing informed strategies in the field and that they can ferret out what is sound, or what works with whom and under what conditions. If integration of research into practice is to be successful, tri-level action might be considered; namely the evidence per se, the organizational context, and means of facilitation (Kitson et al. 1998 as cited by Barratt 2003).

Practice with Children and Families: What Works?

First, there must be some acknowledgment of the status of children within the geopolitical context. Many can be viewed as haves and have-mores, following the description of their families. But that is only part of the picture. In 2007, 28 percent of Caucasian, 50 percent of Hispanic, and 71 percent of African American (or black) children in the United States were raised in single-parent households. Children in such circumstances are at greater risk for poverty, juvenile crime, substandard education and health care, homelessness (including running away and aging out of foster care), violence, and a number of related ills (Barusch 2009; Hopps, Pinderhughes, and Shankar 1995; Shinn 1997; Short 1997). Thus, they are more likely to need help from social work professionals, in the home or other environments, via protective care, kinship care, foster care, family reunification and preservation, and therapeutic care (group or individual), responsible fatherhood programs, and other services. In 2001, a report submitted by the General Accounting Office (GAO) indicated that more than 12,700 children were placed in the child welfare or juvenile justice systems by the parents in a last attempt to get them needed mental health services (cited in The President's New Freedom Commission on Mental Health Report 2003). In fact, more than 3 million referrals involving the abuse and neglect of 6 million children were reported to child protective services in 2006, with approximately one fourth of the cases being substantiated (U.S. Department of Health and Human Services 2008). It is also estimated that 50 percent of children in foster care meet the criteria for a mental disorder diagnosis (Stambaugh, Burns, Landsverk, and Reutz 2007). Former U.S. Surgeon General David Satcher, M.D. stated:

> We need to take three steps: 1) To improve early recognition and appropriate identification of mental disorders in children within all systems serving children; 2) To improve access to services by removing barriers faced by families with mental health needs, with a specific aim to reduce disparities in access to care; and 3) To close the gap between research and practice, ensuring evidence-based treatments for children. (U.S. Public Health Service 2000:15)

The profession has been under pressure to improve quality and effectiveness of service to children for some time, whether the focus of service is family centered or child centered. One scholar commented: "Child welfare services may well be the driest area in the desert of social work scholarship, and the evaluation of psycho-therapeutic outcomes one of the most intensely distorted. Yet their inadequacies are repeated in other fields of practice with similar effects" (Epstein 263, cited in Hopps and Morris 2000).

Much of the work in this subject area is being done in the fields of psychology and psychiatry. Several reviews of evidence-based child welfare interventions reported common positive outcomes such as: decrease in out-of-home placements; changes in child or parent behavior; improved child and family well-being; prevention of recurrence of child maltreatment; reduction in the number of hospitalizations; reduction in the number of runaway episodes; less frequent contact with the criminal system; and reduced risk of increased problem behaviors (Hoagwood et al. 2001; Thomlison 2003). However, due to the numerous external factors involved, it could not be asserted that positive outcomes were the sole result of interventions. For example, the increased parent, family, or community engagement alone could have caused a child's behavior to improve. It should also be noted that the lack of a universal means to measure outcomes, or standards to define outcomes that can be applied across studies, warrants caution.

Families engaged in the child welfare system often face multiple issues that will not be addressed within a single agency. Jonson-Reid and Drake (2008) suggest the use of multisector administrative databases to answer many questions necessary to the generation of evidence-based policy. Interlocking databases will aid in helping professionals understand what services families have received over time and which agency would be best to provide future services should the family return for help. This would also allow for access to interstate and within-state data. Banks, Landsverk, and Wang (2008) evaluated the *Greenbook Initiative*, a collaboration among child welfare courts, domestic violence courts, and juvenile courts. The project was successful in establishing relationships and responding effectively to children and families.

Effective child welfare and foster care program interventions have been documented in the home and community (Olds 2002). Multisystemic therapy, which is a home-based intervention, has been found to have the strongest results in children's services (Hoagwood et al. 2001; Schoenwald, Ward, Henggler, and Rowland 2000). Other programs, such as The Incredible Years parenting curriculum (Webster-Stratton and Taylor 2001) and Early Intervention Foster Care (EIFC) (Fisher et al. 1999); Project 12 Ways/Safe Care for child neglect (Chaffin and Friedrich 2004); and Multidimensional Treatment Foster Care (Fisher and Chamberlain 2000) have been found to yield improved practice outcomes with early intervention (Thomlison 2003). Therefore, the timing of the intervention is also a factor in effectiveness. Early intervention is required to decrease risk factors, alleviate distress, and prevent negative outcomes in adulthood (Thomlison 2003).

Evidence-Based Practice with Children

Conservative estimates currently suggest that around 15 million children have been diagnosed with some form of mental disorder and that about a quarter are receiving evidence-based behavioral health services (American Psychological Association 2008). McCracken and Marsh (2008) suggest that evidence-based practice is the use of client reports, clinician observations, and empirically based findings that aids clinical decision making that promotes collection, interpretation, and utilization of evidence.

The development and implementation of evidence-based practices for children pose a considerable challenge. There are several concerns: debate around the involvement of children in clinical or experimental trials; applicability of interventions tested in research settings to real-life practice contexts; use of treatment manuals that might impede practitioner flexibility; differential outcomes of psychosocial interventions; and cultural context (Devore and Schlesinger 1999; Kendell and Beidas 2007; Lonigan, Elbert, and Bennett Johnson 1998; Ollendick and King 2004).

Social work scholars, for example, are under pressure to expand evidence (or scientific)-based practice for children; however, the effort required to recruit and include parents and obtain permission for their children's involvement in highly controlled clinical trials is daunting. Their children's participation in experimental studies that pose potential risk goes against the judgment of most parents. In addition, mandated treatment prohibits the use of control or comparison groups in which intervention is not provided to clients (Dawson and Berry 2002). Despite parental trepidation, the inclusion of children in controlled clinical studies is a critical facet of developing interventions and practice with this population. Other gatekeepers of children with special needs, who may also have the best interests of children in mind, can impede research efforts that might challenge widely held assumptions about existing service programs (Curtis, Robers, Copperman, Downie, and Liabo 2004).

In 2002, President Bush established the President's New Freedom Commission on Mental Health to address the gaps in the mental health system that affect adults and children. This report specifically focused on children with severe emotional disturbances, 5 to 9 percent of all children. The problem behaviors of children entering services that are frequently discussed in research studies include aggression, behavior and social emotional difficulties, health and development problems, and social skills deficits (Thomlison 2003). These children typically experience physical or sexual abuse and neglect (Cohen and Mannarino 1993; Wolfe 1994); juvenile delinquency (Borum 2003); or exposure to traumatic events (Munson 2002). Research studies (Hoagwood et al. 2001; Ollendick and King 2004) have also found that a significant amount of work has focused on interventions that address specific mental disorders, such as attention-deficit/hyperactivity disorder (ADHD), conduct disorders, anorexia and bulimia, autism, post-traumatic stress disorder (PTSD), bipolar disorder, obsessive-compulsive disorder, panic disorder, substance abuse, and a variety of phobias.

It is difficult to address generally what works with children, as many programs and interventions are tailored to specific individuals and families. However, it is recommended that practitioners use clinical judgment in assessing the applicability of an intervention or program to their client's needs. In addition, it may be considered unethical to fail to engage in developing and testing new services (Thomlison 2003).

Assessing the effects of evidence-based practice in children's services has been made somewhat easier for practitioners through the development of specific criteria to evaluate an intervention (Kazdin 1999). In 1995, the Society of Clinical Psychology's Task Force on Promotion and Dissemination of Psychological Procedures published its report on empirically validated psychological treatments. The two categories of efficacy proposed in the report were well-established treatments and probably efficacious treatments. All others not considered probably efficacious are considered experimental. The task force recommended that well-established treatments: 1) demonstrate efficacy through at least two rigorous between-group experiments, or series, or case studies comparing the intervention to another treatment; 2) utilize a treatment manual in the investigation; 3) clearly describe samples; and 4) replicate intervention effects by at least two different research teams (Chambless et al. 1996). Although several scholars have refined the categories since, these are the most utilized in research to outline best practices.

Until recent movements toward evidence-based practice, there were no findings to summarize, critique, or review in the field of child and adolescent services (Hoagwood et al. 2001). Today, an overview of the literature on practice in the child welfare field reveals hundreds of studies that focus on a variety of child-specific interventions. The majority focus on programs that utilize specific psychosocial or theoretically based interventions; target the caring adults in children's lives (i.e., parents, teachers); or introduce innovative administrative processes within systems for improved child outcomes. With the growth of research in this area, it has been difficult for service providers to initially assess the literature for the most appropriate intervention for their clients. In order to assist their decision making, Garland, Hawley, Brookman-Frazee, and Hurlburt (2008) propose a "complementary approach," reviewing various evidence-based practices with children exhibiting disruptive behavior problems and identifying components of these treatments common to all. These components included "therapeutic content, treatment techniques, aspects of the working alliance, and treatment parameters" (Garland et al. 2008:510). Chorpita, Daleiden, and Weisz (2005) also suggest that there are several benefits to classifying practice elements of evidence-based interventions, such as "potential to facilitate improved understanding of similarities and differences among treatments, to guide treatment selection and matching to clients, to address gaps in the literature, and to point to possibilities for new interventions based on the current research base" (5).

The treatments commonly found to be well established in several scholarly reviews of evidence-based treatments for children with specific diagnoses were: behavior modification (Ollendick and King 2004); videotape modeling, graduated exposure, participant modeling, and reinforced practice (Burns 2003; Hoagwood et al. 2001; Ollendick and King 2004; Weisz et al. 2004). Other studies have identified interventions that are probably efficacious, meaning the treatment group had better outcomes than a comparison or no-treatment group. These interventions included: cognitive-behavioral therapy (Burns 2003; Hoagwood et al. 2001) and multisystemic therapy (Burns 2003; Schoenwald et al. 2000; Thomlison 2003). Many other practices are increasingly being studied in the literature to demonstrate efficacy. Interventions, such as the various methods of child psychotherapy, are being further explored, as they have not met the well-established or probably efficacious criteria (Hoagwood et al. 2001; Lonigan, Elbert and Johnson 1998).

Child trauma has been defined as the "result from any event or series of events that overwhelms, overstimulates, or creates subtle or extreme fear in a child that causes temporary or permanent interruption of normal developmental processes or tasks that occur with or without physical or psychological symptoms and behavioral change" (Munson 2006:215). Children specifically dealing with trauma have been found to have improved outcomes as a result of cognitive-behavioral treatment (Cohen and Mannarino 1997; Deblinger et al. 1999; Stambaugh et al. 2007; Thomlison 2003), parent-child interaction therapy (Eisenstadt et al. 1993; Stambaugh et al. 2007; Ware et al. 2008), and child parent psychotherapy for family violence (Lieberman et al. 2005; Stambaugh et al. 2007).

Over 3 million child outpatient physician visits a year resulted in a prescription for a psychotropic medication (Hoagwood et al. 2001). In their review of evidence-based practices with children, Hoagwood and colleagues found that "careful medication management, including systematic titration to the optimal dosage, was superior to clinical outcomes associated with routine prescription of the same medication delivered in the usual manner in the community" (1184). In particular, there is empirical support for the use of psychostimulants for children with ADHD and selective serotonin reuptake inhibitors (SSRIs) for children with obsessive-compulsive disorder (McClellan and Werry 2003). Strong empirical evidence for the effectiveness of pharmacotherapy with children's disorders other than ADHD is sparse, despite the high percentage of children prescribed medications (Hoagwood et al. 2001). In fact, some psychopharmacology approaches are not considered to be evidence-based (Burns 2003).

Evidence-based practice with children typically involves the collaboration of practitioners with parents, schools, and various community stakeholders. As the systems influencing the family are important, strategies that create collaborative efforts are essential in children's services (Thomlison 2003). For example, 70 to 80 percent of the mental health services received by children who have mental health problems are provided by schools (Hoagwood et al 2001). Classroom-based contingency management and cognitive group interventions have been found to be effective in these settings (Hoagwood et al. 2001).

Across the country, many agencies are beginning to develop effective means to improve their systems and collaborate with other institutions of care. The initial systems-of-care studies by Bickman (1996) showed that system coordination alone improved accessibility of services for children and families, increased satisfaction with services, and also reduced hospitalization. However, there was no improvement in individual outcomes linked to the interventions used (Pullenbank Coffey 2004; Hoagwood et al. 2001). Therefore, the collaboration of agencies in conjunction with evidence-based practices with children might lead to more positive outcomes (Pullenbank Coffey 2004).

A new report on services for children and adolescents recommends better dissemination:

Care should include prevention, early intervention, targeted treatments for particular disorders, an understanding of developmental processes and continuity of care," said task force chair Anne E. Kazak, PhD, ABPP. "Furthermore, treatments should be accessible regardless of age, gender, sexual orientation, disability, race, ethnicity and culture. Lastly, evidence-based practice should be cross-disciplinary and include collaborations with families, schools, practitioners and researchers from various health fields. (APA 2008)

Kendall and Beidas (2007) offered two means through which evidence-based practices can be shared: mediational analyses and "manuals that are alive" (17). In other words, the mediating factors of an intervention, such as comorbidity, the severity of the problem, parents' maladaptive behaviors, early termination of treatment, and service availability, might influence treatment outcomes (Hoagwood et al. 2001). In addition, the creation of treatment manuals that allow therapist creativity is a positive means of disseminating evidence-based practices. Stambaugh et al. (2007) reported that many intervention developers themselves educate local clinicians in an effort to disseminate findings. The clinicians will eventually become teachers to educate others in their local child welfare community. In addition, there are several successful university-community partnerships in which researchers provide consultation and evaluate interventions with practitioners (Palinkas et al. 2008; Schoenwald et al. 2008). Meta-analyses that compile and synthesize results of various intervention studies may also be used to improve the dissemination of evidence-based practices (Usher and Wildfire 2003; Weisz and Hawley 1998). The use of the Internet for training and access to research was also suggested as a means to increase practitioners' use of evidence-based practices with children (Barratt 2003; Kendall and Beidas 2007; Kessler et al. 2005; Usher and Wildfire 2003). Hoagwood and colleagues (2001) state that it is also important to disseminate the results of interventions that did *not* work or caused worse outcomes for the children involved.

Despite statistics that reveal significant increases in the U.S. population of people of color, Munoz and Mendelson (2005) state that there are very few studies on evidence-based interventions that include this cohort in their sample. Further, the mental health needs of children of color receive little attention in the literature (Walker 2002). Given these disparities, the transportability of evidence-based practice into real-world practice with children from diverse populations has been questioned (Lau 2006).

For over twenty years, culturally competent practice has been a central focus in the fields of social work and child welfare (McPhatter and Ganaway 2003). This need is even more critical since a cultural transformation is challenging American society (Austin 2000). Although positive outcomes of culturally competent care, such as increased accessibility to services and improved health status of clients of color, have been found (Callister 2005), "social work education continues to lag in producing a labor force prepared to take on the complexities of culture, race, ethnicity, to maximize positive outcomes for children, families, and communities" (McPhatter and Ganaway 2003:104).

The goal of culturally competent practice is to "exclude the risk of misinterpretation or underplaying significant emotional or behavioral characteristics" (Walker 2002:384). Several assumptions regarding ethnicity-sensitive practice were noted by Schlesinger and Devore (1995): "History affects the genesis and resolution of problems; the 'here and now' is more significant than the past or future. Family functioning capacity is affected by nonconscious phenomena; ethnicity can be both a source of cohesion, identity and strength and at the same time a source of discordance, strain and strife" (Hopps and Kilpatrick 2006:39).

Therefore, staff should embrace antidiscriminatory practices and understand the cultural context and influences that affect the lives of children. Munoz and Mendelson (2005) propose three steps to developing culturally sensitive evidence-based interventions: select clinical theories or principles that have universal relevance; identify appropriate interventions; and gather empirical support for intervention outcomes. Instead of culturally competent practice being the sole responsibility of individual practitioners, Nybell and Gray (2004) argue that the organizational culture, or agency context, must also be addressed. An understanding of both culture and power dynamics and how they play out in practice is also needed (Hopps, Pinderhughes, and Shankar 1995). There must be steps taken within the agency to promote culturally competent policies and service delivery within the context of evidence-based practice for children.

Organizational Culture

Most services are delivered in complex organizations by practitioners. These providers are key stakeholders in the adoption and implementation of evidence-based practice and their perspectives are essential to the success or failure of the endeavor. In one recent study of case managers, several factors were identified as determinants of practitioner buy-in to the efficacy of the intervention, including: whether evidence-based practice was acceptable to the practitioner and the client and suitable to the perceived need of the client; the motivation of the practitioner relative to utilization; the practitioner's experience with education regarding utilization; and the degree of support provided by the agency for enhancing implementation of both service process and outcome (Aarons and Polinkas 2007). Suggestions for addressing these concerns include viewing intervention as a complex process where evaluation, adjustment, dialogue, and negotiation among the developers of evidence-based interventions, agencies, practitioners, and clients could be supported (Aarons and Polinkas 2007). Evidence-based designs need to be viewed separately from delivery and/or implementation at various points that have bearing on the invention and can compromise or even generate "negative appraisal" of evidence-based practice when the problem is operational (Henggeler, Pickal, and Brondion 1999, as cited in Aaron and Palinkas 2007) and managerial.

Glisson and Hemmelgam (1998), for example, investigated the impact of intra- and interorganizational mechanisms used for service coordination on service quality and outcomes, in an effort to improve services to children. They reported that an agency's organizational environment had a direct impact on the children receiving services. Specifically, organizational climate (low conflict, cooperation, role clarity, and personalization) was the primary predictor of positive service outcomes (children's improved psychosocial functioning) and a significant predictor of service quality; and interorganizational coordination had a negative effect on service quality and no effect on outcomes. Several more recent studies are also noteworthy (Gambrill 2003; Glisson and Hemmelgam 1998; Howard, McMillen, and Pollion 2003; Thyer 2004).

Problems associated with quality education, continuing education, and the culture of organizations tend to be influenced more by action than by "reflection and evaluation" in the workplace. These factors highlight the need for quality and accessible supervision, particularly because stress in the organizational environment combined with personal stresses can lead to overwhelming conditions for practitioners. One intervention, Action Learning Sets, was a group method offered to guide professional supervision, to help address irrationality and other problematic circumstances. It proved the benefit and value of a "holding environment" for some practitioners, described metaphorically as managers "holding a boundary around workers, helping them to prioritize and not take responsibility for what cannot be done" (Randall, Cowley, and Tomlinson 2000:351). Now, expanded opportunities to establish virtual and other service groups are available through electronic communication. This means that supervisors can be in touch with their online practitioners constantly; this can lead to fatigue for both but also to increased learning (Hopps and Pinderhughes 1999; Lowe and Korr 2007).

Going Forward

The need for evidence-based child and family services remains a critical domain for research and practice development, complicated by competing demands, needs, values, ethics, and methodological considerations that will slow the full realization of such practice. Although stakeholders rightfully should remain vigilant in their capacity to protect children as a vulnerable population, they must be sure not to serve as barriers to the much-needed research efforts critical for moving the science and effectiveness of service forward. Evidence- (or empirically) based practice in the meantime has become the "gold standard" by which to judge social work practice (Fisher 1973; O'Hare, Tran, and Collins 2002; Thyer 2004). But how is progress to be achieved?

• *Recognize the apprehension for science.* Greater efforts must be made to educate the general public and other stakeholders about the need for scientific verification of children's services to improve practice outcomes. In the meantime, the ongoing development of social work-related research centers and laboratories creates vital venues that will help us in improving the lives of children. For example, the increased work in the area of fatherhood is a result of numerous studies that demonstrated positive children's outcomes when there is quality father involvement—an idea previously not considered to be of importance (Marsiglio, Amato, Day, and Lamb 2000).

• *Focus on family.* We cannot continue to disconnect children in need from the families that are primarily responsible for their well-being. Healthy family development, parenting, and economic support for the powerless and economically disadvantaged must underpin the larger picture and address the bio-psycho-social health of all children. Included in this multisystemic approach is consideration for the well-being of fathers, as many face a broad range of personal and societal challenges (Hopps et al. 1995; Rollins and Lowe in progress).

• *Child welfare re-professionalization.* Social workers, clients, service consumers, and the paying public are all concerned about standards for professional practice and the necessity to ensure that the highest level of service is available to each and every client. This is why legal regulation of practice, licensure, and certification is needed and encouraged. Although all states and the District of Columbia have some form of regulation, the field struggles with minimum standards and some practitioners do not yet possess sufficient practice credentials. In child welfare, along with other areas of public service, there has been a long-standing concern about de-professionalization (Dressel, Waters, Sweat, Clayton, and Chandler-Clayton 1988; Fabricant and Burghardt 1992). Briar-Lawson and Drews (2000) state:

> Human service systems such as child welfare are hard-pressed to achieve effective outcomes. First, rule driven, bureaucratized services tend to impede desired individualized and enfranchising helping approaches. Second, child welfare service paradigms may be based on outdated and flawed assumptions. Third, services are ineffective because people who deliver services are often not *educationally and professionally prepared* for the job. (169) (italics added)

Acting on this observation, the profession ought to assume greater advocacy for professional education at the BSW and MSW levels for this service domain (Perry 2006).

Finally, as the field's original vulnerable population, children and families must remain at the forefront of concern through the development of evidence-based practice interventions that preserve their dignity and at the same time demonstrate good stewardship.

References

Aarons, G. A. and Palinkas, L. (2007). Implementation of evidence-based practice in child welfare: Service provider perspectives. *Administration Policy Mental Health and Mental Health Service Research 34*:411–419.

American Psychological Association (2008). APA task force recommends dissemination of evidence-based practice. *Science Daily.* http://www.sciencedaily.com/releases/2008/08/080813114222.htm (accessed September 19, 2008).

Austin, D. (2000). Greeting the second century: A forward look for a historical perspective in social pedagogy in informal learning. In J. Hopps and R. Morris (Eds.), *Social work at the millenium: Critical reflections on the future of the profession,* 18–41. New York: Free Press.

Banks, D., Landsverk, J., and Wang, K. (2008). Changing policy and practice in the child welfare system through collaborative efforts to identify and respond effectively to family violence. *Journal of Interpersonal Violence 23* (7): 903–932.

Barker, R. L. (2003). *The social work dictionary of English literature,* 5th ed. Washington, D.C.: NASW Press.

Barratt, M. (2003). Organizational support for evidence-based practice within child and family social work: A collaborative study. *Child and Family Social Work 8*:143–150.

Barusch, A. S. (2009). *Foundations of social policy: Social justice in human perspective.* Belmont, CA: Brooks Cole.

Bickman, L. (1996). A continuum of care: More is not always better. *American Psychologist 51*:689–701.

Borum, R. (2003). Managing at-risk juvenile offenders in the community: Putting evidence- based principles into practice. *Journal of Contemporary Criminal Justice 19* (1): 114–137.

Briar-Lawson, K. and Drews, J. (2000). Child and family welfare policies and services: Current issues and historical antecedents. In J. Midgley, M. Tracy, and M. Livermore (Eds.), *The handbook of social policy,* 157–174. Thousand Oaks, CA: Sage.

Burns, B. J. (2003). Children and evidence-based practice. *Psychiatric Clinics of North America 26*:955–970.

Callister, L. C. (2005). What has the literature taught us about culturally competent care of women and children? *The American Journal of Maternal Child Nursing 30* (6): 380–388.

Chaffin, M. and Friedrich, B. (2004). Evidence-based treatments in child abuse and neglect. *Children and Youth Services Review 26*:1097–1113.

Chambless, D. L. et al. (1996). An update on empirically validated treatments. *Clinical Psychology 49* (1): 5–18.

Chorpita, B. F., Daleiden, E. L., and Weisz, J. R. (2005). Identifying and selecting the common elements of evidence-based interventions: A distillation and matching model. *Mental Health Services Research 7* (1): 5–20.

Cnaan, R. A. and Dichter, M. E. (2008). Thoughts on the use of knowledge in social work practice. *Research on Social Work Practice 18* (4): 278–284.

Cohen, J. A. and Mannarino, A. P. (1993). A treatment model for sexually abused pre-schoolers. *Journal of Interpersonal Violence 8*:115–131.

Curtis, K., Robers, H., Copperman, J., Downie, A. and Liabo, K. (2004). "How come I don't get asked no questions?" Researching "hard to reach" children and teenagers. *Child and Family Social Work 9*:167–175.

Dawson, K. and Berry, M. (2002). Engaging families in child welfare services: An evidence-based approach to best practice. *Child Welfare 81* (2): 293–317.

Deblinger, E., Steer, R., and Lippmann, J. (1999). Two-year follow-up study of cognitive behavioral therapy for sexually abused children suffering post-traumatic stress symptoms. *Child Abuse and Neglect 23*:1371–1378.

Devore, W. and Schlesinger, E. G. (1999). *Ethnic sensitive social work practice*. Boston: Allyn and Bacon.

Dinitto, D. (2000). An overview of American social policy. In J. Midgley, M. Tracy, and M. Livermore (Eds.), *The handbook of social policy* 11–26. Thousand Oaks: Sage.

Dressel, P., Waters, M., Sweat, M., Clayton, O., and Chandler-Clayton, A. (1988). Deprofessionalization, proletarianization, and social welfare work. *Journal of Sociology and Social Welfare 15* (2): 113–131.

Eisenstadt, T. H., Eyberg, S. M., McNeil, C. B., Newcomb, K., and Funderburk, B. (1993). Parent-child interaction therapy with behavior problem children: Relative effectiveness of two stages and overall treatment outcomes. *Journal of Clinical Child Psychology 22*:42–51.

Fabricant, M. and Burghardt, S. (1992). *The welfare state crisis and the transformation of social service work*. Armonk, NY: M. E. Sharpe.

Fisher, J. (1973). Is casework effective? A review. *Social Work 18* (1): 5–20.

Fisher, P. A. and Chamberlain, P. (2000). Multidimensional treatment foster care: A program for intensive parenting, family support, and skill building. *Journal of Emotional and Behavioral Disorders 8* (3): 155–164.

Fisher, P. A., Ellis, B. H., and Chamberlain, P. (1999). Early intervention foster care: A model for preventing risk in young children who have been maltreated. *Children's Services: Social Policy, Research, and Practice 2*:159–182.

Fraser, M. W. and Galinsky, M. J. (1997). Toward a resilience-based model of practice. In M. W. Fraser (Ed.), *Risk and resilience in childhood: An ecological perspective*, 265–275. Washington, DC: NASW Press.

Fukuyoma, F. (October 18, 2008). The fall of America. *Newsweek*, 30.

Gambrill, E. (2003). Evidence-based practice: Implications for knowledge development and use in social work. In A. Rosen and E. Proctor (Eds.), *Developing practice guidelines for social work practice: Issues, methods and interventions*, 37–58. New York: Columbia University Press.

Garland, A. F., Hawley, K. M., Brookman-Frazee, L., and Hurlburt, M. S. (2008). Identifying common elements of evidence-based psychosocial treatments for children's disruptive behavior problems. *American Academy of Child and Adolescent Psychiatry 47* (5): 505–514.

Glisson, C. (1992). Structure and technology in human service organizations. In Y. E. Hasenfeld (Ed.), *Human services as complex organizations*, 184–202. Thousand Oaks, CA: Sage.

Glisson, C. and Hemmelgam, A. (1998). The effects of organizational climate and in-ter-organizational coordination on the quality and outcomes of children service systems. *Child Abuse and Neglect 22* (5): 401–421.

Hill, R. B. (2007). Family roles of noncustodial African-American fathers. In L. A. See (Ed.), *Human behavior in the social environment from an African American perspective,* 2nd ed., 117–131. Binghamton, NY: Haworth Press.

Hoagwood, K., Burns, B. J., Kiser, L., Ringeisen, H., and Schoenwald, S. K. (2001). Evidence-based practice in child and adolescent mental health services. *Psychiatric Services 52* (9): 1179–1189.

Hopps, J. G. and Lowe, T. B. (2008). Scope of social work practice. In K. M. Sowers and C. N. Dulmus (Vol. Eds.) and B. White (Section Ed.), *Comprehensive handbook of social work and social welfare, vol. 1: The profession of social work.* New York: Wiley.

Hopps, J. G. and Kilpatrick, A. (with Nelson, J.) (2006). Contexts of helping: Commonalities and human diversities. In A Kilpatrick and T. Holland (Eds.), *Working with families: An integrated model by level of need.* Boston: Allyn and Bacon.

Hopps, J. G. and Morris, R. (Eds.) (2000). *Social work at the millennium.* New York: Free Press.

Hopps, J. G. and Pinderhughes, E. B. (1986). Characteristics of the social work profession. *Encyclopedia of social work,* 18th ed. Silver Spring, MD: NASW Press.

Hopps, J. G. and Pinderhughes, E. (1987). Social work in the United States: History, context, and issues. In M. Hokenstad, S. Khinduka, and J. Midgley (Eds.), *Profiles in international social work,* 163–179. Washington, DC: NASW Press.

Hopps, J. G., Pinderhughes, E. B., and Shankar, R. (1995). *The power to care: Clinical practice effectiveness with overwhelmed clients.* New York: Free Press.

Howard, M. O., McMillen, C. J., Pollio, D. E. (2003). Teaching evidence-based practice: Toward a new paradigm for social work education. *Research on Social Work Practice 13* (2): 234–259.

Jonson-Reid, M. and Drake, B. (2008). Multisector longitudinal administrative databases: An indispensable tool for evidence-based policy for maltreated children and their families. *Child Maltreatment 20* (10): 1–8.

Karger, H. and Stoesz, D. (2006). *American social welfare policy.* Boston: Pearson, Allyn and Bacon.

Kazdin, A. E. (1999). Current (lack of) status of theory in child and adolescent psychotherapy research. *Journal of Clinical Child Psychology 28*:533–543.

Kendall, P. C. and Beidas, R. S. (2007). Smoothing the trail for dissemination of evidence-based practices for youth: Flexibility within fidelity. *Professional Psychology, Research and Practice 38* (1): 13–20.

Kessler, M. L., Gira, E., and Poertner, J. (2005). Moving best practice to evidence-based practice in child welfare. *Families in Society 86* (2): 244.

Lau, A. S. (2006). Making the case for selective and directed cultural adaptations of evidence-based treatments: Examples from parent training. *Clinical Psychology: Science and Practice 13* (4): 295–310.

Lieberman, A. F., Van Horn, P., and Ghosh Ippen, C. (2005). Toward evidence-based treatment: Child-parent psychotherapy with preschoolers exposed to marital violence. *American Academy of Child and Adolescent Psychiatry 44* (12): 1241–1248.

Lonigan, C. J., Elbert, J. C., and Bennett Johnson, S. (1998). Empirically supported psychosocial interventions for children: An overview. *Journal of Clinical Child Psychology 27* (2): 138–145.

Lowe, T. B. and Korr, W. S. (2007). Workplace safety policies in mental health settings: A report from social work supervisors. *Journal of Workplace Behavioral Health* 22 (4): 29–47.

Marsiglio, W., Amato, P., Day, R. D., Lamb, M. (2000). Scholarship on fatherhood in the 1990s and beyond. *Journal of Marriage and Family* 62 (4): 1173–1191.

Mullen, E., Bledsoe, S., and Bellamy, J. (2008). Implementing evidence-based social work practice. *Research on Social Work Practice* 18 (4): 325–338.

Mullen, E. J. and Bacon, W. (2004). A survey of practitioner adoption and implementation of practice guidelines and evidence-based treatments. In A. R. Roberts and K. Yeager (Eds.), *Evidence-based practice manual: Research and outcome measures in health and human services*, 210–218. New York: Oxford University Press.

McClellan, J. M. and Werry, J. S. (2003). Evidence-based treatments in child and adolescent psychiatry: An inventory. *American Academy of Child and Adolescent Psychiatry* 42 (12): 1388–1400.

McCracken, S. G. and Marsh, J. C. (2008). Practitioner expertise in evidence-based practice decision making. *Research on Social Work Practice* 18 (4): 301–310.

McNeish, D., Newman, T., and Roberta, H. (2002). *What works for children? Effective service or children and families*. Buckingham, England: Open University Press.

McPhatter, A. R. and Ganaway, T. L. (2003). Beyond the rhetoric: Strategies for implementing culturally effective practice with children, families and communities. *Child Welfare* 82 (2): 103–124.

Munoz, R. F. and Mendelson, T. (2005). Toward evidence-based interventions for diverse populations: The San Francisco general hospital prevention and treatment manuals. *Journal of Consulting and Clinical Psychology* 73 (5): 790–799.

Munson, C. (2002). Child and adolescent needs in a time of national disaster: Perspectives for mental health professionals and parents. *Brief Treatment and Crisis Intervention* 2 (2): 135–151.

Munson, C. E. (2006). Evidence-based treatment for traumatized and abused children. In A. Roberts and K. Yeager (Eds.), *Foundations of evidence-based social work practice*, 214–230. New York: Oxford University Press.

Nybell, L. M. and Gray, S. S. (2004). Race, place, space: Meanings of cultural competence in three child welfare agencies. *Social Work* 49 (1): 17–26.

O'Hare, T., Tran, T. V., and Collins, P. (2002). Validating the internal structure of the practice skills inventory. *Research on Social Work Practice* 12 (5): 653–668.

Olds, D. (2002). Prenatal and infancy home visiting by nurses. From randomized trials to community replication. *Prevention Science* 3 (3): 153–172.

Ollendick, T. H. and King, N. J. (2004). Empirically supported treatments for children and adolescents: Advances toward evidence-based practice. In P. M. Barrett and T. H. Ollendick (Eds.), *Handbook of interventions that work with children and adolescents: Prevention and treatment*, 3–25. New York: Wiley.

Palinkas, L. A., Schoenwald, S. K., Hoagwood, K., Landsverk, J., Chorpita, B. F., and Weisz, J. R. (2008). An ethnographic study of implementation of evidence-based treatments in child mental health: First steps. *Psychiatric Services* 59 (7): 738–746.

Perry, R. (2006). Do social workers make better child welfare workers than non-social workers? *Research on Social Work Practice* 16:392–405.

Pulleyblank Coffey, E. (2004). The heart of the matter 2: Integration of ecosystemic family therapy practices with systems of care mental health services for children and families. *Family Process* 43 (2): 161–173.

Randall, J., Cowley, P., and Tomlinson, P. (2000). Overcoming barriers to effective practice in child care. *Child and Family Social Work* 5:343–352.

Rollins, L. S. and Lowe, T. B. (in progress). *Unpublished manuscript.*

Schoenwald, S. K., Kelleher, K., and Weisz, J. R. (2008). Building bridges to evidence-based practice: The MacArthur foundation child system and treatment enhancement projects (Child STEPs). *Administration and Policy in Mental Health* 35:66–72.

Schoenwald, S. K., Ward, D. M., Henggeler, S. W., and Rowland, M. D. (2000). Multi-systemic therapy versus hospitalization for crisis stabilization of youth: placement outcomes 4 months post referral. *Mental Health Services Research* 2 (1): 3–12.

Shinn, M. (1997). Family homelessness: State or trait? *American Journal of Community Psychiatry* 25 (6): 755–769.

Short, J. F. (1997). *Poverty, ethnicity and violent crime.* Boulder, CO: Westview Press.

Stambaugh, L., Burns, B. J., Landsverk, J., and Rolls Reutz, J. (2007). Evidence-based treatment for children in child welfare. *Focal Point: Research, policy and practice in children's mental health* 21 (1): 12–15.

Sze, W. and Hopps, J. (1973). *Program evaluation and accountability.* Cambridge: Schenkman.

The President's New Freedom Commission on Mental Health. (2003). *Final Report.* http://www.mentalhealthcommission.gov/reports/reports.htm (accessed October 12, 2008).

Thomlison, B. (2003). Characteristics of evidence-based child maltreatment interventions. *Child Welfare* 82 (5): 541–569.

Thyer, B. A. (2004). Science and evidence-based social work practice. In H. E. Briggs and T. L. Rzepnicki (Eds.), *Using evidence in social work practice: Behavioral perspectives,* 54–65. Chicago: Lyceum Books.

U.S. Department of Health and Human Services, Administration on Children, Youth and Families. (2008). *Child maltreatment 2006.* Washington, DC: U.S. Government Printing Office.

U.S. Public Health Service. (2000). *Report of the surgeon general's conference on children's mental health: A national action agenda.* Washington, DC: Department of Health and Human Services.

Usher, C. L. and Wildfire, J. B. (2003). Evidence-based practice in community-based child welfare systems. *Child Welfare* 82 (5): 597–614.

Waldfogel, J. (2000). Economic dimensions of social policy. In J. Midgley, M. Tracy, and M. Livermore (Eds.), *The handbook of social policy,* 27–39. Thousand Oaks: Sage.

Walker, S. (2002). Culturally competent protection of children's mental health. *Child Abuse Review* 11:380–393.

Webster-Stratton, G. and Taylor, T. (2001). Nipping early risk factors in the bud: Preventing substance abuse, delinquency, and violence m adolescence through interventions targeted at young children (0–8 years). *Prevention Science* 2:165–192.

Weissman, M. M. and Sanderson, W. C. (2001). Promises and problems in modern psychotherapy: The need for increased training in evidence-based treatments. In M. Hager (Ed.), *Modern psychiatry: Challenges in educating health professionals to meet new needs,* 132–165. New York: Josiah Macy Jr. Foundation.

Weisz, J. R., Hawley, K. M., and Doss, A. J. (2004). Empirically tested psychotherapies for youth internalizing and externalizing problems and disorders. *Child and Adolescent Psychiatric Clinics of North America* 13:729–815.

Weisz, J. R. and Hawley, K. M. (1998). Finding, evaluating, refining, and applying empirically supported treatments for children and adolescents. *Journal of Clinical Child Psychology 27* (2): 206–216.

Wolfe, D. A. (1994). The role of intervention and treatment services in the prevention of child abuse and neglect. In G. B. Melton and F. D. Barry (Eds.), *Protecting children from abuse and neglect: Foundations for a new national strategy,* 224–304. New York: Guilford Press.

8 | Social-Behavioral Research in Aging and the Social Work Research Agenda

Barbara Berkman

BILL REID, social work's seminal researcher, believed that research is essential in leading the way to address the significant issues of our time. This is true in gerontology, where research scholars, whose collaborative work with other disciplines on social-behavioral processes, are addressing the emerging issues in aging. Interdisciplinary research is fundamental to the understanding of disease etiology as well as to the promotion of health and well-being.

Recent years have witnessed an explosion of new knowledge and a substantial increase in the number of journals, articles, monographs, books, and other publications related to aging. There has also been a significant upgrade in the quality of research that is published. Theory is richer; databases are larger and more reliable; new methodologies are available; and computing power and techniques have advanced. Until recently, compared with this impressive progress in aging-related research, the field of social work has been lacking. However, today we are making significant strides in our efforts to understand and study issues related to practice with older adults and their families.

During the last several decades, there have been dramatic shifts in the demographics of aging. People are living longer because of advances in public health, health care technology, and treatment and service delivery. The statistics that highlight the increasing proportion of the population older than 65 years and their increasing diversity are familiar to us all. At the end of this decade, the baby boom generation (the largest birth cohort in our history) will begin to turn 65. By 2030, 20 percent of the total U.S. population will be 65 years and older (U.S. Bureau of Census 2000a), with the fastest growing segment being those over age 85 (U.S. Bureau of Census 2000b). This growing older population, by sheer numbers alone, presents opportunities and challenges for research in health care and in social work. In the years to come, unprecedented numbers of elders will face risks of frailty and loss of independence. There will be an opportunity for social and behavioral research to help improve health and functioning and contribute to reduced rates of disability for older people. But there will also be challenges. Social work needs a strong research agenda in aging that can help improve the quality of life for older people and their caregivers.

This chapter begins with a brief overview of a few emerging societal trends and the challenges and opportunities for social work researchers in the fields of aging and health care. The trends chosen are directly linked to the use of health and mental health services, and are the underpinnings for a strong research agenda for social workers in aging. In addition, the major social-behavioral research interests in aging of the National Institute of Health will be discussed and examples of research in these arenas, undertaken by the mentors and scholars in the Hartford Geriatric Social Work Faculty Scholars Program, will be presented.

Social Trends in Health and Aging: Challenges and Opportunities for Research

Chronic Illness

Today, there are significant changes in outcomes of patient care stimulated by technological advances in biomedicine and pharmacology. People are living longer with complex chronic physical and mental health conditions. Four of every five older Americans have at least one chronic health condition, and 69 percent have multiple physical or mental health conditions (Berkman, Silverstone, Simmons, Howe, and Volland 2000). The leading causes of morbidity and mortality are almost all related to chronic diseases, resulting in acute episodes of illness over a lifetime of chronic processes (Paulson 1994). These elderly people often have significant activity impairments and quality-of-life issues (Gonyea, Hudson, and Corley 2004; Burnette and Kang 2003). They will represent an increasing percentage of individuals served by social workers. Social work's dual focus on person-in-environment provides a unique vantage point from which to study social, behavioral, and environmental sources of risk and resilience associated with chronic illnesses.

Community-Based Service

The acute model of care, long the focus of geriatric social work in hospitals, is no longer appropriate because the chronically ill older population needs continuity of care rather than episodic interventions (Berkman, Gardner, Zodikoff, and Harootyan 2006). Social workers, therefore, need to expand their intervention practice skills to ambulatory community-based settings and the prevention of acute care episodes (Berkman 1996). Moreover, given the mental and physical health benefits associated with community living, social work researchers need to develop and test interventions that support continued independence for older adults (Gardner and Zodikoff 2003). Since policy changes in government financing of home health care may lead to significant reduction in services, placing home health patients at a greater risk for negative outcomes, it is particularly important that social workers focus on home health care research.

Increased Diversity

The older adult population is increasingly diverse in terms of age, race, ethnicity, gender, and socioeconomic status. By 2050, about one third of the elderly population will be composed of African Americans, Hispanic Americans, Asian Americans and other nonwhite racial/ethnic populations (U.S. Bureau of the Census 2000c). In the next 50 years, the proportion of Hispanic individuals aged 65 or older is expected to triple, representing an estimated 16 percent of the population (Federal Inter-Agency Forum on Aging Statistics 2000). Estimates of the number of older gay men and lesbians range from as low as 3 percent to as high as 18 to 20 percent (Hooyman 2006). There are vast differences in factors affecting the health care of older adults in terms of emotional reactions, health beliefs, health care utilizations, health risks, and patterns of relationships with family members (Johnson 2005; Maramaldi and Guevara 2003). This is an arena for research where social work brings significant expertise.

Family Caregiving

Another emerging trend that affects social work practice and drives our research agenda is the increasing expectation that families will assume responsibility for home care needs of their loved ones, despite the fact that the number of family members available to provide care continues to decrease. Thus, the burden of care is falling on fewer family members who may have fewer psychological, financial, environmental resources. Living with physical

and mental illness profoundly affects and is affected by an older adult's relationships (or lack of relationships) with family members and other caregivers
(Gardner and Zodikoff 2003).

What is more, older persons are not only receiving care, they also are providing it. Half of all people caring for elderly family members are themselves
older than 60 years of age, and there are 2.5 million families in the United
States that are maintained by a grandparent (Lipsitz and Rosenberg 2002). A
growing number of older women have assumed the role of custodial grandparents, due most often to the biological parent's substance abuse, incarceration, physical disability, or death (Kropf and Wilks 2003). Social work is taking a leadership role in relation to caregiving research.

Social work researchers are beginning to meet the challenges presented
by these trends, focusing on many of the priority areas that the National Institutes of Health (NIH) have identified. For example, the National Institute
on Aging (NIA) Strategic Plan calls for research that can "improve the health
and quality of life for older people, understand healthy aging processes, and
reduce health disparities among older adults and populations," all significant
areas for social work research (NIA 2001).

The Hartford Geriatric Social Work Faculty Scholar's Program selected
five NIH-identified priority areas for social behavioral research in aging and
categorized the Hartford Faculty Scholars' and Mentors' research by primary
focus (Berkman, Kurzban, and Gardner 2005). These areas are: 1) changing
lifestyle behavior for better health; 2) enhancing the end-of-life experience;
3) improving quality of life in chronic conditions; 4) maintaining health and
functioning; and 5) reducing health disparities. The remainder of this chapter will identify examples of current geriatric research in each area undertaken by social workers. These areas are interrelated and the examples offered
could easily fit into more than one.

Changing Lifestyle Behavior for Better Health

The view that illness is a chronic process raises the question of whether an
acute episode can be prevented, placing much more importance on consumers in determining their health care needs and outcomes (Berkman 1996).
The focus of care becomes primary care, with an emphasis on disease prevention and health promotion (Paulson 1994). The growing empowerment of
older adults who wish to participate in decision making regarding their own
health care and treatment is shifting the decision-making role away from the
physician to the patient.

Research has shown that lifestyle and other social environmental influences can influence outcomes of aging. We also know that remaining relatively healthy and emotionally vital into very advanced age is a realistic

expectation. Thus, self care in health promotion is an important area for research in which social workers have been significantly involved. Excellent examples of research led by social workers in this arena are the "Fit and Strong" intervention, a video-based physical activity program for people with arthritis, focused on boosting adherence to the intervention (Hughes, Seymour, Pollak, Huber, and Sharma 2004); and a "Healthy Moves for Aging Well" intervention for homebound people, offering targeted exercises for people with functional deficits (http://healthyagingprograms.org 2005). In another avenue to health promotion, social work researchers have focused on successful aging and the relationship between faith and health (Parker 2003; Ai 2006). The state of knowledge in the area of changing lifestyle behavior is still very basic. We still need interventions designed across the continuum of care that focus on prevention and health promotion.

Maintaining Health and Functioning: Patients and Caregivers

As case managers and counselors to the vulnerable elderly and their families, social workers provide critical support in maintaining older adults in their communities and reducing the cost of health services. Social work researchers are already studying new models of intervention directed at psychosocial and environmental factors that influence the maintenance of health and functioning (Mahoney 2004; Naleppa 2003). These factors can result in serious consequences in terms of quality of life, morbidity, and mortality. In another example, social workers are testing interventions to alleviate geriatric depression, which often goes unreported, undiagnosed, and untreated (Gellis 2004).

In family caregiving research, social work has been in a leadership position, recognizing that family caregivers who help patients maintain functioning have their own health issues, being very prone to depression and physical problems. Seltzer (2001), Greenberg (2001, 2004), and Li (2005) are just a few of the many social work researchers examining the experiences of caregivers, and are testing interventions to help alleviate distress. Other leading social work researchers in family caregiving emphasize that innovative responses to caregivers' needs are required if people with disabilities are to remain in the community with quality of life (Toseland and McCallion 2004).

One risk associated with the increased burden of family caregiving is elder mistreatment. Greg Paveza has been a social work leader in developing the research agenda in this area. He and his colleagues point out that although most social workers are aware of the individual and societal costs of elder mistreatment, there is little known about the incidence, the precipitating factors, the consequences, and effective treatment of this form of family violence (Paveza and Vande Weerd 2003). There remains a serious need for empirical research to address this multifaceted public health concern. Many social workers are leading new efforts in this area (Shibusawa 2005; and Brownell 2002).

Quality of Life in Chronic Conditions

The rapidly increasing number of chronically ill older patients, the majority of whom are living in the community, present complex interacting medical and psychosocial problems. These conditions not only pose significant health and financial burdens for the affected individuals but also affect their families. These patients and their families challenge social workers to enable them to access and utilize social and health care services effectively so as to improve their quality of life (Berkman, Gardner, Zodikoff, and Harootyan 2006). Physical and mental conditions that diminish one's capacity to function independently often lead to a need for long-term care in community or residential settings.

One of our premier social work geriatric researchers in this area has studied the course of depression over time as it affects and is affected by impairment severity, functional ability, and rehabilitation service utilization (Horowitz 2003 and 2005). Other social work researchers have studied the current trend toward substitution of home and community-based nursing care for older adults with neuropsychiatric disorders (Semki 2006).

Enhancing End of Life

There are documented shortcomings in the care of the dying. The state of the knowledge is very limited. But social workers are assuming leadership roles in this growing arena for research. Researchers such as Townsend (2005), Bern-Klug (2001), Kramer (2004, 2005), and Waldrop (2005) are beginning to make distinct contributions in this area. Most research has been focused in hospice settings and there is growing interest in nursing homes. The values and perspectives of our profession, such as person-in-environment and the strengths perspective, can place social work research in the mainstream of this agenda.

Reducing Health Disparities

Health care professionals must be particularly cognizant of cultural diversity among elders living with serious physical and mental health problems, as there are greater disparities in health in later life among minority populations (Maramaldi and Guevara 2003). For example, social work researchers report that older women of color are uniquely vulnerable to chronic conditions such as heart disease, diabetes mellitus, and hypertension, and experience more comorbid conditions than do white women (Chadiha and Adams 2003). We know that disease risk factors, as well as response to treatment, caregiving, and overall quality of life, may be affected by race, ethnicity, gender, and socioeconomic status through discrimination and stigmatization.

In view of the increasing diversity of the older adult population, social work researchers are focusing on designing interventions that effectively address the physical and mental health problems confronting elders and family members from different cultural backgrounds. A recent example of social work-led intervention research in this area is the design and testing of an innovative empowerment intervention for African American women caregivers, which may have a significant effect on positive caregiving outcomes (Chadiha 2003, 2004). We can appreciate intervention research aimed at decreasing barriers to cancer screening for racial and ethnic minority groups by developing culturally and linguistically appropriate communication materials (Maramaldi 2001).

Pondering the Future

The future of social work practice in geriatric health care relies on our ability to generate meaningful research on the epidemiology and theoretical bases of health-related psychosocial problems and to develop and evaluate effective interventions for addressing these concerns (Gardner and Zodikoff 2003). With increasing research, social work educators will be able to integrate evidence-based knowledge into their curricula and teach students to use empirically derived intervention approaches in gerontological practice.

Many of the demographic, social, and health care trends mentioned in this chapter are expected to continue well into the future, as will evolutions in health care and in the practice of social work in aging. The expansion and diversification of the older adult population will most likely generate increasing demand for health care services such as home health and long-term care. As society grows older and a greater proportion of adults experience chronic conditions, our expectations of later life will change dramatically with respect to employment, housing, social relationships, independent functioning, and quality of life. Within this context, social work's dual emphasis on theory and practice and expertise in social health care services have a major contribution to make to the geriatric knowledge base.

The John A. Hartford Foundation's Faculty Scholars and Doctoral Fellows Programs offer the opportunity to increase the number of geriatric social work researchers. With the continued support of funders such as the Hartford Foundation and with increased federal interest in developing research in aging by social workers, such as NIA's funding of a social work faculty research training program, we will continue bringing the social work perspective to the knowledge base in aging.

References

Ai, A. (2006). Depression, faith-based coping, and post-operative global functioning in adult and older patients undergoing cardiac surgery. *Journal of Psychosomatic Research 60* (1): 21–28.

Berkman, B. (1996). The emerging health care world: Implications for social work practice and education. *Social Work 41*:541–553.

Berkman, B. and Harootyan, L. (2003). Introduction. In Berkman, B. and Harootyan, L. (Eds.), *Social work and health care in an aging society,* 1–14. New York: Springer.

Berkman, B., Gardner, D., Zodikoff, B., and Harootyan, L., (2005). Social work in health care with older adults: Future challenges. *Families in Society 86* (3): 329–337.

Berkman, B., Kurzban, S., and Gardner, D. (2005). *Bridging the gerontological research gap: NIH and social work perspective.* Site visit report to the Hartford Foundation.

Berkman, B., Silverstone, B., Simmons W. J., Howe, J., and Volland, P. (2000). Social work gerontological practice: The need for faculty development in the new millennium. *Journal of Gerontological Social Work 34* (1): 5–23.

Bern-Klug, M., Gessert, C., and Forbes, S. (2001). The need to revise assumptions about the end of life: Implications for social work practice. *Health and Social Work 26* (1): 38–48.

Brownell, P. (2002). Elder abuse. In A. Roberts, and G. J. Greene (Eds.), *Social workers desk reference,* 723–727. New York: Oxford University Press.

Burnette, D. and Kang, S. (2003). Self-care by urban, African American elders. In B. Berkman and L. Harootyan (Eds.), *Social work and health care in an aging society,* 123–148. New York: Springer.

Chadiha, L. A., Adams, P., Phorano, O., Ong, S.-L., and Byers, L. (2003). Cases from the field: Stories told and lessons learned from Black female caregivers' vignettes for empowerment practice. *Journal of Gerontological Social Work 40* (1/2): 135–144.

Chadiha, L. A., Adams, P., Biegel, D. E., Auslander, W., and Gutierrez, L. (2004). Empowering urban African American women caregivers: A literature synthesis and practice strategies. *Social Work 49* (1): 97–108.

Federal Interagency Forum on Aging-Related Statistics. (2000). Older Americans 2000: Key indicators of well-being. *FIFAS.* Washington, DC: U.S. Government Printing Office.

Gardner, D. S. and Zodikoff, B. D. (2003). Meeting the challenges of social work practice in health care and aging in the 21st century. In Berkman, B. and Harootyan, L. (Eds.), *Social work and health care in an aging society,* 377–392. New York: Springer.

Gellis, Z. D. (2006). Mental health and emotional disorders among older adults. In B. Berkman and S. D'Ambruoso (Eds.), *Handbook of social work in health and aging,* 129–140. New York: Oxford University Press.

Gellis, Z. D., McGinty, J., Tierney, L., Burton, J., Jordan, C., and Kim, J. (2004). Depression screening in home health care elderly. Paper presented at the Annual New York State Geriatric Mental Health Conference. State University of New York at Albany, Albany, NY.

Gonyea, J. G., Hudson, R. B., and Curley, A. (2004). *The geriatric social work labor force: Challenges and opportunities in responding to an aging society.* Boston: Institute for Geriatric Social Work, Boston University School of Social Work.

Greenberg, J. S., Seltzer, M. M., Krauss, M. W., Chou, R. J. A., and Hong, J. (2004). The effect of quality of the relationship between mothers and adults with disabilities on maternal well-being: The mediating role of optimism. *American Journal of Orthopsychiatry 74*:14–25.

Home Health Services Quarterly Journal. (2006). *Healthy Moves*. http://healthyaging-programs.org (accessed June 9, 2005).

Hooyman, N. (2006). Our aging society. In Berkman, B. and D'Ambruoso, S. (Eds.), *Handbook of social work in health and aging*, 1031–1032. New York: Oxford University Press.

Horowitz, A. (2003). Depression and vision and hearing impairments in later life. *Generations 27*:32–38.

Horowitz, A., Reinhardt, J. P., Boerner, K., and Travis, L. A. (2003). The influence of health, social support quality and rehabilitation on depression among disabled elders. *Journal of Aging and Mental Health 7*:343–350.

Horowitz, A., Reinhardt, J. P., and Kennedy, G. (2005). Major and subthreshold depression among older adults seeking vision rehabilitation services. *American Journal of Geriatric Psychiatry 13* (3): 180–187.

Hughes, S. L., Seymour, R. B., Campbell, R., Pollak, N., Huber, G., and Sharma, L. (2004). Impact of the fit and strong intervention on older adults with osteoarthritis. *The Gerontologist 44*:217–228.

Johnson, J. (2005). Disparities and chronic conditions among African American older adults. *Health and Aging Network, ASA 12* (1): 6–8.

Kramer, B. J. and Bern-Klug, M. (2004). Social work end-of-life research. In J. Berzoff and P. Silverman (Eds.), *Living with dying: A handbook for end-of-life healthcare practitioners*, 792–814. New York: Columbia University Press.

Kramer, B. J., Christ, G. H., Bern-Klug, M., and Francoeur, R. B. (2005). A national agenda for social work research in palliative and end-of-life care. *Journal of Palliative Medicine 8*:418–431.

Kropf, N. and Wilks, S. (2003). Grandparents raising grandchildren. In B. Berkman and L. Harootyan (Eds.), *Social work and health care in an aging society*, 177–200. New York: Springer.

Lee, J. S. and Gutheil, I. (2003). *The older patient at home: Social work services and home health care*. In B. Berkman, and L. Harootyan (Eds), *Social work and health care in an aging society*, 84–86. New York: Springer.

Li, L. W. and Fries, B. (2005). Elder disability as an explanation for racial differences in informal home care. *Gerontologist 45*:206–215.

Lipsitz, L. A. and Rosenberg, R. (2002). *Harvard cooperative program on aging newsletter 31* (2).

Mahoney, K. J., Simon-Rusinowitz, L., Loughlin, D. M., Desmond, S. M., and Squillace, M.R. (2004). Determining personal care consumers' preferences for a consumer-directed cash and counseling option: Survey results from Arkansas, Florida, New Jersey, and New York elders and adults with disabilities. *Health Services Research 39* (3): 643–663.

Maramaldi, P. (2001). *Diagnostic delays following abnormal mammography: A comparison of Latina and White women*, 297–318. Ph.D. diss., Columbia University.

Maramaldi, P. and Guevara, M. (2003). Cultural considerations in maintaining health-related quality of life in older adults. In Berkman, B. and Harootyan, L. (Eds.), *Social work and health care in an aging society*, 297–318. New York: Springer.

McCallion, P., Toseland, R., Gerber, T., Banks, S. (2004). Increasing the use of formal services by caregivers of persons with dementia. *Social Work 49* (3): 441–450.

Naleppa, M. (2003). Gerontological social work and case management. In Berkman, B. and Harootyan, L. (Eds.), *Social work and health care in an aging society*, 97–122. New York: Springer.

Parker, M. W., Roff, L., Klemmack, D., Koenig, H., Baker, P., and Allman, R. (2003). Religiosity and mental health in southern, community-dwelling older adults. *Aging and Mental Health 7* (5): 390–397.

Paulson, L.G. (1994). Special populations among older persons. *Journal of Gerontological Social Work 25*:1–10.

Paveza, G. and VandeWeerd, C. (2003). Elder mistreatment and the role of social work. In B. Berkman and L. Harootyan (Eds.), *Social work and health care in an aging society*, 245–268. New York: Springer.

Seltzer, M. M., Greenberg, J. S., Floyd, F., Pettee, Y., and Hong, J. (2001). Life course impacts of parenting a child with disability. *American Journal of Mental Retardation 106*:282–300.

Semke, J. (2006). Long-term residential settings for older persons with severe and persistent mental illness. In Berkman, B. (Ed.), *Handbook of social work in health and aging*, 637–644. New York: Oxford University Press.

Shibusawa, T., Kodaka, M., Iwano, S., and Kaizu, K. (2005). Interventions for elder abuse and neglect: Frail elders in Japan. *Brief Therapy and Crisis Intervention 5*:203–211.

Toseland, R., McCallion, P., Smith., T., and Banks, S. (2004). Supporting caregivers of frail older adults in an HMO setting. *American Journal of Orthopsychiatry 74* (3): 349–364.

Townsend, A., Ishler, K., Vargo, E., Pitorak, E., Matthews, C., and Shapiro, B. (2005). Assessment of family caregiver strain during end-of-life hospice care. In Bern-Klug, M. (Ed.), *End-of-life perspectives: Families and elders symposium*. 10th Annual Conference of the Society for Social Work and Research, Miami, FL.

U.S. Bureau of the Census. (2000a). *Census 2000 summary file 1 (SF 1)*. Washington, DC: Author.

U.S. Bureau of the Census. (2000b). *Population projections of the United States by age, sex, race, Hispanic origin, and nativity: 1999–2000*. Washington, DC: Author.

U.S. Bureau of the Census. (2000c). *Projections of the total resident population by 5-year age groups, race, and Hispanic origin with special age categories: Middle series, 2050 to 2070 (NP-T4-G)*. Washington, DC: Author.

U.S. Department of Health and Human Services. (2001). *National Institute on Aging, National Institute of Health: 01–4951 (3)*.

Waldrop, D. P., Kramer, B. J., Skrentny, J. A., Milch, R. A., and Finn, W. (2005). Final transitions: Family caregiving at the end of life. *Journal of Palliative Medicine 8*:623–638.

9 | A Culturally Grounded Approach to Drug Use Prevention with Latino Children and Youth

Flavio Francisco Marsiglia

THIS CHAPTER PROVIDES an overview of the theoretical and methodological underpinnings behind the development and testing of empirically based drug abuse prevention interventions with and for ethnic minority children and youth. It reviews culturally based risk and protective factors from an ecosystemic perspective by focusing on existing cultural assets and community resiliency. Strengths and vulnerabilities of Latino youth associated with drug use illustrate the multilevel factors influencing the development of culturally grounded and evidence-based interventions.

The profession of social work has had a strong historical presence in community-based drug abuse treatment settings (Ashenberg Straussner 2001). Its direct practice involvement has focused on research and evaluation efforts, studying what works and for whom. Practice research efforts have generally had a strong methodological emphasis on single-subject design and more general evaluation research, generating empirical and nonempirical knowledge (Knott, Corredoira, and Kimberly 2008).

Since the early 1990s, there has been a concerted effort in the social work field to recognize drug abuse practice research as responsive and to support its development with the best available science (Liddle 2004; Stoffel and Moyers 2004). This has resulted in a renewed engagement of the profession with other disciplines in drug research as a natural phenomenon in need of informed social work practice research. Social work researchers are contributing their professional perspective to a better understanding of the interrelationships of individuals, communities, families, and social institutions. Social work research is also providing evidence from the field for social policies and improved service delivery to address drug abuse. These interdisciplinary collaborations aim at integrating the strengths of the communities within their intervention research models (Montoya, Atkinson, and McFaden 2003).

The strength perspective (Cowger 1994) has inspired a form of quality control to improve competency and applicability of drug abuse interventions for specific individuals, families, and communities. The strength perspective questions the assumptions behind generic drug prevention and treatment interventions and highlights the community's world view and its strengths (Krovetz 1999). This critical approach produces practice-relevant research that validates and integrates community-based narratives and norms throughout the research process and the development of culturally responsive intervention. Culture and identities are considered key components of the intervention research process, not simply add-ons. When culture and research are integrated, practice and research cease to be dichotomous or antithetical, leading to the generation of practice-based research rather than research-based practice (Epstein 1995).

A federally recognized Model Program called *keepin' it REAL* is reviewed as an effective drug prevention intervention with and for ethnic minority youth. Implications and challenges for social work practice research are provided as a means to enhance the profession's involvement in the generation of scientifically robust, culturally meaningful, and innovative interventions.

Epidemiology, Etiology, and Consequences of Substance Abuse

Youth drug abuse is a significant public health concern because it affects the health of the users as well as families, communities, and society at large (Califano 2007). Drug abuse can impede children and youths' ability to achieve their full potential and can cause serious physical and mental health harm (Winters 2003). Youth drug use affects families and can become a burden to society at large, as drug-abusing youth and adults have lower academic achievement, lower productivity levels at work, and greater need for supports than nondrug-using youth (Cartwright 2008).

Since the 1990s, adolescent drug use rates in the United States have slightly declined for some substances, but in the aggregate alcohol and other drug consumption within this age group continues to be disturbingly high (Johnston,

O'Malley, Bachman, and Schulenberg 2007; Donovan 2007). Drug use and abuse can disproportionally lead to chronic illness or death for some subgroups of adolescents; others experience such negative consequences later in life or not at all. Latino drug-related morbidity and mortality rates provide a snapshot of the gravity of drug-related problems and their consequences for the well-being of children and youth (Kanna, Fersobe, Soni, and Michelen 2008). For example, drug-using Latino youth experience greater health-related complications than drug-using youth of other ethnic backgrounds and are overrepresented in the juvenile justice system and in emergency rooms with mental and physical health conditions associated with abuse (Malik-Kane and Visher 2008).

When age, national origin, generational status, gender, socioeconomic status, and migration history are considered, important within-group differences emerge (Ojeda, Patterson, and Strathdee 2008). Recently arrived Latino immigrant children across the age spectrum appear to be protected from substance use through various family and other culture-related factors (de la Rosa 2002). Rates of substance use, however, vary by acculturation levels (Marsiglia and Waller 2002) and acculturation to mainstream American culture has been linked to pro-drug norms and attitudes, leading to higher rates of substance use (Kulis, Yabiku, Marsiglia, Nieri, and Crossman 2007). Greater identification with one's ethnic group has also been recognized as a protective factor against substance use (Holley, Kulis, Marsiglia, and Keith 2006; Marsiglia, Kulis, Hecht, and Sills 2004).

The existing knowledge about ethnic minority youth protective and risk factors associated with drug abuse and other conditions is limited and sometimes inconclusive, in part because ethnic minority children and youth are not proportionally represented in randomized trials (Huey and Polo 2008). Large sectors of ethnic minority communities lack access to culturally tailored psychosocial interventions to prevent and treat drug abuse and other diseases (Miranda, Bernal, Lau, Kohn, Hwang, LaFramboise 2005). This and the lack of access to existing mainstream interventions and randomized trials only exacerbate existing health disparities (Lopez, Bergren, and Painter 2008). A lack of focus on culture not only undermines the quality of the services but also can lead to the design and implementation of interventions that underutilize culturally based resiliencies and protective factors.

Even though Latinos constitute the largest ethnic minority group in the nation (U.S. Census Bureau 2008), relatively little is known about Latino children and youth and their resiliency or vulnerability to drug abuse. When Latinos are represented in samples, they tend to be treated as a homogeneous group without much concern about national origin, generational status, or acculturation status (Marsiglia, Kulis, and Hecht 2001). Results emerging from studies using an ethnic glossing approach (umbrella terms such as "Latino" are used to group very different subgroups) are difficult to disaggregate to address Latino cultural heterogeneity (see Trimble 1990–1991).

Attention to national origin and geographic location has allowed higher levels of specificity in identifying needs and designing effective interventions to address them. For example, depression has been connected with substance use and HIV/AIDS risk in the region along the U.S.–Mexico border, especially among the Mexican migrant population (Valdez, Neaigus, and Kaplan 2008). In order to respond to drug-use treatment and prevention needs and to effectively utilize the assets of community members, prevention and treatment are approached as part of a continuum of care. Much remains to be learned about the great majority of Mexican American and other Latino children and youth who do not use or abuse drugs. This knowledge will help in planning psychosocial interventions that deter nonusers from starting while assisting users to stop or decrease their use.

Culturally Grounded Drug Abuse Intervention Research

The emerging culturally grounded perspective (Marsiglia and Kulis 2008) supports the inclusion of culture in all social work interventions. The key focus is on ethnicity and race, but the approach is also grounded in gender, sexual orientation, religion, social class, and ability status. Culturally grounded social work intervention research integrates the concept of *intersectionality*—approaching culturally grounded drug abuse interventions as a complex and multidimensional phenomenon. Intersectionality is expressed through multiple systems of inequality based on the different statuses occupied by a single individual at a particular place and time (Collins 1998). In the case of immigrant Latino/a youth, the intersection of their acculturation status, gender, ethnicity, and age will be assessed in order to understand and address their unique identities and experiences.

A multidimensional approach to drug-use research recognizes the existing heterogeneity within groups according to the strength of ethnic identity along various dimensions and in combination with other contextual factors. Strength of ethnic identity and ethnic labels together explain more of the variance in drug use among samples of Southwest adolescents than either does alone (Marsiglia, Kulis, and Hecht 2001). Identity is approached as an ever changing, multidimensional, and dynamic process influenced by developmental factors as well as by the various social and cultural contexts influencing children and youth.

Culture is often approached as a source of resilience and support for healthy behaviors, such as family-centeredness in the Latino community.

However, culture of origin and the adjustments to a host culture can be a source of stress. Acculturation stress often emerges when young people attempt to live within two worlds—the culture of origin and the host culture (Smokowski, Rose and Bacallao 2008). Prejudice and discrimination are a source of stress for children and youth, leading to negative health behaviors and outcomes. For example, pro substance-use norms and behaviors of elementary school Mexican American children were found to be more closely associated with perceived ethnic discrimination than with acculturation stress (Kulis, Marsiglia, and Nieri 2008).

Closeness to family and strong parental monitoring as well as a strong connection to the extended family have been identified as strong protective factors (Voisine, Parsai, Marsiglia, Kulis, Nieri 2008). Acculturating into mainstream culture is an inevitable process that can erode some of the existing protections connected to culture of origin. The focus of migration research is not on the absence or presence of acculturation but on how the acculturation processes take place and their consequences for the well-being of children and their families. Acculturation that occurs slowly and promotes bicultural orientations protects adolescents by sheltering them from the risks connected to the developmentally driven expansion of their social networks, a process that makes them more vulnerable for drug use (Marsiglia et al. 2005).

The culturally grounded approach focuses on assets and strengths at the community, family, school, and individual levels. Some of those strengths or assets can be summarized as follows:

- *Individual and peer levels:* Pro-social behaviors, low levels of sensation-seeking, positive peer influence, antidrug norms, high academic achievement, and delayed initiation into alcohol and other drugs.
- *Family level:* Good and effective communication, effective parental monitoring, consistent rules and expectations at home.
- *School level:* Clear academic standards and support, disciplined and nurturing school environment, clear policies regarding alcohol and other drugs.
- *Community level:* Social organization—neighbors know each other and look after each other; neighborhood attachment—residents have a sense of pride in their community and low access to alcohol, tobacco, and other drugs (Sobeck, Abbey, Agius, Clinton, and Harrison 2000; Chambers, Taylor, and Potenza 2003).

Policy makers, practitioners, and researchers play an essential role in partnering with communities to design and test evidence-based interventions that support these protective factors and reduce substance-use risks. Communities have their own tempo and may be ready at different times to engage in these efforts. First, the readiness of a community to be engaged is assessed and future steps are identified accordingly (Hawkins and Catalano 2002). Well-developed tools are available to guide communities through this process (see Communities That Care: http://ncadi.samhsa.gov/features/ctc/resources.aspx).

Culturally Grounded and Evidence-Based Prevention Intervention Research

Prevention interventions are commonly separated into three categories, based on the target population: universal, selective, and indicated (Midford 2008). Universal prevention targets all individuals regardless of their level of risk. Selective prevention targets those at risk for substance abuse due to membership in a vulnerable subgroup, such as dropouts, children of adult alcoholics, or victims of family violence. Indicated prevention targets those already using or who are engaged in related behaviors known to lead to drug use. Selective interventions aim at reducing or eliminating use, and they focus more on the individual and less on community variables than the other two classifications.

A number of research-based prevention programs ranging from universal to selective have been developed and tested in the last two decades. The Substance Abuse and Mental Health Services Administration's (SAMHSA) Effective Substance Abuse and Mental Health Interventions directory, http://modelprograms.samhsa.gov, provides a comprehensive list. Model programs are diverse in their approach and target population. Some address at least in part the variations in substance-use rates by race/ethnicity, culture, gender, sexual orientation, and socioeconomic status. Effective prevention programs acknowledge the unique needs and strengths of each population and ensure that culturally competent services are provided (Resnicow, Soler, Braithwaite, Ahluwalia, and Butler 2000; Sale, Sambrano, Springer, Peña, Pan, and Kasim 2005).

Keepin' it REAL

One example of an effective, culturally grounded substance-abuse prevention program is *keepin' it REAL*. This program was developed by an interdisciplinary team of researchers at the Southwest Interdisciplinary Research Center at Arizona State University's School of Social Work. The intervention was originally evaluated through a large randomized trial (N = 7,000) in 32 Phoenix middle schools, funded by the National Institute on Drug Abuse of the National Institutes of Health.

Keepin' it REAL incorporates specific cultural elements from ethnic cultural communities to enable members of these groups to better respond to the intervention. It has been shown to be effective in decreasing pro-drug outcomes like substance use and increasing antidrug outcomes such as antidrug norms and attitudes and the use of effective drug resistance strategies (Hecht, Marsiglia, Elek, Wagstaff, Kulis, Dustman, and Miller-Day 2003). See table 9.1 for a summary of the results of the multicultural version of the intervention.

The arrows in table 9.1 show the significant changes in the desired direction in the experimental group (youth of all ethnicities) when compared to the control group from pre-intervention (T1) to each of three post-intervention time points (T2 = 2 months, T3 = 8 months, T4 = 14 months). Relative to their counterparts in the control group, Latino youth participating in *keepin' it REAL* also reported better outcomes, including less overall substance use, less recent alcohol and marijuana use, fewer intentions to use substances, greater drug resistance self-efficacy, and smaller estimates of peer substance use (Kulis, Marsiglia, Elek-Fisk, Wagstaff, and Hecht 2005).

The culturally specific content of the intervention enhanced its effectiveness for Latino-heritage youth, but narrow cultural targeting is not essential for the program to be effective. In other words, this experiment shows that programs do not necessarily need to target a single cultural group, but they must integrate in their content some reflection of the groups that will receive the intervention. In other words, children and youth need to connect to the content and recognize themselves in the format and substance of the intervention. They should conclude: *This program is about me and for me.*

Table 9.1 Summary of Partial Results of the Evaluation of *Keepin' it REAL*

| | *Keepin' it REAL versus Control* | | |
	T2	T3	T4
PRO-DRUG USE			
Recent Alcohol Use	↓	↓	↓
Recent Cigarette Use		↓	↓
Recent Marijuana Use			↓
Descriptive Norms	↓	↓	↓
Positive Drug Expectancy	↓	↓	↓
ANTI-DRUG			
Use of R.E.A.L. Strategies	↑	↑	↑
Injunctive Norms: Parents			↑
Injunctive Norms: Friends	↑	↑	↑
Personal Norms	↑	↑	↑
Self Efficacy	↑	↑	↑

Less acculturated Mexican-heritage students (defined as Spanish language dominant or bilingual) reported lower levels of substance use at baseline and at post-treatment tests, while higher-acculturated Mexican-heritage students (English language dominant) reported higher baseline levels of substance use (Marsiglia, Kulis, Wagstaff, Elek, and Dran 2005). Program effects were confined to the higher acculturated students, with those participating in the intervention reporting much smaller increases in substance use (alcohol, cigarettes and marijuana) and less erosion in antidrug norms than those reported by the control group. The less acculturated students generally maintained their preexisting antidrug attitudes whether they were in the intervention or control group.

Acculturation appears to operate differently for Latino boys and Latina girls, with some aspects of culturally prescribed gender roles shielding youth from pro-drug use behaviors and attitudes (Kulis, Marsiglia, and Hurdle 2003). Acculturation was found to have a stronger effect in increasing the substance-use risk of Mexican-origin middle school girls than of their male counterparts (Kulis, Marsiglia, and Hecht 2002). These processes go beyond gender (male/female), as gender identity has a stronger explanatory power. Gender identity—especially in combination with ethnicity and acculturation status—was a much stronger predictor of behavior and attitudes than gender label alone (Kulis, Marsiglia, Chase-Lingard, Nieri, and Nagoshi 2008).

These protective and risk processes do not exist solely at the individual or family levels but are influenced by the broader circles of the child's environment. Subsequent studies considered how factors such as geographic isolation, socioeconomic status, residential instability, and ethnic and racial residential concentration interacted with cultural processes that affect individual health trajectories.

Less-acculturated youth reported less substance use and lower adherence to pro-drug norms when they attended schools with a high enrollment of less-acculturated students (Kulis et al. 2004). A strong presence of recent Latino immigrant families in a neighborhood was identified as having an appreciable protective effect both in the substance-use rates of Mexican-heritage adolescents and in the effectiveness of the prevention program (Yabiku, Kulis, Marsiglia, Lewin, Nieri, and Hussaini 2007).

These social environmental effects highlight the existence of unique protective culture-based ecosystems. Generic or culturally neutral interventions may not be able to utilize the strengths or identify and address the challenges and vulnerabilities of communities. Culturally grounded interventions, in contrast, can identify existing protective and risk factors and address them through culturally grounded content and the modality of the intervention.

Among youth who were already using alcohol and other drugs at baseline, the program was also effective in promoting reduced or discontinued alcohol use (Kulis, Nieri, Yabiku, Stromwall, and Marsiglia 2007). These results show not only how the diversity of groups translates to different responsiveness to interventions but also how culturally specific intervention that accounts for group diversity can be effective.

At present, SIRC researchers are analyzing the results of an additional randomized trial also funded by NIDA/NIH to test the effectiveness of an adapted fifth-grade version of *keepin' it REAL* with a large sample of Phoenix fifth-to-eighth graders. This version is also enhanced with lessons that address acculturation-related issues that may affect both immigrant and U.S.-born Latinos and other youths.

Based on the positive results of the original trial, the intervention was named a Model Program by the Substance Abuse and Mental Health Services Administration (SAMSHA). *Keepin' it REAL* was licensed by ASU and is available through ETR Associates. Although this evidence-based intervention was developed by and for Arizona youth, the program is now in use in thirty-five states and at several international sites.

Cost-Effectiveness of Prevention Efforts

The effectiveness of *keepin' it REAL* and other model programs shows that drug abuse is preventable. Prevention efforts can be cost-effective by reducing the demand for expensive treatment services and collateral costs to society, such as lost work productivity and addiction-related health problems (Kumpfer and Adler 2003). Although cost-benefit information is lacking for many programs, some research shows that benefit-cost ratios for programs that have had them calculated are in the range of 8:1 (Kim, Coletti, Crutchfield, Williams, and Howard 1995). One study estimated that prevention program participation saves society $840 for each student participant (Caulkins, Pacula, Paddock, and Chiesa 2004). National cost estimates for a universal prevention program are $150 per enrolled student (RAND 2002). At this rate, it would cost approximately $550 million annually to offer universal prevention programs to all 3.75 million seventh-grade students. This compares favorably to the $40 billion spent nationally on drug-control efforts (RAND 1999). Thus, a solid commitment to prevention makes for sound economic policy.

Methodological Issues: Intervention Research

Culturally grounded research is evolving and gaining additional scientific rigor, due in part to ongoing efforts to enhance the validity and generalizability of its findings. Listed below are some selected lessons learned and advances in the field.

- *PAR:* In order to start from the needs and strengths of the community, the research team followed a Participatory Action Research (PAR) approach, which supported the active engagement of community partners throughout the research process (Christens and Perkins 2008).
- *Significance:* The significance of the research question should be matched by scientifically sound research designs and methods. Following the NIH criteria for assessing scientific merit is recommended.
- *Rigor:* The research question and aims of the study should guide the choice of theory and methods, emphasizing theory-based designs that acknowledge culture and sociocultural contexts.
- *Mixed methods* appear to be the most appropriate choice for culturally grounded evidence-based studies. The use of qualitative and mixed methods allowed for the integration of culture into the design and for ecological and cultural validity (Castro and Coe 2007).
- *Geographic Information Systems (GIS):* Integrating the social contexts of the subjects, such as peers, family, school, and neighborhoods, was achieved through different methods, most prominently mapping and the use of other data sets such as the U.S. Census, school district data, and city and county data. The use of GIS allowed for the effective manipulation of diverse sources of data within a common geographic spatial area (Shekhar and Xiong 2008).
- *Sampling:* In order to control for many inherent biases that can be introduced from community-based samples, stratified sampling designs are recommended (Peterson et al. 2008).
- *Missing data.* Multiple analysis procedures can be conducted, guided by the main hypotheses and sub-hypotheses, as far as the statistical power of the sample is preserved. Using longitudinal designs adds challenges to the implementation of analysis protocols. The incorporation of techniques such as planned missing data has become more common in social work and allied professions' methodological training (Aiken, West, and Millsap 2008). Such techniques can help research teams control high attrition and mobility rates common in many community-based studies.
- *Training:* Conducting experimental designs in natural settings requires creativity and the commitment of a strong team. *Keepin' it REAL* involved many MSW-level students who served as school liaisons, keeping the experimental and control sites connected to the research team and engaged in all phases of the research process. The students benefited

greatly from such participation, which often was counted as part of their research training and internship requirements.

- *Cost:* Randomized trials are costly and complex, as they often take place in natural settings such as schools. The *keepin' it REAL* randomized trials and follow-up studies conducted to date have been made possible by different awards of the National Institute on Drug Abuse (NIDA) and the National Center on Minority Health and Health Disparities (NC-MHD) of the National Institutes of Health (NIH).

Social work researchers, in partnership with colleagues from other disciplines, have been advancing much-needed knowledge about evidence-based and culturally responsive interventions. It appears imperative that more research be conducted in this area in order to further connect the strengths of historically oppressed communities to innovative interventions supporting their well-being. Further support will enhance the research infrastructure in the schools of social work and continue to diversify their faculties and student bodies. Underrepresented communities need to be community partners, and their members need to be represented in the academy.

Discussion and Social Work Implications

The following conclusions and implications are offered as we move forward.

Demographic Growth

The rapid growth of the Latino and other minority youth populations is both a main challenge and a strong asset. Here is where investments in prevention are likely to have greater payoffs. Prevention efforts should span the spectrum of problem severity and involve both individual-focused and community-focused interventions.

Cultural Diversity

The nation's increasing ethnic, cultural, and language diversity raises the question of how the diverse needs of a diverse community can be met. Although immigration will decline in coming years, the Latino population will continue to increase nationwide (U.S. Census Bureau 2008). A related phenomenon is that the number of monolingual Spanish speakers and bilingual Spanish-English speakers is on the rise.

We must not only address the current need for services that include language diversity but also meet the professional pipeline challenge to ensure that we are educating large numbers of culturally competent service providers and culturally aware researchers. Fortunately, research shows that—at least in the case of substance-abuse prevention—a strict cultural match of program to person is not required for success. Instead, it is important that programs incorporate content from a range of cultures so that participants can find themselves and their culture represented within it. Thus, decision makers should seek programs that are not only evidence-based but also culturally appropriate for the targeted populations.

Cultural Resiliency

Ongoing research shows that recent immigrant youths and their families tend to be very resilient, and that many are able to effectively cope with adversity. Cultural norms and values and a strong connection to family and community appear to buffer youth from risk. Interventions that support those assets and assist youth with their acculturation process are needed in order to strengthen the protective effects of the culture of origin against drug abuse. Anti-immigrant and English-only movements tend to weaken connections to culture of origin and make large numbers of youth more vulnerable to risks.

Cultural Adaptation

Intervention developers are examining ways that efficacious prevention and treatment programs can be adapted for different cultural groups while retaining the core components that make them effective. Collaborations between community practitioners and researchers should be pursued to advance knowledge about adaptation. In the meantime, decision makers responsible for selecting programs for implementation should gather information on the origins of the program to determine whether cultural adaptations are needed, and on any adaptation made, so that their impact on program outcomes can be assessed.

Co-occurring Conditions

The relationship of substance abuse to other social problems, such as mental disorders, crime, and child-welfare problems, needs to be addressed. For example, there is a need to provide comprehensive treatment to youths with substance-abuse histories and high rates of comorbid psychiatric disorders and increased risky sexual behaviors. The complex relationships between drug abuse and other social and health problems means that efforts to address substance abuse in a vacuum should be discontinued and replaced with an integrated approach to substance abuse as a public health concern.

Methodology

Evidence-based practice needs to include prevention interventions grounded in the cultural strengths and assets of ethnic minority communities. Social work practitioner-researchers can play a key role in identifying those strengths and in designing and testing interventions that prevent the erosion of protective factors and the onset of risk factors. Such studies should be conducted in partnership with the targeted communities and in natural settings to increase their translational capacity.

Social work as a profession has well-established community partnerships and a professional ethos that positions it to take a leadership role in developing and testing evidence-based and culturally responsive interventions. The link between evidence-based research and culture will only grow stronger in the future. Professional commitment must be paired with rigorous methodological developments and training because our communities deserve the best available science.

References

Ashenberg Straussner, S. L. (2001). The role of social workers in the treatment of addictions: A brief history. *Journal of Social Work Practice in the Addictions 1* (1): 3–9.

Califano, J. A. (2007). *High society: How substance abuse ravages America and what to do about it.* New York: Public Affairs.

Cartwright, W. S. (2008). Economic costs of drug abuse: Financial, cost of illness, and services. *Journal of Substance Abuse Treatment 34* (2): 224–233.

Castro, F. G., Brook, J. S., Brook, D. W., and Rubenstone, E. (2006). Paternal, perceived maternal, and youth risk factors as predictors of your stage of substance use: A longitudinal study. *Journal of Addictive Diseases 25*:65–75.

Castro, F. G. and Coe, K. (2007). Traditions and alcohol use: A mixed-methods analysis. *Cultural Diversity and Ethnic Minority Psychology 13* (4): 269–284.

Caulkins, J. P., Pacula, R., Paddock, S., and Chiesa, J. (2004). What we can—and cannot—expect from school-based prevention. *Drug and Alcohol Review 23* (1): 79–87.

Chambers, R. A., Taylor, J. R., and Potenza, M. N. (2003). Developmental neurocircuitry of motivation in adolescence: A critical period of addiction vulnerability. *American Journal of Psychiatry 160* (6): 1041–1052.

Collins, P. H. (1998). *Fighting words: Black women and the search for justice.* Minneapolis: University of Minnesota Press.

Cowger, C. D. (1994). Assessing client strengths: Clinical assessment for client empowerment. *Social Work 39* (3): 262–268.

Cristens, B. and Perkins, D. D. (2008). Transdisciplinary multilevel action research to enhance ecological and pychopolitical validity. *Journal of Community Psychology 36* (2): 214–231.

De la Rosa, M. (2002). Acculturation and Latino adolescents' substance use: A research agenda for the future. *Substance Use and Misuse 37* (4): 429–456.

Donovan, J. E. (2007). Really underage drinkers: The epidemiology of children's alcohol use in the United States. *Prevention Science 8* (3): 192–205.

Epstein, I. (1995). Promoting reflective social work practice. In P. McCartt Hess and E. Mullen (Eds.), *Practitioner researcher partnerships*, 83–102. Washington, DC: NASW Press.

Flores, G., Bauchner, H., Feinstein, A. R., and Nguyen, U. S. (1999). The impact of ethnicity, family income, and parental education on children's health and use of health services. *American Journal of Public Health 89* (7): 1066–1071.

Hawkins, J. D. and Catalano, R. C. (2002). *Tools for community leaders: A guide for getting started.* http://ncadi.samhsa.gov/features/ctc/resources.aspx (accessed September 6, 2007).

Hecht, M. L., Marsiglia, F. F., Elek, E., Wagstaff, D., Kulis, S., Dustman, P., and Miller-Day, M. (2003). Culturally grounded substance use prevention: An evaluation of the *keepin' it REAL* curriculum. *Prevention Science 4* (4): 233–248.

Hernandez, M. T., Lemp, G. F., Castaneda, X., Sanchez, M. A., Auki, B. K., Tapia-Conyer, R., and Drake, M. V. (2004). HIV/AIDS among Mexican migrants and recent immigrants in California and Mexico. *Journal of Acquired Immune Deficiency Syndrome 37* (4): 203.

Holley, L., Kulis, S., Marsiglia, F. F., and Keith, V. (2006). Ethnicity versus ethnic identity: What predicts substance use norms and behaviors? *Journal of Social Work Practice in the Addictions 6* (3): 53–79.

Huey, S. J. and Polo, A. J. (2008). Evidence-based psychosocial treatments for ethnic minority youth. *Journal of Clinical Child and Adolescent Psychology 37* (1): 262–301.

Institute of Medicine. (1994). *Reducing risks for mental disorders: Frontiers for preventive intervention research.* Washington, DC: National Academy Press.

Johnston, L. D., O'Malley, P. M., Bachman, J. G., and Schulenberg, J. E. (2007). *Monitoring the future national survey results on drug use, 1975–2006. Volume I: Secondary school students* (NIH Publication No. 07–6205). Bethesda, MD: National Institute on Drug Abuse.

Kanna, B., Fersobe, S., Soni, A., and Michelen, W. (2008). Leading health risks, diseases and causes of mortality among Hispanics in the United States of America (USA). *The Internet Journal of Health 8* (1). http://www.ispub.com/vol8n1/risks.xml (accessed November 14, 2008).

Kim, S. W., Coletti, S. D., Crutchfiled, C. C., Williams, C., and Howard, J. (1995). Benefit-cost analysis of drug abuse prevention programs: A macroscopic approach. *Journal of Drug Education 25* (2): 111–127.

Knott, A. M., Corredoira, R., and Kimberly, J. (2008). Improving consistency and quality of service delivery: Implications for the addiction treatment field. *Journal of Substance Abuse Treatment 35* (2): 99–108.

Krovetz, M. (1999). Fostering resiliency: Expecting all students to use their minds and hearts well. Thousand Oaks, CA: Corwin Press.

Kulis, S., Marsiglia, F. F., Sicotte, D., Hohmann-Marriott, B., and Nieri, T. (2004). Majority rules: The effects of school ethnic composition on substance use by Mexican American adolescents. *Sociological Focus 37* (4): 373–393.

Kulis, S., Marsiglia, F. F., Elek-Fisk, E., Wagstaff, D., and Hecht, M. L. (2005). Mexican/Mexican American adolescents and *keepin' it REAL*: An evidence-based substance abuse prevention program. *Children and Schools 27* (3): 133–145.

Kulis, S., Marsiglia, F. F., and Nieri, T. (2006, August). Perceived discrimination and acculturation stress: Effects on substance use among Latino youth in the Southwest. Paper presented at the annual meeting of the American Sociological Association, Montreal.

Kulis, S., Yabiku, S., Marsiglia, F. F., Nieri, T., and Crossman, A. (2007). Differences by gender, ethnicity, and acculturation in the efficacy of the *keepin' it REAL* model prevention program. *Journal of Drug Education 37* (2): 123–144.

Kulis, S., Nieri, T., Yabiku, S., Stromwall, L., and Marsiglia, F. F. (2007). Promoting reduced and discontinued substance use among adolescent substance users: Effectiveness of a universal prevention program. *Prevention Science 8* (1): 35–49.

Kulis, S., Marsiglia, F. F., and Nieri, T. (2008, October). Relative influence of perceived ethnic discrimination and acculturation stress on substance use among Latino youth in the Southwest. Paper presented at the annual meeting of the American Public Health Association. San Diego, CA.

Kulis, S., Marsiglia, F. F., Chase-Lingard, E., Nieri, T., and Nagoshi, J. (2008). Gender identity and substance use among students in two high schools in Monterrey, Mexico. *Drug and Alcohol Dependence 95* (3): 258–268.

Kumpfer, K. L. and Adler, S. (2003). Dissemination of research-based family interventions for the prevention of substance abuse. In Z. Sloboda and W. J. Bukoski (Eds.), *Handbook of drug abuse prevention: Theory, science, and practice*, 75–100. New York: Kluwer Academic/Plenum Publishers.

Liddle, H. A. (2004). Family-based therapies for adolescent alcohol and drug use: Research contributions and future research needs. *Addiction 99* (Supp. 12): 76–92.

Lopez, C., Bergren, M., and Painter, S. G. (2008). Latino disparities in child mental health. *Journal of Child and Adolescent Psychiatric Nursing 21* (3): 137–145.

Malik-Kane, K. and Vishr, C. (2008). Health and prisoner reentry: How physical, mental, and substance abuse conditions shape the process of reintegration. Research Report. Washington, DC: Urban Institute.

Marsiglia, F. F., Kulis, S., and Hecht, M. L. (2001). Ethnic labels and ethnic identity as predictors of drug use and drug exposure among middle school students in the Southwest. *Journal of Research on Adolescence 11* (1): 21–48.

Marsiglia, F. F. and Waller, M. (2002). Language preference and drug use among Southwestern Mexican American middle school students. *Children and Schools 25* (3): 145–158.

Marsiglia, F. F., Miles, B. W., Dustman, P., and Sills, S. (2003). Ties that protect: An ecological perspective on Latino/a urban pre-adolescent drug use. *Journal of Ethnic and Cultural Diversity in Social Work 11* (3/4): 191–220.

Marsiglia, F. F., Kulis, S., Wagstaff, D. A., Elek, E., and Dran, D. (2005). Acculturation status and substance use prevention with Mexican and Mexican American youth. *Journal of Social Work Practice in the Addictions 5* (1/2): 85–111.

Marsiglia, F. F. and Kulis, S. (2008). Oppression, diversity and change: Culturally grounded social work. Chicago: Lyceum Books.

Midford, R. (2008). Is this the path to effective prevention? *Addiction 103* (7): 1169–1170.

Miranda, J., Bernal, G., Lau, A., Kohn, L., Hwang, W. C., and LaFramboise, T. (2005). State of the science on psychosocial interventions for ethnic minorities. *Annual Review of Clinical Psychology 1*:113–142.

Montoya, I. D., Atkinson, J., and McFaden, W. C. (2003). Best characteristics of adolescent gateway drug prevention programs. *Journal of Addictions Nursing 14* (2): 75–83.

Offord, D. (2000). Selection of levels of prevention. *Addictive Behaviors 25* (6): 833–842.

Ojeda, V. J., Patterson, T. L., and Strathdee, S. A. (2008). The influence of perceived risk to health and immigration-related characteristics of substance abuse among Latino and other immigrants. *American Journal of Public Health 98* (5): 862–868.

RAND. (2002) *What are the true benefits of school-based drug prevention programs?* Drug Policy Research Center Research Brief. http://www.rand.org/pubs/research_briefs/2005/RB6009.pdf (accessed September 12, 2008).

Resnicow, K., Soler, R., Braithwaite, R., Ahluwalia, J., and Butler, J. (2000). Cultural sensitivity in substance use prevention. *Journal of Community Psychology 28* (3): 271–290.

Sale, E., Sambrano, S., Springer, J. F., Peña, C., Pan, W., and Kasim, R. (2005). Family protection and prevention of alcohol use among Hispanic youth at high risk. *American Journal of Community Psychology 36* (3/4): 195–205.

Shekhar, S. and Xiong, H. (Eds.) (2008). *Encyclopedia of geographic information systems (GIS).* New York: Springer

Smokowski, P. R., Rose, R., and Bacallao, M. L. (2008). Acculturation and Latino family processes: How cultural involvement, biculturalism, and acculturation gaps influence family dynamics. *Family relations 57* (3): 295–308.

Sobeck, J., Abbey, A., Agius, E., Clinton, M., and Harrison, K. (2000). Predicting early adolescent substance use: Do risk factors differ depending on age of onset? *Journal of Substance Abuse 11* (1): 89–102.

Stoffel, V. C. and Moyers, P. A. (2004). An evidence-based and occupational perspective of interventions for persons with substance-use disorders. *American Journal of Occupational Therapy 58* (5): 570–586.

Trimble, J. (1990–1991). Ethnic specification, validation prospects, and the future of drug use research. *The International Journal of the Addictions 25* (2): 149–170.

U.S. Census Bureau (2008). Factors for Features: Populations Estimates. Press Release July 9. Washington, DC: U.S. Census Bureau.

Valdez, A., Neaigus, A., and Kaplan, C. D. (2008). The influence of family and peer risk networks on drug use practices and other risks among Mexican American noninjecting heroin users. *Journal of Contemporary Ethnography 37* (1): 79–107.

Voisine, S., Parsai, M., Marsiglia, F. F., Kulis, S., and Nieri, T. (2008). Parental monitoring and adolescent substance use among Mexican/Mexican American adolescents in the Southwest United States. *Families in Society 89* (2): 264–273.

Winters, K. C. (2003). Assessment of alcohol and other drug use behaviors among adolescents. In National Institute of Alcohol Abuse and Alcoholism, *Assessing Alcohol Problems,* 101–123. Bethesda, MD: NIH Publications.

Yabiku, S., Kulis, S., Marsiglia, F. F., Lewin, B., Nieri, T., and Hussaini, S. (2007). Neighborhood effects on the efficacy of a program to prevent youth alcohol use. *Substance Use and Misuse 42*:65–87.

10 | Development of Intervention Models with "New Overwhelmed Clients"

June G. Hopps, Tony B. Lowe, and Ollie G. Christian

SOCIAL WORKERS HAVE historically been in a unique position to develop, confirm, and verify knowledge for practice with clients or client systems. Yet despite advancements in research and acknowledgment of poverty, relatively little has been done with "overwhelmed clients." The relationship between practice and research can perhaps best be described as ambivalent. For social work to move ahead, we must attend to growing questions about both the profession's domain and the efficacy of its knowledge base (Fischer 1973; Haworth 1984; Hopps and Pinderhughes 1986; Hopps, Pinderhughes, and Shanker 1955).

Colleagues at Boston College Graduate School of Social Work began to explore practice effectiveness with very oppressed inner-city clients in the Boston, Massachusetts area. The initial project was funded by the Boston Foundation. At that time, we reported that:

> clinical social work literature was not optimistic about successful interventions with this client population, citing numerous reasons for this state of affairs: poor or insufficient ideas on theories as guides to practice intervention; the use of micro-system strategies—clinical intervention—to address problems stemming from macro-system dynamics—poverty;

the use of methods based on stances and values that perceive this clientele as deviant, pathological, and incompetent; and the fact that research capabilities for assessing interventions are still emerging. (Hopps, Pinder-hughes, and Shanker 1995:4)

This paper reports a "design and development" approach (Rothman and Thomas 1994) to refining effective interventions with such neglected populations.

Overwhelmed Clients in the Inner City

For the purpose of the initial project, "overwhelmed clients" were defined as those clients suffering with multidimensional problems (i.e., physical, emotional, psychological, employment, family, and economic) reinforced by social factors (i.e., race, gender, class, poverty) that not only justified their marginal status but also made them almost powerless and unable to change their level of social functioning. To determine when the social work and mental health establishment were on target in helping to meet the needs of these overwhelmed clients, we examined a random sample of 178 cases drawn from more than 2,000 closed client files. The goal was to identify the interventions and worker characteristics that together operate to move clients to a higher level of functioning, characterized by greater self-esteem, greater sense of mastery, and greater self-sufficiency. Operational definitions of each of these outcomes were developed and utilized in the research. This sample is larger than those in most other studies (usually 50 to 100 cases), thus making it more generalizable. This method permitted researchers to focus on outcomes of intervention rather than merely on the intervention process and worker activity, which is not only timely, but vital given national resource constraints.

Demographics

Participants consisted mostly of women (58 percent) under the age of 19 (68 percent) and single (58 percent). The majority were people of color (African Americans and Hispanics), although Asians and Caucasians used services. Slightly more than 70 percent were unemployed. Women were two times more likely to use services than men. Most clients had some high school education, about 48 percent had completed between 10 and 12 years of education and 15 percent had completed 13 or more years. Clients had learned to control births (e.g., an average of three children). Those delivering service were primarily (80 percent) professionally educated (i.e., MSW, Psy.D, Ph.D., M.D.) and of these, 50 percent were MSWs.

Interventions

The results showed that among interventions, assessment, advocacy, individual, family, and group work were effective strategies. In fact, group work was found to be the most effective approach for alleviating psychosocial distress. In addition,

> What we found in the research . . . is that clinical services with over-
> whelmed clients are effective. When these services are offered by caring,
> flexible practitioners who value education and hold their clients to high
> expectations and believe that they can change and free themselves from
> the entrapping subculture, clients can move to higher levels of function-
> ing. In fact, the best predictor of successful client change is flexible and
> caring practitioners who in their practice expose clients to high goals and
> expect them to rise to the occasion. The clients, 71 percent of whom pre-
> sented with multiple problems, are suffering not solely from psychological
> problems, but from multiple problems—joblessness, drug abuse, domestic
> and street violence—that reinforce one another. The etiology of problems
> is not always personal and psychological, but communal and developmen-
> tal compounded by systems failures. Most clients in this study received
> shorter-term rather than longer-term service, with nearly 70 percent of
> cases terminated within two years. Thus, although most clients did have
> mental health services, they were not receiving treatment for serious per-
> sonality disorders. (Hopps, Pinderhughes, and Shankar 1995:3)

In a word, clinical services can be provided effectively to overwhelmed clients if delivered by competent, adaptive, and compassionate professionals
who hold clients to *high expectations*.

> Clinical work nevertheless is compromised by environment detractors—
> drugs, violence, communities that do not provide adequate nurturing,
> and national policies that do not permit a sufficient range of programs
> and resources to address clients' multiple problems. In fact no agency
> from which the sample was drawn manifested programs and activities
> focused on community building and such changes as safer streets and
> improved environments. Philosophically, agencies may not have tuned
> in to the significance of paid work in the lives of their clients. Practically,
> perhaps they understand all too well the powerlessness of clinicians to
> have an impact on the employment picture. (Hopps, Pinderhughes, and
> Shanker 1995:4)

The circular reinforcing process of these political, economic, and social forces creates a sense of powerlessness that undermines the very skills that are so necessary for coping with them. Joblessness in a work-oriented society is a major barrier to the development of effective coping. It creates serious deprivation since work serves as a psychological and developmental organizer, creating needed structure for both individuals and communities. . . . Too often contributions to lack of success in outcomes with overwhelmed clients lie in the solutions we have fashioned, both in our national policies and intervention strategies and processes. (5)

Based on the findings, the researchers advocated a justice-based model calling for reforms in physical and behavioral health, income maintenance, and major community initiatives, including better housing, safer streets, crime fighting, and community-based jobs.

A New Overwhelmed Population: African Americans with Alzheimer's Disease

The aim of the new initiative is to replicate the 1995 study. The researchers propose to investigate a new group of overwhelmed people, African American seniors with Alzheimer's disease. In contrast to the existing study, the new one will focus on a cohort group that resides in rural Southern communities. This population is deserving of attention, since few efforts document their mental health service use and many are long-term sufferers of injustice and poverty—in a word, oppression. In one effort to document service use, investigators found that over half (58 percent) of "older African Americans with mental health disorders were not receiving care" (Black et al. 1997, as cited by DHHS 2001:65).

At the turn of the twentieth century, 89 percent of African Americans were forced to live in the depths of poverty and in legal subservience (DHHS 2001). African American elders are three times more likely to experience poverty than whites (Ross 2000a, as cited in Kaiser Family Foundation Report). Because black women have greater longevity than black men, single women are particularly vulnerable to poverty and its related disadvantages of poor health care, diet, nutrition, housing, and transportation (DHHS 2001). The impact of stress due to serious economic conditions and inadequate health care means that the incidence of disease will increase (Ross 2000a), and one growing area is Alzheimer's disease.

For African Americans, etiological differences in dementia are recognized at the clinical, molecular, and epidemiological levels. Alzheimer's is most common cause of dementia among African Americans (Auchus 1997; Froehlich,

Bogardus, and Inouye 2001), and African Americans have higher rates than other groups (Folstein et al. 1991; Heyman et al. 1991; Schoenber et al. 1985). Such reports should be carefully reviewed because measurement bias could undergird these differences (Mast, Fitgerald, Steinberg, MacNeil, and Lichtenberg 2001; Fillenbaum et al. 1990; Froehlich 2001). Two studies, for example, found high false positive rates among widely applied diagnostic tools (Anthony, Le-Resche, Nias, Von Korff, and Folstein 1982; Fillenbaum, Heyman, Williams, Prosnitz, and Burchett 1990). Molecularly, studies suggest the presence of a genetic risk factor, an apolipoprotein E (APOE)-4 allele, common among whites but not among African Americans (Tang, Stern, Marder, et al. 1998). Given this finding, the elevated prevalence of the disease reported among older African Americans, who lack this genetic risk factor, is paradoxical. Further investigation is needed to understand the relationship of genetic and environmental determinants. At the community level, a recent investigation of the prevalence of dementia in a multiethnic community in south Florida found that African American men and women suffered higher rates of dementia than either Cuban or white men and women (Demirovic et al. 2003).

Demographic factors are also associated with risk of Alzheimer's disease. First, there is a significant correlation between age and disease rate: as seniors grow older, dramatic increases in risks are reported (156). For instance, between 65 and 85 years of age, the rate multiples almost eighteenfold. Second, *prima facie* evidence suggests gender may be a differentiating factor since higher rates are reported among women. This may be explained by the confounding effect of age, since across racial and ethnic groups, women live longer than men. Third, level of education is a factor because elders with less education have higher rates of dementia (Guland et al. 1997). Questions about the potential of "ethno-racial bias" in the assessment process (Li et al. 1989; Murden et al. 1991) have been raised, namely, the suggestive application of diagnostic exams (e.g., Mini-Mental Health Status) where interpretations are vulnerable to bias.

Health-related factors are also associated with risk. Studies suggest that the 20 percent of those suffering from Alzheimer's disease may also have a co-occurring depressive disorder (Burn et al. 1990; Lyetsos et al. 2000). One study, in a review of closed charts, found a number of health problems associated with race (Zamrini, Parrish, Parsons, and Harrell 2004). Blacks with Alzheimer's disease were more likely to have higher rates of hypertension, while whites were more likely to have atrial fibrillation, cancer, coronary artery disease, high cholesterol, and gastrointestinal disease. Other health problems also associated with Alzheimer's include head injury, stroke, and Down syndrome.

Research studies, coupled with practice efforts, are shedding new light on emerging effective treatments. Although no known cure exists for Alzheimer's, a number of medications (Reminyl, Exelon, Aricept, and Cognex) are currently available to treat mild to moderate forms of the disease. For the severe forms, Namenda has been found to delay progression of some symptoms (DHHS 2004a). A recent investigation suggests that African American clients and those with a milder baseline agitation/aggression may respond better to depression treatment (Steinberg et al. 2003). These findings have broad clinical implications in that they highlight the need to develop racially and culturally based customized evaluation, prevention, and treatment protocols for African American and other clients (Stephenson 2001).

What are the theoretical approaches, intervention repertoire, and other strategies used by social work/mental health professionals in serving a cohort of rural African American seniors with Alzheimer's disease? Given this growing overwhelmed population, research is critical to developing validated knowledge for practice advancement.

References

American Psychiatric Association. (2000). *Diagnostic and statistical manual of mental disorders,* 4th ed. Washington, DC: American Psychiatric Press.

Auchus, A. P. (1997). Dementia in urban black outpatients: Initial experience at Emory Satellite Clinics. *Gerontologist 37*:25–29.

Anthony, J. C., LeResche, L., Nias, U., Von Korff, M. R., and Folstein, M. F. (1982). Limits of the Mini-Mental State as a screening test for dementia and delirium among hospital patients. *Psychological Medicine 12*:397–408.

Austin, B.W. and Young, A. J. (1998). Twenty-first century leadership in the African American community. In F. Hesselbein, M. Goldsmith, R. Beckhard, and R. Schubert (Eds.), *The community of the future,* 199–212. New York: The Peter Drucker Foundation for Nonprofit Management.

Bird, T. D., Sumi, S. M., Nemens, E. J, and Nochlin, D. (1989). Phenotypic heterogeneity in familial Alzheimer's disease: A study of 24 kindreds. *Annual of Neurology 25* (1): 12–25.

Black, B. S., Rabins, P. V., German, P., McGuire, M. and Roca, R. (1997). Need and unmet need for mental health care among elderly public housing residents. *The Gerontologist 37*:6717–6728.

Blythe, B., Tripodi, T., and Briar, S. (1994). *Direct practice research in human service agencies.* New York: Columbia University Press.

Briar, S. and Miller, H. (1971). *Problems and issues in social casework.* New York: Columbia University Press.

Burn, A., Jacoby, R., and Levy, R. (1990). Psychiatric phenomena in Alzheimer's Disease III: Disorders of mood. *British Journal of Psychiatry 157*:81–86.

Demirovic, J., Prineas R., Loewenstein D., Bean J., Duara R., Sevush S., and Szapocznik, J. (2003). Prevalence of dementia in three ethnic groups: The South Florida program on aging and health. *Annual of Epidemiology 13* (6): 472–478.

Federal Interagency Forum on Aging-Related Statistics. (2004). *Older Americans 2004: Key indicators of well-being*. Washington, DC: U.S. Government Printing Office.

Fillenbaum, G., Heyman, A., Williams, K., Prosnitz, B., and Burchett, B. (1990). Sensitivity and specificity of standardized screens of cognitive impairment and dementia among elderly black and white community residents. *Journal of Clinical Epidemiology 43*:651–660.

Fischer, J. (1973). Is casework still effective: A review. *Social Work 18*:5–20.

Folstein, M. F., Spear Bassett, S., Anthony, J. F., et al. (1991). Dementia: Case ascertainment in a community survey. *Journal of Gerontology Series A: Biological Science and Medical Science 46*:132–138.

Froehlich, T. E., Bogardus, S. T., Jr., and Inouye, S. (2001). Dementia and race: Are there differences between African Americans and Caucasians? *Journal of American Geriatrics Society 46*:477–484.

Guland, B., Wilder, D., Lantigua, R., Mayeux, R., Stern, Y., Chen, J., Cross, P., and Killeffer, E. (1997). Differences in rates of dementia between ethno-racial groups. In L. G. Martin and B. J. Soldo (Eds.), *Racial and ethnic differences in the health of older Americans*, 233–269. Washington, DC: National Academy Press.Haworth, G. (1984). Social work research, practice and paradigms. *Social Service Review 58* (3): 343–357.

Heyman, A., Fillenbaum, G., Prosnitz, B., et al. (1991). Estimated prevalence of dementia among elderly black and white community residents. *Archives of Neurology 48*:594–598.

Hopps, J.G. (2000). Social Work: A contextual profession. In J.G. Hopps and R. Morris (Eds.), *Social work at the millennium: Critical reflections on the future of the profession*, 3–17. New York: Free Press.

Hopps, J.G. and Pinderhuges, E. (1999). *Group work with overwhelmed clients*. New York: Free Press.

Hopps, J. G., Pinderhughes, E., and Shanker, R. (1995). *The power to care: Clinical practice effectiveness with overwhelmed clients*. New York: Free Press.

Geismar, L. L. (1972). *Early supports for family life: A social work experiment*. Metuchen, NJ: Scarecrow Press.

Li, G., Shen, Y. C., Chen, C. H., Zhau, Y. W., and Lu, M. (1989). An epidemiological survey of age-related dementia in an urban area of Beijing. *Acta Psychiatrica Scandinavica 79*:557–563.

Lyketsos, C. G., Steinberg, M., Tschanz, J., Norton, M., Steffens, C., and Breitner, J. C. S. (2000). Mental and behavioral disturbances in dementia: Findings from the Cache County Study on memory in aging. *The American Journal of Psychiatry 157*:708–714.

Mast, B. T., Fitzgerald, J., Steinberg, J., MacNeil, S. E., and Lichtenberg, P. A. (2001). Effective screening for Alzheimer's disease among older African Americans. *The Clinical Neuropsychologist 15* (2): 196–202.

Morris, R. (2000). Social work's century of evolution as a profession, choices made, opportunities lost: From the individual and society to the individual. In J. G. Hopps and R. Morris (Eds.), Social work at the millennium: Critical reflections on the future of the profession, 42–69. New York: Free Press.

Mullen, E. F. and Dumpson, J. R. (Eds.) (1972). *Evaluation of social work interventions*. San Francisco: Jossey-Bass.

O'Hare, T. (2005). *Evidence-based practice for social workers: An interdisciplinary approach* Chicago: Lyceum Books.

Reid, W. J. (1994). Research and evaluation. In F. G. Reamer (Ed.), *The foundations of social work knowledge*. New York: Columbia University Press.

———. (1995). Research overview. In R. L. Edward and J. G. Hopps (Eds.), *Encyclopedia of social work*, 19th ed., 2040–2054. Washington, DC: NASW Press.

Reid, W. J. and Hanrahan, P. (1992). Recent evaluation of social work: Grounds for optimism. *Social Work 27*:328–340.

Ross, H. (2000a). Growing older: Health issues for minorities. In *Closing the gap*, a newsletter of the Office of Minority Health, U.S. Department of Health and Human Services. Washington, DC: U.S. Government Printing Office.

———. (2000b). Recognizing and treating depression in older adults. In *Closing the gap*, a newsletter of the Office of Minority Health, U.S. Department of Health and Human Services. Washington, DC: U.S. Government Printing Office.

Rubin, A. (1985). Practice effectiveness: More grounds for optimism. *Social Work* (Nov.–Dec. 1985): 469–476.

Schoenberg, B. S., Anderson, D. W., and Haerer, A. F. (1985). Severe dementia: Prevalence and clinical features in a biracial U.S. population. *Archives of Neurology 42*:740–743.

Segal, S. P. (1972). Research on the outcome of social work therapeutic interventions: A review of the literature. *Journal of Health and Social Behavior, 13*, 3–17.

Stephenson, J. (2001). Racial barriers may hamper diagnosis: Care of patients with Alzheimer's disease. *Journal of the American Medical Association 286* (7): 779.

Sze, W. C. and Hopps, J. G. (1977). *Evaluation and accountability in human service program*. Cambridge, MA: Schenckman.

Tang, M. X., Maestre, G., Tsai, W. Y., et al. (1996). Relative risk of Alzheimer's disease and age-at-onset distributions based on APOE genotypes among elderly African Americans, Caucasians, and Hispanics in New York City. *American Journal of Human Genetics 58*:574–584.

Tang, M. X., Stern, Y., Marder, K., et al. (1998). The APOE-4 allele risk of Alzheimer's disease among African Americans, whites and Hispanics. *Journal of the American Medical Association 279*:751–755.

Thornton, K. A. and Tuck, I. (2000). Promoting the mental health of elderly African Americans: A case illustration. *Archives of Psychiatric Nursing 14* (4): 191–198.

U.S. Department of Health and Human Services. (2001). *Mental health: Culture, race, and ethnicity. A supplement to mental health: A report of the surgeon general*. Office of the Surgeon General, Substance Abuse and Mental Health Service Administration. Washington, DC: U.S. Government Printing Office.

———. (2004a). Alzheimer's disease medications: Fact sheet. *National Institute on Aging and National Institute of Health Publication No. 03–3431*. Washington, DC: U.S. Government Printing Office.

———. (2004b). *Home safety for people with Alzheimer's disease*. National Institute of Health, National Institute on Aging, and Alzheimer's Disease Education and Referral Center. Washington, DC: U.S. Government Printing Office.

Williams, E. and Barton, P. (2003/04). Successful support groups for African Americans caregivers. *Generations* 81–83.

Wood, K. M. (1978). Casework effectiveness: A new look at the research evidence. *Social Work 23*:437–458.

Zamrini, E., Parrish, J., Parsons, D., and Harrell, L. E. (2004). Medical co-morbidity in black and white patients with Alzheimer's disease. *Southern Medical Journal 97* (1): 2–6.

11 | Pulling Together Research Studies to Inform Social Work Practice

The Science of Research Synthesis

Julia H. Littell

OUR EMPIRICAL KNOWLEDGE BASE is cumulative, always evolving, and inevitably incomplete. As results of new studies become available, we can assess their contributions to existing knowledge. New studies can support, contradict, or modify inferences based on previous research. Inferences that rest on a careful synthesis of results across studies are generally stronger than those based solely on a single study or on a subset of relevant studies. A careful synthesis can also raise new questions and highlight current gaps in knowledge. Thus, the synthesis of results across studies is essential for evidence-informed practice and for advances in practice research. Since empirical knowledge is not static, we need periodic syntheses of ever-expanding bodies of evidence.

In 1998, Dr. William J. Reid envisioned a worldwide effort to provide continually updated evidence to inform social work practice and policy. Two years later, the international Campbell Collaboration began to do just that. In the years that followed, much has been learned about the promise and problems of research synthesis.

In this chapter, I discuss methods of research synthesis and their applications to practice research in general, and to questions about the effects (and effectiveness) of interventions. I describe the work of the Campbell Collaboration and its older sister, the Cochrane Collaboration. Finally, I contrast traditional and systematic reviews, using examples from my own syntheses of research on a popular model program.

The Practice of Research Synthesis

Research synthesis is the process of locating, assessing, and summarizing a body of research. Traditional research reviews are narrative summaries of convenience samples of published studies. Traditional reviews are generally conducted as follows: first, reviewers seek pertinent studies, often using an electronic keyword search in one or more bibliographic databases such as PsycINFO or Social Work Abstracts. The searches can be limited to studies published in peer-reviewed journals. Second, reviewers scan titles and abstracts, reading those studies that seem relevant to the topic or question at hand. Third, reviewers write a narrative summary of the studies and their results. Finally, they draw conclusions about similarities and differences among the studies, central patterns, and the overall weight of the evidence.

The traditional review process is rarely transparent to the reader, who cannot tell whether reviewers selected studies based on their results or on some other factor. Further, it is often not clear how results of multiple studies were processed and synthesized to arrive at overall conclusions. Traditional reviews have well-known limitations related to sampling and analysis methods.

Sampling Methods

Traditional reviews are based on unspecified "samples" of studies (e.g., convenience samples of published studies) that may not represent all of the credible research conducted on a particular topic. Many reviewers report the methods they used to locate studies but do not explain how they decided which studies to include and exclude. Thus, readers may be unable to tell whether or not studies were selected because they supported a favored position or on some other basis.

Traditional Method of Analysis

Reviewers rarely explain how they sifted evidence and drew conclusions about overall trends or variations in a body of research. The synthesis of results of multiple studies involves several complex operations that are not performed easily with "cognitive algebra." Studies show that, left to their own devices, reviewers can reach conclusions influenced by trivial properties of research reports (Bushman and Wells 2001).

To address this issue, some reviewers use a process called "vote counting." They sort original studies into two or three categories according to their results, then tally the number of studies with significant positive results, negative results, and null findings (sometimes the negative and null categories are combined). Vote counting offers some advantages over unspecified synthesis methods, because it is more transparent. However, vote counting usually relies on tests of statistical significance in the original studies. Because such tests are heavily influenced by sample size, clinically significant results will be missed in small studies (and those that lack sufficient statistical power to detect meaningful effects) and trivial results will appear to be statistically significant in very large studies. Thus, a vote count is a tally that has no inherent meaning. Carlton and Strawderman (1996) showed that vote counting can lead to the wrong conclusions.

Limitations of Traditional Reviews

Unless the methods of selecting and synthesizing research results are explicit, readers cannot tell whether the review is a comprehensive and fair appraisal of the evidence. Gibbs (2003) noted that practitioners should be able to rely on published research reviews for unbiased syntheses of relevant evidence, but the reviews rarely measure up to these expectations. In fact, traditional narrative reviews are vulnerable to several sources and types of bias.

Sources of Bias in Research Synthesis

Research syntheses can be affected by biases that arise in the original studies, in the reporting and dissemination of results, and in the review process itself. These sources of potential biases are explored next.

Research Design and Implementation

Owing to design and implementation problems, studies can systematically overestimate or underestimate phenomena, which makes their conclusions potentially invalid (Shadish, Cook, and Campbell 2002). In treatment outcome research, some of these problems include selection bias, differential attrition, and experimenter expectancy effects. Related to experimenter expectancies, "allegiance effects" may appear when interventions are studied by their advocates (Luborsky et al. 1999). A careful synthesis of evidence requires critical assessment of the qualities of component studies and the strength and credibility of inferences that can be drawn from them.

Publication and Dissemination Processes

We expect the peer-review process to favor high-quality studies; we do not expect it to introduce bias in terms of the results. Publication bias occurs when the published literature is not representative of all the high-quality studies in a field. A compelling body of literature demonstrates the persistence of publication and dissemination biases in the empirical literature across many fields, including medicine, education, and social science (Begg 1994; Dickerson 2005; Torgerson 2006). The sources of these biases are complex and, while they arise in various ways, publication and dissemination biases lead in the same direction—that is, they tend to inflate estimates of treatment effects. Reasons for this are as follows.

Investigators are more likely to report results that are statistically significant and results that confirm their hypotheses (Dickersin 2005). Negative and null results are apt to be under-reported, i.e., presented with missing information when they are reported at all (Chan, Hróbjartsson, Haar, Gøtzsche, and Altman 2004). Although investigators are the primary source of publication bias (Dickinson 2005), peer reviewers may be biased against manuscripts that counter their expectations or theoretical perspectives (Mahoney 1977). Studies with significant positive results are much more likely to be accepted for publication than studies with null or negative results (for reviews, see Dickersin 2005; Scherer, Langenberg, and von Elm 2007). After acceptance for publication, studies with significant positive results are published more rapidly (Hopewell, Clarke, Stewart, and Tierney 2001) and cited more often (Egger and Smith 1998) than published papers with null or negative results.

The selective reporting, publication, dissemination, and citation of statistically significant results make them more visible and available than other, equally valid findings. These biases are likely to affect research synthesis unless reviewers take precautions to avoid them (Rothstein, Sutton, and Bornstein 2005).

Research Synthesis

The review process is most vulnerable to bias when reviewers sample studies selectively, rely only on published studies, fail to consider variations in study qualities that may affect their validity, and selectively report results. The same biases that can affect primary research may be present in a research synthesis. For example, allegiance effects appear in research syntheses sponsored by companies that have a financial stake in the outcome (Jørgensen, Hilden, and Gøtzsche 2006).

The same principles used to minimize bias in primary research apply to the synthesis of research findings. For example, the development of a public, *a priori* plan for research synthesis limits reviewers' freedom to selectively report results. The introduction of intersubjectivity (inter-rater agreement) can reduce bias and error at many steps in the research and review processes.

The Science of Research Synthesis

Systematic approaches to reviewing research are not new, nor did they originate in the biomedical sciences (Chalmers et al. 2002; Petticrew and Roberts 2006). Meta-analysis, which is the quantitative synthesis of results across studies, was initiated early in the twentieth century and became a regular component in the literature on psychology in the 1970s. From the mid-1980s and onward, Larry Hedges, Ingram Olkin, and others developed the statistical underpinnings of meta-analysis (Hedges and Olkin 1985). Then Harris Cooper cast meta-analysis as one step in a scientific approach to research synthesis. Cooper (1998) compared the process of research synthesis to the process of primary research, noting that both followed the same basic steps (Cooper and Hedges 1994).

The term "systematic review" refers to "a process involving measures to control biases in research synthesis" (Chalmers, Hedges, and Cooper 2002:16). Systematic reviews follow basic steps in the research process to identify, analyze, and synthesize results of previous studies. They use explicit and replicable procedures to minimize bias at each step (Higgins and Green 2008; Littell, Corcoran, and Pillai 2008).

Transparent Intentions and Methods

A protocol for the review should be developed in advance, specifying the central objectives and methods. Steps and decisions are carefully documented so readers can follow and evaluate reviewers' methods (Moher et al. 1999). Conflicts of interest and sponsorship arrangements are disclosed, because these issues can affect reviewers' decisions and conclusions (e.g., Jørgensen, Hilden, and Gøtzsche 2006).

Explicit Inclusion/Exclusion Criteria

Reviewers specify, in advance, the study designs, populations, interventions, comparisons, and outcome measures that will be included and excluded. Reasons for exclusion are documented for each excluded study. This limits reviewers' freedom to select studies on the basis of their results, or on some other basis. Systematic reviews have clear boundaries so they can be replicated or extended by others.

Search Strategies

Reviewers use a systematic approach and a variety of sources to try to locate all potentially material studies. In collaboration with information retrieval specialists, they identify electronic databases and develop appropriate key-

word strings to use in each database. Hand-searching of the contents of journals is often needed to find eligible studies that are not properly indexed
(Hopewell, Clarke, Lefebvre, and Scherer 2006). Reviewers must make vigorous efforts to locate the "gray literature" (unpublished and hard-to-find
studies), to avoid the "file drawer problem" (Hopewell, McDonald, Clarke,
and Egger 2006; Rothstein et al. 2005). This involves personal contacts with
experts, along with scanning conference abstracts and reference lists. The
search process and its results are carefully documented.

Inter-Rater Agreement on All Key Decisions

Two or more raters review all citations and abstracts. Decisions on full-text
retrieval, study inclusion/exclusion, and study coding are made by at least
two independent raters who compare notes, resolve differences, and document reasons for their decisions.

Systematic Extraction of Data from Original Studies

Raters extract data from study reports onto paper or electronic coding forms.
These data are then available for use in the analysis and synthesis of results.
The data forms provide a bridge between the primary research studies and
the research synthesis, and a historical record of reviewers' decisions (Higgins
and Green 2008).

Analysis of Study Qualities

Aspects of research methodology that relate to the validity of a study's conclusions are assessed individually. Reviewers are encouraged to use separate
assessments of different study qualities, instead of an overall study-quality
score (Littell et al. 2008). Campbell's threats-to-validity approach is a useful
framework, as is the assessment of potential sources and types of bias in the
primary studies (Higgins and Green 2008). These assessments may be useful
in analysis and interpretation of data on treatment effects.

Analysis of Study Results

Study findings are represented as effect sizes whenever possible. Effect size
refers to a group of statistics that express the strength and direction of
an effect or relationship between variables. Most effect sizes are standardized to facilitate synthesis of results across studies. Examples include the
standardized mean difference (the difference between two group means
divided by their pooled standard deviation), odds ratio, risk ratio, and correlation coefficient. Raters document the data and formulas used for effect
size calculations.

Synthesis of Results

Transparent methods are used to combine results across studies. Quantitative methods lend themselves to this purpose. Meta-analysis includes a set of statistical techniques used to estimate combined effect sizes, account for variations in the precision of effect size estimates drawn from different samples, explore potential moderators of effects, and examine potential effects of publication bias (Lipsey and Wilson 2001; Littell et al. 2008). It is important to note that some meta-analyses are not embedded in systematic reviews: for example, a meta-analysis of a convenience sample of published studies is not a systematic review. Systematic reviews do not always include meta-analysis.

Reporting Results

Moher and colleagues (1999) developed the Quality of Reporting of Meta-analyses (QUOROM) statement to improve reports on systematic reviews and meta-analyses. The QUOROM statement includes a checklist of items that should be reported and a flow diagram for authors to use to describe how studies were identified, screened, and selected.

Updating Reviews

To remain current and germane for policy and practice, systematic reviews need to be updated regularly.

The Cochrane and Campbell Collaborations

Two international, interdisciplinary collaborations of scholars, policy makers, clinicians, and consumers were developed to bridge the science and practice of research synthesis. The Cochrane Collaboration produces systematic reviews of studies on effects of interventions in health care (see www.cochrane.org). The Campbell Collaboration synthesizes results of research on interventions in social care (education, social welfare, mental health, and crime and justice; www.campbellcollaboration.org). These groups also produce evidence-based guidelines for research synthesis. The evidence for this work comes from methodological research, much of which is contained in the Cochrane Library.

Named for Donald T. Campbell, the American sociologist and author of *The Experimenting Society* (Campbell 1988), the Campbell Collaboration (C2), started in 2000, was initiated by and modeled on the Cochrane Collaboration. Prominent social work scholars have been involved in C2 since its inception.

C2 is a nonprofit, membership organization, led by an international Steering Group, whose members are elected by constituents. The C2 Secretariat (central office) is currently located in Oslo, Norway. Much of the work is conducted by the C2 Secretariat and by five Coordinating Groups (CGs). C2 produces peer-reviewed systematic reviews on topics in social work and social welfare, education, and crime and justice. The C2 Methods group provides training in systematic review methods and meta-analysis. The C2 Users group involves diverse constituents in the formulation, execution, and dissemination of reviews; it also produces plain-language summaries of C2 systematic reviews.

C2 systematic reviews can be initiated by anyone. The first step is to submit a "title" for a C2 review to one of the CGs. C2 reviews are conducted by teams who agree to follow the evidence-based procedures and standards for systematic reviews that have been developed by the Cochrane and Campbell Collaborations. Teams usually include members with expertise in the substantive area, information science, research methodology, and statistics. When both collaborations are interested in the topic, a systematic review can be registered (and produced) in both organizations; this is often done simultaneously, with a joint editorial process that serves the needs of both .

Before embarking on a C2 or Cochrane review, the review team develops a detailed protocol (plan) for the review. This protocol (and, ultimately, the completed systematic review) is vetted by C2 Editors, peer reviewers (substantive and methodological experts), and information retrieval specialists.

Contrary to a popular misconception, C2 reviews are *not* limited to randomized controlled trials (RCTs). However, C2 reviewers conduct separate analyses of RCTs and non-RCTs (because nonrandomized designs do not reliably approximate results of RCTs; Glazerman, Levy, and Myers 2002). C2 reviews and commentaries on them are posted on the C2 Web site (in the Campbell Library). C2 reviews are expected to be updated periodically.

Systematic Reviews of Intervention Effects

Systematic reviews and meta-analysis can be used to synthesize quantitative data on effects of interventions, associations between variables, and the accuracy of diagnostic or prognostic tests. Methods for synthesizing qualitative data and for combining syntheses of qualitative and quantitative data are under development (see, for example, Thomas et al. 2004). Here, I will focus on the synthesis of quantitative data on intervention effects. This choice is not meant to suggest that other empirical questions (e.g., about clients' needs and preferences) and other types of data are not equally important for practice and policy. However, although questions about "what works" (and what

works best for whom) have received considerable attention in health and social services, I argue that there is still much room for improvement in syntheses of research on intervention effects.

Criteria for evaluating the efficacy and effectiveness of therapeutic interventions have been developed by many professional and government organizations. Diverse criteria have been applied to bodies of empirical evidence
to determine what works for various conditions. Results have been used to
create lists of effective or model programs, called evidence-based practices
(EBPs), empirically supported treatments (ESTs), or empirically validated
treatments (EVTs).

Examples of this approach include the prestigious Blueprints for Violence
Prevention series (Mihalic, Fagan, Irwin, Ballard, and Elliott 2004), the National Registry of Evidence-based Programs and Practices (Substance Abuse
and Mental Health Services Administration 2007), and standards developed
by the Society for Prevention Research (Flay et al. 2005) and the American
Psychological Association's Society of Clinical Psychology (Division 12;
Chambless et al. 1998).

Criteria, standards, and classifications are not consistent across these
groups. However, the debate over such standards of evidence has been over-
shadowed by efforts to implement evidence-based practices "however they
are defined" (New Freedom Commission on Mental Health 2005). These des-
ignations affect funding decisions in several states and public agencies.

For the most part, lists of "evidence-based practices" and some of the most
influential reviews of EBPs are based on traditional, narrative review methods (Littell 2008). The practice of research synthesis—as represented by the
proliferation of published narrative reviews and lists—is not well connected
to the science of research synthesis. That is, most lists of EBPs and research
reviews are not informed by the growing body of research on the advantages
and disadvantages of different approaches to the identification, analysis, and
synthesis of empirical evidence. As Chalmers and colleagues observed, "science is supposed to be cumulative, but scientists only rarely cumulate evidence scientifically" (Chalmers, Hedges, and Cooper 2002:12). They also
noted that academics are usually unaware of the fundamental methodological and practical issues in research synthesis.

Systematic reviews and meta-analyses are becoming more common, but
traditional reviews prevail in the social sciences. Many publications that
are called systematic reviews or meta-analyses are not informed by the science of research synthesis. For example, many published meta-analyses
are based on convenience samples of published studies (although publication bias is rarely considered as a rival explanation for positive effects).
These reviews bear little resemblance to standards set by the Cochrane and

Campbell Collaborations and the QUOROM statement. Studies of the quality of systematic reviews and meta-analyses exist in the medical literature (e.g., Shea, Moher, Graham, Pham, and Tugwell 2002), but scant attention has been paid to the methods used in research reviews in the social and behavioral sciences.

Traditional and Systematic Reviews of a Model Program

What criteria and methods have reviewers used to locate, analyze, and synthesize evidence for "evidence-based" practices in the social work, psychology, and related fields? How "systematic" are these reviews? To find out, my colleagues and I analyzed original studies and published reviews of research on the effects of a model program called Multisystemic Therapy (Littell 2008; Littell, Popa, and Forsythe 2005).

Multisystemic Therapy

Multisystemic Therapy (MST) is a short-term, home- and community-based program that addresses complex psychosocial problems. It aims to provide alternatives to out-of-home placement for youth with social, emotional, and behavioral problems (Henggeler, Schoenwald, Borduin, Rowland, and Cunningham 1998; Henggeler, Schoenwald, Rowland, and Cunningham 2002). MST is licensed by a for-profit consulting firm (MST Services Inc.). Licensed MST programs exist in more than 30 states in the United States and in Canada, Australia, New Zealand, England, Ireland, Norway, Sweden, Denmark, and the Netherlands.

MST is one of the model programs identified by the U.S. Substance Abuse and Mental Health Services Administration (SAMSHA 2007) and by Blueprints for Violence Prevention (Henggeler, Mihalic, Rone, Thomas, and Timmons-Mitchell 1998). It has been cited as an effective treatment by the U.S. National Institute on Drug Abuse (1999, 2003), the National Institute of Mental Health (2001), and the Surgeon General's office (U.S. Department of Health and Human Services 1999, 2001).

A Systematic Review

My colleagues and I conducted a systematic review of research on effects of MST. Our review was registered simultaneously in the Cochrane and Campbell collaborations. Our protocol was published in 2004, and the completed review was published in the Cochrane Library and the Campbell Library in 2005 (Littell, Popa, and Forsythe 2005).

The systematic review included randomized controlled trials (RCTs) of licensed MST programs for youth with social, emotional, and behavioral problems (Littell et al. 2005). Studies that assessed effects of MST for young people with medical conditions were not included, nor were studies of programs that were called MST but were not licensed by MST Services Inc.

Search strategies were developed with information specialists and produced over 5,200 "hits." This led us to 266 unique citations (titles and abstracts), which were read by two reviewers. Following an inclusive screening process, we retrieved 95 full-text reports. Two of us read these reports and made independent decisions about whether studies were eligible for our review.

The completed review included eight RCTs with 1,151 families. Six of these studies were conducted by MST developers in the United States. One was conducted in Norway and one was conducted in Canada. All eight RCTs compared MST with another treatment, providing evidence of the relative effects of MST; not its absolute effects.

Data extraction and coding were performed by two raters who worked independently and compared results. During this process, we encountered problems with some of the MST trials that had not been identified in previous reviews. These included discrepancies across multiple published reports on the same study, ambiguous or substandard research procedures, and systematic omission of participants who did not complete treatment (inability to support intent-to-treat analysis). We requested and sometimes received additional data from principal investigators. These issues are documented in the systematic review and in a published debate with MST program developers (Littell 2005, 2006; Henggeler et al. 2006).

Results were synthesized across studies on twenty-one distinct outcome measures, including incarceration, other restrictive out-of-home placements, arrest or conviction, self-reported delinquency, peer relationships, behavior problems, substance use, youth psychiatric symptoms, parent psychiatric symptoms, and family functioning. Forest plots showed results from each study that provided data on an outcome measure. Overall (mean) effects were estimated using random effect models. Results were inconsistent across studies on every outcome measure. No significant differences between MST and treatment as usual were obtained in the largest and most rigorous study: a multisite trial conducted by independent investigators with full intent-to-treat analysis (Leschied and Cunningham 2002). The results of this study are public, but not published. A few significant effects of MST were found in weaker studies; none of the overall effects was statistically different from zero.

These results suggest that MST is *not* consistently better or worse than other services. This does not mean that MST is *in*effective. Low statistical power (too few studies) is a plausible explanation for the null results. In any case, these conclusions are contrary to those of many published reviews that claim that the effectiveness of MST is well established.

Published Reviews of MST

In our search for relevant studies, we found that published reviews of the research on MST are more numerous than original studies. In fact, we identified eighty-six reviews of effects of MST published after 1996 (this does not include the synopses of prior studies typically included in the background sections of original research reports). We obtained sixty-six of these reviews and assessed the methods they used. Many cited other reviews, not primary studies. I took a closer look at the thirty-seven published reviews that cited one or more MST trials and provided some analysis or synthesis of research on effects of MST (Littell 2008). Most (twenty-two) of these reviews relied solely on narrative syntheses of results of convenience samples of studies.

Only eight reviews used explicit inclusion and/or exclusion criteria. Nine used systematic keyword searches of electronic databases. Most distinguished randomized and nonrandomized studies, but variations in study quality within these categories rarely were considered.

Several reviews summarized the evidence in tables of "key findings" on selected outcomes. Some reviewers organized this evidence by outcome domains, using tables that show which studies provided evidence of *favorable* effects of MST within each domain. Others organized the evidence by study, highlighting *positive* results from each. Notably, null results and negative effects were not mentioned in these summaries (we know these results exist because they are in our systematic review). A similar approach was used in some narrative syntheses. Several reviews reported the number of studies that showed statistically significant differences favoring the MST group on one or more outcome measures (vote counting). The practice of highlighting favorable outcomes is an example of *confirmation bias*—the tendency to emphasize results that confirm a hypothesis and ignore evidence to the contrary.

Considerable variation was seen in the methods used and studies included in the reviews, with more consistency in their conclusions. Several reviews classified MST as a "probably efficacious" treatment according to the Chambless criteria mentioned above. Nine reviews provided a caveat about the evidence (e.g., results were not "well established," appeared related to fidelity, and had not been replicated by independent teams). Only three mentioned negative or null effects in their conclusions. Most (twenty-five) reviews offered unqualified support for MST.

Because all of these published reviews included studies that had mixed results, it was uncertain whether or how null and negative results were factored into reviewers' conclusions. How did reviewers determine whether positive results outweighed negative or null findings, especially when they did not use quantitative methods to pool results across studies? The next section takes a closer look at this problem.

Tracing Results from Research Reports to Reviews

To get a closer look at how research results were characterized by reviewers, I selected one MST trial and traced results from the original research report to descriptions of that study in published reviews (Littell 2008). The trial that I selected is (to my knowledge) the only published RCT of effects of MST in a sample of families of abused or neglected children (Brunk, Henggeler, and Whelan 1987). This study was not included in our Cochrane/Campbell review because main effects of MST cannot be calculated from available data. Nevertheless, the Brunk study has been cited as evidence for the effectiveness of MST in cases of child maltreatment. To understand how reviewers arrived at this conclusion, I analyzed the Brunk study and thirteen published reviews that cited it (Littell 2008).

In the Brunk study, 43 families were randomly assigned to MST or parent training (PT) groups. Immediate post-treatment outcome data were reported for 33 (77 percent) of these families. Mean scores were presented for subgroups of abuse cases and neglect cases. Brunk and colleagues reported that they collected data on 30 measures or subscales (client self-reports on 16 items, therapist reports on 3 measures, and 11 observational measures of parent-child interactions). Results were reported on 29 of the 30 measures; subgroup means were provided for 19. Results were mixed. Two comparisons (one self-report and one observational measure) favored PT, 5 observational measures favored MST, and the rest—22 scales—showed no significant differences between groups overall. (Means are missing for 10 of the 22 scales that showed null results.) The investigators described their results in the abstract of the article:

> Families who received either treatment showed decreased parental psychiatric symptomology, reduced overall stress, and a reduction in the severity of identified problems. Analyses of sequential observational measures revealed that multisystemic therapy was more effective than parent training at restructuring parent-child relations. Parent training was more effective than multisystemic therapy at reducing identified social problems. The differential influences of the two treatments were probably associated with differences in their respective treatment contexts and epistemologies. (Brunk et al. 1987:171)

In my judgment, this is a fairly balanced abstract. Authors highlight apparent benefits of each treatment and domains in which the two treatments produced equivalent results. By their own assessment, the study had mixed results.

Next let us see how results of this small RCT were characterized in published reviews. Of the 37 reviews analyzed above, 13 mentioned results of the Brunk study. Most reviewers emphasized statistically significant differences that favored the MST group. In fact, 11 of 13 reviews used a *single* phrase to characterize results of this study; all 11 indicated that MST had favorable outcomes. For example, some reviewers concluded that the Brunk study showed that MST "improved parent-child interactions" (Burns 2000; Henggeler et al. 2002). Although there is evidence to support this statement, it is incomplete and potentially misleading.

Three trends emerged in this analysis. First, the authors conducted some necessary *data reduction*. Second, there is an apparent *reduction in uncertainty*, as many of the null results are underreported in the original study and ignored in most reviews. Finally, reviewers highlight positive results that confirm expected effects of MST; this is a clear example of *confirmation bias*.

Lost in this process is information that MST and PT produce somewhat *different* results but are largely equivalent in terms of their outcomes. This knowledge could be useful to practitioners who are more concerned about some outcomes than others (e.g., parent-child interaction versus parental support). It could also be useful to consumers, especially those who have a clear preference for one treatment modality over another.

Selective Citation and Repetition

Frequent repetition of the same conclusions may be mistaken for replication. In addition to the 37 reviews described above, we found 19 published reviews that relied primarily (or solely) on other reviews (Littell 2008). These include often-cited reviews by Lehman and colleagues (2004), Mihalic et al. (2004), the Office of the Surgeon General (U.S. DHHS 2001), and the NIH State-of-the-Science Conference Statement on Preventing Violence (2004).

For example, the NIH statement cited the Blueprints group as their source of information on effective treatments, and concluded that MST "evaluations demonstrated reductions in long-term rates of rearrest, violent crime arrest, and out-of-home placements" and "positive results were maintained for nearly 4 years after treatment ended" (NIH 2004:12). The statement did not mention negative or null results, nor did it report that only one study had conducted a multiyear follow-up. Moreover, the NIH statement did not rely on the systematic review that was commissioned especially for its purposes. Produced by independent authors (under a contract with the U.S. Agency for

Health Research and Quality), that systematic review did not assess effects of specific interventions because the number of studies was too small to detect differences between programs (Chan et al. 2004).

Discussion and Conclusions

Methods matter. We have seen that different methods of research synthesis can lead to very different conclusions. Traditional reviews are vulnerable to publication, dissemination, selection, and confirmation biases. These biases tend to inflate effect sizes, producing overly optimistic estimates of intervention effects. Systematic review methods are designed to minimize these biases, to produce more accurate estimates of effects.

Critical appraisal of the research base for "evidence-based practices" is scant, but it appears that the literature on MST is not unique. Gorman and others have critically appraised studies of some of the school-based drug abuse and violence prevention programs that appear on many lists of EBPs. Gorman identified problems in this body of evidence that were similar to those we found in MST trials, including substandard research practices that compromised the internal validity of the RCTs (Gorman 2002, 2003a, 2003b, 2005). Similarly, Gandhi and colleagues found that many authors accept very weak evidence of effectiveness (Gandhi, Murphy-Graham, Petrosino, Chrismer, and Weiss 2006).

Some reviewers have not engaged in careful, critical appraisal of the methods used in original studies. It may be that some RCTs have escaped scrutiny, because these designs are considered to be the "gold standard" in research on efficacy and effectiveness. However, RCTs that are not well designed and those that are poorly implemented are unlikely to produce credible results (Shadish, Cook, and Campbell 2002).

Meta-analysts and systematic reviewers have been calling for better reporting on primary research for many years. These calls led to the development of consensus statements to guide reporting of RCTs, meta-analyses, and other types of studies (Moher et al. 1999, 2001; see www.equator-network.org). Many journals have adopted these guidelines.

To check publication and dissemination biases, editors of top medical journals now require the prospective registration of clinical trials in publicly available databases as a condition of publication (De Angelis et al. 2004). If investigators register their protocols before they begin to collect data, reviewers will later have a record that can be used to see whether all outcomes were reported. To facilitate this process, the World Health Organization (WHO) is creating a global platform for prospective registers of treatment research (WHO 2006). The WHO recommends that institutional review boards require prospective registration of studies on human subjects.

There is a tremendous need for education and training in the science of research synthesis, along with support for systematic reviews (e.g., as all or part of a dissertation). The Cochrane Collaboration and the Campbell Collaboration offer opportunities for training, technical assistance, publication, and dissemination of rigorous research syntheses. These collaborations are supported by international, interdisciplinary cadres of volunteers who are devoted to getting research reviews done right.

Social workers, social scientists, and policy makers should embrace the science of research synthesis. Evidence-based, systematic review methods can produce more reliable, unbiased syntheses of evidence for practice and policy. This will provide us with better estimates of the effects of social programs and practices. Some systematic reviews have shown that different treatments produce equivalent results. Under these conditions, practitioners and others can base their decisions on considerations other than effectiveness (e.g., clinical goals, clients' preferences for one treatment modality over another, resource constraints). Ultimately, this empirical evidence should inform and enhance practice, "increasing, not dictating, choice" (Dickersin, Straus, and Bero 2007).

References

Brunk, M., Henggeler, S. W., and Whelan, J. P. (1987). A comparison of multisystemic therapy and parent training in the brief treatment of child abuse and neglect. *Journal of Consulting and Clinical Psychology 55*:171–178.

Bushman, B. J. and Wells, G. L. (2001). Narrative impressions of literature: The availability bias and the corrective properties of meta-analytic approaches. *Personal and Social Psychology Bulletin 27*:1123–1130.

Campbell, D. T. (1988). The experimenting society. In E. S. Overman (Ed.), *Methodology and epistemology for social science: Selected papers,* 290–314. Chicago: University of Chicago Press.

Carlton, P. L. and Strawderman, W. E. (1996). Evaluating cumulated research I: The inadequacy of traditional methods. *Biological Psychiatry 39*:65–72.

Chalmers, I., Hedges, L. V., and Cooper, H. (2002). A brief history of research synthesis. *Evaluation and the Health Professions 25*:12–37.

Chambless, D. L., Baker, M. J., Baucom, D. H., Beutler, L. E., Calhoun, K. S., Crits-Christoph, P., et al. (1998). Update on empirically validated therapies, II. *The Clinical Psychologist 51*:3–16.

Chan, A. W., Hróbjartsson, A., Haar, M. T., Gøtzsche, P. C., and Altman, D. G. (2004). Empirical evidence for selective reporting of outcomes in randomized trials: Comparison of protocols to published articles. *Journal of the American Medical Association 291*:2457–2465.

Chan, L. S., Kipke, M. D., Schneir, A., Iverson, E., Warf, C., Limbos, M. A., et al. (2004). *Preventing violence and related health-risking social behaviors in adolescents*

(No. AHRQ Publication No. 04-E032–2). Rockville, MD: Agency for Healthcare Research and Quality.

Cooper, H. (1998). *Synthesizing research: A guide for literature reviews,* 3rd ed. Thousand Oaks, CA: Sage.

Cooper, H. and Hedges, L. (1994). *Handbook of research synthesis.* New York: Russell Sage Foundation.

De Angelis, C., Drazen, J. M., Frizelle, F. A., Haug, C., Hoey, J., Horton, R., et al. (2004). Clinical trial registration: A statement from the International Committee of Medical Journal Editors. *New England Journal of Medicine 351*:1250–1251.

Dickersin, K. (2005). Publication bias: Recognizing the problem, understanding its origins and scope, and preventing harm. In H. R. Rothstein, A. J. Sutton, and M. Borenstein (Eds.), *Publication bias in meta-analysis: Prevention, assessment, and adjustments.* Chichester, UK: Wiley.

Dickersin, K., Straus, S. E., and Bero, L. (2007). Evidence-based medicine: Increasing, not dictating, choice. *British Medical Journal 334*:s10.

Egger, M. and Smith, G. D. (1998). Bias in location and selection of studies. *British Medical Journal 316*:61–66.

Flay, B. R., Biglan, A., Boruch, R. F., Castro, F. G., Gottfredson, D., Kellam, S., et al. (2005). Standards of evidence: Criteria for efficacy, effectiveness and dissemination. *Prevention Science 6*:151–175.

Gandhi, A. G., Murphy-Graham, E., Petrosino, A., Chrismer, S. S., and Weiss, C. H. (2006). The devil is in the details: Examining the evidence for "proven" school-based drug abuse prevention programs. *Evaluation Review 31*:43–74.

Gorman, D. M. (2002). The "science" of drug and alcohol prevention: The case of the randomized trial of the Life Skills Training program. *International Journal of Drug Policy 13*:21–26.

——. (2003a). Prevention programs and scientific nonsense. *Policy Review* (February and March):65–75.

——. (2003b). The best of practices, the worst of practices: The making of science-based primary prevention programs. *Psychiatric Services 54*:1087–1089.

——. (2005). Does measurement dependence explain the effects of the Life Skills Training program on smoking outcomes? *Preventive Medicine 40*:479–487.

Gibbs, L. E. (2003). *Evidence-based practice for the helping professions: A practical guide with integrated multimedia.* Pacific Grove, CA: Brooks/Cole-Thompson Learning.

Glazerman, S., Levy, D. M., and Myers, D. (2002). *Nonexperimental replications of social experiments: A systematic review.* Princeton, NJ: Mathematica Policy Research.

Hedges, L.V. and Olkin, I. (1985). *Statistical methods for meta-analysis.* Orlando, FL: Academic Press.

Henggeler, S. W., Mihalic, S. F., Rone, L., Thomas, C., and Timmons-Mitchell, J. (1998). *Blueprints for violence prevention, book six: Multisystemic therapy.* Boulder, CO: Center for the Study and Prevention of Violence.

Henggeler, S. W., Schoenwald, S. K., Borduin, C. M., Rowland, M. D., and Cunningham, P. B. (1998). *Multisystemic treatment of antisocial behavior in children and adolescents.* New York: Guilford Press.

Henngeler, S. W., Schoenwald, S. K., Borduin, C. M., and Swenson, C. C. (2006). Methodological critique and meta-analysis as Trojan horse. *Children and Youth Services Review 28*:447–457.

Henggeler, S. W., Schoenwald, S. K., Rowland, M. D., and Cunningham, P. B. (2002). *Serious emotional disturbances in children and adolescents: Multisystemic therapy*. New York: Guilford Press.

Higgins, J. P. T. and Green, S. (Eds). (2008). *Cochrane handbook for systematic reviews of interventions, version 5 (updated February 2008)*. http://www.cochrane-handbook.org/.

Hopewell, S., Clarke, M., Stewart, L., and Tierney, J. (2001). Time to publication for results of clinical trials. *Cochrane database of methodology reviews, 2001, Issue 3*, Art. No.: MR000011. DOI: 000010.001002/14651858.MR14000011.Chichester, UK: Wiley.

Hopewell, S., McDonald, S., Clarke, M., and Egger, M. (2006). Grey literature in meta-analyses of randomized trials of health care interventions. *The Cochrane database of systematic reviews, Issue 2*. Chichester, UK: Wiley.

Jørgensen, A. W., Hilden, J., and Gøtzsche, P. G. (2006). Cochrane reviews compared with industry supported meta-analyses and other meta-analyses of the same drugs: Systematic review. *British Medical Journal 333*:782–785.

Lehman, A. F., Goldman, H. H., Dixon, L. B., and Churchill, R. (2004). *Evidence-based mental health treatments and services: Examples to inform public policy*. New York: Milbank Memorial Fund.

Leschied, A. W. and Cunningham, A. (2002). Seeking effective interventions for young offenders: Interim results of a four-year randomized study of multisystemic therapy in Ontario, Canada. London, Ontario: Centre for Children and Families in the Justice System.

Lipsey, M. W. and Wilson, D. B. (2001). *Practical meta-analysis*. Thousand Oaks, CA: Sage.

Littell, J. H. (2005). Lessons from a systematic review of effects of multisystemic therapy. *Children and Youth Services Review 47*:445–463.

———. (2006). The case for multisystemic therapy: Evidence or orthodoxy? *Children and Youth Services, 28*:458–472.

———. (2008). Evidence-based or biased? The quality of published reviews of evidence-based practices. *Children and Youth Services Review 30*:1299–1317.

Littell, J. H., Corcoran, J., and Pillai, V. (2008). *Systematic reviews and meta-analysis*. Oxford: Oxford University Press.

Littell, J. H., Popa, M., and Forsythe, B. (2005). Multisystemic therapy for social, emotional, and behavioral problems in youth aged 10–17. *The Cochrane database of systematic reviews, issue 4*. Chichester, UK: Wiley.

Luborsky, L., Diguer, L., Seligman, D. A., Rosenthal, R., Krause, E. D., Johnson, S., et al. (1999). The researcher's own therapy allegiances: A "wild card" in comparisons of treatment efficacy. *Clinical Psychology: Science and Practice 6*:95–106.

Mahoney, M. J. (1977). Publication prejudices: An experimental study of confirmatory bias in the peer review system. *Cognitive Therapy and Research 1*:161–175.

Mihalic, S., Fagan, A., Irwin, K., Ballard, D., and Elliott, D. (2004). *Blueprints for Violence Prevention* (No. NCJ 204274). Washington, DC: U.S. Department of Justice Office of Juvenile Justice and Delinquency Prevention.

Moher, D., Cook, D. J., Eastwood, S., Olkin, I., Rennie, D., Stroup, D. F., et al. (1999). Improving the quality of reports of meta-analyses of randomised controlled trials: The QUOROM statement. *The Lancet 354*:1896–1900.

Moher, D., Schultz, K. F., Altman, D. G., for the CONSORT Group (2001). The CONSORT statement: Revised recommendations for improving the quality of reports of parallel-group randomized trials. *The Lancet 357*:1191–1194.

National Institutes of Health. (2004). NIH State-of-the-Science Conference statement on preventing violence and related health-risking social behaviors in adolescents. *NIH Consensus and State-of-the-Science Statements*, Oct. 13–15, *21* (2): 1–34.

National Institute of Mental Health. (2001). *Youth in a difficult world*. NIH Publication No. 01–4587. Washington, DC: NIMH.

National Institute on Drug Abuse. (1999). *Principles of drug addiction treatment: A research-based guide*. (NIH Publication 99–4180). Bethesda, MD: Author.

——. (2003). *Effective drug abuse treatment approaches: Multisystemic therapy. NIDA Behavioral Therapies Development Program*. http://www.nida.nih.gov/BRDP/Effective/Henggeler.html.

New Freedom Commission on Mental Health. (2005). *Subcommittee on Evidence-Based Practices: Background Paper. DHHS Pub. No. SMA-05–4007*. Rockville, MD: Author. http://www.mentalhealthcommission.gov/reports/EBP_Final_040605.pdf.

Nickerson, R. S. (1998). Confirmation bias: A ubiquitous phenomenon in many guises. *Review of General Psychology 2*:175–220.

Petticrew, M. and Roberts, H. (2006). *Systematic reviews in the social sciences: A practical guide*. Oxford: Blackwell.

Reid, W. J. (1998). *Empirically-supported practice: Perennial myth or emerging reality?* Distinguished Professorship Lecture. School of Social Welfare, University at Albany, November 13.

Rothstein, H. R., Sutton, A. J., and Bornstein, M. (Eds.). (2005). *Publication bias in meta-analysis: Prevention, assessment, and adjustments*. Chichester, UK: Wiley.

Scherer, R.W., Langenberg, P., and von Elm, E. (2007). Full publication of results initially presented in abstracts. *Cochrane database of systematic reviews, 2007, issue 2*. Chichester, UK: Wiley.

Shadish, W. R., Cook, T. D., and Campbell, D. T. (2002). *Experimental and quasi-experimental designs for generalized causal inference*. Boston: Houghton Mifflin.

Shea, B. J., Grimshaw, J. M., Wells, G. A., Boers, M., Andersson, N., Hamel, C., et al. (2007). Development of AMSTAR: a measurement tool to assess the methodological quality of systematic reviews. *BMC Medical Research Methodology, 7*. http://www.biomedcentral.com/1471–2288/7/10.

Shea, B., Moher, D., Graham, I., Pham, B., and Tugwell, P. (2002). Comparison of the quality of Cochrane reviews and systematic reviews published in paper-based journals. *Evaluation and the Health Professions 25*:116–129.

Substance Abuse and Mental Health Services Administration. (2007). *National registry of evidence-based programs and practices*. http://www.nrepp.samhsa.gov/ (accessed August 1, 2007).

Thomas, J., Harden, A., Oakley, A., Oliver, S., Sutcliffe, K., Rees, R., Brunton, G., and Kavanagh, J. (2004). Integrating qualitative research with trials in systematic reviews. *British Medical Journal 328*:1010–1012.

Torgerson, C. J. (2006). Publication bias: The Achilles' heel of systematic reviews? *British Journal of Educational Studies 54*:89–102.

U.S. Department of Health and Human Services. (1999). *Mental health: A report of the surgeon general*. Rockville, MD: Author.

——. (2001). *Youth violence: A report of the surgeon general*. Washington, DC: Author.

World Health Organization. (2006). International Clinical Trials Registry Platform (ICTRP). http://www.who.int/ictrp/en/.

PART THREE | *An Example of Empirical Model Development and Dissemination*

The Task-Centered Model

12 | The Intellectual Legacy of William J. Reid

Lynn Videka and James A. Blackburn

WILLIAM J. REID (1928–2003) shaped the scholarly agenda and the practice of social work throughout his thirty-five-year career. Reid's work on time limits in treatment, the task-centered practice model, and the role of science in knowledge development for social work transformed the profession from one that had little investment and stake in empirical knowledge development for practice to one that is deeply invested in scientifically based practice approaches. At the time of Reid's earliest work, the prevailing practice methods were psychodynamic, with the leading texts Hollis's (1964) *Casework: A Psychosocial Therapy*, Turner's (1968) *Differential Diagnosis and Treatment in Social Work*, and Helen Harris Perlman's (1957) *Social Casework: A Problem Solving Process*. Although behavioral theory books had begun to interest some social workers, this theory was far from mainstream. And although social work had begun paying attention to research in works such as *Motivation, Capacity, and Opportunity* (Ripple, Alexander, and Polemis 1964) and *Women in Marital Conflict: A Casework Study* (Hollis 1949), the profession was far from using empirical methods as a standard tool for developing knowledge to inform practice. William J. Reid was a visionary of his day; he saw the potential for new, more efficient, and more effective social work practice based on empirical demonstration of effectiveness. He saw that this approach could revolutionize the practice of social work.

This chapter will review the intellectual basis of William J. Reid's scholarship contributions to social work over the past four decades in the context of the developing profession as discussed by Feldman (this volume, chapter 1). It begins with Reid's traditional social casework education and training, the lens through which social work practice was viewed in the 1950s and early '60s. This chapter also describes Bill Reid's enduring commitment to scientific discovery that will improve social work practice and to data-driven inquiry over ideology-driven decisions.

The 1960s Context in Social Work

In the 1960s social work was just beginning to lay the foundation for its identity as a scholarship-based profession. There were only ten doctoral programs (Feldman 2005). Kirk and Reid (2002) assert that though social workers, in the Charity Organization Society's scientific philanthropy, strove to be scientific from the start, early social work can be thought of a "proto-science" rather than a true science (30). This is because members of the young profession, after the landmark Flexner lecture in 1915 (Flexner 1915), agreed that scientifically based knowledge is a hallmark of every profession, but social work did not have established scientific methods or a body of science to call its own. Early social work emulated science in works such as Mary Richmond's *Social Diagnosis* (1917). Practice was characterized by an emphasis on evaluation of the facts in a case and rational decision making about case interventions by the social worker. But the young profession had not yet embraced university education, did not have trained scientists among its ranks, and produced no direct scientific inquiry that would build a theoretical knowledge base to guide the profession.

During the 1950s and '60s the number of studies of social work practice increased. Social work research began to focus on topics more relevant to social interventions, such as the treatment process and factors that influenced the continuance of treatment. New works included *Motivation, Capacity and Opportunity* (Ripple 1964), a study of the effects of client motivation and ability on social work treatment outcomes; *Patterns of Use of Family Agency Service* (Beck 1962), a descriptive study of the clientele of family service agencies; and "Continuance and Discontinuance in Martial Counseling" (Hollis 1968), a study of factors that predicted marital counseling drop-out. These studies defined social work intervention in broad, nonspecific terms. They focused on practical problems that vexed social work practitioners, such as treatment engagement and drop-out rates, and on descriptors of the client population.

In the 1950s and into the 1960s the profession began to produce a series of studies of social work intervention outcomes. The best known include

Girls at Vocational High, a study of intervention with female juvenile delinquents (Meyer, Borgatta, and Jones 1965), the Cambridge Somerville Youth
Study (Powers and Witmer 1951), and the Chemung County Study (Wallace
1967). These studies reflected the changing orientation of social policies and
programs toward service outcomes. This reflected the shift toward rational,
outcomes-based decision criteria for American social policies, the hallmark
of the Kennedy administration, led by Robert McNamara in the Department
of Defense (Sorensen 1965; McNamara 1995). McNamara's idea was to use
economic analytic methods to make public policy decisions and to judge
the outcomes of public policies. Based on McNamara's corporate experience,
this method was known as Planning, Programming and Budgeting Systems
(PPBS). First developed in the defense department, PPBS brought planning
and rational and empirical decision making to public policy and became
deeply influential in domestic as well as military policy. One conclusion, that
social programs should be evaluated to see whether they produced the results
for which they were designed, dramatically influenced social work and social
policy in the United States. The era of accountability in government, in government services, and in social work was born.

Collectively these 1960s social work studies examined the then very blunt
tool of social work practice, typically "whatever the social worker did," reflecting the lack of implementation of systematic intervention theories in the
field. Their findings were disappointing. Study after study showed that social
work interventions produced results no better than the control group condition (Kirk and Reid 2002).

William Reid was beginning his career during this period, having received
his doctoral degree from Columbia University in 1963. His first publication
(Reid 1964) was entitled "Practitioner and client variables affecting casework
treatment." The study laid the groundwork for Reid's enduring interests in
social work treatment outcomes and his orientation to the treatment process.
It also reflected the influence of his teachers at Columbia University, including Florence Hollis, who was pioneering research on her casework intervention typology at the time. Reid's work reflects Hollis's deep commitment to
the practice of social casework, as social work practice was called at the time
(Hollis 1964). Reid sustained a lifelong interest in studying the practice of
social work.

Defining Themes for a Lifetime of Work

In the first of Bill Reid's landmark works, *Brief and Extended Casework,* Reid
and Shyne (1969) employed a rigorous experimental research design. Setting a
standard for all of Reid's work to come, the study was set in a real-world social

service setting, the Community Service Society of New York. Also launching a lifetime focus, the study was motivated by questions concerning the effectiveness and efficiency of social work services, one of the first efforts to focus on effectiveness given the enduring labor shortages that characterized the expanding field (Wenocur and Reisch 1989). Reid and Shyne begin with the following statement, "While caseworkers continue to be in short supply, the clienteles of casework continue to grow. The search for briefer methods has resulted in considerable controversy, much of it over the question of how much treatment is desirable or necessary" (1969:1).

In this book, Reid defined the positions that formed the intellectual backbone of his career. He based his ideas on the philosophy of pragmatism, following the thinking of Helen Harris Perlman (1957), stating that, "Given our limited resources, it [short-term treatment] is the only practical means of providing help to growing numbers of needful people" (Reid and Shyne 1969:2). In his later works, such as *The Task Planner* (Reid 2000), this underlying philosophical point of view was expressed in a multimodal compendium of problem-oriented treatment strategies that draw from theories as diverse as behavioral interventions, cognitive strategies, and family systems approaches such as paradoxical interventions. This philosophy also positioned Reid's work and the field to eschew theoretical ideology in favor of whatever approaches work best.

In *Brief and Extended Casework*, Reid and Shyne referred to social work intervention as a "learning process." This foreshadowed the increasingly behavioral orientation that Reid's work would take over the years; it began at a time when behavioral intervention models were well outside of the profession, which was still largely steeped in psychodynamically influenced models and argued over the nuances of Freudian, Kleinian, and Rankian theory.

Brief and Extended Casework also established empiricism as the epistemology for social work intervention in the second half of the twentieth century and beyond. The findings of the study, including that brief intervention produced better outcomes than long-term treatment, laid the groundwork for the development of Reid's task-centered model of social work practice. In chapter 9, "Program Implications," Reid and Shyne (1969) state, "The findings of the present experiment, together with the results of related research, provide an empirical basis for the wide use of briefer, more economical and better structured approaches" (194).

The Design and Evolution of Task-Centered Practice

The Task Force on Social Work Research commissioned by the National Institutes of Mental Health cited Reid's task-centered practice approach as creating "major changes in the practice of social casework over the past 20 years"

(Task Force on Social Work Research 1991:5). Task-centered practice heralded a new era of scientifically developed, eclectic practice models and is perhaps the only empirical practice model to be created uniquely within social work. It still sets a standard as an empirically developed social work practice intervention model that yields theoretically coherent knowledge and is generalizable to many practice situations and client groups, a special feature that is important given the diversity of social work practice settings and clientele.

In *Task-Centered Casework*, Reid and Epstein (1972) set out to create a model for short-term practice based on Reid and Shyne's (1969) earlier work in *Brief and Extended Casework*, and on their newest thinking. They acknowledged the ideas of teachers who influenced them, stating, "We are unable to say where their ideas leave off and ours begin" (vi). These predecessors included Helen Harris Perlman (1957), whose problem-solving approach provided the theoretical underpinnings for task-centered practice, which eliminated the psychodynamic and some of the functionalist thinking that Perlman integrated and provided further structured steps to guide the problem-solving intervention process. Reid and Epstein also acknowledged Howard Parad (1968a, b), who was one of the foremost writers on crisis intervention at the time, and Florence Hollis, his teacher and mentor at the Columbia University School of Social Work, who pioneered the descriptive study of social work practice process in couples therapy. Hollis focused on treatment strategies, which led to her typology (1964) and influenced Reid to concentrate on treatment actions, a hallmark of the task-centered model.

Reid and Epstein (1972) lay out an eclectic practice approach that is meant to be dynamic and evolutionary over time, based on new empirical findings. They state in the book's introduction, "We have drawn on a range of theories and practices" (1972:1), and make clear their commitment to evolution of thought, especially when it can be based on new empirical findings— "We have been guided by the findings of our research . . . and by our clinical experience when empirical evidence was lacking"—and go on to say that, "Our . . . system is, by design, . . . open to infusions from other points of view and to modifications indicated by subsequent research" (1972:1). Task-centered practice, as described in this book, is based on three studies detailed in chapter 11 (1972:216–260). The first, based on a series of eight case studies in a hospital social work department, demonstrated and tested the elements of the task-centered practice, including investigating client and practitioner perspectives in task definitions. Not surprisingly, identifying workable tasks that were doable, yet relevant to complex problems was one of the early challenges to be addressed by the model.

The second, considered by Reid and Epstein to be the major study in creating the model, focused on twenty second-year MSW students, also in a

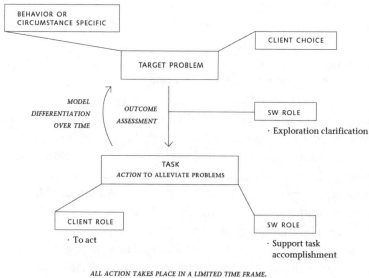

FIGURE 12.1 Task-Centered Treatment Model (1972–2000)

medical social work setting. The intervention model was well-defined. The study found problem resolution and client satisfaction high among the treated cases. The third study replicated the second with six cases in a psychiatric clinic. The methods of developing the intervention model and the science embodied the ideals of the "social research and development model" that Reid so admired and that Rothman and Thomas would later write about in their own books (Rothman and Thomas 1994).

Task-centered practice was the first social work practice model to focus on the *client's* actions, supported by the social worker, to reduce the client's problems, the "task" in task-centered practice. Figure 12.1 lays out a conceptual model of task-centered practice.

Defining the Problem

The client's problem is central in defining the tasks of social work intervention.Task-centered practice jettisoned the long-held tradition of social work intervention being centered on an assessment that included the client's childhood and early experiences. Task-centered practice does not reject historical information that is pertinent to the problem, but does not require an extensive social history either. Instead of focusing on development and past life experiences, the practitioner focuses on the here and now of the client's life. The client's point of view is essential in defining the problem for work.

Problems are taken at face value; additional meaning is not read into the client's statements and target problems are not reinterpreted to mean other problems. The problems that the social worker and client agree to work on together inform the choice of tasks that can be undertaken.

Task-centered treatment, with its explicit problem focus, led the way for more client-centered and transparent approaches to social work intervention. In psychodynamic theory, most popular and influential in social work in the 1960s and '70s, the social worker was the expert, identified the client problems, and directed the intervention based on psychodynamic principles, which were unknown and not typically explained to the client, except in infrequent insight-oriented casework. The caseworker had a different, higher status than the client. Professional expertise led the social worker to control the course of treatment and to require client compliance, as in traditional approaches to medical care. In task-centered practice, the power gradient between client and worker is reduced. The client determines the problem focus. In the case of a mandated intervention, the client still identifies the problem; the social worker is not the aloof expert, but rather is a teacher, advocate, and supporter of the client's own problem-solving actions.

The Task: The Central Action of Social Work Intervention

In task-centered practice, the central construct is the client's actions to reduce the target problem identified by the client. This is the "task," the action of the intervention. This action can be taken by the client, or at times by the social worker. It may be a group task (shared by a family or classmates), a solo task, or an action that the social worker undertakes on her own on the client's behalf. Tasks and task review are the central elements of the intervention session with the client. Tasks are structured and influenced by several factors, including the client's preferences and the social worker's intervention.

The Client's Role

The client's role in task-centered treatment is an active one; the aim is for the client to act on their own behalf to solve their problems. Although these actions do not preclude cognitive or mental actions, such as rethinking a problem situation or reflecting on the pros and cons of making one decision or another, the social work intervention is not restricted to a verbal and mental process. Throughout task-centered practice the client role involves a good deal of choice and preference. The client determines the problem; there are no problems for work other than those to which the client explicitly agrees. Client actions, the tasks, are central in solving the problem. Many involve work in between sessions with the social worker. The extent of client choice and the power of the client in setting priorities and making choices throughout treatment were highly innovative ideas about social work intervention in 1972.

The Social Worker's Role

The social worker's role in task-centered practice is to explore, clarify, offer guidance, advocate, and support. The social worker facilitates—but does not direct—definition of the client's problem. She or he explores and clarifies in order to help the client identify tasks that will aid problem resolution. A major role for the practitioner is to structure the intervention so that the client is following an orderly problem-solving process that will produce positive results in eight to twelve weeks. The social worker may also identify tasks to be completed during a session, such as rehearsing an action prior to the client's task implementation on their own. The social worker supports and praises task accomplishment. She also helps clients to anticipate if possible, to identify, and to overcome barriers to task completion between sessions. She helps clients evaluate the effectiveness of the task in helping them reach goals, works with clients to modify or revise tasks for more effective problem resolution, and helps clients identify problem change over time.

Lasting Effects on Social Work Practice

The task-centered model heralded new approaches to social work practice. Social workers now regularly use time limits, focus on the here and now, use transparency and client-driven choices in treatment, and pay careful attention to evaluation. Through the 1970s and 1980s Reid and his colleagues developed a wide body of evidence that showed that task-centered practice was effective in a variety of social work practice settings including health care, mental health services for people with serious and persistent mental illnesses, in schools and working with children, and in family and couples therapy. Several more books and dozens of articles on task-centered practice were published.

In *The Task Planner,* Reid (2000) created a compendium of task or problem-solving ideas for a diverse set of more than 100 problems ranging from addiction to couples conflict and communication, to common mental disorders of depression and anxiety, to immigration acclimation to a new culture, to unemployment. For example, task strategies suggested for couples' communication problems include paraphrasing the partner's statements before replying to check accuracy of the message received, validating the partner's feelings, and agreeing to temporarily disengage when conflict reaches a high level. For these tasks Reid drew on the empirically based couples communication work of Gottman (1994) and Jacobsen and Margolin (1975).

Task-centered practice revolutionized social work practice, transforming it from tradition and ideology-based approaches to empirically based practice. In addition to the couples communication example above, *The Task Planner* (2002) offered theoretically diverse, scientifically based ideas for tasks, such as using public health approaches for addiction relapse prevention and structural family therapy approaches for parent-child enmeshment. In *Gerontological Social Work* (2003), Naleppa and Reid adapted task-centered practice to a wide range of problems faced by older people and their caregivers.

Task-centered practice has always been a dynamic form of practice. The model was designed to change over time, and change it did. Reid and his colleagues developed task repertoires that varied with respect to client problems. Task-centered practice became increasingly eclectic. The approach retains coherence through the consistent use of problem solving and the focus on problem-solving actions and practice outcomes by the client-social worker partnership. It is eclectic in that almost any theoretically and empirically informed theory can be incorporated.

Task-centered practice was client centered and client driven even before empowerment and strengths-based practice became the mantra of the profession and curriculum education policy. As what Reid called a "generic" theory, it anticipated generalist practice. Task-centered practice is entirely adaptable to a generalist practice framework, as Tolson, Reid, and Garvin laid out in *Generalist Practice: A Task-Centered Approach* (2002). The model is readily integrated into teaching, practice, and research, the unification challenge of the profession in our time.

William J. Reid's Legacy: Building Knowledge for Practice

In the later period of his work, Reid increasingly focused on the larger landscape of science and knowledge. Although a leader in the empirical practice movement, he embraced intellectual pluralism throughout his career. At the time that intellectual battle lines were drawn between quantitative empiricists and experiential relativists (eventually in fully postmodern discourse), Reid solidified his stance on intellectual pluralism. In the midst of the quantitative (mislabeled "logical positivist") –qualitative (mislabeled "constructivist" or "postmodern") debate about preferred research methods in social work, Reid, a known empiricist, coedited *Qualitative Research in Social Work* (1994) with Edmund Sherman. This book is a compendium of qualitative research approaches in social work. Reid's own research blended qualitative case studies with experimental designs, using the methodology that was appropriate for the research questions.

In "Long term trends in clinical social work" (Reid 1997), Reid identified trends likely to influence the field for some time to come. These included many themes that informed his work over the decades, such as eclecticism, consumerism, client power, and the influence of empirically based practice. He also identified trends such as the diminishing of single-theory hegemony in favor of multitheory eclecticism.

In "The scientific and empirical foundations of clinical social work" (Reid 2001), Reid gave an intellectual history of empirical practice and pointed to the future of multimethod approaches and the challenges of postmodern thinking. Reid distinguished postmodern thinking, which he defines as embracing the rational empiricism of Popper, Dewey, and other twentieth-century philosophers, from constructivism, in which the relative positions of power, language, and discourse are viewed as determinants of what a society takes as knowledge.

In *Science and Social Work: A Critical Appraisal* (2002), Stuart Kirk and Reid considered the historically ambivalent stance that social work had taken toward empirically based knowledge and the challenge posed by the complexity of problems on which social workers concentrate. They offered a comprehensive historical view of science in the profession, from its earliest days and the infamous critique of the profession by Abraham Flexner (1915) to today's issues, including the applied science of social work, technological advances and implications, methodological pluralism, and research tools in social work practice. Kirk and Reid saw signs of progress in the perennial challenge for the profession to define its knowledge base and its science. They identified the trend toward evidence-based practices, forecasting the tsunami that has washed over many fields of practice since the book's publication in 2002.

William J. Reid's Legacy for the Future of the Profession

Reid's thinking and scholarship will continue to influence the social work profession's knowledge base for generations to come. His philosophy and inquiry have set us on a course of a commitment to empirical epistemology for building knowledge, but without the frequently presumed narrow view of this approach. His work sets the stage for diverse methods of inquiry, a steady focus on the practice of social work, and the client's role in driving the focus of practice. These features culminate in diverse, pluralistic models of practice that strive to achieve the highest degree of efficacy possible.

References

Beck, D. F. (1962). *Patterns of use of family agency service.* New York: Family Service Association of America.

Flexner, A. (1915). Is social work a profession? *Proceedings of the National Conference of Charities and Correction.* Chicago: Hildmann Printing Co., 1915.

Gottman, J. (1994). *Why marriages succeed or fail.* New York: Simon and Schuster.

Hollis, F. (1949). *Women in marital conflict: A casework study.* New York: Family Service Association of America.

——. (1964). *Casework: A psychosocial therapy.* New York: Random House.

——. (1968). Continuance and discontinuance in martial counseling. *Social Casework* 41:431–445.

Jacobson, N. S. and Margolin, G. (1979). *Marital therapy: Strategies based on social learning.* New York: Brunner/Mazel.

Kirk, S. and Reid, W. J. (2002). *Science and social work.* New York: Columbia University Press.

McNamara, R. (with VanDeMark, B). (1995). *In retrospect: The tragedy and lessons of Vietnam.* New York: Times Books.

Meyer, H., Borgatta, E., and Jones, W. (1965). *Girls at vocational high.* New York: Russell Sage Foundation.

Parad, H. J. and Parad, L. G. (1968a). A study of crisis-oriented planned short-term treatment, part 1. *Social Casework* 49:346–55.

——. (1968b). A study of crisis-oriented planned short-term treatment, part 2. *Social Casework,* 49:418–426.

Perlman, H. H. (1957). *Social casework: A problem solving process.* Chicago: University of Chicago Press.

Ripple, L., Alexander, E., and Polemis, B. W. (1964). *Motivation, capacity, and opportunity: Studies in casework theory and practice.* Chicago: School of Social Service Administration.

Reid, W. J. (1964). Practitioner and client variables affecting casework treatment. *Social Casework* 44:33–39.

——. (1997). Long-term trends in clinical social work. *Social Service Review 71* (2): 200–213.

——. (2001). The role of science in social work: The perennial debate. *Journal of Social Work 1* (3): 273–293.

——. (2001). The scientific and empirical foundations of clinical social work practice. In H. Briggs and K. Corcoran, *Structuring change* (2nd ed.). Chicago: Lyceum Books.

——. (2000). *The task planner: An intervention resource for human service professionals.* New York: Columbia University Press.

Reid, W. J. and Epstein, L. (1972). *Task-centered casework.* New York: Columbia University Press.

Reid, W. J. and Sherman, E. (Eds.). (1994). *Qualitative research in social work.* New York: Columbia University Press.

Reid, W. J. and Shyne, A. W. (1969). *Brief and extended casework.* New York: Columbia University Press.

Rothman, J. and Thomas, E. (Eds.). (1994). *Intervention research: Design and development for human service.* New York: Hayworth Press.

Sorensen, T. C. (1965). *Kennedy.* New York: Harper and Row.

Task Force on Social Work Research. (1991). *Building social work knowledge for effective services and policies: A plan for research development.* Washington, D.C.: Task Force on Social Work Research.

Tolson, E., Reid, W. J., and Garvin, C. D. (2002). *Generalist practice: A task-centered approach.* New York: Columbia University Press.

Turner, F. J. (1968). *Differential diagnosis and treatment in social work.* New York: Free Press.

Wallace, D. (1967). The Chemung County evaluation of casework services to dependent multi-problem families: Another problem outcome. *Social Service Review* 41:379–389.

Wenocur, S. and Reisch, M. (1989). *From charity to enterprise: The development of American social work in a market economy.* Urbana: University of Illinois Press.

13 | Task-Centered Practice in the United States

Ronald H. Rooney

THE TASK-CENTERED APPROACH has made a signal contribution to empirically oriented practice in social work in the United States and around the world. In this chapter, I will present a brief history of the approach, outline its key elements, describe how it has been used and adapted in the United States, suggest contributions and challenges stimulated by the approach, and finally, point to the future.

Origins of the Task-Centered Approach

In the 1960s, it was generally assumed that casework effects were beneficial and more treatment would produce greater effects. Reid and Shyne conducted an experimental study of the relative effects of planned short-term (PSTS) and extended service to family service clients. Contrary to conventional wisdom, clients receiving PSTS received as much long-lasting assistance as those receiving extended service (Reid and Shyne 1969). In addition, clients were less likely to drop out in PSTS, and those receiving extended service had relatively few additional sessions with more unilateral terminations. This social work study was consistent with later results from other helping professions supporting the efficacy of time-limited treatment (Hoyt 2000; Wells and Gianetti 1990).

Reid concluded that if clients receiving PSTS could do as well as those receiving continued service (CS), without having a specific model of treatment prescribing more than length of service, treatment might be better with a model to guide it that was designed to produce results in a brief time period. Hence Reid and Epstein began to develop a model to explicitly guide social workers in time-limited practice (Reid and Epstein 1972). The model was based on two principles: work was to be aimed at assisting clients in resolving target problems of their own choosing, and work should be guided where possible by empirical research. Integral to the model was an ongoing testing of the method: continual, public assessment of progress was owed to clients as much as to agencies and funders. Spiritually akin to the problem-solving model (Perlman 1957), the task-centered approach focused on very specific problems in living. The central theme was the mutual design of tasks to alleviate problems in the environment. Problems were to be described in measurable terms such that the success or lack thereof could be accessible to client and worker. The model was to be a collaborative one in which the practitioner was expert in helping clients reduce problems, not in prescribing or dictating what the problem was or how it should be approached.

Outline of the Approach[1]

The task-centered practitioner is guided to be alert to the priorities of a referral source, yet clear about the model's aim to pursue problems as perceived by clients, as together they explore potential target problems. These are problems in living that are acknowledged by the client and feasible for reduction or resolution in a limited time period. The task-centered practitioner then works with the client to prioritize identified target problems and specifically describe them in such a way that the success of efforts to improve will be measurable. Specific goals are then set that include measurable indicators of progress. Finally, an explicit contract for a set number of sessions is developed.

After establishing the basic contract, the social worker and client identify general tasks or strategies that they plan to use to address the problem. The tasks are a blueprint to guide efforts. Such strategies should draw on available empirical data about effective methods, but are decided upon conjointly with the client. General tasks are then elaborated into specific tasks for the client and social worker to complete between sessions. A key aspect of the approach is the anticipation of obstacles that might prevent success in achieving the task. Finally, task plans are summarized.

The middle phase includes a review of how the target problems are changing and of details of task-completion attempts. The task-centered practitioner
praises efforts and returns with the client to explore obstacles that may have
blocked achievement. In support of task development efforts, role plays or
guided practice are often constructed to practice tasks in a safe environment.
In addition, incentives may be constructed to enhance task efforts.

The social worker and client prepare for termination from the beginning
session as they regularly review the number of remaining sessions and tailor
efforts toward the time remaining. The final session then includes a mutual
assessment of progress and a review of learning about the steps in problem
solving. As problems are seldom fully resolved, this stage often includes planning for further work with other formal and informal resources. In some
cases, services may be extended or new contracts enacted if the client wishes
it and there is reason to believe that the efforts will be successful.

Research Results and Adaptations for the United States

Research on the task-centered approach has included eight controlled studies that generally supported its efficacy (Reid 1997; Gibbons et al. 1985; Gibbons et al. 1978; Larsen and Mitchell 1980; Newcome 1985; Reid 1975; Reid
1978; Reid, et al. 1980; Reid and Bailey-Dempsey 1995; Colvin et al. 2008a).
Studies have been conducted with psychiatric outpatients and with school-
related problems, with reports of changes persisting over time in two studies
(Reid 1997).

One of the signal contributions of the task-centered approach has been its
flexibility. It has been found useful in a range of public and private settings
with varied populations: case management with the frail elderly (Naleppa
and Reid 2000), child welfare (Rooney 1988; Rzepnicki,1985), clients with
serious and persistent mental illness (Gibbons et al. 1985), students in elementary and high schools (Bailey-Dempsey and Reid 1996; Reid et al. 1980;
Colvin et al. 2008a, Colvin et al. 2008b), and sibling aggression (Caspi 2008),
as well as in supervision (Caspi and Reid 2002). Although most applications
have been to voluntary clients in a variety of settings, the approach has also
been integrated into approaches for work with clients who are involuntary or
do not seek service (Magnano 2008; Rooney 1992; Trotter 2006).

Contributions

The task-centered approach has made at least five signal contributions to
social work practice. First, Reid and Epstein described a metamodel for how

social work models or approaches could be constructed (Reid and Epstein 1972). Social work has long struggled with how to utilize approaches developed outside the field. Reid and Epstein suggested that the criteria by which information should be selected include the value base of social work emphasizing collaboration, empirical evidence, and applicability to social work settings and issues. Those criteria remain pertinent as social work strives to incorporate evidence-based practice appropriately.

Second, the task-centered approach has consistently modeled an empirical orientation to practice, seeking the best available knowledge as sources of information to assist clients in making informed decisions (Kelly 2008). The creators consistently modeled this value through continual testing and revision of the approach. In addition, the model incorporated ongoing evaluation for the benefit of client and practitioner as well as agency. More recent contributions detail the empirically derived development of practice guidelines (Caspi 2008) and continued revision based on data of the Partnership in Prevention program (Colvin et al. 2008a, Colvin et al. 2008b).

Third, the task-centered approach has embodied the social work value of self-determination and supported client empowerment and facilitated strengths (Gutierrez et al. 1998; Saleebey 1997). The approach has been used to teach practical problem-solving skills to clients through developing goals, assessing possible task strategies, anticipating obstacles, and then reviewing what might have gotten in the way of task completion.

Fourth, the approach has proven quite flexible in adapting to varied settings and circumstances ranging from resource provision to counseling. Most competing approaches focus on one area, generally aimed at psychological assistance or therapy (Kelly 2008).

Finally, that flexibility has extended to recognizing the circumstances of clients who are not voluntary. Reid and Epstein were among the first social work theorists to address involuntary treatment circumstances (Epstein and Brown 2002; Reid 1978). The task-centered approach has played a prominent role in two leading approaches to work with involuntary clients (Trotter 2006; Rooney 1992).

Limitations

One of the challenges facing the approach is also a strength: brief treatment is not the treatment of choice for all situations and the task-centered approach is not an all-purpose model (Gambrill 1994). Indeed, one of the strengths of the task-centered approach has been its acknowledgment of limitations (Reid and Epstein 1972). For example, clients who are grieving or have primarily expressive needs are guided to Rogerian techniques such as reflective listening. Advocates of strengths-oriented and solution-focused approaches have suggested that the task-centered approach, and problem-solving approaches in general, may neglect client capacities and resources and focus on pathology (De Jong and Berg 2002). While some problem-solving approaches may indeed focus on pathology and ignore resources, the task-centered approach has consistently focused on enhancing client resources and building on strengths. Gambrill suggested that it has borrowed some behavioral techniques without accurately applying them (Gambrill 1994). It might be argued that borrowing some empirically based techniques and applying them in a new structure of practice is a hallmark of model development (Rothman and Thomas 1994). Much of the initial research on the approach was conducted by proponents. However, that initial development has led to more than 200 books, articles, and dissertations, most contributed by people who were not the original developers (Kelly 2008).

Future Directions

William J. Reid and Laura Epstein had little patience for polemic, all-or-nothing struggles between problem-oriented approaches and strengths-oriented approaches or between empirically based approaches and all others, choosing to focus on areas of common interest rather than areas of disagreement (McMillen, Morris, and Sherraden 1994; Shaw 2004). Indeed, one of the major contributions of task-centered practice in the future may capitalize on the sturdy, flexible technology that adapts to so many social work practice contexts (Kelly 2008:199). The future may include more productive exploration of how such approaches can contribute to and be appropriately blended with one another. For example, certain solution-focused techniques such as asking coping questions, scaling questions, and forms of the miracle question may be integrated as useful adjuncts to task-centered techniques (De Jong and Berg 2002). However, the solution-focused approach appears to lack a technology for assessing what happens when well-planned goals go awry. Further, while the solution-focused approach is generally admirable in its exploration and facilitation of client resources, proponents might better guide practitioners in situations that are beyond some clients' experience, and outside information can contribute to informed decision-making. Rather than focusing on shortcomings of other models, however, exploration of appropriate blending may draw on the strengths of both approaches. For example, the motivational interviewing approach offers considerable promise and an evidence base for assisting clients who do not currently acknowledge problems of concern to others (Miller and Rollnick 2002). Integrating techniques designed to assist clients in pre-contemplation, in which they do not see a problem, or in contemplation, in which they have not made a decision to act on a concern, could be a useful adjunct to the problem-search phase for task-centered clients who do not initially perceive a concern recognized by others. Such blending with other approaches can augment them as well by incorporating the task-centered approach's valuing of client-perceived concerns and focus on modifying the environment, rather than the more narrowly psychological focus of many other therapeutic approaches.

The context for social work practice, including managed care and concerns for effectiveness in public service, continues to support the relevance of the task-centered approach to helping clients address problems or goals of concern to them and doing so in a timely fashion.

Finally, social work students now and in the future may assume that focusing on developing discreet, measurable, and feasible goals with clients around their own expressed concerns is and always has been simply good social work practice. They may not know that this conventional wisdom is in large part a contribution of the task-centered approach (Kelly 2008). There are worse outcomes than being absorbed into a general model of good practice.

Note

1. The following section draws largely from Reid 2000 and Epstein and Brown 2002.

References

Bailey-Dempsey, C. and Reid, W. J. (1996). Intervention design and development: A case study. *Research on Social Work Practice* 6:208–228.
Caspi, J. (2008). Building a sibling aggression treatment model: Design and development research in action. *Research on Social Work Practice* 18:575–585.
Caspi, J. and Reid, W. J. (2002). *Educational supervision in social work.* New York: Columbia University Press.
Colvin, J., Lee, M., Magnano, J., and Smith, V. (2008a). The Partners in Prevention Program: The evaluation and evolution of the task-centered case management model. *Research on Social Work Practice* 18:607–615.
——. (2008b). The Partners in Prevention Program: Further development of the task-centered case management model. *Research on Social Work Practice* 18:586–595.
De Jong, P. and Berg, I. K. (2002). *Interviewing for solutions.* Pacific Grove, CA: Wadsworth.
Epstein, L. and Brown, L. (2002). *Brief treatment and a new look at the task-centered approach,* 4th ed. New York: MacMillan.

Gambrill, E. (1994). What's in a name? Task-centered, empirical, and behavioral practice.*Social Service Review 68* (4): 578–599.

Gibbons, J. S., Butler, J., Urwin, P., and Gibbons, J. L. (1978). Evaluation of a social work service for self-poisoning parents. *British Journal of Psychiatry 133*:111–118.

Gibbons, J., Bow, I., and Butler, J. (1985). Task-centered social work after parasuicide. In E. M. Goldberg, J. Gibbons, and I. Sinclair (Eds.), *Problems, tasks and outcomes: The evaluation of task-centered casework in three settings*, 169–257. Boston: George Allen and Unwin.

Gutierrez, L. M., Parsons, R. J., and Cox, E. O. (1998). *Empowerment in social work practice: A source book*. Pacific Grove, CA: Brooks-Cole.

Hoyt, M. F. (2000). *Some stories are better than others: Doing what works in brief therapy and managed care*. Philadelphia: Brunner/Mazel.

Kelly, M. (2008). Task-centered practice. In T. Mizrahi and L. Davis (Eds.), *Encyclopedia of Social Work*, 20th ed., 197–199. Washington, DC: NASW Press.

Larsen, J. and Mitchell, C. (1980). Task-centered strength-oriented group work with delinquents. *Social Casework 61*:154–163.

Magnano, J. (2009). *Partners in success: An evaluation of an intervention for children with severe emotional disturbances*. Albany: State University of New York Press.

McMillen, J., Morris, L., and Sherraden, M. (2004). Ending social work's grudge match: Problems versus strengths. *Families in Society 85* (3): 317–325.

Miller, W. R. and Rollnick, S. (2002). *Motivational interviewing: Preparing people to change addictive behavior,* 2nd ed. New York: Guilford.

Naleppa, M. J. and Reid, W. J. (2000). Integrating case management and brief-treatment strategies: A hospital-based geriatric program. *Social Work in Health Care 31* (4): 1–23.

Newcome, K. (1985). Task-centered group work with the chronically mentally ill in day treatment. In A. E. Fortune (Ed.), *Task-centered practice with families and groups*, 78–91. New York: Springer.

Perlman, H. (1957). *Social casework: a problem-solving process*. Chicago: University of Chicago Press.

Reid, W. J. (1975). An experimental test of a task-centered approach. *Social Work 20*:3–9.

——. (1978). *The task-centered system*. New York: Columbia University Press.

——. (1997). Research on task-centered practice. *Social Work Research 21* (3): 132–137.

——. (2000). *The task planner: An intervention resource for human service professionals*. New York: Columbia University Press.

Reid, W. J. and Bailey-Dempsey, C. (1995). The effects of monetary incentives on school performance. *Families in Society 76*:331–340.

Reid, W. J. and Epstein, L. (1972). *Task-centered casework*. New York: Columbia University Press.

Reid, W. J., Epstein, L., Brown, L. B., Tolson, E. R., and Rooney, R. H. (1980). Task-centered school social work. *Social Work in Education 2*:7–24.

Reid, W. J. and Shyne, A. W. (1969). *Brief and extended casework*. New York: Columbia University Press.

Rooney, R. H. (1988). Measuring task-centered training effects on practice: Results of an audiotape study in a public agency. *Journal of Continuing Social Work Education 4*:2–7.

——. (1992). Strategies for work with involuntary clients. New York: Columbia University Press.

Rothman, J. and Thomas, E. (Eds.). (1994). *Intervention research design and development for human service.* New York: Haworth.

Rzepnicki, T. L. (1985). Task-centered intervention in foster care services: Working with families who have children in placement. In A. E. Fortune (Ed.), *Task-centered practice with families and groups,* 172–184. New York: Springer.

Saleebey, D. (1997). (Ed). *The strengths perspective in social work practice,* 2nd ed. Needham Heights, MA: Allyn-Bacon.

Shaw, I. (2004). William J. Reid: An appreciation. *Qualitative Social Work* 3:109–115.

Trotter, C. (2006). *Working with Involuntary Clients,* 2nd ed. Thousand Oaks, CA: Sage.

Wells, R. and Gianetti, V. J. (1990). *Handbook of the brief psychotherapies.* New York: Plenum.

14 | Task-Centered Practice in Great Britain

Peter Marsh

FROM RELATIVELY EARLY DAYS the task-centered model has featured strongly in United Kingdom social work; the model is taught within social work courses, and practice research contributes directly to the development of the model. It has been widely used in almost all settings: from hospital to child welfare, from adult care to mental health care, and from probation to child protection. The substantial development work has had three broad phases. First was early work on outcomes and comparative studies. Once task-centered work became more established, its development became part of the UK's strong emphasis on service user involvement in decision making and the promotion of a partnership-based approach within social work. The final phase, in the light of evidence that adoption and continuing use of the task-centered model needed a good deal of investment of time and skill, has been to examine and test the ways the model can be implemented and supported.

In more recent years the model has suffered, alongside all practice development, from a government-led move within social work away from a professionally driven practice model and toward a procedure-driven practice primarily by managers rather than by practitioners.

History and Research Results

Professional social work education in UK universities began in earnest in the early 1960s and had major growth in the 1970s. A key driver of this growth in the quantity and quality of social work education was the foundation in 1961 of the National Institute for Social Work (NISW), based in central London. The institute combined a substantial practice development program with training, a research unit, and a dedicated library. It became a center for the dissemination of the latest work on professional practice, examining a range of models and engaging in their development. Prominent among these was task-centered social work, and Nano McCaughan and Anne Vickery led a program that combined training courses held throughout the country with active debate and examination of the model (see for example McCaughan and Vickery 1982). This work continued as a powerful force until the end of the 1980s.

From the early 1970s the development of task-centered practice was taken up by the NISW research unit, headed up by the redoubtable Tilda Goldberg. A program of work to develop practice via research was established, linking with the training function of NISW and spreading out to colleagues in various universities and social service agencies. The research on task-centered work examined a range of practice settings, the model's suitability for different problems, and effectiveness studies. It contributed to the growing UK debate about the role of casework within the social worker's portfolio, and highlighted the notable value of task-centered work. An overall summary of three major studies provided a remarkably detailed examination of many aspects of task-centered practice (Goldberg, Gibbons, and Sinclair 1985). The first was a comparative study of task-centered social work against other forms of mental health practice in the case of parasuicide (suicide attempts) that highlighted quite dramatically the potential for the model (Gibbons, Bow, and Butler 1985). Another study, on probation work with offenders (Goldberg and Stanley 1985) in the Differential Treatment Unit (an experimental team), tested a range of different practice approaches within criminal justice. Task-centered work within a court order proved feasible, and was again showing promise as an effective problem-solving model. The final study, of initial work with service users within social services intake teams (Sinclair and Walker 1985), indicated a wide variation (from 10 to 55 percent of cases) in implementation of the model within different teams.

Application

In the early 1980s, UK social work began to develop an overall approach to practice that became characterized as partnership-based. Essentially the approach emphasized the value, from both a research and a citizenship perspective, of social workers and service users engaging in partnership that emphasized the need for both parties to have maximum understanding of each other's position and to tackle problems as an explicitly joint endeavor. This approach was particularly prominent in work with children and families in the care system. It is at the heart of the 1989 Children Act, which is the current legislative base for work with children and families, and provided an excellent platform for task-centered practice. Another strong current of the times was the growing recognition of the need to take more account of ethnicity and culture, and again task-centered work was recognized as being well suited to this emphasis on "respectful" practice (Ahmad 1990).

Building on these themes, the Social Work in Partnership project, led by Peter Marsh and Mike Fisher, began a series of practice-based studies looking at task-centered work as the basis of a partnership approach within both children and adult services. In particular, the studies examine implementation, support, and practice development issues (Marsh and Fisher 1992), as well as the key elements of successful training (Newton and Marsh 1993).

Adaptations

The practice development work in the UK continued with studies by Peter Marsh and Mark Doel. These provided new ways of delivering some aspects of the model (such as using a newspaper metaphor to aid with problem exploration) and an approach to training that was based in practice examples (Doel and Marsh 1992). Their most recent work with a practice team examined implementation, supervision, and agency support issues in detail (Marsh and Doel 2005).

The Prominence of Task-Centered Practice

Task-centered work is now a mainstream practice model in teaching texts in the UK. It is, for example, one of the five approaches to practice in the classic *Assessment in Social Work* (Milner and O'Byrne 1998), where an interesting map metaphor characterizes the task-centered approach as the "Handy Tourist Map," recognizing its "real world" strengths and its potential for use in a wide range of settings. Task-centered work is given even higher prominence in the widely used practice text by Coulshed and Orme (2006), where it is one of only four "methods" (accompanied by counseling, dealing with loss and change, and cognitive-behavioral work). Social work students in the UK will find task-centered work alongside about six other approaches in the Davies's encyclopedic class text, *Companion to Social Work,* and within eight areas of "intervention" in Lishman's major field practice text designed to support student supervision (see Marsh 2007, 2008).

Limitations

However, the overall position of practice development in the UK from the late 1990s onward has not been as promising as in earlier periods. For example, in the major study of UK social work education in the early 1990s (Marsh and Triseliotis 1996) the confusion about different models/interventions/approaches was clearly shown. Task-centered work was self-reported as well known by 14 percent of students, with only "counseling," at 15 percent, better known by qualifying year students, but it featured as one of more than 80 theories and theorists (Marsh and Triseliotis 1996:51). The lack of widespread research into practice, the muddling descriptions of approaches and the standards that should be used to judge them, and the managerialism that has affected all services in the UK has greatly weakened professional social work practice in recent years. Task-centered work is a victim of these trends.

Strengths and Weaknesses

Task-centered work in the UK has had serious research attention. Indeed, it has been at the forefront of developmental research and has had a strong base in the partnership approach to social work that is promoted throughout the UK. The growing emphasis on evidence-based approaches is a positive boost for the model, and the work on implementation provides a sound base for continuing development. But the lack of funding for, and lack of attention to, practice-based research is a serious problem for continuing development (Marsh and Fisher 2005), and the current manager-led approach to social work is a threat to all models of professional practice. Some serious attention to the status of professional practice is required if we are to ensure that the excellent past work of building effective practice continues.

References

Ahmad, B. (1990). *Black perspectives in social work*. Birmingham: Venture Press.
Coulshed, V. and Orme, J. (2006). *Social work practice*, 4th ed. Basingstoke: Macmillan.
Doel, M. and Marsh, P. (1992). *Task-centred social work*. Aldershot: Ashgate.
Gibbons, J., Bow, I., and Butler, J. (1985). Task-centred work after parasuicide. In E. M. Goldberg, J. Gibbons, and I. Sinclair (Eds.), *Problems, tasks and outcomes: The evaluation of task-centred casework*, 169–247. London: Allen and Unwin.

Goldberg, E. M., Gibbons, J., and Sinclair, I. (1985). *Problems, tasks and outcomes: The evaluation of task-centred casework in three settings*. No. 47 National Institute for Social Work Library. London: Allen and Unwin.

Goldberg, E. M. and Stanley, S. J. (with Kenrick, J.) (1985). Task-centred casework in a probation setting. In E. M. Goldberg, J. Gibbons, and I. Sinclair (Eds.), *Problems, tasks and outcomes: The evaluation of task-centred casework*, 87–168. London: Allen and Unwin.

Marsh, P. (2002). Task-centred work. In M. Davies (Ed.), *The Blackwell companion to social work*, 106–113. Oxford: Blackwell.

———. (2007). Task-centred practice. In J. Lishman (Ed.), *Handbook for practice learning in social work and social care knowledge and theory*, 188–200. London: Jessica Kingsley.

———. (2008). Task-centred work. In M. Davies (Ed.), *The Blackwell companion to social work*, 121–128. Oxford: Blackwell.

Marsh, P. and Doel, M. (2005). *The task-centred book*. London: Routledge.

Marsh, P. and Fisher, M. (1992). *Good intentions: Developing partnership in social services*. York: Joseph Rowntree Foundation.

———. (2005). *Developing the evidence for social work and social care practice*. London: Social Care Institute for Excellence.

Marsh, P. and Triseliotis, J. (1996). *Ready to practise? Social workers and probation officers: Their training and first year in work*. Aldershot: Avebury.

McCaughen, N. and Vickery, A. (1982). Staging the play. *Social Work Today 14* (2): 11–13.

Milner, J. and O'Byrne, P. (1998). *Assessment in social work*. London: Macmillan.

Newton, C. and Marsh, P. (1993). *Training in partnership—translating intentions into practice in social services*. York: Joseph Rowntree Foundation.

Sinclair, I. and Walker, D. (1985). Task-centred casework in two intake teams. In M. Goldberg, J. Gibbons, and I. Sinclair (Eds.), *Problems, tasks and outcomes: The evaluation of task-centred casework*, 11–88. E. London: Allen and Unwin.

15 | Task-Centered Practice in the Netherlands

Nel Jagt and Louwerus Jagt

History

The task-centered model was introduced in the Netherlands in 1977 with the translation of Reid and Epstein's *Task-Centered Casework*, followed by the translation in 1980 of *Task-Centered Practice* and in 1982 of *The Task-Centered System*. Marie Kamphuis,[1] a social work pioneer, had a hand in this.

When he retired as a staff member of the school of social work in The Hague, Gerard Kal commented on the introduction of task-centered work (Kal 1987). Looking back on his experiences as a social worker (he was a student of Marie Kamphuis in Groningen) he had discovered the limitations of the psycho-social casework theories he learned. Too often extensive anamneses were followed by poor intervention plans. Task-centered casework seemed to him the model he was looking for: it offered a "no-nonsense" way of helping, it bore the emancipatory hallmark of client participation, and it gave room for the client to decide what the problem was and what goals were worthwhile. He especially appreciated a clear structure that could be understood by clients from start to finish.

Both of us, Nel and Lou Jagt, at that time teaching in schools of social work in Rotterdam and Breda, shared Kal's opinion on the task-centered model. We thought it important to concentrate on target goals and to work with time limits. We were impressed by the possibilities of the task concept and the research base of the model, and we believed that the task-centered approach could boost social work in the Netherlands. So it worked indeed. A later statement by Kirk and Reid (2002:172) summarized our experience: "While attention to research in social work was expanding, the issues of its dissemination and use were largely neglected." We considered dissemination of the task-centered model in the Netherlands as one of our primary tasks.

Important Steps in Dissemination

Two big steps in the last decade of the twentieth century were writing a book on TCP in Dutch and initiating an international TCP congress in the Netherlands. The first edition of *Taakgerichte hulpverlening in het maatschappelijk werk* was published in 1990. Based on Reid's books, it "translated" the TCP model to Dutch social work practice, explaining differences and congruence with known theories and models, giving case examples, and relating the model to the Professional Profile of the NVMW, the Dutch association of social workers. The book had several reprintings, was revised in 1995, and was in 2004 completely rewritten in the light of new theories by Reid and others, changes in our society, and changes in social work practice. Since 1990 about 20,000 copies have been sold, and we have been informed by accreditation committees that since then all social work students have been more or less educated in the TCP model.

Each chapter of the book ended with learning tasks for students. Many students (and teachers) were enthusiastic about TCP, because it helped them to find answers on "how-to" questions. TCP also gave a rationale for the short-term approach. Before this, short-term work was frequent, but often seen as inferior. Now social workers were entitled to be proud of their work and able to structure it better in a "real social work way." For more advanced students we translated and adapted Reid's *Task-Centered Strategies* in 1995, and published articles on TCP in professional journals and books.

An international congress on TCP was realized in Breda in 1998, in cooperation with the school of social work from Hogeschool Brabant, the Dutch Association of Social Workers, and the publisher of our books. The congress had 450 attendees (social work staff, teachers, and social scientists). Contributions were made by William Reid (overview and current developments), Cynthia Bailey-Dempsey (TCP with school-aged children and their parents), Ronald Rooney (TCP work with involuntary clients), Peter Marsh (effective training for TCP), and Lou Jagt and Geert van der Laan (application of the TCP model in the Netherlands).

The next day, two more congresses were held: one in Breda with about 150 students and presentations from Anne Fortune, Reid, and Bailey-Dempsey; and a second in Amsterdam with about 250 attendants and Glenda and Ronald Rooney. In this way, TCP became quite well known in the Netherlands. It helped that general textbooks on social work, as a rule, spent a chapter or paragraph on the model.

Limitations

Does this mean TCP is overall understood well? Not always; in the Netherlands we meet the same misunderstandings as Marsh and Doel report from the UK—for instance, that TCP is easy to apply and meant for concrete and practical problems. Often the model is underestimated. Indeed, it is easy to explain (to clients for instance), but not easy to *do* for workers. It does not suffice to have learned about the TCP model just once in initial professional education; social workers have to maintain their knowledge and competences. How does this happen?

Application

TCP has been taught in refresher courses for social workers, but especially in in-service training. Peter Marsh from the UK gave his train-the-trainers course to social work teachers. Some of them—and us—trained the staff in agencies, including those for community social work, medical social work, school social work, occupational social work, and youth care. In these and other contexts, the TCP model was taught with actual cases from the agencies concerned.

Furthermore, TCP has been demonstrated in quite elaborate cases in the nationwide online project Casus Consult (CC). CC was started in 2000 by and for social workers in order to exchange and discuss practice experiences and knowledge via the Internet. Although many workers showed enthusiasm, it turned out to be quite a challenge to write readable texts that would inform colleagues. But the project is still running and attracts new and eager participants. Sharing and developing knowledge in this way holds promise for the future.

A computerized registration model, based on the clear structure of TCP, was developed in 2000 in cooperation with an Information Communication Technology professional, to match agencies' registration and social case recording. The aims were to give practitioners more grip on their practice and to capture data for research. However, most agencies prefer software devised for their own specialized branch of practice.

Inspired by the work of Ronald Rooney, Lou published in 2001 a book on work with involuntary clients. In common with Rooney, a connection was made with the TCP model. The presented strategies had a noticeable impact on new methods developed by the Association of Probation in our country.

Future Directions

We conclude this account about maintaining and developing TCP knowledge with some signals from other areas that indicate that TCP methods are indeed valued and being further developed:

- In 2005, a regional developmental agency studied evaluated and validated methods used by social agencies in its region and reported that: "Our most important finding is that on the list with nineteen social work methods only one evaluated and validated method occurred; the task-centered model. The other models are descriptive and not scientifically evaluated. A remarkable but poor result."
- In 2007, a training college for physiotherapy started a course based partly on the task-centered model to help patients with psychosomatic symptoms. The students appreciated the possibilities that TCP offered them to strengthen their profession.
- Last, but not least, some workers and agencies are informing their colleagues by means of professional journals or Internet sites about experiences with TCP in their field of specialization; for instance, social work with immigrants.

In the end we can say that the task-centered model is quite well disseminated in social work practice in the Netherlands, but there is still work to do. What has to be developed in the near future is intervention research. For the last decade, two universities have had a chair in social work and the twenty schools of social work (in Hogescholen for professional education) have had funds to appoint researchers, and they have made these appointments on a large scale. So in the future there will be more than dissemination of methods that have been developed elsewhere.

Note

1. Marie Kamphuis (1907–2004) was in the United States for two long periods just after the Second World War to study social casework. In the last edition of her book *What Is Social Casework?* (11 printings/several editions from 1950 to 1977) she writes

about TCP. Kamphuis had a big impact on the professionalization of and education for social work. The current Marie Kamphuis Foundation aims to strengthen the relation of social work and science.

References

Jagt, L. (2001). *Moet dat nou? Hulpverlening aan onvrijwillige cliënten*. Houten: Bohn Stafleu van Loghum.

Jagt, N. and Jagt, L. (2004). *Taakgerichte hulpverlening in social work*. Houten: Bohn Stafleu van Loghum.

Kal, G. (1987). "Over *taakgericht* casework." In H. de Kler and H. Pos, *Maatschappelijk werk in verandering*. Den Haag: Ruward.

Kirk, S. and Reid, W. J. (2002). *Science and social work*. New York: Columbia University Press.

Marsh, P. and M. Doel. (2005). *The task-centred book*. London: Routledge.

Reid, W. (1995). *Taakgerichte strategieën*. Houten: Bohn Stafleu van Loghum.

16 | Task-Centered Practice in Germany

Matthias Naleppa

History

The task-centered model was introduced to German social work through a translation of the first book by Reid and Epstein (1979). Its clear structure and focus on time limits and a straightforward strategy make it a model that fits well with the very task-oriented nature of Germans. However, the model initially did not receive much attention. Several factors may have contributed to this. German social workers were—and continue to be—very guarded about applying practice models that come from a different cultural context. The 1970s, when the model was introduced, also saw an intense discussion about the usefulness of casework models for German social work practice (Müller 2006). Task-centered practice did not benefit from this discussion. Moreover, "task" is a term that is difficult to translate into German. The term *"Aufgabe"* comes the closest. It includes the meaning of task, but it also used as a word for homework and thus conveys a negative connotation for some. Finally, while the model was published in German, no protagonists were on hand to provide training and promote the model. All of these factors are currently changing and the task-centered model is beginning to gain foothold and popularity in some regions of Germany.

Application

Over the past decade, a series of workshops and training projects were implemented in Munich, Nürnberg, Bamberg, Würzburg, and other southern German locations. Practitioners trained in the model come from the fields of family counseling, services for the homeless, substance abuse treatment, services for older adults, and child welfare services. Depending on the practice setting, the task-centered model is applied as a straightforward model as presented by Reid and Epstein (1979) or in combination with case management as described by Naleppa and Reid (2000). Because group work approaches are widely used, the model is also applied in groups. No major adaptations except for language are needed. The model fits well into the cultural context, and practitioners using it consistently provide positive feedback regarding its applicability to the local practice reality.

Social work in Germany can be characterized as less clinical and counseling/therapy-oriented than in countries such as the United States and as having a stronger focus on more traditional fields of welfare services. Practitioners tend to act more autonomously, drawing from their experience rather than trusting theory (Dewe, Peters, and Stüwe 1987). The practice models used by social workers are usually more systems-based and administrative approaches, often strongly shaped by routines and standards required by institutions (Spiegel 2006). Typical social work activities include administration of welfare benefits, case management, referral, accessing and coordination of services, management and leadership of organizations, as well as group work practice and some community organizing. While counseling and communication competencies are an important part of social work practice, they are used as skills within these activities rather than directly for therapy. The task-centered model lends itself well to integration into such forms of practice.

Challenges

Social workers are increasingly trying to enter the fields of counseling and therapy. Structural conditions make this fairly difficult. A major obstacle that the task-centered model and other therapeutic practice models face is the very restrictive German laws and regulations regarding psychotherapy. They currently only allow insurance reimbursement for psychologists with training in behavior therapy, psychoanalysis, or depth psychology. Significant changes to these restrictions are not anticipated in the near future, but social workers are increasingly integrating counseling techniques into their practice repertoire.

Research Results

Only a limited amount of country-specific research on task-centered practice exists, since the practice model is still in its early phase in Germany. The evaluation of the model and dissemination of findings occurs only at the agency level. Several agencies have participated in training sessions and then used single-subject designs to evaluate the outcomes. Projects used task-centered practice with methadone maintenance and other substance abuse clients (Naleppa, Bohnert, and Fassler 2000). A series of single-subject designs pointed to positive treatment outcomes. Feedback from practitioners was affirmative. Especially beneficial for German social work practice were the clear focus on client-acknowledged problems, the straightforward structure of the model that enables active client participation, the use of time limits and related expectancy effects, the use of task schedules and other practice forms, and the fairly effortless integration of accountability measures into day-to-day practice.

Future Directions

Currently, an increased effort is under way to promote the task-centered model in Germany. An original German language textbook on task-centered practice is in process and should be available shortly (Naleppa, in progress). A number of schools of social work are offering courses that include a strong emphasis on task-centered practice. Several individuals are now skilled to provide in-depth training in task-centered practice. Empirically based practice is gaining significance in Germany (Spiegel 2006). Thus, it should be anticipated that the task-centered model will continue to gain acceptance in Germany.

References

Dewe, B., Peters, F. and Stüwe, G. (1987). Professionelle Arbeit kann warten, bis man sie braucht (Professional work can wait until it is needed). *Sozialmagazin* 2:30–36.

Müller, C. W. (2006). *Wie Helfen zum Beruf wurde: Eine Methodengeschichte der Sozialen Arbeit (How helping became a profession: A history of social work methods)*, 4th ed. Weinheim and Munich, Germany: Juventa.

Naleppa, M. J., Bohnert, A., and Fassler, A. (2000). Ergebnisse eines Tests des Task-centered Modells in der Caritas Fachambulanz für Suchtkranke Miesbach (Outcomes of a test of task-centered practice in the Caritas outpatient program for substance abusing clients Miesbach). Miesbach, Germany: Author.

Naleppa, M. J. and Reid, W. J. (2000). Integrating case management and brief treatment strategies: A hospital-based geriatric program. *Social Work in Health Care 31*: 1–23.

Reid, W. J. and Epstein, L. (1979).*Gezielte Kurzeitbehandlung in der sozialen Einzelhilfe (Task-centered casework)*. Freiburg i. Br., Germany: Lambertus.

Spiegel, Hiltrud von. (2006). *Methodisches Handeln in der Sozialen Arbeit: Grundlagen und Arbeitshilfen (Social work methods: Foundations and skills)*. Munich, Germany and Basel, Switzerland: Ernst Reinhardt.

17 | Task-Centered Practice in Switzerland

Alexander Kobel and Matthias Naleppa

History

The task-centered model (termed *"aufgabenzentrierte, zeitlich befristete Beratung"* or AZB in Switzerland) was first introduced to Swiss social work practice through a translation of the seminal work of William Reid and Laura Epstein (Reid and Epstein 1979). Despite its scientifically founded, praxis-oriented, and social work-specific methods, the task-centered model until very recently did not receive due recognition in Switzerland. Other practice approaches such as problem-solving, systems theory-based models, and case management were at the center of attention. The recent acknowledgment and reappearance of task-centered practice is related to developments in the Swiss public welfare system. In many locations, especially the urban centers, social welfare departments are confronted with an increasing need for services and limited financial and personnel resources available to address the demand. The consequences are dire, ranging from declining quality to unmotivated practitioners who change to less taxing fields of practice.

Such pressure challenges service providers to better account for service outcomes while maintaining acceptable working conditions for employees.

With this backdrop, the School of Social Work of Bern in collaboration with the Social Welfare Office of Zurich and the Institute for Community-Based Social Work (ISSAB) of the University Duisburg-Essen/Germany developed a practice concept (Sozialdepartement der Stadt Zürich 2005) that enables a systematic appraisal and steering of limited resources while concurrently supporting a resource-oriented approach to social work. It was decided to integrate task-centered practice as a key practice feature. To make better use of the task-centered model, a translation of an Epstein and Brown book (2006) was initiated to supplement the German edition of the Reid and Epstein (1979) publication. The following section will illustrate the adaptation of the task-centered model to this practice reality.

Adaptation

The starting point for our developmental work was the concept of service bundles (so-called *Dienstleistungspakete*). A service bundle includes a description of the services needed and the time required to address them. All services—even financial and public assistance and legally mandated services—are provided within the assigned service bundle by the same social worker. The following table provides an overview of the types of service bundles used.

Capacity planning and management occurs through a guidance system that uses specific allocation criteria to compare data on current service bundle needs with the resource *staff time* available (annual staff working hours and average time required for each service bundle) to address this demand. The

Table 17.1 Service Bundles

Service Bundle	Service	Approximate Time and Frequency
Intake/Assessment	Assessment of general client situation and needs. Identification and negotiation of general framework for individual, financial, and legally mandated services. Triage to one of the three following service bundles.	1–3 sessions in first month 4–5 hours per month
Counseling (*Beratung*)	Task-centered, time-limited counseling and assistance in one or more problematic areas of living according to client-prioritized list.	4–6 sessions over three months; 3–4 hours per month
Guidance (*Begleitung*)	Reoccurring assistance, especially to protect client and welfare department interests. Includes monitoring of services and enforcing mandates.	3–4 sessions over six months; 1–2 hours per month
Maintenance (*Bearbeitung*)	Updating of financial supports and monitoring of services provided by third parties. Counseling not needed or possible.	1–2 sessions per year; ½–1 hour per month

professionals then decide how to adapt their service bundles to the existing capacities. They can accomplish this, for example, by offering fewer counseling bundles or by changing guidance into maintenance bundles. Through specific priority criteria that show when certain service bundles can no longer be offered, staff develop a strategy to address the lack of capacities.

Application

The task-centered approach is the key practice approach in the *counseling* service bundle. For these clients, the task-planning and implementation sequence begins during assessment. The primary focus of assessment is the collaborative evaluation of the situation, leading to an account of client service needs and problems to be addressed. An important element is the explicit resource orientation: the focus is not only on problems in living but also on the resources that can be activated to address the needs. Our experience shows that when integrating this step into the assessment, for example through the joint development of a resource list, clients and social workers appraise the situation more optimistically and already begin to identify potential problem-solving strategies. Assessment is standardized and includes:

- Reason for contact and areas of living posing a problem in the words of client(s).
- Areas to be addressed, prioritized by client(s).
- Service providers that are or should get involved.
- Resources that can be activated to address the problems (resource list).
- Anticipated amount of services required.
- Explicit client agreement and commitment to assessment and planned service bundle.

In the service bundles counseling and guidance, goals and tasks are formulated together with the clients; for maintenance clients, this step is skipped. The contract includes two parts. The first section includes problems, goals, and client tasks, as well as tasks for professionals, other persons, and institutions in the client's social environment. A second section—clearly distinguishable—includes the legal mandates that clients must comply with in order to receive financial and public assistance. This separation assists in clarifying the workers' dual role of providing individual assistance and counseling and controlling financial means and public assistance. Upon completion, service bundles are evaluated by client and social worker. This evaluation serves the purpose of reinforcing achieved outcomes for clients and making the outcomes more apparent for social workers and third parties. It also serves as foundation for the decisions regarding the client's needs for another service bundle. If additional assistance is required, a determination for a new service bundle is made.

Future Directions

Currently, we are in the phase of introducing and establishing task-centered practice in Switzerland. A systematic evaluation still has to be completed. It is hoped that such data will benefit agency leadership in the social-political dialogue about staffing and resources. Initial experiences with the model indicate that task-centered practice integrated with a capacity planning and management system can help professionals better manage the resource "staff time." It also provides the foundation for systematic outcome evaluation, an important task for strained social welfare departments.

References

Epstein, L. and Brown, L. B. (2006). *Aufgabenzentrierte, zeitlich befristete Beratung in der Sozialarbeit (Task-centered, time-limited counseling in social work)*. Luzern, Switzerland: Interact.

Reid, W. J., and Epstein, L. (1979). *Gezielte Kurzeitbehandlung in der sozialen Einzelhilfe. (Task-centered casework)*. Freiburg, Germany: Lambertus.

Sozialdepartement der Stadt Zürich. (2005). *Fallsteuerung: Hintergründe und Praxis eines zukunftsfähigen Modells (Managing cases: Background and practice of a sustainable model)*. Zürich, Switzerland: Author.

18 | Task-Centered Practice in Norway

Rita Elisabeth Eriksen

IN THIS CHAPTER, I will focus on two major topics: the dissemination and documentation of Task-Centered Practice (TCP) and some important factors in adjusting TCP to Norwegian fieldwork and users.

History

TCP was introduced in Norway in the early 1970s (G. A. Askeland, personal communication, Oct. 10, 2007). Mari-Anne Zahl translated a summary (Zahl 1987) of Epstein's book: "Helping people. The task-centered approach." Zahl used this summary in teaching at the University of Trondheim, School of Social Work and in her research (Zahl 1989). As one of her master students at that time, I was inspired to practice TCP.

With comprehensive support from the Norwegian State's Social and Health Department (1990–1998), TCP has been developed primarily in the local social services departments. TCP has also inspired social workers and health professionals in settings like child care, probation, occupational social work, school social work, psychiatric clinics, and medical hospitals. The public documentation of this practice is casual. Some scattered documents are available, for example, using TCP to improve housing for users with addiction problems (Steen 2002), to prevent marginalization of the users' living conditions (Fredrikstad 2006), and to rehabilitate youngsters with drug problems (Hjelme 2007). The projects combine TCP and "change-oriented consultations" (Barth, Børtveit, and Prescott 2001) (these Norwegian psychologists have further developed the work of Miller and Rollnick 1991).

Since 1987, TCP has been more systematically explored in research, practice, lecturing, teaching, and guidance. The participants were students and practitioners, but different leaders also have been pleased to use TCP in administrating their staffs (Nordstrand 1993, 1995; Eriksen 1994, 1998).

Dissemination

In 1990–1992 a project with unemployed youth was carried out in a local social service department in Oslo (Tronsmo 1992). Mark Doel and Peter Marsh (1992) from the University of Sheffield shared their knowledge about TCP, and I was engaged as a consultant. The youth expressed satisfaction in working this way.

In the 1990s the Norwegian State's Social and Health Department supported two national programs whose aim was to increase knowledge of social work practice in local social service departments. Several projects focused on trying out TCP. Nordstrand (1993) taught social work students TCP and focused on how they practiced in the field. TCP influenced the students to concentrate more on their relations with their users rather than the systems they worked within. Two other projects documented the users' progress in goal attainment and how the social workers practiced TCP (Eriksen 1994, 1998). A textbook on TCP was completed (Eriksen and Nordstrand 1995), as well as a handbook (Eriksen 1999a) and several teaching videos (Eriksen 1999b). Several schools of social work still use the TCP textbook in their curricula.

Haram and Amundsen's (1995) book about short-term methods in social work included TCP in Norway. For some years Nesset and Eriksen worked to refine TCP in the context of local social services departments and with different groups of users. Nesset (2001), as a practitioner, emphasized the experiences concerning TCP and Eriksen (2001), as a researcher and lecturer, elaborated on the organizational context. Eriksen also developed programs for TCP training. Participants appreciated the systematic way of working and building on their previous knowledge (Halås 2002). The participants stressed the importance of practicing TCP in their own working contexts in order to understand its essence (Eriksen 2003).

Adaptations

I will mention some examples of adaptations of TCP to Norwegian fieldwork. The examples are mainly from my own projects, since I know them best.

Social Benefits Make the Users Dependent on the Social Workers

In the Norwegian welfare state we have a system to secure the citizens' living conditions:

1. A social security system with universal rights for all citizens, financed by the state.
2. A social benefit system financed by the local governments. Citizens must be entitled to receive services from the local social service departments. The services might be money, housing, treatment, training, education, or work. The aim is to strengthen the citizens' resources in ways that enable them to take better care of themselves.

   (A new reform has been introduced: The New Work and Welfare Administration [NAV] [St.meld. nr. 14, 2002–2003], which implies one administration of our welfare system.)

In the 1990s, social workers in the local social service departments had much individual authority to grant social benefits to the best of their judgments. Users felt economically dependent on their social workers. Some users worked hard with tasks, hoping to get increased benefits, while others were more interested in how they could get more social benefits without efforts to improve their life situations. The interactions between the users and the social workers were influenced by an imbalance in power in several unfortunate ways (Eriksen 1994). A follow-up project aimed to empower the users instead of making them dependent on social benefits. The administrative staffs became responsible for dealing with the applications for benefits. The users and social workers concentrated on TCP and promoted more meaningful services for the users (Eriksen 1998). The results from these projects led to organizational changes in some local social service departments, with applications for social benefits in one department and counseling in another.

A Short-Term Intervention with a Long-Term Perspective

The users of the social services departments are a heterogeneous group (Underlid 2005; Eriksen 2007). Many have complex social problems that have accumulated over years and cannot be resolved in the short time (three months) recommended by Epstein (1992) and Reid (1992). The numbers of consultations (interviews) in a user's TCP period varied from one to eleven. The average was five consultations (Eriksen 1994). Both the users and the social workers were surprised that so much work could be done in such a short time. In this project the collaboration ended when the users expressed that they could finish the remaining work on their own or together with their informal network (family, friends, neighbors, or colleagues). Consequently, social service departments used TCP for intensive periods of work with the option of future contracts. Some of the users later called upon their social workers to start a new period of TCP. If so, a new contract was made with new or revised problems and goals to be reached. The users gradually learned how to work in a TCP partnership and how to solve their problems better. The project participants reported that the ending of each TCP period was easier to carry out when the users had the possibility to make new contacts later.

An Explicit Motivation Phase First, Then a Problem-Solving Phase

Another adaptation in Norway was to add a motivation phase before the problem-solving phase. Users who had struggled with their problems for many years needed consultations and serious reflection to believe in possible changes in their life situations. The social workers had to work explicitly with these users' motivations for a period of time without expectations to carry out tasks in action (Eriksen 1998). In the first phase, they listened actively to the users' disappointments, grief, and losses. At the same time they pointed out the users' resources and what they had gained so far. Many of these users reported that they did not have much faith in themselves and their possibilities for solving their problems. When the social workers systematically asked for their resources, they became more aware of their own coping strategies and what social support their informal network provided. In this period they only had "reflection tasks" concerning what life situations they really wanted. Gradually as the users expressed will and belief in changes, the partners began to be more action-oriented in their tasks. Some users who were strongly ambivalent decided to take a break from TCP in the motivation phase. Later on they wanted new consultations, and at that time they really were motivated and impatient to start their problem-solving process. A few did not come back to the project at all.

Conclusions

TCP has been quite well disseminated in the local Norwegian social service departments and has left some "footprints" in other settings of social work practice. Users report that they like to work in a TCP partnership to get a better grip on their life situations. Social workers valued work in TCP's systematic and concrete ways. More research and documentation is necessary to refine how TCP might be further developed in the Norwegian culture and context.

References

Barth, T., Børtveit, T., and Prescott, P. (2001). *Endringsfokusert rådgivning (Change-focused counseling)*. Oslo: Gyldendal Akademisk Forlag.

Doel, M. and Marsh, P. (1992). *Task-centred social work*. Hants, Ashgate: Aldershot.

Epstein, L. (1992). *Brief treatment and a new look at the task-centered approach*, 3rd ed. New York: Macmillan.

Eriksen, R. E. (1994). *Fra passivitet til aktivitet—målrettede endringer i livssituasjonen (From passive to active citizen: Goal-oriented changes in everyday life)* (Project report). Oslo: Diakonhjemmet høgskolesenter and Sosial- og helsedepartementet (Diakonhjemmet University College and The Ministry of Social and Health Affairs).

——. (1998). *Fra klient til deltaker—et perspektiv på sosialt arbeid ved sosialkontor (From client to participant: Perspectives on social work at social service departments)*. (Project report). Oslo: Diakonhjemmet høgskole and Sosial- og helsedepartementet (Diakonhjemmet University College and The Ministry of Social and Health Affairs).

——. (1999a). Arbeidshefte i innføring i oppgaveorientert tilnærming (Workbook on introduction to the task-centered approach). Oslo: Diakonhjemmet høgskole (Diakonhjemmet University College).

——. (1999b). Hvordan lære seg oppgaveorientert tilnærming (OOT)? Del I: OOTs teorigrunnlag. Del II: Praktiske tilnærminger (How to learn the task-centered approach (TC)? Part one: TC's theoretical basis. Part two: Practical approaches). Oslo: Diakonhjemmet høgskole(Diakonhjemmet University College).

——. (2001). Fagutvikling gir bedre service (Professional orientation gives better services). *Embla (Journal)* 3:44–50.

——. (2003). Oppgaveorientert tilnærming—anvendbar kunnskap ved norske sosialkontor (The task-centered approach: Applicable knowledge in Norwegian social services) . I. M.-A. Zahl (Ed.), *Sosialt arbeid: refleksjon og handling (Social work: Reflection and action)*, 191–214. Bergen: Fagbokforlaget.

——. (2007). *Hverdagen som langtids sosialklient:—deres mestring i et (bruker)medvirkning sperspektiv (Everyday life of long-term social service clients: Coping in a user perspective)*. Dr. polit. Avhandling (Thesis for the doctorate). Trondheim: ISH, NTNU.

Eriksen, R. E. and Nordstrand, M. (1995). *Innføring i oppgaveorientert tilnærming (OOT) (An introduction to the task-centered approach [TC])..* Oslo: Diakonhjemmet høgskole, Høgskolen i Sør Trøndelag og Sosial- og helsedepartementet (Diakonhjemmet University College, Sør Trøndelag University College and The Ministry of Social and Health Affairs).

Fredrikstad community, The social service department. (2006 Nov.) På egne ben. Prosjektskisse ("On their own footing"). (Project report).

Halås, C. T. (2002). Opplæringsprogram i oppgaveorientert tilnærming i Nordland (A teaching program in the task-centered approach in Nordland County). (SOFUS)

(Sosial- og familieavdelingens Utadrettede satsing) (The Department of Social and Family Affairs for Outreach Efforts). No. 2. http://www.fylkesmannen.no/fagom .aspx?m=21298 (accessed October 10, 2007).

Haram, R. A. and Amundsen, R. H. (1995). *Korttidsmetodikk: en sosialfaglig arbeidsmetode. (Short-term interventions: A social work approach)*. Oslo: Ad Notam Gyldendal.

Hjelme, S. (2007, Sept. 30). Åpen dør for rusmisbrukere. *Tidsskrift for avmakt til handlekraft (Open doors for drug addicts)*, 9–12. http://multimedia.api.no/www .frifagbevegelse.no/archive/01487/Ungdom_innmatL_1487567a.pdf (accessed November 19, 2007).

Miller, W. R. and Rollnick, S. (1991). *Motivational interviewing: Preparing people to change addictive behavior*. New York: Guilford Press.

Nesset, C. B. (2001). Korttidsinnsats med langtidsvirkning (Short-term interventions with long-term effects). *Embla (Journal)* 4:52–58.

Nordstrand, M. (1993). *Klient eller system: forsøk med målrettet praksisopplæring i sosialarbeiderutdanning (The client or the system: Goal-oriented field practice in social work)*. (Project report). Trondheim: Sosialhøgskolen (Sør Trøndelag University College).

——. (1995). Oppgaveorientert tilnærming og ledelse (The task-centered approach and management). In Hippe, K., and Hyrve, G. (Eds.), *Der skoen trykker: lederutvikling for barnevern- og sosialledere ("Where the shoe pinches": Development of management in child care and social services)*. Oslo: Kommuneforlaget.

Reid, W. (1992). *Task strategies*. New York: Columbia University Press.

Steen, G. (2002, December) Bedre botilbud til rusmiddelmisbrukere (Better housing for drug addicts). http://www.rus.no/?module=Articles;action=Article.publicShow ;ID=254 (accessed September 28, 2007).

Tronsmo, E. (1992). Oppsummering av ungdomsprosjektet (Summarizing the youth project). Oslo: Majorstua sosialsenter (Majorstua Social Service Department).

St.meld. nr. 14 (Announcement from the Norwegian Parliament No. 14) (2002–2003). Samordning av aetaten, trygdeetaten og sosialtjenesten (Coordination of Employment Services, Social Security, and Social Services).

Underlid, K. (2005). *Fattigdommens psykologi (The psychology of poverty)*. Oslo: Det norske samlaget.

Zahl, M.-A. (1987). *Å hjelpe mennesker gjennom en oppgave orientert tilnærming (Helping people by a task-centered approach)*.. Et norsk sammendrag av Laura Epstein's bok: "Helping People. The Task-Centered Approach." (A Norwegian summary of the book of L. Epstein: Helping people). Trondheim: Universitetet i Trondheim, Institutt for sosialt arbeid.

——. (1989). *Lillestrøm-prosjektet (The project in Lillestrøm)*. Trondheim: Universitetet i Trondheim, Institutt for sosialt arbeid.

19 | Task-Centered Practice in Australia

Christopher Trotter

Application

Task-centered practice and variations of it are used widely in Australia. It is used with both families and individuals, in settings including mental health, corrections, child welfare and child protection, social security, school welfare, intellectual disability, and family support.

The practice of task-centered work is also discussed in a number of social work publications. The biggest selling general social work text in Australia, written by Ian O'Connor and colleagues (2006), outlines a problem-solving model very similar to the stages of task-centered work. It also refers specifically to task-centered work in its outline of the stages of care management for the aged. Another popular Australian publication, *Working with Involuntary Clients* (Trotter 2006), makes extensive use of task-centered and problem-solving approaches. The inspirational work of William Reid is acknowledged in the introduction.

A number of publications have examined the nature of the work carried out by Australian social workers and found that task-centered principles are often used. For example, a study by Osmond and O'Connor (2006) in child protection referred to the use of task-centered approaches. Jane Squires and

Natasha Kramaric-Trojak (2003) found in an analysis of approaches with young people seeking social security benefits that task-centered and problem-solving were among several approaches used by workers (alongside, for example, solution focused, systems, and crisis intervention). A study I undertook in child protection in Australia found that child protection workers often use key task-centered strategies of defining problems with clients and developing tasks to address those problems. When workers used those strategies, their clients had good outcomes (Trotter 2004).

Adaptations

One particular adaptation of task-centered work in Australia relates to work with involuntary clients. Involuntary clients include those on parole, probation, or other court orders; those in the child protection system; and on occasion, those in the mental health and education systems. For the most part these clients receive social work services because they are required to rather than because they choose to. In work with this client group, engaging clients, reaching agreement about which problems should be the focus of the intervention, and dealing with pro-criminal, antisocial, and self-defeating attitudes have a particular importance.

These issues have been addressed by a number of authors including Rooney (1992), Jones and Alcabes (1993), and Ivanoff and colleagues (1994). I have also addressed these issues through a number of research studies in Australia (Trotter 1996, 2004, 2006, 2007). My studies in child protection (Trotter 2004) and in corrections settings (Trotter 1996, 2006) have found that role clarification and pro-social modeling have particular importance in work with involuntary clients and can complement and enhance task-centered strategies.

Role clarification involves the worker discussing with clients issues such as the purpose of the intervention; the worker's dual role as helper and investigator; the worker's authority and how it can be used; negotiable and nonnegotiable areas; and who might have access to information about the client.

Pro-social modeling involves the worker 1) consciously identifying pro-social behaviors and comments, for example, the client talking about and mixing with noncriminal peers; 2) rewarding those comments and behaviors by, for example, the use of praise or reduced frequency of appointments; 3) modeling pro-social behavior, for example, following up on tasks; and 4) identifying and discouraging pro-criminal and antisocial client comments and behaviors. As mentioned, my work in this area suggests that these skills add another dimension to task-centered work with involuntary clients and this in turn improves client outcomes.

Research Results

Task-centered practice and problem-solving approaches have proved to be effective in work with a range of clients in research studies undertaken in Australia. For example, a study with criminal offenders under supervision in the community found a strong correlation between the use of problem-solving practices by probation officers and a higher rate of completion of probation orders by clients (Trotter 1996). A study in child protection also found that when task-centered practices were used by workers the cases were closed earlier, children were less likely to be removed, and both workers and clients were more satisfied with the outcomes (Trotter 2004). One particularly interesting result from this study was that the outcomes were better if the workers as well as the clients completed tasks. Studies using William J. Reid's family problem-solving model (1987) have also pointed to the advantages of the use of the model with involuntary clients (Trotter, Cox, and Crawford 2002).

Strengths and Weaknesses

One of the great strengths of task-centered work in Australia is in its endurance. It has been forty years since William Reid and his colleagues began to publish material on task-centered work. The principles continue to be utilized not only in many Australian social work texts (e.g., O'Connor et al. 2006; Trotter 2006) but also in the day-to-day practice of social workers. Jim Ife, well known in social work circles in Australia, pointed out in his book *Rethinking Social Work* (1996) that problem solving "is very much part of the mainstream" and used by the majority of social workers. The key task-centered principles of helping the client to define problems, setting goals, and developing tasks to address those goals continue to be used today and have certainly stood the test of time.

Perhaps the greatest challenge to task-centered work in Australia has come from supporters of solution-focused and strengths-based approaches. Solution-focused work in particular is based on a view that social work interventions should focus on solutions rather than problems and that detailed problem definitions are unnecessary in order to achieve change (DeShazer 1988; DeJong and Millar 1996). Despite this view, however, task-centered principles continue to be used by Australian social workers and continue to be promoted at least in some Australian social work literature—no doubt because they provide a practical and client-friendly approach to social work and because the research continues to support their effectiveness.

References

DeJong, P. and Miller, S. (1996). How to interview for client strengths. *Social Work 40* (6): 729–36.

DeShazer, S. (1988). *Clues: Investigating solutions in brief therapy.* New York: Norton.

Ife, J. (1997). *Rethinking social work.* Melbourne: Longman.

Ivanoff, A., Blythe, B., and Tripodi, T. (1994). *Involuntary clients in social work practice.* New York: Aldine de Gruyter.

Jones, J. A. and Alcabes, A. (1993). *Client socialization: The Achilles heel of the helping professions.* Westport, CT: Auburn House.

Osmond, J. (2006). A quest for form: The tacit dimension of social work practice. *European Journal of Social Work 9* (2): 159–181.

Osmond, J. and O'Connor, I. (2006, March). Use of theory and research in social work practice: Implications for practice. *Australian Social Work 59* (1): 5–19.

O'Connor, I., Hughes, M., Turney, D., Wilson, J., and Settlerlund, D. (2006) *Social work and social care practice.* London: Sage.

Reid, W. (1985). *Family problem-solving.* New York: Columbia University Press.

Rooney, R. (1992). *Strategies for work with involuntary clients.* New York: Columbia University Press.

Squires, J. and Kramaric-Trojak, N. (2003, Dec). Centrelink: How social workers make a difference for young persons: A model of intervention. *Australian Social Work 56* (4): 293–304.

Trotter, C. (1996). The impact of different supervision practices in community corrections. *Australian and New Zealand Journal of Criminology 29* (1): 29–46.

——. (1999). Don't throw the baby out with the bathwater—in defence of problem solving. *Australian Journal of Social Work 52* (4): 51–55.

——. (2004). *Helping abused children and their families.* Thousand Oaks, CA: Sage.

——. (2006). *Working with involuntary clients.* Thousand Oaks, CA: Sage.

——. (2007). Probation and parole. In R. Sheehan, G. McIvor, and C. Trotter (Eds.), *What works with women offenders,* 124–141. London: Willan Publishing.

Trotter C., Cox, D., and Crawford, K. (2002). Family counselling in juvenile justice. *Australian Social Work 55* (1): 119–127.

20 | Task-Centered Practice in Japan

Fujie Ito

JAPAN FACES SEVERAL SOCIAL ISSUES, including a rapidly aging population and the lowest birthrate among developed countries. It also has a significant increase in the number of young people with difficulties in school, or with mental problems. There is also a rise in the number of cases of child abuse. As a result, the demand for social services and competent social workers is increasing.

Social Workers in Japan

Japan did not have a national qualification for social workers until the Certified Social Workers and Care Workers Act of 1987. As of June 2008, there were about 108,000 registered social workers working in fields such as elderly, children and family, people with disabilities, and people who need economic support. Social workers provide counseling, advice, and case management at private or public agencies, but the majority take care of service users in residential settings.

Japanese social workers learned social work theories and practices mainly from the United States, starting from casework by Mary Richmond to the life model by Carol Germain and Alex Gitterman, to empowerment practices, to the strengths model. However, there are several barriers to fully adapting these approaches to Japan. First, Japanese social welfare used a measure-oriented system for a long time, in which the government decided and administered the social services for the users. While the quality of services was uniform, social workers themselves did not have much incentive to apply new practices. Second, because family social work agencies are less developed than family services in the United States, the institutions that encouraged social workers to use social work skills and knowledge as a profession were limited. Third, supervision and on-the-job-training in everyday work was not provided systematically. This situation prevented social workers from developing social work models.

History of Task-Centered Practice

The task-centered model was introduced to Japan in the late 1970s. *Task-Centered Casework,* written by William J. Reid and Laura Epstein, was translated into Japanese in 1979 and some casework scholars reviewed it (Komatsu 1978). In the 1980s, many social work textbooks covered a task-centered model as a structured short-term treatment. Task-centered casework was introduced to Japan relatively early and while it seems to have been acknowledged, it has not been widely applied among social workers.

The Japanese Society of Social Work Practice conducted a survey of 1,343 social workers working in the elderly and child welfare fields, focusing on the acknowledgment and application of social work models in 1997 (JSSW 1997). The survey asked whether social workers knew and used six social work models in their fields. These included a psychosocial model, a problem-solving model, a task-centered model, a behavior modification model, a life model, and a systems model.

The percentage of respondents answering that they knew a task-centered model was 57.1 percent, the highest among the social work models, but the percentage of respondents who used this model in their settings was 38.7 percent. Few Japanese social workers applied a task-centered model, which is why there have been few reports on task-centered practice.

Application of Task-Centered Practice

A short-term treatment that draws upon task-centered practice was implemented for juvenile delinquents on probation in 1994 (Matsumoto 1996). Its aim is to limit the term of probation to within six to seven months by carrying out tasks in order to terminate probation. The delinquents selected are seen as being not highly problematic and are expected to be rehabilitated in the short term by intensive guidance.

The short-term probation proceeds as follows. First, delinquents make a pledge to meet a probation officer one or two times every month and report their circumstances. Second, a probation officer determines a field of guidance, such as daily life, school life, working conditions, family relationships, or friend relationships, based on advice presented by the Family Court. Third, tasks are planned by a probation officer and the written plan is explained to the delinquents. Fourth, the youth tackle the tasks with the guidance of a probation officer and report their achievement. If some obstacles or difficulties achieving tasks are found, the probation officers are flexible and change the field of guidance and tasks. After six months, if the tasks are completed and no delinquency occurs, probation is terminated.

Here are case studies of three boys who were on short-term probation due to habitually inhaling paint thinner (Ito 1996). Boy A was instructed to lead a well-regulated life at his workplace and was given the tasks of writing the date and the reason of absence and recording his view about the experience of the workplace. Boy B was instructed to establish a good relationship with his family, and his tasks were to discuss the consequences of inhaling paint thinner with his family and to write about it and to write about how his family saw him. Boy C was also instructed to establish a good relationship with his family and was given the task of recording how he felt about the comments of his parents. Their tasks were monitored carefully. Although many juvenile delinquents find writing something down difficult, Boys A, B, and C made efforts to achieve the tasks within six months and were released from probation. Their families reported that the boys' daily lives for the most part were improved and the communication within their families became smoother.

The characteristics of short-term probation are consistent with task-centered practice in regard to setting limits for the probation term, planning and achieving the action tasks toward a goal, and getting clients to agree to the plan. Structured treatment like task-centered practice is applicable to involuntary clients on probation because it is easy for them to grasp what they should do and to understand what is expected of them. However, in order to develop short-term probation in line with task-centered practice, we need to get delinquents involved more in clarifying and defining their own problems and in planning tasks. We also need to establish a partnership with probation officers through the process, and to collect more case data to analyze the effectiveness of this treatment.

Future Directions

There are several changes going on in the social work field in Japan. The social welfare system has been shifting to a contract-oriented system in which users can select services through contracts. In conjunction with this, many private organizations have joined as service providers, so the working fields for social workers are increasing. Concerning social work education, the number of schools and graduate schools is increasing, as well as the number of students who proceed to doctoral courses. The Certified Social Workers and Care Workers Act was amended in 2007 and the new curricula for certified social workers began in 2009. The curricula emphasize training competent professionals not only for clinical work but also for community welfare.

The current situation has led Japanese social workers to take new steps, including the development of original social practice models. For example, a case management model for child abuse was developed by the process of modified design and development (Shibano 2002), and a mediation model for school class breakdown was developed through qualitative and quantitative surveys by a school social worker (Otsuka 2008). These models are good examples of addressing pressing social problems and of development through systematic feedback from practices.

We have gained ground in the development of empirically based practice like the task-centered model. It is hoped that researchers, including "practice doctorates" mentioned by Reid (1979), can collaborate with practitioners to develop social work models with strong agency support in Japan.

References

Ito, F. (1996). Applications of the task-centered approach [in Japanese]. *Bulletin of St. Catherine Women's College* 8:17–33.

Japanese Society of Social Work Practice. (1997). *Survey report on Japanese social workers* [in Japanese].

Komatsu, G.. (1978). A task-centered approach [in Japanese]. *Serial of Mental Health* 10:19–23.

Matsumoto, S. (1996). Theory and practice of a short-term probation [in Japanese]. *Rehabilitation and Crime Prevention 122*:7–24.

Otsuka, M. (2008). *School class breakdown and school social work* [in Japanese]. Tokyo: Aikawashobou.

Reid, W. J. (1979). The model development dissertation. *Journal of Social Service Research 3*:215–225.

Shibano, M. (2002). *Theory and practice of social work practice model development* [in Japanese] Tokyo: Yuhikaku.

21 | Task-Centered Practice in South Korea

Nam-Soon Huh and Yun-Soon Koh

History

Task-centered practice was acknowledged as an attractive alternative for social workers who were looking for effective and structured practice approaches in South Korea at the beginning of the 1990s. At that time, many welfare centers in poverty-stricken neighborhoods were opened and counseling centers for children and adolescents were revitalized with the help of the government's interest and investment. Seoul Dong Bu Child Guidance Center was one of several agencies that experimented with task-centered practice with the help of Professor Hye-Ran Kim from the Department of Social Welfare, Seoul National University, who was trained by Professor Laura Epstein from the University of Chicago. The center found task-centered practice, which focuses on task achievement in a short period of time and cooperation with the client, was useful for runaway adolescents who lacked structured life experience and refused guidance from adults. The center offered training and supervision using the task-centered model, translated task-centered books, and published case studies and research results on task-centered practice.

However, task-centered practice was not widely utilized in other social work practice fields in South Korea until the late 1990s when the Department of Social Welfare, Hallym University, sponsored workshops with Professor William Reid from the University at Albany, State University of New York and Professor Matthias Naleppa from Virginia Common Wealth. Since then, task-centered practice has spread to diverse fields including schools, youth centers, local welfare centers, senior centers, and hospitals.

Adaptations

Currently task-centered practice is one of the essential intervention approaches in South Korea, especially in treatment centers and schools for maladjusted adolescents and in local welfare centers for case management. When agencies use task-centered practice in adolescent groups, they integrate it with individual counseling and other structured approaches rather than using it as a single independent approach. These include structured approaches for self-esteem, interpersonal skills, social skills, Ego-gram, and sports activities to not only solve the adolescents' target problems and reduce the dropout rate from the programs but also to improve adolescents' self-efficacy, self-control, and adjustment in schools.

Social workers believe that integrating other approaches for self-efficacy and self-control can motivate adolescents for successful task performance. Considering the developmental characteristics of adolescents, combining sports activities with the task-centered approach effectively reduced program dropouts and increased completion of tasks (Nam 1993). Integration of play therapy, art therapy, and personality tests for problem assessment created opportunities to explain problems, helped build rapport, and improved motivation among Korean adolescents who were poor in language expression and understanding problem solving (Lee 2005; Oh 1998).

When social workers used case management with the task-centered model with community-dwelling elderly, the term "contract" was unfamiliar and uncomfortable to Korean aged. Using a less burdensome term (e.g., "appointment") was helpful. Many elderly clients could not successfully achieve the planned tasks even though they had strong motivation unless detailed information regarding methods to achieve the tasks was provided. Accurate and sufficient information on the planned tasks and how to perform these, plus making sure the client understood the information, was helpful to achieve the tasks (Huh 1997).

Research Results

Initial studies of the feasibility of task-centered practice with delinquent adolescents used single-subject designs and a qualitative analysis of the group process (Kim 1996; Kim 1995; Nam 1993). In the late 1990s, there were several evaluation studies using Reid's Task-Centered Scale and scales of self-esteem, self-control, and self-efficacy (Huh 1997; Oh 1998; Lee 2005). Lee (2005) conducted a randomized experimental study with a group of potential school dropout students who had records of absences and leaving early. The experimental group received twelve weeks of treatment including an initial interview, group therapy for five weeks, individual therapy for five weeks, and a final evaluation session. There was no special intervention for the control group other than teachers' usual disciplinary remarks or no intervention. The experimental group improved target problems, self-efficacy, and self-control. At the end of the experiment, five of eight students in the control group were dropouts and three other were in a very risky situation, while no one dropped out of the experimental group.

Oh (1998) studied middle school students with school-adjustment issues. She used structured approaches of "expressing emotions" and "understanding myself" in the beginning and a task-centered approach later with two different groups referred by teachers. After eight weeks of intervention, there was improvement in reduction of target problems and in self-efficacy and responsibility.

Kim (1995) used a single-subject method with AB design for a runaway adolescent admitted to Seoul Dong Bu Child Guidance Center. Ten weeks of a task-centered program with individual counseling resulted in improvement in all three target problem areas ($p < .05$): smoking cigarettes, intermittent awakening during the night, losing temper, and shouting at junior residents.

These studies reported effectiveness of the task-centered practice. However, there are several limitations in the studies by the South Korean researchers. First, it is necessary to have follow-up studies to see the long-term effect because all of these studies were designed with short-term interventions. Second, most South Korean researchers were also practitioners in the field with expectations for success, which might have had an positive impact on the results.

In addition to these studies with delinquent adolescents, one study addressed the feasibility of task-centered practice as a case management approach for the elderly (Huh 1997). Three social workers and two social work interns in four different welfare centers performed case management with task-centered practice, measuring target problems and task performance. The elderly were active and more able than expected; problems were more easily solved when identified by clients than by case managers. Also, the problems that the clients identified were more simple and practical than the social workers had thought. The social workers also found out that they did not understand well what the clients saw as the problems. Eighty-three percent of target problems were improved while 37 percent and 42 percent of tasks were performed by clients and case managers respectively. Case management with the task-centered approach was an effective model for South Korean elderly even though there was difficulty with problems related to family issues because the clients did not want the case managers to intervene with their families.

Other South Korean studies have reported positive results of the task-centered model with psychiatric patients (Hong 1996), homeless people with alcohol problems (Shin 2001), and parents of disabled children (Yoo 2000). However, those studies are more exploratory, so they need more evidence-based research to determine effectiveness.

Strengths

Task-centered practice is an attractive model for South Korean social workers, who have a burden of heavy caseloads, are very goal-oriented, and readily accept the characteristics of task-centered practice such as short-term oriented, highly structured intervention methods and utilization of diverse other theories and skills. Historically, social workers have had difficulty in cooperating with clients who have a cultural tendency to express their needs poorly and yet strong expectations for problem solution by the social worker. Task-centered practice encourages clients' participation in the selection of target problems and tasks. Because of this, the task-centered model provides both social workers and clients with opportunities to cooperate, respecting client-oriented problem identification and task formulation.

Limitations

Task-centered practice requires an intensively structured intervention, usually in a short time period, which can be burdensome for South Korean social workers who have a heavy caseload of 80–100 clients. Also, there are difficulties in intervening with environments, including family, because of lack of family cooperation and community resources (Kim 1996; Huh 1997). While South Korean practitioners need more training on environmental and family intervention, task-centered practice seems appropriate with new clients suffering from multiple problems.

Future Directions

South Korean scholars, social workers, and policy makers are searching for evidence-based approaches to improve the quality of services. Because of its short-term and goal-oriented approach, task-centered practice continues to be used with adolescents at schools and youth centers and as a case management model at community centers and senior centers (Bu-Cheon Ohchung-ku Senior Center 2007; Huh and Koh 2007). The model is expected to be tried out in diverse fields such as social services, mental health, family services, and community development, in diverse formats (individual counseling, group work, etc.), with flexibility to integrate other approaches (sports, play therapy, art therapy, etc.) to improve other individual, group, and family functions.

References

Bu-Cheon Ohchung-ku Senior Center. (2007). *Application and understanding of case management in the social welfare practice field: Focusing on the task-centered approach.* Seoul, Korea: Hakhyunsa.

Epstein, L. (1999). *Brief treatment and a new look at the task-centered approach.* Trans. Seoul Dong Bu Child Guidance Center, Korea. New York: Macmillan.

Huh, N.-S. (1998). A study on the application of the task-centered model: Case management for the in-home elderly. *Korean Social Welfare* 35:399–426.

Huh, N.-S. and Koh, Y.-S. (2007). *Theory and practice in case management for the elderly: Focusing on the task-centered approach.* Hallym: NURI-Project, Hallym University.

Hong, K.-M. (1996). *A study on the application of the task-centered model for pre-discharged psychiatric patients.* MSW thesis, Catholic University.

Lee, J.-H. (2005). *A study on the effectiveness of an integrated program for potential school dropouts to improve school adjustment.* MSW thesis, Graduate School of Hallym University.

Nam, K.-C. (1993). *A study on social work practice in a community welfare center: Focused on the task-centered model case in the group program.* MSW thesis, Seoul National University.

Kim, E.-.S. (2003). *A case study of high risk youth's self-control and self-efficacy using the task-centered model.* MSW thesis, Graduate School of Hallym University.

Kim, H.-R. (1996). A study on the application of the task-centered model: Focused on the foster care case. *Korean Social Welfare* 30:25–47.

——. (1996). *A case study on the task-centered model application for initial stage adjustment for a juvenile runaway.* MSW thesis, Graduate School of Ewha Womans University.

Oh, S. Y. (1998). *A study on the effectiveness of group work for the maladjustment of adolescents in school: Applied to the task-centered model.* MSW thesis, Graduate School of Hallym University.

Shin, W. (2001). *A study on the possible application of the task-centered model for the homeless with alcohol problems.* *Korean Social Studies,* Seoul National University 23 (1): 149–178.

Yoo, Y.-S. (2000). *Group work with parents of disabled children: Focusing on the task-centered approach.* Liberal Art and Social Science Studies 29.

22 | Task-Centered Practice in Hong Kong

T. Wing Lo

History

In Hong Kong, task-centered practice has been taught in social work training programs for almost twenty years. In the early 1990s, a group of social work educators published a textbook on casework intervention and task-centered practice was incorporated as one of six essential intervention approaches (Wong 1992), but the application of task-centered practice in Hong Kong has not been well documented.

Since the mid-1990s, Lo (2005) has taught task-centered group work to students in social work intervention classes based on the group models introduced in Fortune (1985). In 1997, he trained social workers in a welfare organization to apply task-centered group work to help people with problems in dating (Hon et al. 1997; Lai undated). He also facilitated numerous groups for social workers who faced personal, family, and work-related problems (Lo 2005). Every year he trains about 200 social workers and social work students who, upon graduation, are employed in various settings, including youth service centers, elderly homes, family service centers, rehabilitation services for the handicapped, drug treatment services, and services for delinquents and offenders.

Nonetheless, social workers in Hong Kong have never been crazy about adopting task-centered practice in their daily work. Many prefer more trendy or fashionable theories, such as narrative theory, cognitive-behavioral theory, or solution-focused approaches, although sometimes it is not surprising to see the shadow of task-centered practice when the other intervention approaches are applied. Because task-centered practice is a fundamental social work approach in Hong Kong, many social workers have in fact learned the concepts and sequence of problem, goals, and tasks in their professional training. They put them into daily practice, but they seldom identify those concepts as originating from the task-centered practice model. Moreover, there is a tendency for social workers to integrate task-centered practice with other intervention theories, rather than using it on its own.

Adaptations

An example of such an integration comes from Lo (2005), who teaches task-centered practice in his group counseling courses, supplemented and complemented by person-centered therapy, rational emotive behavior therapy, and psychodrama. His own intervention model uses person-centered therapy as the heart (genuineness and congruence) of intervention, task-centered practice as the skeleton (intervention structure), rational emotive behavior therapy as the brain (cognitive ability), and psychodramatic techniques as the hands and feet (skills) of social workers.

Task-centered practice has a neat and systematic intervention structure and is simple to learn and use. However, Hong Kong Chinese are quite reserved and thus, in many instances, time and space are required for warm-up. Person-centered skills are usually used for ice breaking and rapport building. Because many problems originate from clients' own irrational beliefs, cognitive-behavioral skills are used to dispute irrational thoughts. After building a working relationship, task-centered practice is used to help clients identify goals and set tasks during the problem-solving stage.

Because Hong Kong is a fast-moving society, its people tend to prefer "fast-food" type social services; the time-limited feature of task-centered practice is particularly attractive. Indeed, in individual casework, eight to twelve sessions are too many for some clients. Normally four to eight intervention sessions are more appropriate. In group work, however, more sessions are typically necessary for the reserved Chinese to build rapport with one another before they are ready to share their problems and emotions in front of strangers. This is also necessary when members have to resolve group conflicts for healthy group development.

Research Results

Task-centered practice has not been well researched in Hong Kong. A recent study (Li 2007) explored counselors' choice of four counseling approaches: task-centered practice, person-centered therapy, rational emotive behavior therapy, and psychodrama. In a sample of 143 social workers, counselors, and trainee counselors, no correlations were found between their choice of counseling approaches and their personal backgrounds. However, there were significant correlations between the counselors' choice of task-centered practice and their perceptions of the degree of helpfulness of six (out of eleven) therapeutic factors developed by Yalom (1995): task-centered practice had the strongest correlation with "universality" (Pearson's $r = .287$, $p < .01$) and "imitative behavior" (Pearson's $r = .246$, $p < .01$). "Universality" is about identifying commonalities in behavior, experiences, thoughts, problems, and feelings. The respondents agreed that task-centered group work promotes these elements and helps assure members that they are not alone. "Imitative behavior" is probably the easiest way to learn from fellow members. Watching others cope with and overcome similar problems successfully motivates members to take action to face their own problems.

Task-centered practice correlated with "instillation of hope" (Pearson's $r = .231$, $p < .01$), the only one of the four counseling approaches to do so. The defined goals in task-centered practice give clients a sense of direction, which in turn may instill hope. "Altruism" was also correlated (Pearson's $r = .187$, $p < .05$). In altruism, group members help one another through giving and receiving and sharing of feelings and experiences. Finding meaning in helping others can boost self-confidence. This is done through providing support, reassurances, and suggestions.

Task-centered practice also had weak correlation with "catharsis" (Pearson's $r = .169$, $p < .05$), the venting of emotions that helps relieve the burden experienced by clients. Clients ventilate about what troubles them and the counselors interpret the meaning of these cathartic experiences and help clients develop insight. Finally, there was a weak correlation with "existentiality" (Pearson's $r = .063$, $p < .05$), which refers to the search for purpose and meaning in life. The setting of goals and tasks helps clients take responsibility for their own actions and destiny.

Strengths

As mentioned earlier, Hong Kong is a fast-moving society and its people prefer time-limited and "fast-food" type services. What is most appealing about task-centered practice is that it helps clients identify problems and set clear goals to be achieved within a short period of time. Hong Kong Chinese are very pragmatic (Wong and Liu 2001). They prefer practical advice rather than "empty-word" counseling. Specific and concrete tasks are helpful because they provide clear directions for clients to solve their problems of living. Attainable tasks help clients develop a sense of achievement, and no matter how superficial the improvement, the clients' confidence is established following completion of tasks.

Such practical and task-oriented principles are also in concordance with the local Chinese culture. Chinese are reserved and less willing to share their feelings and emotions openly. Insofar as face-saving is highly valued among Chinese adults, task-centered practice's emphasis on "problems of living" serves to normalize the clients' problems as personal and thus reduces labeling and stigma. Moreover, the roles of social workers and clients are like those of mentors and mentees. This "teaching and learning" attribute is consistent with the learning style of Chinese who grow up in an authoritarian, "duck-feeding" education system.

Limitations

Because task-centered practice demands that clients be autonomous and independent in problem solving, it is difficult to apply it to clients with low motivation and high resistance, such as school bullies referred to social workers by teachers. Task-centered practice, focusing rationally on problems, goals, and tasks, is criticized by frontline workers as unsuitable for clients who need constant emotional support, especially those in the beginning phase of bereavement and loss. Some elderly clients cannot catch up with the fast pace of task-centered practice despite having clear goals. They feel as though they lose face in the group when they fail to complete tasks within the prescribed period.

Moreover, frontline workers opined that the approach is often incapable of reaching the root of the problem. When clients' problems are highly complex, task-centered practice has to be integrated with other intervention approaches. Another shortcoming is that it focuses mainly on an individual's problem rather than on the environment that contributes to the problem. A common dilemma faced by school social workers is deciding to what extent students' behavioral problems are the result of inappropriate school management. Lastly, the merits of the systematic and structured features of task-centered practice might become constraints if social workers cannot apply them flexibly in clients' ever-changing situations.

Future Directions

Task-centered practice is an empirical and eclectic model. This approach falls in line with the recent trend of integration of social work services in Hong Kong. Under this philosophy, social workers should integrate intervention methods to meet clients' needs. Task-centered practice, because of its neat intervention structure, must have a place in the core of intervention methods.

References

Fortune, A. E. (Ed.). (1985). *Task-centered practice with families and groups*. New York: Springer.

Hon, E. K., Poon, W. H., Law, S. K., and Fung, W. L. (1997). *New phenomena of 1997*. Unpublished manuscript. Hong Kong: Caritas [in Chinese].

Lai, K. Y. (undated). *Task-centered group work approach* [in Chinese]. Hong Kong: Youth and Community Service Division, Caritas-Hong Kong.

Li, K. H. (2007). *Of counselors-in-training: Therapeutic factors and approaches*. MSSc research project, City University of Hong Kong.

Lo, T. W. (2005). Task-centered group work: Reflections on practice. *International Social Work 48* (4): 455–465.

Wong, C. P. Y. (1992). The task-centered approach. In L.P.C. Ko (Ed.), *Casework: Theories and case illustrations* [in Chinese], chap. 4. Hong Kong: The Writers' and Publishers' Cooperative.

Wong, C. P. Y. and Liu, L. W. J. (2001). The task-centered approach [in Chinese]. In L. P. C. Ko and C. K. Au (Eds.), *Casework: Theories and case illustrations*, 137–168. Hong Kong: Chinese University Press.

Yalom, I. D. (1995). *Theory and practice of group psychotherapy*, 4th ed. New York: Basic Books.

23 | Task-Centered Practice in Taiwan

Yueh-Ching Chou and Ronald H. Rooney

History

The task-centered model/approach (任務/職務中心方法) (短期處遇) has been known in Taiwan since the 1990s. The task-centered approach (TCA) was introduced in 1987 by a senior social work instructor (Zong-lee Liao/廖榮立) in his book on social work theories. The TCA has been included in subsequent books as a social work theory and is part of the teaching content in master's degree programs in universities. Test questions on the TCA currently appear in the social work licensing examination. However, the amount of influence of the TCA on actual practice by social workers on the front line is undetermined.

There are 75 universities and 70 colleges in Taiwan. Twenty-four offer training at the BSW level for social work practitioners with a total enrollment of about 2,000 students each year. Sixteen universities provide master's programs and five offer Ph.D. programs in social work or social welfare, with a total of 320 master's students and 20 Ph.D. students registered each year. Social work education in Taiwan has been modeled after the educational program in the United States including textbooks, curricula, and professional systems such as licensing. Furthermore, the majority of instructors with a Ph.D. have been trained in the United States (Chou, Haj-Yahia, Wang, and Fu 2006). The TCA is taught as one of the social work theories in all the universities that offer master's degree programs. Students are also usually introduced to the psychosocial model, cognitive model, crisis intervention model, systems theory model, ecological perspective, feminist theory model, life model, behavior modification model, Marxist approaches, and radical social work. Additionally, the TCA is described in books on social work theories or direct service in Chinese in Taiwan (Song, Tzen, Su, and Chen 2002; Liu 2002; Shu 1999). The approach is explicitly presented in the Taiwanese *Caseru Social Work Encyclopedia*, which covers its historical development, theoretical perspectives, basic assumptions, practice procedures, operational skills, and evaluation (*Caseru Social Work Encyclopedia* 2008). The TCA or brief treatment is recommended for working with students who are truant from schools (Chen 2008), with sexually abused children (Shieh 2002), and as a general problem-solving method in social work practice (Chang 2004).

Research Results

The TCA has been tried with families whose child has developmental disabilities and in group work with abused women. Chou developed an eight-session intervention program to work with families who had a child with developmental disabilities (Chou 1992). In a second study, Chou and students engaged families who had a preschool child with a developmental delay, but who had earlier rejected intervention services because it would have required a medical diagnosis for their child (Chou et al. 2001). One of Chou's students (Shu 2004) conducted another intervention study with families who had a preschool child with a developmental delay. The intervention guidelines were improved again based on the feedback from the clients and practitioners involved in the project. In addition, in 2001, Chou used the task-centered approach to conduct group work with abused women.

All four studies utilized the design and development (D & D) paradigm of Edwin J. Thomas and Jack Rothman to develop practice guidelines for the practitioners to follow for use in practice (Rothman and Thomas 2004). The quantitative and qualitative evaluations included semi-experimental designs (Chou 1992; Chou et al. 2001; Shu 2004) and single-system designs (Chou et al. 2002); the dependent variables included perceptions of having a child with developmental disabilities, client's well-being, marital relationships, family relations, social support, and services satisfaction. Based on these four studies, intervention/recording formats have been developed and modified, including practice guidelines for sessions.

Feedback from the clients included comments such as: the social worker was active and intensive, the goals and tasks of the service were clear, and the family could participate as well, which made them feel respected and involved in working on their problems. Families particularly appreciated having regular sessions; the intensity helped them face their problems and plan for changes. Social workers also thought that the intensity of intervention, particularly in the early stages, and the family's participation were the primary reasons that the interventions were successful. The schedule of sessions was also useful for building a trusting relationship. However, the social workers recommended that the frequency and ordering of the sessions needed to be flexible and reversible, particularly when working with single-parent families or with families who have limited communication skills.

Limitations

Limitations of the TCA as seen by practitioners included: eight-session intervention contracts were more successful when the caseload size was limited; social workers had to begin work before they were fully familiar with the TCA, so they had less success than if they had known more about the approach before they began work; families required concrete resources as well as counseling assistance, and a combination of hard and soft services worked best.

Strengths

Major advantages of the TCA were that its values can fit the local culture because it focuses on the clients' wishes instead of the practitioner's views; it is systematically constructed; and the clients have a clear understanding of what work together will be like and how long it might last. Taiwanese people are usually not comfortable discussing personal relationships with strangers. However, clients served by social workers using the TCA felt respected by the social workers who focused on their wishes.

Application

While most social work students in Taiwan have learned the TCA, it is unknown how many apply it after graduation. Their academic training focuses more on social administration and policy making than on the development of practice skills (Chou et al. 2006). Unlike in the United States, social work education in Taiwan has not emphasized competence-based education. Organizations tend not to focus on service effectiveness or practice methodologies.

This gap between training/education and actual practice is common in Taiwan. Studies by Chou and her students are beginning efforts to structure systematic interventions and study their effectiveness.

Future Directions

More work can be done to convince organizations in Taiwan of the TCA's usefulness:

1. Convey that the TCA can be useful in helping them and their clients to reach goals.
2. Disseminate knowledge so that instructors learn to practice the TCA before teaching it to their students in their classes.
3. Integrate the TCA into students' practicum and field agencies.
4. Utilize videotaped models of task-centered working processes in teaching methods.
5. Increase the fidelity of TCA translations (Chinese) to ensure that these are more consistent and the terms are described as they were intended. The TCA provides a useful model for implementing an approach that is found useful by families and is amenable to evaluation. It is a promising approach for addressing the divide between training/education and actual practice in Taiwan.

References

Caseru Social Work Encyclopedia. (2008). Task-centered perspective (任務中心取向). http://www.casehsu.org/mediawiki/index.php/%E4%BB%E5%8B%99%E4%B8%AD% [in Chinese] (accessed May 18, 2008).

Chen, S. Y. (2004). Introduction of social work brief treatment. *Community Development Journal 105*:400–410. [in Chinese]

Chen, Z. L. (2008). School social work dealing with students who are truant from school. http://www.tosun.org.tw/database/ 900307/socil/socil.htm [in Chinese] (accessed May 18, 2008).

Chou, Y. C. (1992). *Developing and testing intervention services for assisting Taiwanese families who have a child with developmental disabilities.* Ph.D. diss., University of Minnesota.

Chou, Y. C., Chu, F. Y., Hsu, C. Y., Liu, Y. S., Tsai, S. M., Huang, L. Y., and Huang, S. W. (2001). Developing and evaluating a service program for assisting involuntary families who have a child with developmental delay. *Journal of Social Work of the Taiwan University 4*:97–161 [in Chinese].

Chou, Y. C., Haj-Yahia, M. M., Wang, F. T. Y., and Fu, L. Y. (2006). Social work in Taiwan: An historical and critical review. *International Social Work 49* (6): 767–778.

Chou, Y. C., Lee, S. L., and Shu, Y. P. (2002). Group social work for battered women: A program development and evaluation in Taipei. *National Taiwan University Social Work Review 7*:59–125 [in Chinese].

Hsieh, R. S. (2002). An experimental model to construct social work treatment for sexually abused children. *Chau-Yang Human Literature and Social Journal 1* (1): 71–100 [in Chinese].

Liao, Z. L. (1987). *Social work theoretical models*. Taipei: Wu-nan Publications [in Chinese].

Liu, M. S. (2002). *Social work case study: Methods, exploration, and treatment*. Taipei: Hong-yeh Publications [in Chinese].

Rothman, J. and Thomas, E. (Eds). (1994). *Intervention research design and development for human service*. New York: Haworth.

Song, L. Y., Tzen, H. Y., Su, C. Y., and Chen, L. C. (2002). *Social work theories: Treatment and case examples*. Taipei: Hong-yeh Publications [in Chinese].

Shu, C. Y. (2002). *Developing an intervention model working with families who have a preschool child with developmental delay in Taipei*. Master's thesis, School of Social Work, Soochow University [in Chinese].

Shu, L. K. (1999). *Social work direct services: Theory and techniques*. Taipei: Hong-yeh Publications [in Chinese].

PART FOUR | *Future Directions*

24 | The Question of Questions

An Agenda for Social Work
Practice Research

Enola K. Proctor

How well is the social work research enterprise meeting the profession's needs? Are researchers pursuing questions that have significance for society and for the profession? Social work research needs to be focused on the most pressing questions—those that have the potential to inform and improve social work practice. This chapter explores the knowledge needs of social work as a profession, asserts the primacy of five research questions, and encourages the pursuit of these as a means to strengthen the social work knowledge base.

Social Work Research: Progress and Challenges

As a profession with a public mandate, social work receives societal sanctions for its practice. Such sanctions rest on assumptions of a current and solid knowledge base (Rosen and Proctor 2003b). By establishing its training role through undergraduate and graduate education for practice and through doctoral and postdoctoral training for research, the profession has a recognized and self-proclaimed responsibility for its own knowledge base. Social work's stature may be only as good as this base, and responsibility for developing it is lodged within social work research.

Several conferences, articles, and books have focused on practice research in the past decade. The Rosen Lecture at the annual Society for Social Work and Research (SSWR) conference was launched in 2002 to underscore the need for research that is capable of guiding social work practice and to highlight knowledge development from programs of practice research. SSWR's program of awards further recognizes high-quality research. Several schools of social work have convened conferences around professionwide issues, including one on the practice-research interface hosted by the Columbia University School of Social Work in 1993 and one on social work practice guidelines convened by the George Warren Brown School of Social Work in May 2000. These events and the growing number of research centers established in schools of social work reflect an ever-stronger infrastructure for social work research.

Yet social work faces real and daunting challenges to its stature as a profession. Over the past two decades, key areas of practice have defaulted to other professions (Marsh 2003), including hospital social work (Proctor, Morrow-Howell, and Kaplan 1996), case management, and disaster response. Nurses now claim professional expertise in several areas that previously were the clear "turf" of hospital social workers, including responding to hospitalized patients' psychosocial needs, working to resolve family crises, providing needed information and facilitating adjustment to disease, supporting patient and family adherence to illness-related care regimens, and assessing and coordinating community resources for posthospital care. Case management—despite the complexity of its component of psychosocial assessment, motivational enhancement, family therapy, and resource procurement—is now often assumed to require little if any human services education or training. In many models of collaborative depression care, nurses—not social workers—have been the providers of choice for assessing depression and providing motivational interviewing, psychosocial support, and problem-solving therapy. Coupled with the erosion of social work's turf is the growing challenge of recruiting talented individuals to the profession. This may be a problem of the field's own making, as it has accredited a rapidly growing number of schools, year after year, to compete for a relatively flat applicant pool.

Where social work remains vibrant, the performance stakes have risen. In nearly every social service sector, stakeholders and contractors expect agencies to monitor and improve quality. Clyman (1999) characterizes the shift toward increased accountability in the human services as perhaps "the largest scale social experimentation since the New Deal in the United States" (p167). Yet remarkably little is known about the quality of social work services (McMillen, Proctor, Megivern, Striley, Cabassa, Munson, and Dickey 2005). Social work's virtual silence on quality of care, its retrenchment in several practice arenas, and its difficulty competing with other fields on both the practice and recruitment fronts converge to portend a potential crisis for its professional stature. To meet these challenges, social work researchers must pursue new questions, using more robust methods, and in short order.

This chapter addresses the challenges of meeting the profession's needs for knowledge and for evidence. It proposes a research agenda guided by five questions, the pursuit of which can strengthen social work's foundation for practice and potentially its professional stature.

Five Pressing Questions:
A Social Work Research Agenda

Fundamentally, this chapter poses questions about questions, specifically: What kind of research is needed for social work practice? What research questions should be asked in this social era, at this point in the profession's history? Are social work researchers asking and addressing the right research questions? How rich is our knowledge around each of these questions?

The basis for this chapter is rooted in a concern that social work researchers have not, unfortunately, focused attention and activity around the most important research questions. The chapter asserts the primacy of five research questions that if pursued, can inform and improve the delivery of social work services and demonstrate the profession's social value:

1. What are the practices in social work practice?
2. How does social work practice vary?
3. What is the value of social work practice?
4. What practices should social workers use?
5. How can social work practice be improved?

"Social work practice" is used broadly and inclusively. Although "practice" in the social work literature often connotes direct service with individuals, families, or groups, here it refers also to administrative, community, and policy practice. This caveat notwithstanding, the chapter's examples and citations overemphasize topics with which the author is most familiar, including direct social work practice, agency-focused research, mental health services, and quality improvement.

What Are the Practices in Social Work Practice?

Fundamentally, this question is about what social workers *do*: What interventions do social workers employ? Can these interventions be named and described?

The importance of this question would seem to be a "no-brainer." Describing the professional activities of social workers is fundamental to the profession's self-definition, self-depiction, and assertion of its means of influence. Yet remarkably little effort to address this question is evident in either social work practice or social work research.

In 2000, the National Association of Social Workers launched a Practice Research Network (PRN), an ambitious project to query 2,000 consenting members of NASW and systematically capture critical information. Through this initiative, new information was gleaned about social workers' employment conditions, salaries, and demographics. The PRN methodology has unique potential to collect information about the "practices" or interventions used in day-to-day practice—potential on which the American Psychiatric Association capitalized through its own PRN (Zarin, Pincus, West, and McIntyre 1997). With funding from the Center for Substance Abuse Treatment, the NASW PRN explored social workers' use of substance-abuse related practice in the year prior to the survey. Nearly two thirds of social workers had referred substance abuse clients to treatment, but over one fourth had engaged in no activities related to substance abuse (NASW 2001). Except for this gross survey of activity over a one-year time period, the social work PRN has not been used to advance knowledge about the interventions used by social workers.

Nor have researchers focused sufficient attention on the question, "What are the practices in social work practice?" Although intervention research is widely recognized as of preeminent importance (Fraser 2000; Thyer 2000; Rubin 2000; Rosen, Proctor, and Staudt 2003), it constitutes a small proportion of empirical studies in social work. Rosen, Proctor, and Staudt (1999) classified published articles in 13 major social work journals, the journals they deemed most likely to publish articles about social work intervention. Of the 1,849 articles published in these journals from 1994 to 1997, only 15 percent were classified as empirical articles that addressed interventions. Only 3 percent of published articles described the intervention or its components in sufficient detail for replication in either research or practice. Even descriptive studies of social work interventions, relying on such methods as practitioner surveys or agency record analyses, are rare.

The actual identification of the "practices in social work practice" is an important function of practice research. A practice, or intervention, is defined as behavior that can be volitionally manipulated and purposefully engaged in to achieve a professionally relevant condition (Rosen and Proctor 1978). Social work interventions vary widely in their complexity, ranging from discrete behaviors to treatment or prevention programs and packages

(Rosen and Proctor 1978). Without attempting an exhaustive review, here are a few examples of such research and its usefulness.

Rosen, Proctor, and Staudt (2003) identified and classified the interventions tested in the published intervention studies and grouped the interventions in the form of a guideline prototype—that is, repertoires, or sets, of interventions used to address specific outcomes or conditions. The repertoires varied considerably in scale: while 103 different interventions addressed psychiatric conditions, only one addressed agency functioning and only one addressed housing needs. Of course the journals selected for such studies may influence the yield of interventions for different areas of practice. Using similar methodology, Staudt, Cherry, and Watson (2005) assembled a taxonomy of 33 different interventions that have been researched for school social work practice. Studying practice itself and deriving data from agency records, Jonson-Reid, Kontak, Citerman, Essma, and Fezzi (2004) identified and reported the frequency of use of seven services in school social work practice. Similar studies are needed for other areas of practice, including community practice, whose interventions have not been sufficiently specified, documented, captured in intervention protocols, or evaluated for fidelity (Coulton 2005).

Researchers need to address other related questions about the practices in social work. For example, are the terms used to capture distinct practices employed reliably and consistently? Do the terms within a taxonomy of interventions differentiate and discriminate different practices with specificity and sensitivity? Beyond the realm of terminology, are interventions or practices operationalized, and have manuals and protocols to guide practitioners been developed and implemented (Fraser 2003)? The NASW Press has launched a treatment manuals series to support these important developments (see, for example, Fraser et al. 2000).

"What are the practices in social work practice?" How important and how useful is research on this question? Such research is fundamental to social work's capacity to characterize its activity. All professions require a commonly understood language, a set of terms to express what they do. A clear lexicon of social work practices is essential to professional training and continuing education. Moreover, medical insurance reimbursement requires that services be described by procedure codes. Although this research is descriptive in nature, identifying, naming, and classifying social work practices are prerequisite tasks for research on relative effectiveness, assessing cost-benefit ratios, and establishing practice guidelines. Research on the interventions most frequently used or needed by social workers constitutes a crucial first question in an agenda to inform social work practice.

How Does Social Work Practice Vary?

Variability in social work practice is a second topic for social work's research agenda. Important questions include: How do social work practices vary in use? Are certain procedures underused? Are other procedures overused? Does observed variation correspond with theories and principles that guide the profession, its values and mission, and tenets of social science? For example, do interventions vary by problem severity, duration, comorbidity? Does use of a given intervention vary by client demographic characteristics? By practice setting? By providers? By provider training? By payment source and structure? Do some groups of clients get more, or less, service than others?

The significance of such questions rests on a simple assumption: interventions are not universally appropriate. No practice is a "magic bullet," equally applicable and effective for all the changes social work strives to achieve. Rather, practices have particular usefulness and appropriateness, and it follows that they should be used differentially. Although this assumption is so obvious that it may be universally held, we currently know very little about how social work practice varies. We do not know the extent to which social work interventions are used differentially and what factors are associated with variation. Nor do we know the extent to which observed variability is rational in that it corresponds to principles that guide practice.

Although research on practice variation is well established in medicine, it is scarce in social work. There are, however, some examples in social work research. Proctor, Morrow-Howell, Choi, and Lawrence (2005) found that case managers' notation of client depression in agency records varied substantially, with no record of depression in three fourths of the records of clients with established depression. Monnickendam, Savaya, and Waysman (2005) report variability in social workers' thinking processes and use of a clinical decision support system; variation was associated with the typicality of the client's case. Jonson-Reid (2002) reports that investigations of child maltreatment vary by age of child and gender: they decrease as child age increases, and are more often conducted for girls than boys. McMillen, Scott, Zima, Ollie, Munson, and Spitznagel (2004) found significant race and geographical variation in use of various mental health services for youth in the child welfare system: city-dwelling youth and youth of color in several regions of the state studied were significantly less likely to receive outpatient mental health therapy. The investigators interpreted these findings as signaling problems with quality of care. Racial variations have also been documented in adoption (Barth, Courtney, Berrick, and Albert 1994; Finch, Fanshel, and Grundy 1986) and kinship care (Wulczyn and Hislop 2000). Warner, Pottick, and Bilder (2005) recently identified income and organizational variations in youth mental health care.

And a hospital social work study found evidence of significant variation in implementation of discharge plans; low-income elders experienced signifi-cantly more discrepancies between planned and implemented services (Proc-tor, Morrow-Howell, and Kaplan 1996).

Once such variation is observed, the question remains: "Are the observed patterns of variation rational and acceptable?" Answering it requires that ob-served patterns be juxtaposed against theory, understanding of best practice, or well-established principles of service delivery. For example, the Andersen (1995) behavioral model of health service use posits that variance in service use other than that associated with need and preference signals inequitable care. From the examples cited above, it appears that need influenced service less than did client demographics, age, gender, geography, or income. Stud-ies of practice variation by race, culture, gender, or income can extend social work's historic social justice perspective to an agenda on disparities in care. Moreover, variation research is the cornerstone for research on the quality of care (McMillen, Proctor, Megivern, Striley, Cabassa, Munson, and Dickey 2005). Overuse, underuse, and misuse of treatments are commonly viewed as threats to quality. Before we assume such threats, we need to know more about the use, overuse, underuse, and misuse of social work practices.

What Is the Value of Social Work Practice?

A third question, particularly crucial for the profession's stature, addresses the value of social work practice. What is our profession's "value added"? With social work, what is the benefit? Without social work, what is missing? Posing such questions reflects the author's assumption that social work practice has an impact, likely a decidedly positive one. But the field cannot rely on asser-tion; its challenge is to calibrate, calculate, and communicate that impact.

What criteria can capture the contribution of social work as a profession? A decade of research has enabled the profession of nursing to claim that nurs-ing saves lives. Nurse staffing ratios have been associated with in-hospital and thirty-day mortality, independent of patient characteristics, hospital charac-teristics, or medical treatment (Person, Allison, Kiefe, et al. 2004). In marked contrast, social work has too often described—indeed advertised—itself as the *low-cost* profession. The promise of "cheapest service" is used for strategic advantage in turf competition with other professions. But in the market, the lowest bidder may not win. Working "cheap" will likely compromise the cali-ber of professionals employed, quality of care provided, change effected, and ultimately professional stature. Social work will be better served when, on the basis of data, the profession can demonstrate and thereby claim its position as the "high value" profession.

Research on the profession's value needs to begin with the identification of the outcomes that social work practice can achieve. Particularly for a profession that is poorly understood, outcomes must be clearly depicted (Proctor, Rosen, and Rhee 2002). A small number of research studies have tackled this challenge by striving to empirically identify, name, and classify in a taxonomic scheme the outcomes associated with social work practice. Proctor, Rosen, and Rhee (2002) collected data from health and mental health social workers, who recorded the outcomes they pursued with their collective 332 clients over a four-month period. The practitioners listed a total of 733 outcomes, from which researchers then constructed a taxonomy of seven outcome domains. In order of relative frequency, these domains were: clinical symptoms, life satisfaction, resource procurement, functional, acceptance, welfare/safety, and knowledge gain. Not surprisingly, the relative emphasis varied by practice domain, with medical and psychiatric social workers differing in their pursuit of the various outcomes. Zeira and Rosen (1999) identified 1,001 different "intermediate" outcomes and classified them into 13 categories; this data reflects the practice of 69 social workers, working with 141 clients in community-based family agencies in Israel. Two additional studies identified and classified social work outcomes from published research literature. Rosen, Proctor, and Staudt (2003) identified 300 outcomes from five years of published social work research and classified them into 39 outcome categories, within eight larger domains. The outcome domain focused on by the largest percent of studies (32.7 percent) was improvement in clinical status, followed in order by life satisfaction/fulfillment, functional status, and environment/resource use. Using a similar methodology, Staudt and colleagues identified and classified 70 outcomes identified in school social work literature, including, in order of frequency, improvements in child functioning, symptoms, and consumer perspectives (satisfaction, attitudes).

Such classifications of social work outcomes reflect what the profession can contribute to society. They provide empirical support to statements that social workers strive to help people reduce or stabilize disabling symptoms associated with their emotional and behavioral problems, get and stay housed, find and keep jobs, and function in the face of disability, mental disorder, substance abuse, and chronic illness. Social work's impact can be gauged through safety and healing for victims of violence and trauma; and through the numbers of children who attend school, are teachable in the classroom, and stay in school to complete their education. Similar research is needed to identify, classify, and document outcomes in community practice, policy practice, and management.

Beyond the important work to identify and classify types of outcomes, research is needed to quantify social work's impact. The value of social work outcomes can be quantified through a range of metrics, few of which appear in social work research or in relation to social work practice. Accordingly, the following questions remain largely unanswered: How much does social work intervention improve individual, family, organizational, community, and/or societal functioning? How much do social work interventions cost to deliver? What is the comparative cost to deliver different interventions? And what is the cost-benefit ratio? Unfortunately, few studies actually quantify the value of social work practice. Changing this picture requires that social work researchers partner with economists and that social work doctoral programs teach the next generation of researchers the methods required to calculate professional "value added."

Rosen et al. (2003) caution that taxonomies of outcomes should be based on careful conceptual work about what should be assessed in terms of social work impact, rather than on what can be easily assessed with readily available instruments and measures. Similarly, research on social work's value should not be limited to the outcomes that *are* pursued in current practice. It is important also to think critically and creatively about the outcomes that *could be* and *should be* pursued in practice and then examined in research. Toward this end, Proctor and Rosen (2003b) urge that social work outcomes be considered also from the perspective of societal needs, potential impact, and professional "niche."

What Practices Should We Use?

Answering the fourth question for social work research requires addressing a number of other, familiar questions, including: What interventions are effective? Which ones are effective for attaining a particular outcome? Raising the bar a bit, which are most effective for a given outcome? Which interventions correspond to client preferences? Which are most effective for particular client groups? Incorporating information about value, which are most cost-effective? Proctor and Rosen (2003a) characterized these questions as "building block research," the answers to which constitute the basic ingredients for evidence-based practice and for practice guidelines.

From both within and outside the profession, momentum has increased over the past decade for evidence-based social work practice. While researchers and educators have pondered the value of an evidentiary approach to practice, questioned what constitutes "evidence" itself, and bemoaned the sufficiency of social work's evidence base, the field has moved ahead to embrace—and demand—evidence-based practice. Some states now restrict public funds to reimbursement for those practices that meet criteria for "evidence-based practices." Unfortunately, social work itself has not driven the discourse, conducted sufficient research, determined criteria of evidence, or identified practices that cross the threshold of "evidence." The field too often defaults to advocacy groups, state governments, and other professions the crucial decisions about which practices clients should receive, even when social workers most often provide them.

Such reactivity is unnecessary in many areas of practice, given recent increases in the quantity and quality of intervention research in social work. Reid and Fortune (2003) identified 107 social work practices, or "programs," that produced positive outcome findings and were described in sufficient detail for replication. In one of his last and most ambitious papers, William Reid worked with colleagues to critically assess and evaluate the state of social work practice knowledge in an effort to "establish an evidentiary base for social work treatments of choice" (Reid, Kenally, and Colvin 2004:79), that is, to assess what treatments work, for which problems, better than other available treatments. Over three fourths of the interventions tested showed significant differences in one or more measures of impact, and in most cases the differences were clinically important. The review suggests that social work research increasingly can answer the question, "What practices should we use?"

But social work is far from able to answer it definitively. Intervention research continues to comprise only about one fourth of empirical studies (Fraser 2003). Many areas of practice remain particularly understudied (Coulton 2005). Important questions of optimal dosage, ordering of treatment components, and moderator variables have yet to be addressed (Proctor and Rosen 2003a). The field especially lacks research on which interventions are appropriate, acceptable, and effective with different client groups (Zayas 2003; Videka 2003), a critical issue made more pressing by the diversity of clientele (Proctor and Rosen 2003b).

But determining what interventions should be used requires another type of scholarly activity, that of consolidation and synthesis (Proctor and Rosen 2003a 2003b). Scholars need to review and assemble evidence from studies of practice effectiveness, critically assess the evidence, and synthesize the findings. Moreover, this work requires use of systematic methods, whether of consensus, critical reviews, or meta-analysis. Synthesis is important for three reasons. First, reviews can help ensure that data—especially outlier data—are viewed within context; consequently, the conclusions reached through systematic reviews often differ from individual studies (Proctor 2004). Littell's (2005) review of research on multisystemic therapy, using methods of the Campbell Collaboration, exemplifies the influence of review method on conclusions supported. Second, systematic methods reduce the risk of simply choosing a study that justifies one's personal practice and beliefs (Clancy and Kamerow 1996). Finally, conclusions reached through reviews of multiple studies have more impact: people are more influenced by "ideas" than by discrete pieces of data (Lavis, Robertson, Woodside, McLeod, and Abelson 2003). The scholarship of research synthesis has been too rare in social work (Proctor 2001).

To be optimally useful, the findings of systematic reviews should be consolidated into easy-to-use practice guidelines (Rosen and Proctor 2003b). These can overcome the barriers that most practitioners face in accessing and critiquing research-based reports. Social work researchers have only recently begun the discourse about practice guidelines and identification of their associated conceptual, methodological, and organizational challenges. Guideline development is increasingly recognized as the purview and responsibility of professional and service delivery organizations (Hefland 2005; Rosen and Proctor 2003a).

How Do We Improve Social Work Practice?

The fifth and final question in this proposed agenda is "How do we improve social work practice?" Although quality is not a new concern for social work (McMillen et al. 2005), there is a dearth of research on quality and quality improvement (Proctor 2002b). Important work remains for researchers, starting with the challenges of identifying and developing quality indicators that are appropriate for social service agencies and social work practice (McMillen et al. 2005). Professional training needs to be focused around best practices, and strategies for improving quality of care need to be conceptualized and tested. The roll-out of real-world quality improvements provides new opportunities for creative partnerships between social work researchers and agency partners.

This research, like that to calculate the value of social work practice (question 3 above), requires methodologies new to most social work researchers. These include research methods to capture stakeholder preferences; research on decision support tools, including electronic agency records, to prompt use of best practices and improve the quality of care provided; and implementation research, a science that requires using distinct outcomes such as acceptability, feasibility, sustainability, and fidelity (Proctor 2002a). Once best practices are identified (through pursuit of research questions 3 and 4 above), social work will require knowledge of dissemination and implementation strategies that are also evidence-based to move these practices into the field.

How can social work researchers prepare for and begin to engage in research to improve social work practice? The results of research must be "implementable." Several factors can shorten the time and reduce the barriers between intervention development and real-world intervention uptake. Researchers should keep in mind the goal of quality improvement for all practice research. Too few social work programs of intervention development carry the product to the crucial implementation phase. Interventions and treatment programs should be based on solid understanding of the practice landscape acquired through "services" research; too few studies address questions about problem epidemiology (including clinical epidemiology and differential prevalence across client groups), barriers to care, and the organizational and community contexts through which care is provided (Proctor 2003a). Forging academic–agency partnerships at the front end will also help: intervention development work should incorporate the perspectives of key stakeholders in practice, including consumers, frontline providers, supervisors, executive directors, and those who make payment and policy decisions (Proctor 2003b). Finally, social work researchers can benefit from partnerships with experts in other disciplines: marketing, organizational and industrial psychology, and engineering and technology. Industry researchers and health care quality researchers can provide crucial conceptual and methodological expertise. Tackling the problem of community adoption of effective prevention strategies, Hawkins (2005) surveyed the "stages of adoption" literature and challenged social workers to better use media for community activation, prevention program marketing, and education.

Conclusion

Pursuit of these five research questions can significantly advance the state—and most of all the usefulness—of social work practice knowledge. However, the field must acknowledge and address the challenges that complicate work on this proposed agenda. One major challenge derives from the very breadth of social work as a field. The many areas of practice, populations of concern, social problems addressed, and levels of intervention each carry unique knowledge demands. No individual researcher, no group of social work researchers, no school of social work can tackle the totality of the field's knowledge needs. There is a dire need for centers of research focused on particular questions, fields of practice, or interventions. Social work practice has become more specialized, as reflected in the recent establishment of "member sections" within the National Association of Social Work. Social work research needs to become similarly specialized.

Advances notwithstanding, the limits of the research infrastructure pose another set of challenges. Social work has too few doctoral graduates, provides too little postdoctoral research training, and suffers from a limited range and depth of methodological expertise among its researchers. The impact of most studies is limited by their small scope and scale, consequences of too little external funding. Knowledge grows slowly and piecemeal. Social work research needs to be better prioritized and more purposely conducted. Specific research questions and individual projects need to be rationalized within the context of long-range agendas. Several recent publications offer research agendas, including Morrow-Howell and Burnette's agenda for research on aging (Morrow-Howell and Burnette, in press), McMillen and colleagues' agenda for research on social service quality (McMillen et al. 2005), and Rosen and Proctor's agenda for developing practice guidelines (Rosen and Proctor 2003a). Several thematically focused research centers now advance knowledge development in such areas as aging, stimulated by the Hartford Foundation initiative in gerontology; mental health and substance abuse, stimulated by the social work center programs of the National Institutes of Mental Health and on Drug Abuse, respectively; and in areas of prevention, child welfare, and social work practice, stimulated by several research centers supported by individual schools of social work. Such programs enable individual researchers to identify manageable portions of a long-range agenda and plug their work into the cumulative body of knowledge and research conducted by other investigators. Research agendas also enable assessing what we know, which often builds confidence, undergirds advocacy, and spurs creativity in launching new projects.

Unfortunately, social work continues to suffer from a shortage of well-trained researchers and a weak research infrastructure. So long as resources remain limited, the "questions of questions" will remain a critical issue for researchers: "Are social work researchers asking questions that will advance social work practice?" Social work can ill afford for scarce research resources to be directed to any but the most important questions. But by pursuing the right questions, social work researchers can inform practice, clarify the profession's contributions to society, and help improve the quality of care.

References

Andersen, R. M. (1995). Revisiting the behavioral model and access to medical care: Does it matter? *Journal of Health and Social Behavior* 36:1–10.

Barth, R. P., Courtney, M., Berrick, J., and Albert, V. (1994). *From child abuse to permanency planning: Child welfare services pathways and placements*. New York: Aldine DeGruyter.

Clancy, C. M., Kamerow, D. B., and Hoadley, J. F. (1996). Evidence-based medicine meets cost-effectiveness analysis. *Journal of the American Medical Association* 276:329–330.

Clyman, R. B. (1999). A systems perspective on research and treatment with abused and neglected children. *Child Abuse and Neglect* 24:159–170.

Coulton, C. (2005). The place of community in social work practice research: Conceptual and methodological developments. *Social Work 29* (2): 73–86.

Finch, S., Fanshel, D., and Grundy, J. (1986). Factors associated with the discharge of children from foster care. *Social Work Research and Abstracts 22*:10–18.

Fraser, M. W. (2003). Intervention research in social work: A basis for evidence-based practice and practice guidelines. In A. Rosen and E. K. Proctor (Eds.), *Developing practice guidelines for social work interventions: Issues, methods, and research agenda,* 17–36. New York: Columbia University Press.

Fraser, M. W., Nash, J. K., Galinsky, M. J., and Darwin, K. E. (2000). Making choices: Social problem-solving for children. Washington, DC: NASW Press.

Hawkins, J. D. (2005). Science, social work, prevention: Finding the intersections. Aaron Rosen Lecture, Society for Social Work and Research, January 14, Miami, Florida.

Hefland, M. (2005). Incorporating information about cost-effectiveness into evidence-based decision-making. *Medical Care 43* (7, II): 33–43.

Jonson-Reid, M. (2002). After a child abuse report: Early adolescence and the child welfare system. *Journal of Early Adolescence 22* (1): 24–48.

Jonson-Reid, M., Kontak, D., Citerman, B., Essma, A., and Fezzi, N. (2004). School social work case characteristics, services, and dispositions: Year one results. *Children and Schools 26* (1): 5–22.

Lavis, J. N., Robertson, D., Woodside, J. M., McLeod, C. B., and Abelson, J. (2003). How can research organizations more effectively transfer research knowledge to decision makers? *Milbank Quarterly 81* (2): 221–248.

Littell, J. H. (2005). Lessons from a systematic review of effects of multisystemic therapy. *Children and Youth Services Review 27*:445–463.

Marsh, J. (2003). Organizational and institutional factors in the development of practice knowledge and practice guidelines in social work. In A. Rosen and E. K. Proctor (Eds.), *Developing practice guidelines for social work interventions: Issues, methods, and research agenda,* 236–252. New York: Columbia University Press.

McMillen, J. C., Proctor, E. K., Megivern, D., Striley, C., Cabassa, L., Munson, M., and Dickey, B. (2005). Quality of care in the social services: Research agenda and methods. *Social Work Research 29* (3): 181–191.

McMillen, J. C., Scott, L. D., Zima, B. T., Ollie, M. T., Munson, M. R., and Spitznagel, E. (2004). Use of mental health services among older youths in foster care. *Psychiatric Services 55* (7): 811–817.

Monnickendam, M., Savaya, R., and Waysman, M. (2005). Thinking processes in social workers' use of a clinical decision support system: A qualitative study. *Social Work 29* (1): 21–30.

Morrow-Howell, N., Burnette, D., and Chen, L. (2005). Research priorities for gerontological social work: Researcher and practitioner perspectives. *Social Work Research 29*:231–242.

National Association of Social Workers. (2001). Substance abuse treatment activities. *Practice Research Network 1* (4). http://www.naswdc.org/naswprn/surveyOne/substance.pdf.

Person, S., Allison, J., Kiefe, C., Waver, M., Williams, O., Centor, R., et al. (2004). Nurse staffing and mortality for Medicare patients with acute myocardial infarction. *Medical Care 42* (1): 4–12.

Proctor, E. K. (2001). Building and consolidating knowledge for practice (Editorial). *Social Work Research 25*:195–196.

——. (2002a). Decision making in social work practice (Editorial). *Social Work Research* 26:3–5.

——. (2002b). Quality of care and social work research (Editorial). *Social Work Research* 26:195–197.

——. (2003). Developing knowledge for practice: Working through "trench-bench" partnerships (Editorial). *Social Work Research* 27:65–128.

——. (2003). Research to inform the development of social work interventions (Editorial). *Social Work Research* 27:3–5.

——. (2004). Leverage points for the implementation of evidence-based practice. *Brief Treatment and Crisis Intervention 4* (3): 227–242.

Proctor, E. K., Morrow-Howell, N., and Kaplan, S. J. (1996). Implementation of discharge plans for chronically ill elders discharged home. *Health and Social Work 21* (1): 30–40.

Proctor, E. K. and Rosen, A. (2003a). The structure and function of practice guidelines. In A. Rosen and E. K. Proctor (Eds.), *Developing practice guidelines for social work interventions: Issues, methods, and research agenda,* 108–127. New York: Columbia University Press.

——. (2003b). Advancing the development of social work practice guidelines: Directions for research. In A. Rosen and E. K. Proctor (Eds.), *Developing practice guidelines for social work interventions: Issues, methods, and research agenda,* 271–289. New York: Columbia University Press.

Proctor, E. K., Rosen, A., and Rhee, C. W. (2002). Outcomes in social work practice. *Social Work Research and Evaluation 3* (2): 109–125.

Reid, W. J. and Fortune, A. E. (2003). Empirical foundations for practice guidelines in current social work knowledge. In A. Rosen and E. K. Proctor (Eds.), *Developing practice guidelines for social work interventions: Issues, methods, and research agenda,* 59–79. New York: Columbia University Press.

Reid, W. J., Kenaley, B. D., and Colvin, J. (2004). Do some interventions work better than others? A review of comparative social work experiments. *Social Work Research 28* (2): 71–81.

Rosen, A. and Proctor, E. K. (1978). Specifying the treatment process: The basis for effectiveness research. *Journal of Social Service Research 3* (1): 15–23.

——. (2003). Practice guidelines and the challenges of effective practice. In A. Rosen and E. K. Proctor (Eds.), *Developing practice guidelines for social work interventions: Issues, methods, and research agenda,* 1–16. New York: Columbia University Press.

Rosen, A., Proctor, E. K., and Staudt, M. (1999). Social work research and the quest for effective practice. *Social Work Research 23* (1): 4–14.

Rubin, A. (2000). Social work research at the turn of the millennium: Progress and challenges. *Research on Social Work Practice 10* (1): 9–14.

Staudt, M. M., Cherry, D. J., and Watson, M. (2005). Practice guidelines for school social workers: A modified replication and extension of a prototype. *Children and Schools 27* (2): 71–81.

Thyer, B. (2000). A decade of research on social work practice. *Research on Social Work Practice 10* (1): 5–8.

Warner, L., Pottick, K., and Bilder, S. (2005). Clinical and organizational correlates of medication for youths in U.S. mental health services. *Social Service Review 79* (3): 454–481.

Wulczyn, F. and Hislop, K. B. (2000). Experience of children 12–17 entering care: Findings from the Multistate Foster Care Data Archive. In *Transition from foster care: A state-by-state database, overview, executive summary,* 10–11. Seattle: Casey Family Programs.

Videka, L. (2003). Accounting for variability in client, population, and setting characteristics: Moderators of intervention effectiveness. In A. Rosen and E. K. Proctor (Eds.), *Developing practice guidelines for social work interventions: Issues, methods, and research agenda,* 169–192. New York: Columbia University Press.

Zarin, D. A., Pincus, H. A., West, J. C., and McIntyre, J. S. (1997). Practice-based research in psychiatry. *American Journal of Psychiatry 154*:1199–1208.

Zayas, L. H. (2003). Service delivery factors in the development of practice guidelines. In A. Rosen and E. K. Proctor (Eds.), *Developing practice guidelines for social work interventions: Issues, methods, and research agenda,* 193–206. New York: Columbia University Press.

25 | Building Capacity for Intervention Research

Jack M. Richman

A SUBSTANTIAL BODY OF LITERATURE suggests that a serious lag exists between the generation of knowledge about best practices through social intervention research and practitioners' acceptance and implementation of this knowledge (Brekke, Ell, and Palinkas 2007; Fixsen et al. 2005; Glasgow, Lichtenstein, and Marcus 2003). Therefore, it is imperative that social work research and practice professionals engage in and extend their involvement in social intervention research so that they can bring evidence-based models to the practice community, enabling practitioners to more effectively address the variety of social and health problems.

Critical Connection Between Evidence-Based Practice and Social Intervention Research

"Evidence-based practice" refers to the process of making practice decisions based on the best available evidence. However, such decisions are often plagued by a shortage of research-based evidence, or the evidence that is available may not be of the quality or rigor needed to provide the strongest support for a specific intervention choice (Mullen and Streiner 2004). Evidence-based practice involves considering a hierarchy of evidence ranging from meta-analysis of randomized controlled trials to expert opinion (Shaya and Gu 2006). The hierarchy proposed by Shaya and Gu (2006) includes seven types of evidence: systematic reviews of randomized controlled trials, with or without meta-analyses; randomized controlled trials; cohort studies; case-control studies; case series studies; case reports; and expert opinion. The reality is that practitioners will use the range of best available evidence as noted on the hierarchy, whether it is at the level of a randomized controlled trial or the expert opinion.

Once the best available evidence has been identified, the principles of evidence-based practice require the practitioner to engage in a process of reviewing the research, client preferences, practice circumstances, and the practitioner's expertise as a basis for making practice decisions (Haynes, Devereaux, and Guyatt 2002). This emands that the practitioner employ his or her experience and clinical expertise, engage in a therapeutic relationship with the client, and negotiate the practice sequence of assessment, mutual problem identification, and development and implementation of a plan with high potential for producing a positive outcome. In addition, the process of implementing an evidence-base practice should include the review of relevant intervention research literature. This model is applicable to all practice levels, including interventions designed for the individual, the family, a group, an organization, or the community.

At this point, intervention research and evidence-based practice converge in a collaborative effort. The growth and development of intervention research are critical because those exploratory efforts are needed to provide practice directions, potential solutions, and templates that practitioners may implement within the context of their experience, skills, and expertise. Without professional social workers engaged in intervention research, practitioners would be deprived of adequate evidence and the range and depth of research needed to guide clinical practice. To ensure the future capacity of social intervention research, stakeholders in both the practice community and the university community must understand their roles in the research process and make a commitment to enhancing and fulfilling them. At least three models offer a framework by which social intervention research can be promoted, encouraged, and advanced.

Models for Implementing Social Intervention Research

To ensure that social intervention research is properly implemented and will be productive, those involved should give careful consideration to the guidelines offered by the following three research models: the practitioner–

scientist model, the agency research unit model, and the university–agency partnership model.

In the practitioner–scientist model, universities teach student practitioners how to understand, design, and implement research in the practice arena. After learning the important relationships among research, data, and practice, students are then given the opportunity by their employer to conduct themselves as a practitioner–scientist in their work environment by combining research, data, and intervention skills in real-world settings (Pepinsky and Pepinsky 1954).

In the agency research unit model, the community agency provides the resources to hire an individual (or individuals) with expertise in research design and implementation. In addition, the community agency provides the resources needed to implement a research agenda. In turn, the agency research unit disseminates their findings and relevant information to the agency's practitioners as well as to the larger professional community through presentations and publications.

The university–agency partnership model involves establishing a collaborative relationship between a university and a community agency or set of agencies. University faculty members and students work as partners with agency personnel in designing and carrying out social intervention research (Bellamy, Bledsoe, Mullen, Fang, and Manuel 2008). These collaborative efforts are focused on developing relevant evidence-based practices for use in the community agency.

Among the three models, the university–agency partnership model appears to provide the best potential and opportunity for both developing and sustaining social intervention research. Moreover, it is consistent with the current direction set by the National Institutes of Health (NIH) for translational research (NIH 2008). Equally important, this model provides a framework for synthesizing the resources and motivation of both universities and agencies, and directing their combined efforts toward a common goal of better research with better outcomes for clients. Further, recent advances in the ways that universities define scholarship have encouraged increased community-engaged scholarship that is a good fit with the university–agency model. Community-engaged scholarship is defined as "the collaboration between institutions of higher education and their larger communities (local, regional/state, national, global) for the mutually beneficial exchange of knowledge and resources in a context of partnership and reciprocity" (Carnegie Foundation for the Advancement of Teaching 2007:3). Although it is likely that this model will become common, its implementation will present challenges to the various stakeholders.

Intervention Research Stakeholders: Practice Community

Agency administrators and community practitioners must recognize not only the importance of social intervention research but also their critical role in the development and implementation of data-driven, evidence-based practices. It is through interactions with the practice arena that researchers are most likely to develop important questions related to policy and practice. In the community settings of organizations and agencies, practitioners' expertise will help researchers implement pilot tests and eventually, full-scale projects to test the effectiveness and efficiency of new intervention models. Thus, the agency personnel are a critically important part of this team effort. Practitioners need to remain connected to their practice skills and put their clients' concerns, values, goals, and preferences at the forefront of both practice and research. They must continue to assess the relevant areas of concern, including a client's situation, strengths, culture, ethnicity, and existing support systems. Furthermore, agencies and organizations must actively support the partnership by providing practitioners with the requisite time and technology to engage in research, review, and synthesis. Practitioners must have the motivation, knowledge, and supportive supervision to implement evidence-based practices and new practice methodologies with fidelity.

Within this model of university–agency partnership, social agencies not only deliver services but also function as learning organizations. Therefore, they must purposefully engage in and support the processes of social intervention research and evidence-based practice. The goal is to develop a team of agency personnel, including administrators, supervisors, and practitioners, who support collaboration with university-based research teams and engage in creative dialogue and clinical or community-level implementation that is informed by social intervention research and data. Developing and sustaining this team is a resource issue in that administrative systems must understand and support the intersecting roles of intervention research and practice, and funding sources must recognize and support these collaborative activities as well as the resulting time obligations. As shown in figure 25.1, agency administrators and practitioners must consider and contemplate numerous issues in preparation for developing a research agenda and entering into collaborative research endeavors with universities.

Administrative Concerns

Community agency management must understand the importance of research in enhancing the work and effectiveness of their practitioners. In addition, they need to be reassured that research findings, which may or may not support the implemented practice models, will not be published in a way that will violate confidentiality or reflect negatively on the reputation of the agency, the community, or the clients served. Administration needs to understand that as researchers and practitioners collaborate, adequate staff, training, supervision, and other resources need to be made available.

Community Considerations

The agency that is working to implement new evidence-based interventions will have to consider the relevance and receptivity of the intervention for the community and the population being served. Ethnic, racial, gender, and cultural issues must be contemplated and accounted for during implementation.

Agency Factors

Agencies, and the administrators and practitioners in them, create a functioning organizational culture. Part of this culture involves the willingness to accept and implement new ideas, including methods of changing or expanding agency practice, to be more effective and efficient. According to Peter Senge, learning organizations are "where people continually expand their capacity to create the results they truly desire, where new and expansive patterns of thinking are nurtured, where collective aspiration is set free, and where people are continually learning to see the whole together" (1990:3).

These organizational factors, including the openness or resistance to change on the individual, administrative, and agency policy levels, are likely to act as supports or barriers and serve as obstacles or assets for the "buy-in" and acceptance to support the implementation of new models of practice. Resources also become a critical factor in terms of the expense of purchasing new evidence-based programs and continual availability over time to ensure program implementation.

Professional Staff Considerations

E. M. Rogers (1995) suggests that when an intervention is being introduced in an agency setting, the new methodology must satisfy five criteria to have the best chance of persisting over time in practice. Three of the criteria Rogers (1995) notes relate to the professional staff; the intervention should be: no more complex than existing services, easy to implement, and likely to produce tangible results recognizable by authorities as important. These are essential as agency staff members begin the implementation of new intervention strategies. An agency may have a positive culture of learning, but if new practice models do not meet these criteria, they may be difficult to sustain in the agency over time.

The Intervention

The other two criteria Rogers (1995) proposes as needed to ensure agency acceptance and continued implementation are: the new intervention should be superior to services as usual and the intervention should be compatible with agency practices. Practitioners have training and successful experience in specific methods and models of practice, and altering their methods and strategies over time is complex and often not easy. Expectation for more positive outcomes and clarity and ease of intervention are encouraging factors in the implementation process.

Obviously developing, testing, and implementing evidence-based practices and sustaining these new practice models over time is a daunting task. Bellamy, Bledsoe, Mullen, Fang, and Manuel (2008) echo this notion when writing about university and agency partnerships: "Results from this study suggest that EBP training and partnership with researchers at Schools of So-

FIGURE 25.1 **Building Agency Capacity for Intervention Research**

cial Work can be effective for motivating social work practitioners to adopt the EBP model but are not sufficient to support the implementation of EBP" (Bellamy et al. 2008:70).

Bellamy et al. highlight these two process that may indeed be separate—developing, testing, and adopting evidence-based practices and sustaining their continuous implementation in agency practice. The latter of these two processes is at least as challenging as the former.

Intervention Research Stakeholders: University Community

Universities also play a critical role in developing collaborative arrangements with the agencies and practitioners with whom they will engage in social intervention research. Faculty members have a twofold responsibility: to engage in social intervention research as part of their research agenda and to train graduate students to understand this area of concern. University graduate programs are the logical environments in which to train future professionals so they will understand intervention research and how it can be effectively implemented within a community context. For example, curricula in schools of social work, psychology, public health, and nursing should teach the integration of social intervention research, evidence-based practices, and practice expertise. Universities must focus on teaching practice strategies that are supported by data, such as cognitive-behavioral therapy, family psychoeducation, social skills training, multisystemic family therapy, and dialectical behavioral therapy. They must commit to teaching the skills that are critical to program implementation, including methods such as group work and family intervention.

Social intervention research requires a rethinking of research design and methodology. This research does not take place in isolation, but depends upon critical relationships with agency personnel, clients, and community partners who have crucial roles that affect implementation, design fidelity, and effectiveness testing. Intervention research will require prior consent, involve complicated issues requiring institutional review board approval, demand consideration of language issues, and necessitate complying with agency protocols and current practice realities. In addition, social intervention research faces challenges such as smaller sample sizes, possible lack of control groups, the inability to withhold treatment or services to clients, and nonrandomized samples; these are all issues that are likely to be encountered on a regular basis and must be addressed and overcome. Furthermore, if the findings of such research are to be useful to practitioners and agency personnel, those involved must give careful consideration to publication and presentation of their research.

Universities will have to review and amend their traditions concerning knowledge creation and dissemination, publications and presentations, and tenure and promotion requirements. If social intervention research is to flourish, universities and their funders must recognize that research may take longer and be of greater intensity when it is based in a community agency and conducted in collaboration with agency personnel. Engaged scholarship, by its very nature, will challenge existing university tenure and promotion procedures and guidelines. This is likely to affect the productivity, type, and quality of research in which faculty members are engaged and may have implications for the tenure and promotion process at many research universities.

Conclusion

Building capacity for social intervention research is complicated. Although social intervention research has proven itself effective, its continued success depends on the often fragile determinants of collaboration, cooperation, flexibility, openness to new perspectives, and willingness to learn and experiment with new ideas and practices. Intervention research and the translation of its findings into practice require collaboration from the beginning among practitioners, their clients, and researchers. This process encompasses various steps, including question and problem formulation, specification of the program theory, development of the intervention program, refinement and confirmation of the program components, effectiveness testing through real-world implementation and testing for impact, and dissemination of findings (Fraser, Richman, Galinsky, and Day 2009). Given the multifaceted nature of this process, it is best implemented through the university–agency partnership model described earlier.

The quality and quantity of social intervention research must be attended to by involving all the stakeholders who recognize the importance of this type of research. It is of critical importance that universities alter their systems in ways that will encourage service and promote community-engaged scholarship. Such adjustments must be based on the understanding that researchers cannot be successful in providing solutions to current social and health issues unless collaboration with the practice community is evident and an integral part of the initial steps in the intervention research process. Researchers must understand that the significant questions affecting communities emanate from and are tested within the context of practice. The wealth of clinical expertise and practice wisdom residing within the practice setting is critical to the development and implementation of research and the translational processes. Therefore, researchers need to seek input and cooperation from community and agency partners regarding problems and solutions. Similarly, the practice community must recognize that university-based researchers bring resources to the table that can provide for more effective practice methods that will ultimately benefit the agency clientele. The findings from these collaborative research efforts may well result in new practice directions. Agencies and their personnel will have to work to maintain their motivation and willingness to accept emerging practice modalities while abandoning the familiar, comfortable practice models that remain untested and lack evidence of effectiveness (Aarons 2004). As true collaborators, both researchers and practitioners need to demonstrate flexibility as they implement research that is both rigorous and relevant to each partner's perspective.

Through the collaborative process that characterizes social intervention research, agency practitioners and university-based researchers will begin to understand how innovations are developed, tested, and implemented in field practice. An overarching goal and hope is that as collaborations and partnerships among university researchers and agency practitioners develop, the knowledge gained will provide directions for practice that will help the clients we serve. This, of course, is the real import of the future of social intervention research.

References

Aarons, G. A. (2004). Mental health provider attitudes toward adoption of evidence-based practice: The evidence-based practice attitude scale (EBPAS). *Mental Health Services Research* 6:61–74.

Bellamy, J. L., Bledsoe, E. S., Mullen, E. J., Fang, L., and Manuel, J. I. (2008). Agency–university partnerships for evidence-based practice in social work. *Journal of Social Work Education* 44:55–75.

Brekke, J. S., Ell, K., and Palinkas, L. (2007). Translational science at the National Institute of Mental Health: Can social work take its rightful place? *Research on Social Work Practice* 17:123–133.

Carnegie Foundation for the Advancement of Teaching. (2007). *Community engagement elective classification.* http://www.carnegiefoundation.org/classifications/index.asp?key=1213 (accessed October 9, 2008).

Fixsen, D. L., Naoom, S. F., Blasé, K. A., Friedman, R. M., and Wallace, F. (2005). *Implementation research: A synthesis of the literature.* Tampa: University of South Florida, Louis de la Parte Florida Mental Health Institute, The National Implementation Research Network (FMHI Publication #231). http: //www.fpg.unc.edu/~nirn/resources/publications/ Monograph/pdf /Monograph_full.pdf (accessed October 9, 2008).

Fraser, M. W., Richman, J. M., Galinsky, M. J., and Day, S. (2009). *Intervention research: Developing social programs.* New York: Oxford University Press.

Glasgow, R. E., Lichtenstein, E., and Marcus, A. C. (2003). Why don't we see more translation of health promotion research to practice? Rethinking the efficacy-to-effectiveness transition. *American Journal of Public Health* 93:1261–1267.

Haynes, R. B., Devereaux, P. J., and Guyatt, G. H. (2002). Clinical expertise in the era of evidence-based medicine and patient choice. *Evidence-Based Medicine* 7:36–38.

Mullen, E. J. and Streiner, D. L. (2004). The evidence for and against evidence-based practice. *Brief Treatment and Crisis Intervention* 4:111–121.

National Institutes of Health. (2008). *The NIH roadmap for medical research: Re-engineering the clinical research enterprise.* http://nihroadmap.nih.gov/clinicalresearch/overview-translational.asp (October 18, 2008).

Pepinsky, J. B. and Pepinsky, N. (1954). *Counseling theory and practice.* New York: Ronald Press.

Rogers, E. M. (1995). *Diffusion of innovations,* 4th ed. New York: Free Press.

Senge, P. M. (1990). *The fifth discipline: The art and practice of the learning organization.* London: Random House.

Shaya, F. T. and Gu, A. (2006). Deriving effectiveness information for decision making. *Expert Reviews of Pharmoeconomics and Outcomes Research* 6 (1): 5–7.

26 | Building Evidence-Based Intervention Models

Anne E. Fortune, Philip McCallion,
and Katharine Briar-Lawson

THIS CHAPTER ADDRESSES selected issues in building social work intervention models through research. These include whether the research focus is problem based or intervention based, approaches to developing evidence-based models, and translating empirical knowledge into practice.

Although the amount and quality of research conducted by social workers has increased since 1990 (Jenson, Briar-Lawson, and Flanzer 2008), the amount of research focused on interventions is small and not increasing as rapidly (Fraser 2009; Rosen, Proctor, and Staudt 1999; Simons, Shepherd, and Munn 2008). There are many practical reasons for difficulty in conducting intervention research: the need for well-conceptualized and well-specified models to test (Fraser 2009), the expense and difficulty of recruiting and retaining clients for experimental studies; continued ethical concerns about withholding or manipulating intervention; issues in practitioners' fidelity to planned intervention (Fraser 2004; Rubin 1977); the difficulty of building a tenured career based on intervention research; the attractiveness of large representative national databases, the increasing quantitative skill of new researchers, and so on. These challenges may be overcome in various ways, but there are also broader issues that affect the utility of the results for practice.

Problem-Focused or Intervention-Focused Research

One issue is whether the research on effective interventions is conceptualized as problem focused or as intervention focused. In the former, the primary interest is reducing or preventing a particular problem, such as substance use (see Marsiglia ch. 21; Catalano et al. ch. 17), depression (Gellis 2008), or hoarding (Stekee 2003). The investigator crafts interventions eclectically to address particular problems. Some interventions are selected from previously tested interventions (e.g., cognitive-behavioral techniques), or the investigator may create new interventions using a D & D (design and developmental) model (Rothman 1994; Fraser 2009). Development and testing are often theoretically complex and sophisticated. One prominent example is Mark W. Fraser and colleagues' Making Choices Program, a social-cognitive group intervention that teaches elementary school children social problem-solving competencies that build relationships with peers. Initially, they tested several pieces of the intervention with a small sample. Based on results, the program was revised and targeted for younger children, retested, and revised again by adding a family intervention. Another effectiveness trial determined that the program worked on a larger scale, more than 500 children from two schools. Finally, a fourth effectiveness trial confirmed the efficacy of the intervention in 14 elementary schools matched and randomized to receive Making Choices or routine services (Fraser, Richman, Galinsky, and Day 2009; Fraser, Nash, Galinsky, and Darwin 2000; Nash, Fraser, Galinsky, and Kupper 2003; Nash, Fraser, Galinsky, and Kupper 2003; Fraser, Day, Galinsky, Hodges, and Smokowski. 2004; Fraser et al. 2005).

By contrast, intervention-focused research concentrates on generalizable interventions that may be used in many situations. Once an intervention is developed (also often using D & D approaches), it is tested with many populations, problems, and intensities. Examples include the task-centered model (see part 2 of this volume), Lawrence Shulman's interactional model (Shulman 1981, 2008), and solution-focused therapy (De Shazer 1985, 1988; De Shazer and Dolan 2007). The interventions may be whole "packages" or microinterventions, for example, the task-centered model's task-planning and implementation sequence (Reid 1985, 1990, 1994) or termination interventions to generalize client learning (Fishman and Lubetkin 1980; Goldstein and Kanfer 1979).

Another form of intervention-focused practice research is the search for "common elements" in psychotherapy. Evidence from controlled experiments suggested that interventions from different psychotherapeutic approaches had similar outcomes (Luborsky, Singer, and Luborsky 1975). The equivalence was called the "tie-score effect" or the "dodo bird verdict" from

Alice's Adventures in Wonderland, where the dodo bird declares "Everyone has won and all must have prizes" (Carroll 1988:22). The dodo bird verdict led to an extensive search for common elements that might explain the equivalence of therapies, such as benevolent relationships, expectations of success, or an experience of mastery (Weinberger 1995). There is now ample literature and research on the commonalities among approaches to intervention. These include conceptualizations of the client–therapist relationship such as therapeutic alliance (Elvins and Green 2008) and the working alliance (Horvath and Greenberg 1994, 2002), as well as therapist contributions such as positive regard and empathy (Bohart, Elliott, Greenberg, and Watson 2002; Farber and Lane 2002). Another common factor is the clients' expectations—of success or positive change, of their own role in the therapy outcome, and of locus of control (Delsignore and Schnyder 2007).

In social work, William J. Reid (1997) refuted the dodo bird effect, finding differential outcomes among the range of problems and interventions of concern to social workers. Perhaps the equivalencies are in "talk therapy" and do not carry over to more active social work interventions. Nevertheless, these conceptualizations of common factors appear throughout standard practice textbooks as basic communication or relationship skills. (For examples, see Bradford W. Sheafor and Charles R. Horejsi's [2006] chapter "Basic Communication and Helping Skills" and Dean H. Hepworth et al.'s [2010] chapter "Building Blocks of Communication: Communicating with Empathy and Authenticity").

A different conceptualization of common elements is as discrete clinical techniques that can be packaged as modules for larger intervention plans. A review of social work experiments found the most common clinical techniques to be formal instruction (56 percent), homework, reinforcement and feedback, and practicing skills in treatment sessions (34 percent each) (Reid and Fortune 2003). The techniques tended to cluster together in intervention packages: mental health intervention programs relying on case management, concrete service, and relationships; cognitive-behavioral group interventions including skills training (parenting, assertiveness, anger, problem solving), skills practice, and homework. In a similar vein, Bruce F. Chorpita (2007) determined effective common techniques like relaxation, cognitive restructuring, and self-monitoring. He built a partly structured evidence-focused practice program called MATCH that combines appropriate effective elements into protocols designed for children's anxiety, depression, conduct problems, and traumatic stress.

Problem-focused intervention research is prevalent in social work today (see, for example, the problem- or population-based organization of Vaughn, Howard, and Thyer [2009] and part 3 of this volume). Funders are usually interested in particular problems, encouraging this trend. Because both the problem and the interventions are particularized and specific, it may also be easier to assess change and to conduct randomized clinical controls (Furman 2009), further encouraging problem-focused interventions.

Consequences of Problem-Focused Intervention Research

The predominance of problem-focused intervention research poses a dilemma for individual practitioners. There are multitudes of proprietary and public domain intervention packages, intervention protocols, practitioner manuals, and Web sites. Most of these EBPs—Evidence-Based Practice defined as tested effective interventions—are for narrowly defined problems and populations. Such precision and specificity facilitates well-controlled research but often results in narrow problem definitions that do not include the systemic concerns, extended social networks, and environmental interventions that are hallmarks of the issues social workers deal with. The narrow scope also makes it more difficult to transfer interventions to broader situations or different problems, so effectiveness may be compromised. Furthermore, social work clients rarely have one highly delimited problem.

Practitioners thus encounter a maze of available EBP interventions, many of which are narrowly focused and few of which are taught in graduate education. The dilemma is how to select, learn, and correctly implement them. The current solution to the choice dilemma is training practitioners to be experts in information retrieval and evaluation of research results. This process of making practice decisions based on evidence constitutes a common second definition of EBP. According to Sackett and colleagues (1996:271), "Evidence-based medicine is the conscientious, explicit, and judicious use of current best evidence in making decisions about the care of individual patients." In social work, the EBP decision-making process has been well elaborated by Eileen Gambrill and Leonard Gibbs (Gambrill 2006; Gibbs 2003; Gambrill and Gibbs 1999). Others have emphasized traditional social work contributions to EBP, for example, data from consumer wisdom and practice wisdom and decision-making criteria related to ethics, values, and consumer preference (Furman 2009; Petr and Walter 2005). A fuller definition, crafted from several sources, is:

> In EBP, the social work practitioner combines well-researched interventions with practice experience and ethics and client preferences and culture to guide and inform the delivery of treatments and services. The EBP decision-making process includes the best possible scientific research

available, the clients' context (including culture, values, attitudes, actions, needs and preferences), the practice circumstances (including organization, professional culture, ethical considerations and economic factors), theory, and the individual practitioner's skills, practice wisdom, and values and ethics. (adapted from IASWR 2009 and Danya International 2008)

Recently, there is a concerted national effort to integrate EBP decision-making processes into social work curricula. Danya International (2008), with funding from the National Institutes of Health and collaboration of seven national social work organizations, developed and promoted a proprietary curriculum guide for teaching students evidence-focused decision making (Reach-SW) at the B.A., MSW, and Ph.D. levels.

In addition to finding appropriate evidence-based interventions, practitioners are expected to implement them, often without special training. Systemwide implementation of an EBP can take 18 to 24 months and still not reach acceptable standards of fidelity (Gioia 2007; Gioia and Dziadosz 2008). Some of the barriers to implementation include practitioner characteristics—anxiety, suspicion, lack of knowledge about translating research into practice, and isolation (Bellamy, Bledsoe, and Traube 2006; Gioia and Dziadosz 2008; Hayes 2005; Mosely and Tierney 2005; Osterling and Austin 2008). Barriers also include organizational climate—encouraging action rather than reflection, risk-averseness, workloads too heavy to permit time for searching, lack of support and reward for innovation, lack of resources to access literature, etc. In addition, both practitioners and agency directors complain of the lack of fit between the research evidence and their practice—a dearth of research, irrelevant research, or EBPs that do not translate to their populations or situations (Osterling and Austin 2008; Proctor, Knudsen, Fedoravicius, Hovmand, Rosen, and Perron 2007; Simons, Shepherd, and Munn 2008).

By contrast, if practice is based on intervention-focused research rather than problem-focused research, practitioners can learn a particular approach that is useful for multiple situations, for example, cognitive-behavioral, task-centered, or interpersonal approaches. The drawback is that the practitioner must assess honestly if a situation is indeed appropriate for the intervention; the risk of using a hammer because it is available is high. Nevertheless, the research about dissemination suggests that the intervention-focused approach that incorporates tested elements into general practice—indirect research utilization—may lead to wider utilization of research-based interventions than other approaches (Reid and Fortune 2003). However, we do not know if this approach is effective enough to replace problem-focused EBP. Presumably the intervention-focus approach would need to be reasonably flexible to address different problems, like the task-centered model or Chorpita's MATCH program (Chorpita 2007; Reid and Epstein 1977).

Infrastructure for Building Intervention Models

One may build evidence-based intervention models using either problem-focused research or intervention-focused research. In either instance, the process is facilitated by a systematic mechanism for development and replication. We have already described the D & D approach to building intervention models (Fraser et al. 2009; Rothman and Thomas 1994), and we turn here to issues of infrastructure, or coordinating and systematizing such research.

One approach is that used by William J. Reid: a solo researcher with few grants who nevertheless systematically constructed, tested, adapted, replicated, and disseminated an intervention model (the task-centered model). Reid's work shows that practice research does not have to be a high-cost endeavor, at least in the pilot phase. Reid worked strategically with his students and with leaders in their field agencies. For example, an entire class of students tested a family problem-assessment and problem-solving tool (Reid 1987). Over time, Reid engaged students and practitioners in writing manuals he called "task planners," miniprotocols or strategies for addressing the types of target problems the students and their clients encountered, thus extending applications of task-centered practice to diverse populations and problems (see, for examples, Reid 1992, 2000; Naleppa and Reid 2003).

Reid saw failures and successes as generative, enabling the development process to be a trial-and-error, self-corrective process. In the formative stages of testing an intervention, funders are reluctant to support pilot research (Kirk and Reid 2002), but intense nonexperimental study can suggest promising interventions. For example, Reid tested single-intervention approaches embedded in complex service programs, conceptualizing how the single intervention can be beneficial when it is part of a larger, complex intervention (Reid 1987).

In contrast to the "solo researcher" are grant-funded intervention research centers, what Marilyn Flynn and colleagues call a thematic center, with research expertise and resources organized around a topic such as intervention research in substance abuse (Flynn, Brekke, and Soydan 2008). For example, the Social Intervention Group (SIG) at Columbia University was established "to develop, adapt, and test sociobehavioral interventions designed to ameliorate social problems among low-income urban populations . . . [particularly] HIV prevention and drug abuse" (Schilling 1997:177). SIG organized teams of researchers into subgroups: a design and measurement group, a data collection team, and an intervention work group. Such centers have become more common since 1990 as the National Institutes of Health (NIH) and other federal entities have supported research infrastructure development in social work (Jenson, Briar-Lawson, and Flanzer 2008). As many as 40 percent of graduate schools of social work have at least one research center (Briar-Lawson et al. 2008). However, despite the proliferation of centers and training opportunities for advanced research methods, it is unclear how many focus on intervention. Furthermore, because research centers rely on short-term funding—usually around areas designated by the funder, not the researcher—it is difficult to establish a systematic trajectory of model-building research.

Reid (1987) believed that the profession should embrace a model-building approach because social work requires innovation in practice to meet changing human needs. Research would be iterative with successive substudies over time. Whether the infrastructure is "solo researcher" or research center, model-building research involves collaboration between schools of social work and community agencies, jointly the site for such research. Collaborative model-building research can support an evidence-based movement and especially culturally congruent EBPs.

Partnerships for Intervention Model Building and the Engaged University

Universities and agencies need a simultaneous renewal of this model-building strategy. Building partnerships with service delivery agencies and increasing their research infrastructure is essential to ensure sustainable research that bridges the gap between "bench and trench" (Proctor, McMillen, Haywood, and Dore 2008; Shera 2008). Agencies have knowledge of practice and client problems, as well as the clients. Universities have the research expertise and infrastructure. Unlike the teaching hospital in which the physician-professor spends several days in practice and conducts practice research, there is rarely a systematic parallel structural arrangement for social work. Moreover, social work faculty often undertake explanatory research on policy or human behavior subjects rather than intervention research. Although such explanatory knowledge is essential because etiological and epidemiological findings inform such work (Fraser 2003), the move to intervention research is critical, but it is hard to build facilitating environments without embedding the researcher, practitioner, and student practice researcher within a strong model-building culture (Thomas and Rothman 1994).

Opportunities for such a model-building culture abound. Agency practitioners hold microtheories that inform their interventions (Fraser 2003); many of these are promising and deserve research. University-based faculty liaisons to field agencies have the opportunity to work with a cluster of agencies around key practices that warrant more adaptation and testing. Units of students doing fieldwork could provide a "research engine" for agencies while engaging practitioners in testing and moving their microtheories into pilot studies. There are examples of schools of social work that have experimented with faculty outstationed in agencies. This partial faculty collocation in an agency may help with building the research engine in the agency. Several faculty with endowed professorships and chairs have offices in agencies, increasing the likelihood of agency-based research.

Despite these opportunities, currently the social work profession is seen as more of a consumer of knowledge and research than an engineer or model builder as envisioned above. To advance renewal, the engaged university movement offers some tools for rethinking university–community structural relationships (Kellogg Commission 1999). The engagement agenda compels a rethinking of how the university relates to the community and especially to its problems. An engaged university is organized to respond to today's needs, enriches students' experiences through research and practical opportunities, and puts its knowledge and expertise to work on the problems of its community. It is characterized by responsiveness, respect for partners, academic neutrality, accessibility, integration, coordination, and resource partnerships (Kellogg Commission 1999:10, 12). In social work, the engaged university suggests an agenda of working with community agencies to research and resolve local social problems, i.e., undertaking action research and intervention model-building research that engages students, practitioners, faculty, and community members.

Translating Empirical Knowledge Into Practice

An important challenge for practice research is successful dissemination leading to widespread adoption, faithful delivery, and sustained interventions. There is yet little research on the success of implementation of EBPs, and most has focused on barriers and difficulties. Earlier studies of research utilization in clinical social work were discouraging. Despite emphasis in educational programs, few postgraduate social workers used research methodologies (for example, Rapid Assessment Instruments or single-system designs) (Reid and Fortune 1992; Reid and Kirk 2002). Nor did they use research findings designed to be relevant to practice or decision-making processes that employed research. By the turn of the century, Kirk and Reid (2002) reported some increase in utilization, particularly indirect utilization—using intervention techniques that have research support, and instrumental utilization—research-based decision making. However, Rubin and Parrish worried about widespread ambiguity and uneven teaching about EBP among MSW social work educators (Rubin and Parrish 2007). Even if EBP skills are taught consistently, students may not learn important skills; in one study, students did not improve on critical appraisal skills—a key component of the EBP decision-making process (Smith, Cohen-Callow, Hall, and Hayward 2007).

As we have discussed, there are many barriers to implementation of EBP. The research processes that enhance credibility of research findings also reduce their applicability to everyday practice (Hoagwood and Johnson 2003). Randomized controlled trials by definition seek to control the environment in which a practice intervention is implemented and tested. These trials benefit from protocols, practitioner training and supervision, and researcher oversight to ensure fidelity. Participants are screened and selected as being likely to benefit from the intervention, which also increases research control. Implementation in real-world settings is less controlled and multiple challenges derail many new interventions.

Hoagwood and Johnson (2003) offer a framework of issues to consider when attempting to implement an EBP (see figure 26.1). Regardless of research evidence for an intervention's efficacy, implementation may not be supported within reimbursement and regulatory requirements (extra-organizational context). Nor is implementation easy if the intervention (or research itself) conflicts with the organization's culture or with the way services are delivered (organizational fit). Even when regulatory and organizational support is present, practitioners may not adopt the intervention because its underpinnings conflict with their practice philosophies and training, or supervisory staff may not be able to provide the type or intensity of supervision needed (intervention processes). Additionally, real-life clients may not be as ready for the challenges and opportunities of the intervention as were the volunteer and prescreened participants in the research studies. There may be a conflict of values or different level of engagement (consumer/family choice and control).

The issues delineated in figure 26.1 speak to many of the reasons "good" interventions fail to be adopted or do not realize the potential promised by the efficacy studies. To get an intervention from research to day-to-day practice is difficult. Wilson and Fridinger (2008) posit three phases in developing and implementing an intervention: research, translation, and institutionalization. The first phase, research, is focused on discovery (the underpinnings of the intervention), efficacy (will desired benefits emerge? usually tested in a randomized control trial), and implementation (the effective local use of the intervention in real-world settings). However, much practice research does not complete even the research phase, ending with assessment of efficacy.

FIGURE 26.1 Challenges in Practice Delivery

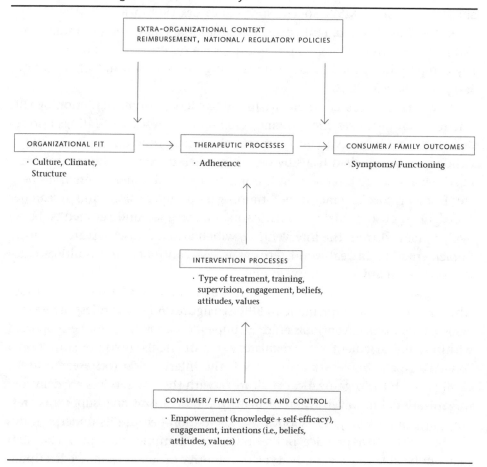

Adapted from Hoagwood and Johnson 2003

Practice research must be pushed further to demonstrate that controlled evaluation findings may be repeated in real-world settings.

But completing the research phase is not enough; attention must move on to translation. Translation means dissemination (the active participation and collaboration of stakeholders, mobilizing resources and influencing systems to change policies, programs, and practices; adoption by local agencies and providers; and practice (implementation of evidence-based interventions at the individual, organization, community, and policy levels) (Wilson and Fridinger 2008).

Translation requires an expanded research agenda and a repertoire of additional research methods. To organize the agenda, the public health field employs conceptual frameworks and methods that may be useful to social work. For example, to move from research to translation and then to maintenance or institutionalization, Glasgow and colleagues (2001) propose the RE-AIM framework, which focuses on individual and institutional outcomes along five dimensions (see table 26.1). Using this framework ensures that the most needy are served and that an intervention may be delivered faithfully using available staff within the resources of an agency.

In such a contextual framework, the focus is not simply on participant outcomes but also on extra-organizational outcomes, organizational fit, intervention processes, and participant choice and control. Practice research therefore concerns macro- as well as micropractice social workers, and research teams need to be expanded to reflect these horizontal levels. For example, organizational components of culture (resistance, proficiency, rigidity), climate (functionality, engagement, stress), and work attitudes (morale or organizational commitment) vary among children's mental health clinics (Glisson, Landsverk, Schoenwaald, Kelleher, Hoagwood, Mayberg, and Green 2008). These variations have important consequences for successful implementation of EBPs in mental health care (Hemmelgarn, Glisson, and James 2006; Schoenwald et al. 2008). This is likely true for other service areas.

Table 26.1 The RE-AIM Framework and Associated Research Questions

---

- *Reach into the target population, especially to those who can most benefit*

What percentage of the target population will be reached by the intervention?
Does the intervention reach those most in need?
Will participants be representative of persons served by the provider?

- *Efficacy or effectiveness*

Does the program achieve greater key targeted outcomes compared with other interventions?
Does it produce unintended adverse consequences?
How will or did it affect quality of life (QoL)?

- *Adoption widely in a range of settings, particularly agencies working with populations most likely to benefit*

Will organizations with underserved or high-risk populations use the intervention?
Does the intervention help the organization address its primary mission?

- *Implementation—consistency of delivery of intervention by staff members with moderate levels of training and expertise*

How many staff members within a setting will try the intervention?
Can different levels of staff implement the program successfully?
Are the different components of the intervention delivered as intended?

- *Maintenance of positive intervention effects (and minimal negative effects) in individuals and populations over time at reasonable cost*

Does the program produce lasting effects at the individual level?
Can organizations sustain the program over time?
Are those individuals and settings that show intervention maintenance those most in need?

Adapted from Glasgow et al. 2001.

At the same time that translational research deals with the expansion to larger contexts, there is a concurrent concern that the different components of an intervention be delivered as intended. This speaks to the need to manualize interventions and to develop treatment fidelity protocols so that faithfulness is facilitated, easily maintained, and monitored in real-world settings. Perhaps this is an issue to which more attention should be paid in the discovery and efficacy stages of an intervention, even as further work is needed in implementation and translation. Collaborative and action research perspectives may be helpful as a practice intervention moves through phases of development, and the process will benefit again from linkages between university and social work faculty researchers and community agencies.

Conclusion

In this chapter, we have raised issues in conducting intervention research, including the topics chosen and the consequences of those topics. Most intervention research in the United States focuses on interventions to resolve specific, narrowly defined problems that may or may not be typical of social work clients. One consequence of problem-focused research is that it tends to ignore both macro- and nano-level causes and resolutions of problems, for example, the role of neighborhood poverty, its contribution to family stress, and the neurological consequences for children's brain development ("I am just a poor boy" 2009). A second consequence of problem-focused research is that practitioners who have diverse clientele—arguably, most social workers—must search for EBPs as varied as their clients. Thus, conscientious practitioners must learn a complex set of information retrieval and evaluation skills while facing both individual and organizational barriers to using them. One solution is to reemphasize intervention-focused research with attention to generalizability across populations and problems. A second solution is to augment the research on common factors, perhaps focusing on cognitive-behavioral or other active techniques and then developing interventions that embed the techniques, as Chorpita (2007) has done. A third approach is to take problem-focused EBPs and test their generalizability more systemically.

All these approaches to intervention model building favor a systematic thematic research program, whether a "solo researcher" or a research center behind it. With uncertain funding and continuity, such extended model building is rare. In retrospect, the development of the task-centered model is extraordinary, starting with solo practitioners (William J. Reid and Laura Epstein) and spreading to developers throughout the world.

Finally, it is imperative that the social work profession take responsibility for developing its own intervention models that alleviate complex problems. A legitimate critique of most EBPs is their narrow, limited problem and individual-centered focus, whereas social workers address individual and social problems with complex, multilevel causes that are often better addressed at a primary prevention and community level. Social workers have been involved in developing broader, more complex evidence-based interventions in mental health, for example, psychoeducation (Anderson, Hogarty, and Reiss 1986) and Assertive Community Treatment (ACT) (Stein and Test 1980), although the interventions are rarely attributed to social work. There is some work, albeit not systematic, on evidence for community-level interventions (Gorey, Thyer, and Pawluck 1998; Ohmer and Korr 2006). In general, however, there is a need for more intervention research that integrates biological, neurological, social, and environmental knowledge and addresses complex social problems.

To implement such an ambitious model-building strategy requires close attention to partners in research. Community partners—agencies or funders—are critical to defining relevant research questions that make sense to practitioners and clients. Such partners are also critical to dissemination; interventions developed in partnerships are more likely to be relevant and respond to the agency contexts that can be major barriers to dissemination.

Intervention research, then, is an area where potential is still greater than achievements to date. The infrastructure in terms of university and community agency linkages, question identification from the field, and an emerging body of both problem-focused and intervention-focused findings has emerged. Further, the work of William J. Reid has illustrated the potential for building significant bodies of intervention research at low cost and by linking faculty, students, and community practitioners. Emerging frameworks such as RE-AIM, a new emphasis on university engagement, growing encouragement for the adoption of EBPs, and increasing attention to mechanisms for managing fidelity (Resnick, Inguito, and Orwig 2005) have supported expansion from the testing of interventions to the translation of demonstrated interventions for more general use in practice. There remains the challenge for practice settings of resources, time, and the management of organizational and environmental constraints, and for social work faculty, addressing the incongruence of this work with tenure and other expectations. Clearly further development will require considerable practitioner and faculty commitment; Reid's solo researcher model continues to be relevant.

References

Bellamy, J. L., Bledsoe, S. E., and Traube, D. E. (2006). The current state of evidence-based practice in social work: A review of the literature and qualitative analysis of expert interviews. *Journal of Evidence-Based Social Work 3* (1): 23–48.

Bohart, A. C., Elliott, R., Greenberg, L. S., and Watson. (2002). Empathy. In J. C. Norcross (Ed.), *Psychotherapy relationships that work: Therapist contributions and responsiveness to patients*, 89–108. New York: Oxford University Press.

Briar-Lawson, K., Korr, W. S., White, B., Vroom, P., Zabora, J., Middleton, J., Shank, B., and Schatz, M. (2008). Advancing administrative supports for research development. *Research on Social Work Practice 32* (4): 236–241.

Carroll, L. (1988). *Alice's adventures in wonderland.* New York: Knopf.

Chorpita, B. F. (2007). *Modular cognitive-behavioral therapy for children.* New York: Guilford.

Danya International. (2008). REACH: Research and empirical applications for curriculum enhancement in social work. http://www.danya.com/reach/ (accessed March 29, 2009).

De Shazer, S. (1985). *Keys to solution in brief therapy.* New York: Norton.

——. (1988). *Clues: Investigating solutions in brief therapy.* New York: Norton.

De Shazer, S. and Dolan, Y. (with Korman, H., Trepper, T., McCollum, E., and Berg, I. K.). (2007). *More than miracles: The state of the art of solution-focused brief therapy.* Binghamton, NY: Haworth Press.

Delsignore, A. and Schnyder, U. (2007). Control expectancies as predictors of psychotherapy outcomes: A systematic review. *British Journal of Clinical Psychology 46*:467–483.

Elvins, R. and Green, J. (2008). The conceptualization and measurement of therapeutic alliance: An empirical review. *Clinical Psychology Review 28* (7): 1167–1187.

Farber, B. A. and Lane, J. S. (2002). Positive regard. In J. C. Norcross (Ed.), *Psychotherapy relationships that work: Therapist contributions and responsiveness to patients*, 175–194. New York: Oxford University Press.

Fishman, S. F. and Lubetkin, B. S. (1980). Maintenance and generalization of individual behavior therapy programs: Clinical observations. In P. Karoly and J. J. Steffen (Eds.), *Improving the long-term effects of psychotherapy: Models of durable outcome.* New York: Gardner.

Flynn, M., Brekke, J. S., and Soydan, H. (2008). The Hamovitch Research Center: An experiment in collective responsibility for advancing science in the human services. *Social Work Research 32* (4): 260–268.

Fraser, M. W. (2004). Intervention research in social work: Recent advances and continuing challenges. *Research on Social Work Practice 14*:210–222.

Fraser, M. W., Day, S. H., Galinsky, M. J., Hodges, V. G., and Smokowski, P. R. (2004). Conduct problems and peer rejection in childhood: A randomized trial of the Making Choices and Strong Families programs. *Research on Social Work Practice 14* (5): 313–324.

Fraser, M. W., Galinsky, M. J., Smokowski, P. R., Day, S. H., Terzian, M. A., Rose, R.A., and Guo, S. (2005). Social information-processing skills training to promote social competence and prevent aggressive behavior in the third grade. *Journal of Consulting and Clinical Psychology 73* (6): 1045–1055.

Fraser, M. W., Nash, J. K., Galinsky, M. J., and Darwin, K. M. (2000). *Making choices: Social problem-solving skills for children.* Washington, DC: NASW Press.

Fraser, M. W., Richman, J. M., Galinsky, M. J., and Day, S. H. (2009). *Intervention research: Developing social programs.* New York: Oxford University Press.

Furman, R. (2009). Ethical considerations of evidence-based practice. *Social Work 54* (1): 82–84.

Gambrill, E. D. (2006). *Social work practice: A critical thinker's guide.* Oxford and New York: Oxford University Press.

Gellis, Z. D. and Kenaley, B. (2008). Problem-solving therapy for depression in adults: A systematic review. *Research on Social Work Practice 18* (2): 117–131.

Gibbs, L. E. (2003). *Evidence-based practice for the helping professions: A practical guide with integrated multimedia.* Pacific Grove, CA: Cengage Learning Brooks/Cole.

Gibbs, L. E. and Gambrill, E D. (1999). *Critical thinking for social workers: Exercises for the helping professions.* Thousand Oaks, CA: Pine Forge Press.

Gioia, D. (2007). Using an organizational change model to qualitatively understand practitioner adoption of evidence-based practice in community mental health. *Best Practices in Mental Health 3* (1): 1–15.

Gioia, D. and Dziadosz, G. (2008). Adoption of evidence-based practices in community mental health: A mixed-method study of practitioner experience. *Community Mental Health Journal 44*:347–357.

Glasgow, R., McKay, H. G., Piette, J. D., and Reynolds, K. D. (2001). The RE-AIM framework for evaluating interventions: What can it tell us about approaches to chronic illness management? *Patient Education and Counseling 44*:119–127.

Glisson, C., Landsverk, J., Schoenwald, S., Kelleher, K., Hoagwood, K. E., Mayberg, S., and Green, P. (2008). Assessing the organizational social context (OSC) of mental health services: Implications for research and practice. *Administration and Policy in Mental Health 35* (1/2): 98–113.

Goldstein, A. P. and Kanfer, F. H. (Eds.). (1979). *Maximizing treatment gains: Transfer enhancement in psychotherapy.* New York: Academic Press.

Hayes, R. A. (2005). Evaluating readiness to implement evidence-based practice. In C. E. Stout and R. A. Hayes (Eds.), *The evidence-based practice: Methods, models, and tools for mental health professionals,* 255–279. Hoboken, NJ: Wiley.

Hemmelgarn, A. L., Glisson, C. and James, L. R. (2006). Organizational culture and climate: Implications for services and interventions research. *Clinical Psychology: Science and Practice 13* (1): 73–89.

Hepworth, D. H., Rooney, R., Dewberry Rooney, G., Strom-Gottfried, K., and Larsen, J. A. (2010). *Direct social work practice: Theory and skills,* 8th ed. Pacific Grove, CA: Brooks/Cole.

Hoagwood, K. and Johnson, J. (2003). School psychology: A public health framework I. From evidence-based practices to evidence-based policies. *Journal of School Psychology 41* (1): 3–21.

Horvath, A. O. and Bedi, R. P. (2002). The alliance. In J. C. Norcross (Ed.), *Psychotherapy relationships that work: Therapist contributions and responsiveness to patients,* 37–69. New York: Oxford University Press.

Horvath, A. O. and Greenberg, L. S. (1994). *The working alliance: Theory, research, and practice.* New York: Wiley.

Institute for the Advancement of Social Work Research. Evidence-Based Practice resources. http://www.iaswresearch.org/ (accessed April 7, 2009).

Jenson, J. M., Briar-Lawson, K., and Flanzer, J. P. (2008). Advances and challenges in developing research capacity in social work. *Social Work Research 32* (4): 197–200.

Kellogg Commission on the State of Public and Land-Grant Universities. (1999). *Returning to our roots: The engaged institution.* Report 3. National Association of State University and Land-Grant Colleges. https://www.aplu.org/NetCommunity/Document.Doc?id=183 (accessed April 10, 2009).

Kirk, S. J. and Reid, W. J. (2002). *Science and social work: A critical appraisal.* New York: Columbia University Press.

Luborsky, L., Singer, B., and Luborsky, L. (1975). Comparative studies of psychotherapy. *Archives of General Psychiatry 32*:995–1008.

Moseley, A. and Tierney, S. (2005). Evidence-based practice in the real world. *Evidence and Policy 1* (1): 13–19.

Nash, J. K., Fraser, M. W., Galinsky, M. J., and Kupper, L. L. (2003). Early development and pilot testing of a problem-solving skills-training program for children. *Research on Social Work Practice 13* (4): 432–450.

Osterling, K. L. and Austin, M. J. (2008). The dissemination and utilization of research for promoting evidence-based practice. *Journal of Evidence-Based Social Work 5* (1/2): 295–319.

Proctor, E. K., Knudsen, K. J., Fedoravicius, N., Hovmand, P., Rosen, A., and Perron, B. (2007). Implementation of evidence-based practice in community behavioral health: Agency director perspectives. *Administration and Policy in Mental Health 34*:479–488.

Proctor, E. K., McMillen, C., Haywood, S., and Dore, P. (2008). Advancing mental health research: Washington University's Center for Mental Health Services Research. *Social Work Research 32* (4): 249–259.

Reid, W. J. (1985). *Family problem solving.* New York: Columbia University Press.

——. (1987). Service effectiveness and the social agency. *Administration in Social Work 11* (3/4): 41–58.

——. (1990). Change process research: A new paradigm? In L. Videka-Sherman and W. J. Reid (Eds.), *Advances in clinical social work research,* 130–148. Silver Spring, MD: NASW Press.

——. (1994). Field testing and data gathering on innovative practice interventions in early development. In J. Rothman and E. J. Thomas (Eds.), *Intervention research,* 245–264. New York: Haworth Press.

——. (1997). Evaluating the dodo's verdict: Do all interventions have equivalent outcomes? *Social Work Research 21* (1): 5–18.

Reid, W. J. and Epstein, L. (1977). *Task-centered practice.* New York: Columbia University Press.

Reid, W. J. and Fortune, A. E. (1992). Research utilization in direct social work practice. In A. J. Grasso and I. Epstein (Eds.), *Research utilization in the social services: Innovations for practice and administration,* 97–115. Binghamton, NY: Haworth.

Reid, W. J. and Fortune, A. E. (2003). Empirical foundations for practice guidelines in current social work knowledge. In E. K. Proctor and A. Rosen (Eds), *Developing practice guidelines for social work intervention: Issues, methods, and research agenda,* 59–79. New York: Columbia University Press.

Resnick, S. G., Inguito, P., and Orwig, D. (2005). Monitoring research fidelity. *Journal of Vascular Nursing 23*:155–156.

Rosen, A., Proctor, E. K., and Staudt, M. M. (1999). Social work research and the quest for effective practice. *Social Work Research 23*:4–14.

Rothman, J. and Thomas, E. J. (1994). *Intervention research: Design and development for human service.* New York: Haworth Press.

Rubin, A. (1997). The family preservation evaluation from hell: Implications for program evaluation fidelity. *Children and Youth Services Review, 19* (1/2): 77–99.

Sackett, D. L., Rosenberg, W. M. C., Muir Gray, J. A., Haynes, R. A., and Richardson, W. S. (1996). Evidence-based medicine: What it is and what it isn't. *British Medical Journal 312* (7023): 71–72.

Schilling, R. F. (1997). Developing intervention research programs in social work. *Social Work Research 21* (3): 173–180.

Schoenwald, S. K., Chapman J. E., Kelleher K., Hoagwood, K. E., Landsverk, J., Stevens, J., Glisson, C., and Rolls-Reutz, J. (2008). A survey of the infrastructure for children's mental health services: Implications for the implementation of empirically supported treatments (ESTs). *Administration and Policy in Mental Health 35* (1/2): 84–97.

Shera, W. (2008). Changing organizational culture to achieve excellence in research. *Social Work Research 32* (4): 275–280.

Shulman, L. (1981). Identifying, measuring, and teaching helping skills. New York: Council on Social Work Education; Ottawa, Canada: Canadian Association of Schools of Social Work.

——. (2008). *The skills of helping individuals, families, groups and communities,* 6th ed. Belmont, CA: Thomson Learning Wadsworth.

Simons, K., Shepherd, N., and Munn, J. (2008). Advancing the evidence base for social work in long-term care: The disconnect between practice and research. *Social Work in Health Care 47* (4): 392–415.

Steketee, G. and Frost, R. (2003). Compulsive hoarding: Current status of the research. *Clinical Psychology Review 23* (7): 905–938.

Smith, C. A., Cohen-Callow, A., Hall, D. M. H., and Hayward, R.A. (2007). Impact of a foundation-level MSW research course on students' critical appraisal skills. *Journal of Social Work Education 43* (3): 481–495.

Vaughn, M., Thyer, B., and Howard, M. O. (Eds.). (2009). *Readings in evidence-based social work.* Thousand Oaks, CA: Sage.

Weinberger, J. (1995). Common factors aren't so common: The common factors dilemma. *Clinical Psychology 2*:45–69.

Wilson, K. M. and Fridinger, F. (2008). Focusing on public health: A different look at translating research to practice. *Journal of Women's Health 17* (2): 173–179.

Index